THE IMPACT OF JESUS OF NAZARETH

Historical, Theological, and Pastoral Perspectives

VOLUME 2
SOCIAL AND PASTORAL
STUDIES

Edited by
Peter G. Bolt and James R. Harrison

SCD Press
2021

CGAR SERIES, NO 2

The Impact of Jesus of Nazareth:
Historical, Theological, And Pastoral Perspectives

Volume 2: Social and Pastoral Studies
CGAR Series, No 2
Edited by Peter G. Bolt and James R. Harrison

© SCD Press and Contributors 2021

SCD Press
PO Box 1882
Macquarie Centre NSW 2113
scdpress@scd.edu.au

ISBN-13: 978-1-925730-41-8 (Paperback)
ISBN-13: 978-1-925730-42-5 (E-book)

Cover design and typesetting by Lankshear Design.

THE IMPACT OF JESUS OF NAZARETH

Historical, Theological, and Pastoral Perspectives

VOLUME 2
SOCIAL AND PASTORAL
STUDIES

Edited by
Peter G. Bolt and James R. Harrison

SCD Press
2021

CGAR SERIES, NO 2

CGAR Series:

1. Peter G. Bolt & James R. Harrison (eds.), *The Impact of Jesus of Nazareth: Historical, Theological, and Pastoral Perspectives.* Vol. 1: *Historical and Theological Studies* (Macquarie Park, NSW: SCD Press, 2020).

2. Peter G. Bolt & James R. Harrison (eds.), *The Impact of Jesus of Nazareth: Historical, Theological, and Pastoral Perspectives.* Vol. 2: *Social and Pastoral Studies* (Macquarie Park, NSW: SCD Press, 2021).

CONTRIBUTORS

Darrell L. Bock is Senior Research Professor of New Testament Studies at Dallas Theological Seminary in Dallas, Texas. He also serves as Executive Director of Cultural Engagement for the Seminary's Center for Christian Leadership. His special fields of study involve hermeneutics, the use of the Old Testament in the New, Luke-Acts, the historical Jesus, gospel studies and the integration of theology and culture. He has served on the board of Chosen People Ministries for over a decade and also serves on the board at Wheaton College. He is a graduate of the University of Texas (B.A.), Dallas Theological Seminary (Th.M.), and the University of Aberdeen (Ph.D.). He has had four annual stints of postdoctoral study at the University of Tübingen, the second through fourth as an Alexander von Humboldt scholar (1989-90, 1995-96, 2004-05, 2010-2011). He also serves as elder emeritus at Trinity Fellowship Church in Richardson, Texas, is a writer for *Christianity Today*, served as President of the Evangelical Theological Society for the year 2000-2001, and has authored over forty books, including a New York Times Best Seller in non-fiction and award winning commentaries on Luke and Ephesians. He is married to Sally and has three married children (two daughters and a son), three grandsons and a granddaughter.

Dr **John Collins** works as lecturer in practical and pastoral theology and is head of the discipline 'Christian Life and Ministry' at the Catholic Institute of Sydney. John is actively involved in pastoral supervision for clergy and marriage and relationship education. He has been happily married to Dr Sandra Carroll for thirty years. John is also currently the president of the Association for Practical Theology in Oceania Inc. and is a candidate for the permanent diaconate for the Catholic Diocese of Parramatta.

Doru Costache is Senior Lecturer in Patristic Studies at St Cyril's Coptic Orthodox Theological College (Sydney College of Divinity) and Honorary Associate of the University of Sydney's Department of Studies in Religion. His particular area of research is the intersection of Christianity and culture, focusing upon early Christian representations of reality. He is the coauthor of *Dreams, Virtue and Divine Knowledge in Early Christian Egypt* (Cambridge University Press, 2019).

Rev Dr **Sally Douglas** is an Honorary Research Associate and Associate Lecturer at Pilgrim Theological College, within the University of Divinity. Douglas' interdisciplinary research spans Biblical Studies and Systematic Theology as she reflexively attends to Biblical and Early Church evidence, and to the potential implications of re-engaging with often suppressed texts in contemporary context. Her highly acclaimed first monograph *Early Church Understandings of Jesus as the Female Divine: The Scandal of the Scandal of Particularity* was published in the Library of New Testament Studies series by Bloomsbury in 2016. Douglas' current research focuses on questions of soteriology, gender and discipleship. Rev Dr Douglas works in the mode of scholar-pastor. She lectures and publishes in the fields of Biblical Studies and Theology, is a Uniting Church Minister with an inner city parish, and regularly contributes to theological discussion in the public square.

Joseph D. Fantin is professor on New Testament at Dallas Theological Seminary where he has taught since 2003. He has published monographs on Greek Grammar and Roman Imperial ideology and Paul. His research interests include the first-century world, Greek language and linguistics, exegetical method, and exegesis of the Gospel of John and Hebrews.

Dr **Rocío Figueroa** is a Peruvian Theologian, Lecturer in Systematic Theology at Catholic Theological College in Auckland and an External Researcher at the Centre for Theology and Public Issues at the University of Otago, Aotearoa New Zealand. She has a bachelor's degree and licence in theology from the Pontifical Faculty of Theology in Lima, and her doctorate in theology from the Pontifical Gregorian University in Rome. She has previously lectured in Peru, Italy, and Mexico. She worked in the Holy See as head for the Women's section in the Pontifical Council for the Laity. Figueroa's present research focus is theological and pastoral responses for survivors of Church sexual abuse.

Greg Forbes is the Head of the Department of Biblical Studies at the Melbourne School of Theology. He teaches New Testament, Greek Language and Hermeneutics. Greg's research interests are in Synoptic Gospels, General Epistles and Greek grammar as it relates to exegesis.

Deborah Guess is an Honorary Research Associate and Adjunct Lecturer at Pilgrim Theological College, University of Divinity, Melbourne. Her primary research areas are eco-theology and Christology. She is currently writing a monograph exploring the eco-theological meaning/s of place. Recently published book chapters include: 'Earth as Home-Place: Eco-Theology and the Incarnation', in Darrell Jackson, et al. (eds.), *Reimagining Home: Understanding, Reconciling and Engaging with God's Stories Together* (Macquarie Park: Morling Press, 2019); and 'Oil Beyond War and Peace: Rethinking the Meaning of Matter', in Anne Elvey, Deborah Guess & Keith Dyer (eds.), *Ecological Aspects of War: Religious and Theological Perspectives from Australia* (Adelaide: ATF Press, 2017). Deborah has recently co-edited (with Joseph Camilleri) a volume *Toward a Just and Ecologically Sustainable Peace: Navigating the Great Transition* (Singapore: Palgrave Macmillan, forthcoming).

James R. Harrison studied Ancient History at Macquarie University and graduated from the doctoral program in 1997. Professor Harrison, FAHA, is the Research Director at the Sydney College of Divinity. His recent monographs include *Paul and the Imperial Authorities at Thessalonica and Rome* (Mohr Siebeck, 2011), *Paul and the Ancient Celebrity Circuit* (Mohr Siebeck, 2019), and *Reading Romans with Roman Eyes* (Lexington/Fortress, 2020). He is also the chief editor of *New Documents Illustrating the History of Early Christianity Vols. 11-15* (forthcoming), co-editor with L. L. Welborn of *The First Urban Churches Vols. 1-6* (SBL, 2015-2020; Vols. 7-9 forthcoming 2021-2023), and is editor of the Cascade collection of E. A. Judge, *The Conflict of Cultures: The Legacy of Paul's Thought Today* (Cascade, 2019).

Norlan Julia, a Catholic priest, is the Rector of St. John Vianney Theological Seminary in Cagayan de Oro, Philippines, where he also teaches Fundamental and Dogmatic Theology. He holds a doctorate in Theology from Heythrop College, University of London. In his book, *Man of the Word: Rahner and Asian Priesthood* (2016), he writes about the challenges of priestly ministry in a multi-cultural, multi-religious, and pervasively poor context of Asia.

Jacob Kavunkal SVD is an Indian Missiologist who was Reader in Missiology at the Jnana Deepa Vidyapeeth, Pontifical Institute of Philosophy and Religion, Pune, and Head of the Department of Theology as well as the Coordinator of Post Graduate Studies at JDV. On retirement from JDV he was Associate Professor and Head of the Department of Mission and Ministry at the Yarra Theological Union/University of Divinity, Melbourne and retired in 2018. He has authored four books and has published over a hundred Missiological articles as well as taught Missiology as a visiting lecturer in countries like Myanmar, the US, the Philippines, and Sri Lanka.

Associate Professor **Peter R Laughlin** (BEng, BTh(Hon), PhD(ACU)) joined the Australian College of Ministries, a member institution of SCD, as Dean of the Alliance Institute for Mission and Head of Theology in 2017. Prior to this he was the Director of the Alliance College of Australia in Canberra. His research interests include the intersection between historical Jesus studies and atonement, divine justice, theodicy, human well-being, pneumatology and theological method. His major work *Jesus and the Cross: Necessity, Meaning and Atonement* [Pickwick Publications, 2014] was published in the *Princeton Theological Monograph Series* and he has recently contributed to the edited work *Justice, Mercy and Well-being: Interdisciplinary Perspectives* [Pickwick Publications, 2020]. He serves as the chair of the International Commission for Theological Education for the Alliance World Fellowship and is also published in areas relating to the Christian and Missionary Alliance, most recently contributing to *Advancing the Gospel* [Forthcoming].

Wagdy Samir is a part-time PhD (Theology) candidate at the Sydney College of Divinity. Wagdy is a Coptic (Egyptian) Orthodox student who is interested in patristics. In his dissertation, Wagdy explores the notion of union with the divine, comparing the commentaries on the Gospel of St John of two fathers, St Cyril of Alexandria (c.378-444) and Fr Matta al-Miskīn (1919-2006). Wagdy's contribution to this volume is a paper on St Cyril of Alexandria's eucharistic theology in the context of humankind's union with the divine.

David M. Shaw is lecturer in Biblical Studies at Perth Bible College, Western Australia and Extraordinary Research Fellow in Bibliological Perspectives at North-West University in Potchefstroom, South Africa. He completed his PhD at the University of Exeter, focusing on the use of the Old Testament narrative in the development of Christian identity and mission in the letter of 1 Peter. David's research interests revolve around the use of Social Identity and Narrative theories in relation to the New Testament.

CONTENTS

1. Peter G. Bolt, *The Impact and Implications of such an Historical Figure as Jesus of Nazareth* 1

Part A: From Rejection to Affirmation: Changing Attitudes to Jesus of Nazareth

2. Darrell Bock, *What Got Jesus into Trouble? Understanding the Significance of Jesus' Ministry by Looking at Its Jewish Context. Part Two—Trouble Solidified* 11

3. Jim Harrison, *Reactions of Roman Officialdom to Christ and His Followers in the Early First Century AD: A Case-Study of Pontius Pilate* 27

4. Joseph D. Fantin, *Early Christian Reactions to Jesus: Paul as a Paradoxical Test-Case* 83

Part B: Social Legacy of Jesus of Nazareth

5. David M. Shaw, *Narrating a New Identity: The Role of Isaiah's Suffering Servant in 1 Peter 2:22-23* 125

6. Sally Douglas, *Jesus' Impact on Understandings of Gender: Attending to First-Century Dialogue* 155

7. Peter Laughlin, *From Passover to Covenant: Exploring the Symbolic Meaning of the Last Supper* 179

8. Wagdy Samir, *St Cyril of Alexandria on the Eucharistic Context of Humankind's Union with the Divine in Commentary On John* 199

9. Doru Costache, *The Teacher and His School: Philosophical Representations of Jesus and Christianity* 227

Part C: The Pastoral and Ecclesial Legacy of Jesus of Nazareth

10. Norlan Julia, *Becoming a Merciful High Priest: The New Ratio Fundamentalis for Seminary Formation* 255

11. Greg Forbes, *Jesus and the Art of Parable: Emulating the Teaching Method of Jesus* 283

12. Rocío Figueroa, *Jesus Christ as a Victim: A Christological Light for Contemporary Survivors of Sexual Abuse* 301

13. Deborah Guess, *Nowhere to Lay His Head: An Eco-theological Reflection on Homelessness* 317

14. John Francis Collins, *Social Sin and Social Grace: Christ risen, Healing and Creating in Historyy* 339

15. Jacob Kavunkal SVD, *Reformation and Vatican II: Challenge of a Ministry-Centred Understanding of Jesus of Nazareth* 367

CHAPTER 1

Introduction:
The Impact and Implications of such an Historical Figure as Jesus of Nazareth

Peter G. Bolt

Wherever his heritage is celebrated and remembered, Jesus of Nazareth continues to make an impact. Writing from a variety of perspectives, the essays in *The Impact of Jesus*, volumes 1 and 2, explore the impact of Jesus of Nazareth on his own and subsequent times. After Volume 1 collected historical and theological essays, volume 2 moves from the historical and theological, towards the wider impact of Jesus on pastoral practice in our contemporary world.

As three samples of Jesus' social impact on the mid first-century, Part A explores the reason for his rejection in the Jewish context (Bock), and seeks to better understand Pontius Pilate, the official ultimately responsible for his death, as a sounding from the Roman context (Harrison), before turning to his acceptance by Paul, one of the earliest persecutors of the Christian movement, who then incorporated his teaching into his own (Fantin).

In part one of his study (*Impact of Jesus*, Vol. 1, Chap. 2), **Darrell Bock** set the context for his essay in this volume by looking at the irritants of Jesus' claims to authority and what provoked a skeptical reaction to him by the Jewish leadership. He considered evidence in Jesus' Jewish context for a 'middle' Jesus — a figure operating between more official Judaism and the practices of the later church — finding claims of deep personal authority tied in to his associations, forgiveness of sins, his Sabbath practices, and his discussions on purity. This claim went beyond that of a teacher or even a prophet, for it was a more direct claim to represent God and his new program. In this second part, Bock examines the events of the end of Jesus' ministry in Jerusalem, testing for their core authenticity and the narrative coherence they may possess, in order to make sense out of what got Jesus into trouble. These final events solidified the earlier skepticism into concrete reaction and led to Jesus being brought before Pilate to be crucified.

Overlapping with Pilate's role in these final events, **James Harrison** argues that a *Roman* historical assessment of Pilate's rule as the prefect of Judea is particularly difficult. The literary sources are sparse, confined to flash-points in Pilate's prefecture, and, in some instances, rhetorically jaundiced. The Gospel accounts present four different portraits of Pilate: each adopting a distinctly evaluative stance towards him as an historical figure and animated by wider theological concerns. The archaeological evidence is also slender, being confined to a fragmentary inscription at Caesarea Maritima, a few numismatic issues, and a recent material find at Jerusalem. Moreover, certain scholarly theses, such as Ethelbert Stauffer's hypothesis about Pilate's *amicitia* with the praetorian prefect Sejanus at Rome during Tiberius' reign, have had a longevity that they do not deserve. This chapter reassesses the literary, epigraphic, numismatic, and archaeological evidence and the commonalities in the Gospel narratives, including one distinctive Johannine tradition, from a Roman viewpoint. It is hoped that by such a methodological case study of Pilate that the wide range of Roman officialdom mentioned in the New Testament can be similarly evaluated so that we might gain a sense of how Rome perceived its role in governing an increasingly troublesome province.

As a bridge towards Jesus's impact on the people of later periods, **Joseph Fantin** turns to his impact upon the apostle Paul. Whereas some argue that Paul was not influenced by Jesus and created his own version of Christianity, others view Paul as a faithful minister of Christ. Fantin recognises that Paul's life was certainly paradoxical. Entering the historical record as a zealous persecutor of Jesus' followers, claiming to have encountered Christ, he became one of Christ's most devoted witnesses. Fantin's essay explores Paul's reaction to Jesus in two areas. After considering the life of Paul and trying to explain his drastic change, it examines the teaching of Paul in order to evaluate whether or not he was influenced by Jesus's life and teaching. Specifically, focusing upon Paul's teaching on divorce (1 Cor. 7:10–16), the analysis suggests that something very real happened to Paul, influencing him and causing his change of direction.

The five essays in Part B explore the Social Legacy of Jesus of Nazareth. In his examination of 1 Peter, **David Shaw** explores the influence of Isaiah's suffering servant upon the letter, utilising Narrative Transportation and Social Identity theories. In particular, he argues that 1 Peter 2:18–25 shapes the corporate identity and missional posture of Peter's readers, in a way that both surprises and undermines typical social identity processes, towards what might best be described as resident-alien-ness.

Noting that Jesus' impact was immediate, costly and scandalous, **Sally Douglas** notes his engagement of women in his movement in transgression of androcentric religious and cultural expectations. As a further case-study in this trajectory, she investigates claims made in 1 Corinthians and 1 Timothy in relation to the contrary claims made in the orthodox, first-century text of *1 Clement*. By attending to the evidence of this first-century dialogue the disruptive significance of Jesus' impact on understandings of gender is revealed.

One of the primary means of cultivating the memory of Jesus' death in the Christian movement has been the regular celebration of the Lord's Supper in Christian communities. Noting that this partaking of the 'body' and 'blood' of the Lord is an act that embodies the hope of Christian atonement, forgiveness, peace, and reconciliation, **Peter Laughlin** enters the debate over the authenticity of the Gospels' words of institution, and suggests the consideration of the symbolic praxis of the meal.

For St Cyril, the eucharist was more than simply symbolic, but it was understood as part of his theology of progressive human participation in the divine. Focusing upon the eucharistic dimension of humankind's union with the divine, **Wagdy Samir** shows that, for St Cyril, communicants partake of the real, vivifying flesh of the Word, leading to humankind's dual sanctification, spiritual and corporeal. Union with Jesus Christ is achieved through the interplay of two aspects, divine action and human response, and this union resembles the Christological reality of the hypostatic union.

But Jesus' impact was not felt simply when Christians gathered for communal worship. **Doru Costache** turns to the early Christians' view of Jesus, beyond his divine and human identity, as an accomplished philosopher who revealed to his disciples the highest philosophy. Rather than Jesus founding a religion, he founded a school which resembled the philosophical schools of the time. Centred on the experience of teaching and learning, the goal of his 'school' was the transformation of the human person, indeed the community of believers, by way of successive stages of initiation. In various aspects of its life, the church manifested its philosophical dimension in and to the world.

The six essays in Part C move further forward to discuss aspects of the legacy of Jesus of Nazareth in contemporary pastoral practice.

Taking as his point of departure the latest *Ratio Fundamentalis* on priestly formation issued by the Vatican Congregation for the Clergy, **Norlan Julia** notes the emphasis placed on two key areas in the training of future priests: human accompaniment and discernment. The *Ratio* envisions 'priests with friendly traits, who are authentic, loyal, interiorly free, affectively stable, capable of weaving together peaceful interpersonal relationships and living the evangelical counsels without rigidity, hypocrisy or loopholes'. This chapter explores how the portrait of Jesus as the High Priest is helpful in the reception and implementation of the *Ratio* in seminary formation in the Philippines and in Asia more generally. An appreciation that the priesthood of Christ is characterised by humanity, solidarity in suffering, and mercy towards humanity is crucial for a more comprehensive understanding of the role of priests today and in drawing up a formation program that can better prepare those in training to embrace the vocation of being 'ministers of mercy'.

Noting that Jesus the master teacher used parables as his mode of conveying truth regarding God and his kingdom, **Greg Forbes** asks why emulation of Jesus is normally construed in terms of ethics, patient suffering, or commitment to mission, rather than in his teaching method. He argues that there is something in the nature of story in general, and parable in particular, that the church needs to recapture in the way it passes on its doctrine and ethics. Because Biblical truth is a sacred story and our lives have an essential narrative flow, the use of narrative to communicate the Christian message is indispensable. Story not only stimulates curiosity, but it confronts us by evoking images that facilitate a shift in perspective. Story ties us to reality.

The essay by **Rocío Figueroa** gives voice to eight survivors of sexual abuse from the Sodalicio movement in Peru. It explores the spiritual consequences associated with the abuse and the secondary victimization that survivors suffered from the community. As a theological response, it proposes Jesus as a victim of sexual abuse and questions whether this conceptualisation could help survivors in their journey.

The theme of 'homelessness' in relation to Jesus and his disciples has often been interpreted eschatologically, thereby endorsing 'cosmic homelessness', which poses a problem for ecological theology. **Deborah Guess** draws on three aspects of Halvor Moxnes' discussion of the spatial aspects of the historical Jesus: (1) the radical nature of Jesus' leaving of home and the way it was impelled by structural (social, economic and political) factors; (2) the trauma that it would have likely entailed; and (3) the ambiguous question of whether an alternative or new home is indicated in the Gospels. Developing Moxnes' three aspects, the essay finds several eco-theological resonances with today's context. A radical challenge is posed to contemporary understandings of 'home', especially as places of consumerism; ecological devastation sometimes causes unacknowledged distress; and, lastly, the question of what any kind of new home might mean remains somewhat ambiguous.

John Collins's essay is an interdisciplinary exercise in pastoral or practical theology, focused on the notion of social grace, understood as the cooperative interaction between the Word and Holy Spirit of God and human agents as the necessary antidote to social sin. In the first of five main parts, Part 1 turns to Object Relations theory, interpreted through the light of neuroscience, to support the argument that social sin is the fruit of the condition theologically understood as original sin and accumulated personal sin. This allows an explanatory schema for understanding original sin as the tendency towards psychological splitting, followed by conceptual justification of the psychological phenomenon leading to action. Part 2 introduces Robert Doran's notion of Social Grace as an antidote of the theological category of Social Sin. After providing some background to the relationship between God and Politics, as proposed by Neil Ormerod, Part 3 investigates the influence of original and personal sin on individuals, the social sphere, and the cultural spheres manifested under the category of politics. Part 4 draws on both the work of Doran and Ormerod to explore the divinely-initiated solution to the problem of evil, as systematically developed, through an overview of the operation in history of the Scale of Values. Bringing together the insights of the first four sets of ideas, Part 5 identifies ways to facilitate God's grace to effectively heal political division and to develop creative ways of cooperation.

Closing the volume, **Jacob Kavunkal** argues that the close occurrence of the fiftieth anniversary of Vatican II and the five hundredth anniversary of the Martin Luther-inspired Reformation presents a challenge for the Christian community and scripture scholars to retrieve the roots of Christian discipleship which lay in the ministry of Jesus of Nazareth. After outlining the significance of ecumenism, the essay underlines two key emphases of Luther, the centrality of the Bible and the common priesthood of Christians. Since they had an impact on Vatican II as well, these emphases present a challenge to the Christian community to focus on the ministry of Jesus, with its priority of wholeness of life for all, especially for those on the margins.

The greatness of Jesus of Nazareth was supremely displayed in his moment of greatest weakness on the cross. Depicting himself as the

Servant of the Lord who gave his life as a ransom for many, he descended to the depths of the typical human social scales of greatness and honour, in order to overturn and surpass them once and for all. Those who felt his immediate impact either chafed under his teaching, or embraced it, but rarely did anyone remain untouched by him. The impact of the one preached throughout the world as the crucified Saviour ripples across cultures throughout the world, and times, even down to our own. The mystery of his salvific death inspires; the power of his resurrection hope sustains; and his impact continues to work its way outwards in manifold implications as his gospel finds a hearing, wherever and whenever that might be.

PART A:
FROM REJECTION TO AFFIRMATION:
CHANGING ATTITUDES TO JESUS OF NAZARETH

CHAPTER 2

What Got Jesus into Trouble? Understanding the Significance of Jesus' Ministry by Looking at Its Jewish Context. Part Two: Trouble Solidified

Darrell L. Bock

In part one of our study (*Impact of Jesus*, Vol. 1, Chap. 2), we set the context for this essay. We looked at the irritants of Jesus' claims to authority and what provoked a skeptical reaction to him by the Jewish leadership. We considered evidence for a 'middle' Jesus, a figure operating between more official Judaism and the practices of the later church. We looked for this in the evidence coming from the Jewish context of which Jesus was a part. We found claims of deep personal authority tied to his associations, forgiveness of sins, his Sabbath practices, and his discussions on purity. This claim was not that of a teacher or even a prophet, but was a more direct claim to represent God and his new program as proclaimed by Jesus.

In part two we look at the events of the end of Jesus' ministry in Jerusalem. These are the events that led to Jesus being brought before Pilate to be crucified. The table of skepticism had already been set. These final events solidified that position into concrete reaction. As with part one, we test these events for their core authenticity and the narrative coherence they may possess in order to make sense out of what got Jesus into trouble.

Major Incident 1: Temple and Temple Cleansing.

Jesus displayed a mixed relationship to the temple in his various remarks and activities associated with it. In many ways, that mix is much like his approach to issues of law in general. Some things are affirmed, while other remarks show that the temple would not remain the center of activity that it had been.

It is debated whether Jesus' act in clearing out the temple's money changers was a (1) call of cleansing, (2) a prophetic reform for the temple, (3) a symbolic picture of its destruction pointing to the arrival of the eschaton, or (4) some type of combination where renewal and a messianic claim on the temple are made (John 2:13–22; Matt 21:12–13 = Mark 11:15–17 = Luke 19:45–46).[1]

In favor of a symbolic act picturing destruction are (1) the following fig tree incident; (2) the remarks of John 2:19, which suggest a concern about another temple more important to God's plan than the physical temple; and (3) Jesus' predictions in the Olivet discourse of the temple's coming destruction (Matt 24 = Mark 13 = Luke 21:5–37). However, in support of symbolism tied to a cleansing reform are the remarks about the temple being either a place of prayer (Matt 21:13) or a place for the nations (Mark 11:17). This appears to foresee a time when the temple will continue to function in line with its rationale for existing. In addition, the early church kept its attachment to the temple, so that any idea that it ceased to have value or was totally obsolete appears not to have been adopted by the earliest church that responded to this act.

---

1   For the destruction view see Wright, *Jesus and the Victory of God*, 413–28; for that of a prophetic declaration of a destruction with the expectation of a renewed temple, see Sanders, *Jesus and Judaism*, 61–76; for the view 'more probably' of a symbolic cleansing as a messianic act tied to entry, see Witherington, *The Christology of Jesus*, 107–16. As the above studies show, even more disputed is why the cleansing/destruction was required. Was it for economic reasons (Sadducees taking unfair economic advantage), purity reasons (sacrifices did not really belong to the worshiper but merely were purchased, or sacrifices were moved into the holy space of the court of the Gentiles), both, or a challenge to the temple as a national symbol for Israel's nationalism? This is less than clear, although I prefer the option that both economic and worship ideals were being compromised by the recent move of the money changers into the court. See discussion of the passage in Bock, *Jesus according to Scripture*. Meyer, *The Aims of Jesus*, 197, rightly calls it several things: a demonstration, a prophetic critique, a fulfillment event, and a sign of the future. The temple cleansing pledges the 'perfect restoration of Israel' (p.198). Where there is restoration in a Jewish context, there very likely is the invocation of Messiah.

As the range of views discussed about this event shows, it is usually regarded as an authentic act of Jesus. What is debated is its significance.

Jewish background is important here. Many Jewish texts reflect a view that the temple would be part of what would be renewed in the last times. This belief appears to be part of the backdrop of Jesus' action, pointing slightly more to a cleansing (*1 Enoch* 90.28–30; Zech 14:21; *Shemoneh Esreh,* Benediction 14).[2] These factors appear to suggest that the temple was being cleansed with a prophetic-like call to the nation to behave appropriately. No doubt that if covenantal unfaithfulness continued, then judgment would come (Mark 13:2 = Matt 24:2 = Luke 21:5–6). The lessons of the blessings and cursing in the Law, plus those of past exile, pointed in such a direction for Jews concerned about the potential impact of unfaithfulness. The event means this at the least.

However, once again, there is more than what appears to be the case on the surface. It is better to see Jesus acting as a messianic claimant and not just discussing the role of the temple. He is making his statement about the need for reform of the temple to prepare for the new era. This is like the prayer in Benediction 14 of *Shemoneh Esreh*, which links together messianic hope and the temple, just as the later inquiry of Jesus before the Council will move from the topic of the temple to messiahship. The fact that this, according to the Synoptics, is Jesus' first act after entering the city as a regal figure makes this view likely. Jesus allowed this symbolism initiated by him and his disciples to frame his entry into the city. It sets a backdrop to his first action in the city at

---

2   1 Enoch 90:28–29 reads: 'And I stood up to see till they folded up that old house; and carried off all the pillars, and all the beams and ornaments of the house were at the same time folded up with it, and they carried it off and laid it in a place in the south of the land. And I saw till the Lord of the sheep brought a new house greater and loftier than that first, and set it up in the place of the first which had been folded up: all its pillars were new, and its ornaments were new and larger than those of the first, the old one which He had taken away, and all the sheep were within it'. It looks to building of a new house of God in the end. Tobit 14:5–7a anticipates a rebuilt temple and reads: 'But God will again have mercy on them, and God will bring them back into the land of Israel; and they will rebuild the temple of God, but not like the first one until the period when the times of fulfillment shall come. After this they all will return from their exile and will rebuild Jerusalem in splendor; and in it the temple of God will be rebuilt, just as the prophets of Israel have said concerning it. Then the nations in the whole world will all be converted and worship God in truth. They will all abandon their idols, which deceitfully have led them into their error; and in righteousness they will praise the eternal God'. Psalms of Solomon 17–18 points to a powerful figure who is a part of such a renewal.

the temple. This is a narrative link to these events where one casts a shadow on the other. Once again, understanding these events means not 'dividing and conquering' but keeping the link and sequence of events in place, especially in the tightly linked sequence that belonged to the last segment of Jesus' ministry. If Jesus' claim meets with rejection, then the nation stands culpable of covenantal unfaithfulness tied to her most holy space and the potential arrival of the new era and its central figure.

Jesus' act in the temple would have been seen as most provocative by the Jewish leadership. They had the most to lose from his action. Where the other areas already mentioned would have been irritants, to the extent they were public claims, this act on the most sacred space overseen by the high priest, Sadducees, and Sanhedrin could not be ignored. It was too direct a challenge to the leadership's authority, now carried out in the most sensitive of locations and social contexts.

Again, to make such a move by itself could have been seen as merely prophetic, but placed alongside and linked to Jesus' eschatological claims, his entry, and other actions that touched on legal questions, a more messianic, restorative association is present with implications for the kingdom's arrival. Jesus is challenging holy space and claiming a right to oversee it by what he does here. To see oneself as having the authority to exercise judgment over the central religious symbol of the nation was to perform an act that assumed a claim to divinely connected authority as well as enacting an authoritative claim that undercut the leadership that saw itself as responsible for such sacred space. This leadership authority was so great and sensitive that Rome even allowed the leaders to control and keep the peace in this sacred space. This is precisely why the cleansing raises the leaders' question after the event about the source of Jesus' authority (Matt 21:23–27 = Mark 11:27–33 = Luke 20:1–8). They ask, 'Who gave you the right to do these things?' It was exactly the right question. They got Jesus' point and saw him as encroaching on their space.

The nature of Jesus' act both fits with and is distinguished from both the Jewish and later Christian views about the temple. We see the 'middle' Jesus again. He does not enter the city to declare his reform with the power of a military leader who conquers. His tone is very distinct from both Jewish eschatological and Greco-Roman political expectation, what Brent Kinman has called an 'atriumphal' entry.[3] This 'humble' element to his entry also stands in contrast to the eventual emphasis of the early church on the unreserved glory of the Messiah, not to mention how by the time the Gospels are written the temple has taken on a more irrelevant role for many followers of Jesus, a direction that predated the temple's destruction.

So, like the handling of the law, Jesus' treatment of the temple suggests an authority over the most sacred of Israel's sites, the very place where God dwells. At the least we have a figure confident of how closely he works with God, one who expresses the divine will in the face of the seeming authority of those who oversaw the temple before Rome and who saw themselves as overseeing the will of God among God's chosen people.

However, if this temple act is linked to other actions associated with Jesus' entry into Jerusalem, then it is more likely that Jesus is making claims beyond that of a prophet. He is a messianic claimant exercising authority over the temple. He himself functions as the hub of what the promised restructuring requires. One could perhaps debate whether the picture is of a messiah or an eschatological prophet. However, if it is an eschatological prophet, then the model is of a leader-prophet like Moses, who himself functioned as the people of God's prime leader, much as a Messiah was anticipated to do in the eschaton. Such a core role for Jesus within God's plan coheres with what our next event also shows. This next event took place in private but that gives insight into how Jesus saw what was taking place in the final phase of his ministry.

---

3 Kinman, 'Jesus' Royal Entry'.

Key Explanation 1: Redesigning Liturgy for a New Era.[4]

Underscoring what has been said about the law is how Jesus handles sacred liturgy rooted in the law as evidenced in the Last Supper (Matt 26:17–30 = Mark 14:12–26 = Luke 22:7–23). This event is also multiply attested as it is found in Mark 14:22–25 and in a tradition reflected in Paul's report in 1 Corinthians 11:23–26 and followed by Luke. What appears to be a Passover meal is reinterpreted in terms of Jesus' approaching death (Mark 14:2 with 22–25; Luke 22:15 makes a clear identification with the Passover meal). Chronological questions between John and the Synoptics most contribute to raising the question of what type of meal is present, since John seems to place Jesus' crucifixion at the time of the sacrifices for this Passover meal (John 18:39; 19:14). At the least we have a meal offered during Passover season that evokes the establishing of a new relationship with God on terms that Jesus creates. The connection to Passover imagery is likely, given that they are eating the meal as pilgrims in Jerusalem for Passover, even if we cannot be absolutely sure that a Passover meal was the occasion.[5] A sacred meal, or at least imagery tied to a sacred season and event, the exodus, is reshaped into a message about the new era of eschatological deliverance.[6]

---

4   This is the one private event these two essays cover. However, it is not presented as a 'troublemaking' event. Rather this event gives insight into how Jesus saw events unfolding in this critical culminating period of his ministry and how he ritualized what was about to happen for his disciples. This rite came to take on so much meaning that it became memorialized among early believers as the one regular practice they would engage in as a community act. Surely the event's explanatory and solemn context helped to give it such ongoing life and memory for the church.

5   There is debate whether a Passover meal is at the base of the Last Supper, although this does seem likely. The Gospel texts we have make the connection. Even if it is not, the event took place so close to Passover that these associations would exist. The classic work arguing for a Passover meal is Jeremias, *The Eucharistic Words of Jesus*. In contrast stands the thesis of Bruce Chilton, *The Temple of Jesus*, 148–54, who argues that the Passover connection is anachronistic and favors seeing the meal in terms of Jesus' view of cultic purity and his practice of forgiveness as seen in his meals and associations. This approach seems to ignore the background inevitably raised by the festal occasion, regardless of what we can or cannot know exactly about the form of a Passover meal at the time. To speak of a death at Passover time in the context of a work of deliverance naturally would lead to this association. Thus, a Passover backdrop is still more likely here. So Goppelt, *Theology*, 1.215. McKnight, *The Death of Jesus*, also argues against a Passover connection. As we argue above, the point we make is possible regardless of the precise historical scenario. I have discussed the issue of the setting in detail in Bock & Glaser, *Messiah in the Passover*. Marshall, 'The Last Supper', has a full discussion of all the issues tied to this scene.

6   For other details about the event, see Bock, *Jesus according to Scripture*, unit 264.

So what does this recasting in terms of sacrifice and covenant mean about Jesus? The remarks about the meal clearly present Jesus as a sacrifice opening up the way to the new covenant relationship with God. As such, it fits the eschatological and kingdom emphasis in Jesus' teaching. But there is more. He is the means through which forgiveness is given. That this result is associated with the kingdom is clear from Jesus' remark about not drinking of the cup again until he drinks it anew in the kingdom of God, which is a look to the kingdom at the time of the full consummation of God's promise which will come sometime after God's vindication of Jesus. The bread (body) and cup (blood) imagery emphasizes the issues tied to what Jesus provides through his death (covenant, forgiveness). So Jesus stands at the hub or base of a new era and makes provision for the establishment of a fresh way of relating to God in a fresh context of forgiveness. Both the bread and the cup picture what Jesus offers 'on your behalf'. The blood pictures what is 'poured out for many' (Matt 26:28 = Mark 14:24). Here Isaiah 53:12 stands in the background, while the Passover stands as the illustrative event. The meal was a promise that what Jesus was about to do would provide a context for a new relationship with God that had been promised long ago.[7] Thus Jesus and his upcoming death are portrayed as the authoritative basis for the opening of the new era.

As great a role as that is, there is even more here. That Jesus could take sacred exodus imagery and transform it with fresh meaning speaks to his view as interpreter of both God's law and plan. The portrait here also reinforces the point previously made under the discussion of the law. Jesus claims an ability to take on a creative role in that plan, to author and perfect a traditional act of worship that was rooted in God's action in saving Israel and tied to the law (Exod. 12). He acts as the unique, sent revelator of God. Jesus exercises authority over worship tied to the law. It is also like the authority he asserts in the temple. Jesus is expanding and reforming most of the major images of Judaism—and

---

7 When one adds the portrait of John's Gospel here, the results are interesting. John does not depict the Last Supper with its bread and cup, but what he does highlight in this time frame is the announcement of the coming of the Paraclete (the Holy Spirit), yet another key dimension of the new covenant promise. John's role in supplementing well-known tradition is seen here. Most see John as understanding that Jesus taught a Supper theme because of imagery present in John 6.

he is very much part of the point. The question that is raised by all of this legal and Jewish halakhic activity is, 'What sort of person is this that he is able to recast old sacred rites?'[8] Jesus is not merely establishing a new rite, which Judaism often did. He is modifying one of the most sacred, Torah-based rites of Israel, the picture of Passover that stood for the nation's salvation. To have the self-belief that he came to do this reflects a self-claim that Jesus knew God's way and will. The one sent by God alters a God-given sacred rite. Again, authority is the issue here.

It is interesting that the church did not limit this celebration only to an annual observance of the event. It was celebrated periodically across the year, unlike events in the Jewish calendar which were part of a regular annual Jewish worship schedule. This difference may well indicate a move where Jesus again is the middle figure in the development of the practice.

Major Incident 2: Jesus' Declaration before the Jewish Leadership—A Claim of Vindication to Come.

Jesus' hope and confidence of vindication occurs in the Gospels during his Jewish examination, leading to his being condemned to the cross. The moment of seeming defeat is the very moment of disclosure of how God will bring him victory. When Jesus appeals to Psalm 110:1 upon being asked if he is the Christ, he is claiming that rather than being the defendant before the council, he will one day be their judge, operating from the very side of God.[9] One day, they will see the Son of Man seated at the right hand of the Father. Matthew and Luke intensify this remark, noting that 'hereafter' (Matthew) or 'from now on' (Luke) they

---

8   Goppelt, *Theology of the New Testament*, 1.220, says it this way: 'Jesus now vouchsafed forgiving fellowship by giving himself as the One who died for the benefit of all others. It is not a heavenly body, not a pneumatic substance, that was given, and also not only an atoning power, but Jesus as the One who died for all'.

9   The detailed explanation and defense of the historicity of this scene is the burden of Bock, *Blasphemy and Exaltation*, 184–237, updated in Bock, 'Blasphemy and the Jewish examination of Jesus' (2009). A related discussion on authenticity appears in my article, 'Blasphemy and the Jewish Examination of Jesus' (2007). All of these works present a detailed case of the essential authenticity of this scene, working through one at a time the series of objections raised against such a positive view of the material.

will see this exercise of authority. This remark becomes the reason Jesus is sent to the Roman governor to be crucified. To the Jewish leadership he has claimed a level of equality with God that is seen as blasphemous. The leadership turns this into a political charge for Pilate, leading to Jesus' death because Pilate would not care less about Jewish blasphemy but would care about a claim to be a king whom Rome did not appoint.

What does Jesus mean besides referring to the fact that he will possess judgment authority one day and gather his elect for their final redemption (the apocalyptic Son of Man texts, esp. Mark: Matt 24:29–31 = Mark 13:24–27 = Luke 21:25–28; M: Matt. 25:31–46)? I Enoch 62:5–9 gives us a clue of how Jews saw such imagery. It reads:

> And one portion of them shall look on the other, and they shall be terrified, and they shall be downcast of countenance, and pain shall seize them, when they see that Son of Man sitting on the throne of his glory. And the kings and the mighty and all who possess the earth shall bless and glorify and extol him who rules over all, who was hidden. For from the beginning the Son of Man was hidden, and the Most High preserved him in the presence of His might, and revealed him to the elect. And the congregation of the elect and holy shall be sown, and all the elect shall stand before him on that day. And all the kings and the mighty and the exalted and those who rule the earth shall fall down before him on their faces, and worship and set their hope upon that Son of Man, and petition him and supplicate for mercy at his hands.

So clearly, as anticipated in Jewish terms, Jesus presents his authority in relationship to final judgment and the position he shares with God in anticipation of vindication.

J. D. G. Dunn's important overview of this scene and its use of Daniel 7 and Psalm 110 summarizes well the current state of discussion on the authenticity of this passage.[10] Dunn defends the likelihood that Jesus expected some form of vindication by this point in his ministry drawn from Daniel 7:13–14. In analyzing Psalm 110:1, he argues that the use

---

10 Dunn, "Are You the Messiah?", 11–21.

of the term 'Power' is neither a Jewish nor Christian way of speaking about God. I have challenged this idea with respect to Judaism, noting how numerous texts in the Midrashim consistently used the phrase of God's Power as a shorthand way to refer to God's saving acts and power in Exodus.[11]

Dunn notes three possible origins for this expression: (1) a Philonic type Christian innovation, (2) an early rabbinic formulation taken over by Christians, or (3) an innovation by Jesus. He argues there is little to choose from these options, but also notes that in combination with Psalm 110:1 the balance may be tipped in favor of an early Jewish Christian use versus one from Jesus, a remark I take as his preference for the second option. Our evidence suggests a fourth option. 'Power' was one of many ways to refer indirectly to God without using his sacred name, a reference that also looked to his power to deliver, something that fits the setting here. Given the numerous such indirect references to God in this scene, Jesus' reply shows respect for God equal to the manner in which the Council's question to him was raised. This touch shows a sensitivity to the significance of the context and the delicate nature of the question being raised about Jesus at the examination.

Dunn goes on to argue that the seating and coming on the clouds combination assumes a second coming and likely demonstrates early Christian influence, yet another argument against authenticity. He sees Psalm 110:1 as inserted into the exchange. However, Psalm 110:1 is a text that gives evidence of being part of a messianic dispute between Jesus and his opponents in the last week of Jesus' ministry where the second coming plays no part (Mark 12:35–37 par.). In the earlier dispute over this text, Jesus simply raises a dilemma between the Messiah being the Son of David and being Lord—and does so in a very Jewish rhetorical manner, posing as an opposition something that needs prioritizing. The ambiguous manner of this challenge and its form suggest authenticity versus early church creation. It also points to the likelihood that Jesus had already thought of this text as an important one in his

---

11 Bock, *Blasphemy and Exaltation in Judaism*, 217–220. The distribution of the expression among these later texts suggests its potential age. It appears in *Sifre* on Numbers (§ 112 on 15:31) and Deuteronomy (§ 319 on 32:18), as well as in *Targum Job* 5.8, *Aboth Rabbi Nathan A* (37:12), and numerous texts in *Mekilta*.

own messianic understanding. The extensive use of this text far more explicitly in the early church also suggests this passage may well be one rooted in Jesus' own initial reflections. The ambiguous nature of Jesus' remark at the trial also suggests an earlier, not a later usage. It reflects a 'middle' Jesus. Even more interesting is that the key allusion to Psalm 110 and the idea of seating appears in all forms of the tradition to this scene. It is not the coming on the clouds that is omnipresent, as Luke's version lacks a reference to the clouds. So one could argue the remark about the clouds is added later to draw more out of the Son of Man allusion without arguing that Psalm 110:1 is the later insertion by the church. All Jesus needs for the Psalm 110:1 allusion is to believe in his and God's close linkage and the hope of vindication, something Dunn already has affirmed as likely and something other events in this essay have already shown. The activity of Jesus in his ministry and the nature of his argument, multiply attested, shows he very likely understood himself as in a unique, close relationship to his Father.

In other words, all the elements here reflect coherence with the larger tradition and point to the likelihood of authenticity for a Daniel 7-Psalm 110 linkage by Jesus, even if not every element was present in that linkage. This is especially the case when there has not been, at the time of the writing of any of the Gospels, any actual sighting of the Son of Man on the clouds, as Jesus' claim makes. So either we have an allusion to the near coming of Jesus, as yet unfulfilled, or the reference to seeing only points to observing the effects of Jesus' being seated, which is more likely. Those effects might include the formation and growth of this group and their acts invoking Jesus, and their changed lives in boldly speaking about Jesus. This alternative, pointing to authenticity, is an option Dunn does not raise. A strong case can be made for it being the more likely option. Dunn's article does argue that (1) something like blasphemy probably did come out of the real scene as the charge framed in Jewish terms and (2) that debate about why Jesus was killed makes it likely something about this scene did get out into public venues. The point in pursuing this discussion in some detail is that it is more likely that Jesus did use a Psalm 110-Daniel 7 combination in his reply than only one text or the other. For Jesus, the key point was the picture of the Son of Man seated by God, a key summary of his understanding of his authority uttered at the most crucial moment of all, when his life was on the line. This view also explains the hope of vindication he had as he faced the prospect of his martyrdom for his view of the kingdom.

When one adds to this all the irritants in terms of Jesus' claims of authority, then one can see why those who did not believe Jesus' claims thought him worthy of death. If he was not who he claimed to be, one sent by God and able to sit with the Glory in heaven, then he was guilty of blasphemy. The inner Jewish debate over whether there could be a second power in heaven taking place in this period only enhances how such a claim would be seen if it were not accepted.[12]

In sum, Jesus' claim of vindication points to Jesus' being given a place at the side of God in line with his own earlier claims of authority tied to righteousness, the Law, the Sabbath, the divine calendar, the liturgy, and forgiveness of sin. The church saw this vindication confirmed in the resurrection. The church proclaimed Jesus' unique place as part of the heart of the church's kerygma. The result was the church's belief that Jesus was alive and that for early Christians there was life after death and a judgment/vindication to come because of their connection to the one raised and vindicated by God. This seating and the vindication this claim represented meant that all people are accountable to the vindicated one, a point that also opened up the proclamation of the kingdom to all nations. The reception of this act also pointed to the identity of the one who sits at God's side mediating God's blessing (John 14–16; Acts 2). He is the one qualified to share in God's very presence, brought there by God's act. As a result Jesus can distribute God's blessing, bring in God's kingdom with more fullness yet to come, and execute God's

---

12 Working through this background is the burden of my study, *Blasphemy and Exaltation in Judaism*. The possibility of such a figure is seen in 1 Enoch 37–71, and the *Exagoge of Ezekiel* 68–85. It is challenged in 3 Enoch 12–16, where Metatron is punished for making such a suggestion about himself and in remarks made to Rabbi Aqiba about his view that David would sit next to God in *b. Hagigah* 14a. The rabbi's view is met with rejection and the retort, 'How long will you profane the Shekinah?' This is an implicit warning not to commit blasphemy against the unique glory of God.

judgment.[13] As we have seen throughout these essays, the stress is not merely on understanding who Jesus is through his own verbal claims. Rather the key to understanding Jesus is to appreciate what his array of actions meant in their Jewish context. They are presented as God's acts reinforcing his claims and unique identity as the Son of Man.

Summary of Events and Acts of Jesus

It is the scope and ultimate unity of all of these acts that point to Jesus' uniqueness. There is a deep coherence across the strands of tradition in the narrative flow of this account that does not suggest a haphazard stitching together of post-Easter reflections. Taking most of these categories one by one, we can find parallels with activity by other human divine agents. However, no one attempted or achieved the combination of acts that Jesus is portrayed as performing. It is the scope of these acts that establishes his uniqueness. The claim was that Jesus is more than a human agent commissioned with divine authority. The Gospels argue that the full array of Jesus' acts explain that Jesus the promised Messiah is also the divinely vindicated Lord. So Jesus shares not only in divine authority but also in sharing a place with God in heaven. All this is done in very Jewish terms in the Gospels. Many of the events reflect a 'middle' Jesus. The crucifixion is the ground from which God builds his plan of redemption through a uniquely worthy sacrifice. The miracles, and especially the exorcisms, show the scope of Jesus' authority and against whom he is battling to bring victory. The reconfiguring of imagery tied to feasts shows that a new era has come. Jewish background gives a context for such claims, but Jesus' acts show a contrast between what

---

13 This view of resurrection fits Jewish background from groups like the Pharisees and some Jews at Qumran, as well as possibly the Essenes as noted by Hippolytus, *Refutatio* 9.27, 'they acknowledge the flesh will rise again and that it will be immortal, in the same manner that the soul is already imperishable'. For a survey of Jewish views, see Puech, 'Jesus and Resurrection Faith', who notes the following relevant texts: Isa 26:14–19; Ezek 37:1–14; Dan 12:1–3; 4Q385 2–3; Ben Sira 48:11; 4Q504 1–2 vi 14–15; 4Q548 1–2 ii 12–14; 1 Enoch 22, 104:5; 2 Macc 7, esp. v 23; Wis 3:1, 3; 5:17–23; 4Q416; 4Q418; CD 7:6; 1QS 3:13–4:26; 1QH 24:6–13, along long portions of 1QH 11, 14, 5 19, 4 and 24; and 4Q521 2 ii 12; 7:5–6. The Christian appeal to resurrection has one very important distinction from all of this. Jesus is raised within history, rather than at the end of history as Jewish expectation had it. Apparently the event tied to Jesus led to this variation.

Judaism's expectations in these areas were and what the church later made of these same issues. Jesus sits as the 'middle' and central figure in the transition. Most sensitive of all these claims of authority was the claim to be able to share directly in God's presence through vindication.

The resurrection-ascension came to serve as the ultimate vindication of these claims. Resurrection becomes God's vote in the dispute between the rejection of the Jewish leaders and Jesus' claims, serving as the 'irritant *par excellence*'[14] leading to early Jesus community views that eventually led to the split between Judaism and what became Christianity. For these original Jewish messianics, Jesus' seated position at the side of God and in his execution of forgiveness and the bestowal of covenantal blessings affirms his position as Lord (Acts 2:16–38). He is the one who is both Lord and Christ. He has brought God's promised new era and with it a new community filled with new promise and enablement. It is the combination of all these acts by Jesus that got him into trouble and led to his crucifixion. The Christian tradition tied to Jesus is quite honest about these causes of conflict operating at multiple levels, especially when seen against the backdrop of Jewish expectation. It does not hide the controversy. The tradition's final claim, however, is that in resurrection God showed which side of the conflict and which set of claims the deity favored. These irritants and conflicts have a solid claim to be historical. The 'middle' Jesus helps us find the historical Jesus, even using the standards applied to testing the distribution and quality of that tradition at individual points. In this way, synthesis and analysis can both be honored as we consider who Jesus was in his Jewish context, what got him into trouble, and why the early church preached him to be at the center of activating a long hoped for promise of deliverance.

---

14 I owe this phrase and observation to my colleague, Mike Burer, who made this point when he graciously read the draft of this essay.

Bibliography

Bock, D.L., & M. Glaser (eds.)   *Messiah in the Passover* (Grand Rapids: Kregel, 2017).

Bock, D.L.   *Jesus according to Scripture* (Grand Rapids: Baker, ²2017 [2002]).

Bock, D.L.   'Blasphemy and the Jewish examination of Jesus', in D.L. Bock & R.L. Webb (eds.), *Key Events in the Life of the Historical Jesus. A Collaborative Exploration of Context and Coherence* (WUNT 247; Tübingen: Mohr Siebeck, 2009; Grand Rapids: Eerdmans, 2010), 625–56. [same pagination in both editions]

Bock, D.L.   'Blasphemy and the Jewish Examination of Jesus', *BBR 17* (2007), 53–114.

Bock, D.L.   *Blasphemy and Exaltation in Judaism and the Final Examination of Jesus: a Philological-Historical Study of the Key Jewish themes impacting Mark 14:61–64* (WUNT 2.106; Tübingen: Mohr Siebeck, 1998).

Chilton, B.   *The Temple of Jesus: His Sacrificial Program within a Cultural History of Sacrifice* (University Park, Pa.: Pennsylvania State University Press, 1992).

Dunn, J.D.G.   '"Are You the Messiah?": Is the Crux of Mark 14:61–62 Resolvable?', in D.G. Horrell & C.M. Tuckett (eds.), *Christology, Controversy and Community: New Testament Essays in Honour of David R. Catchpole* (NovTSupp 99; Leiden: Brill, 2000), 1–21.

Goppelt, L.   *Theology of the New Testament* (2 Vols.; Grand Rapids: Eerdmans, 1981–82 [German: 1976]).

Jeremias, J.   *The Eucharistic Words of Jesus* (New Testament Library; N. Perrin, trans.; New York: Scribner, ²1966 [1955]).

Kinman, B.   'Jesus' Royal Entry into Jerusalem', *BBR 15* (2005), 223–60.

McKnight, S.   *The Death of Jesus* (Waco: Baylor University Press, 2005).

Marshall, I.H.	'The Last Supper', in D. L. Bock & R. L. Webb (eds.), *Key Events in the Life of the Historical Jesus: A Collaborative Exploration of Context and Coherence* (WUNT 247; Tübingen: Mohr Siebeck, 2009; Grand Rapids: Eerdmans, 2010), 481–588. [same pagination in both editions]
Meyer, B.F.	*The Aims of Jesus* (London: SCM, 1979).
Puech, E.	'Jesus and Resurrection Faith in Light of Jewish Texts', in J.H. Charlesworth (ed.), *Jesus and Archaeology* (Grand Rapids: Eerdmans 2006), 639–659.
Sanders, E.P.	*Jesus and Judaism* (London: SCM, 1985).
Witherington, B., III	*The Christology of Jesus* (Minneapolis: Fortress, 1990).
Wright, N.T.	*Jesus and the Victory of God* (London: SPCK, 1996).

CHAPTER 3

Reactions of Roman Officialdom to Christ and His Followers in the Early First Century AD: A Case-Study of Pontius Pilate

James R. Harrison

Abstract

A *Roman* historical assessment of Pilate's rule as the prefect of Judea is particularly difficult. The literary sources are sparse, confined to flashpoints in Pilate's prefecture, and, in some instances, rhetorically jaundiced. The Gospel accounts present four different portraits of Pilate: each adopts a distinctly evaluative stance towards him as an historical figure and is animated by wider theological concerns. The archaeological evidence is also slender, being confined to a fragmentary inscription at Caesarea Maritima, a few numismatic issues, and a recent material find at Jerusalem. Moreover, certain scholarly theses, such as Ethelbert Stauffer's hypothesis about Pilate's *amicitia* with the praetorian prefect Sejanus at Rome during Tiberius' reign, have had a longevity that they do not deserve. This chapter reassesses the literary, epigraphic, numismatic, and archaeological evidence and the commonalities in the Gospel narratives, including one distinctive Johannine tradition, from a Roman viewpoint. It is hoped by such a methodological case study of Pilate that the wide range of Roman officialdom mentioned in the New Testament can be similarly evaluated so that we might gain a sense of how Rome perceived its role in governing an increasingly troublesome province.

The reactions of elite Roman officials to Christ and the *Christianoi* is a fascinating but methodologically complex study. The New Testament documents record several encounters of Christ and the first believers with elite Roman officials from the thirties to the late fifties.[1] The arraignment of Christ before the Roman prefect Pontius Pilate is graphically depicted in the Gospels, as are the apostle Paul's meetings with Roman proconsuls and procurators (Sergius Paulus, Lucius Junius Gallio Annaeanus, Marcus Antonius Felix, Porcius Festus) in the book of Acts. Crucially, all of these encounters with elite Roman officials are mediated to us through the narratives of Christian writers. A full-scale study of official Roman responses to the early Christians would require us to situate each prefect, proconsul and procurator in his literary, epigraphic, numismatic, and archaeological context as a precursor to any meaningful discussion of Roman officialdom in the New Testament. Because such a task is properly the subject of a monograph,[2] this chapter will focus on Pontius Pilate as an important test-case, but will bring into play all the genres of evidence noted above.

The methodological challenge is to penetrate behind the theological rhetoric of the Gospels, while respecting their differently redacted historical traditions and the varying evaluative perspectives from which each evangelist approaches Pilate, his retainers, and the anonymous crowds of Jerusalem. In concentrating upon the commonalities of the Gospel narratives regarding Christ's arraignment before Pilate (Mark 15:1–25; Matt 27:11–26; Luke 23:1–25; John 19:28–19:16), in which the full array of the material and literary evidence relating to Pilate will

---

1   Throughout I employ the name 'Christ' as opposed to 'Jesus', not due to its messianic import, but because this is the name by which Romans consistently referred to Jesus and his followers (Tacitus, *Ann.* 14.44; Suetonius, *Claud.* 25; *Nero* 15; Pliny [the Younger] *Ep.* 10.96; cf. Acts 11:26).
2   For a discussion of Roman political reactions to the early Christians from the post-Easter period to the reign of Hadrian, see Harrison, 'Persecution'. On Luke's presentation of the proconsuls, procurators and other officialdom in Acts, see Rowe, *World Upside Down*, 53–89.

be brought to bear in our assessment, it is hoped that a Roman viewpoint of Pilate's role will emerge from the interpretative overlay of the Gospels and, concomitantly, we will gain a stronger sense of why the Romans found Christ a confronting figure worthy of execution. The result will necessarily be a 'minimalist' portrait, but hopefully historically secure nonetheless.

One independent Gospel tradition (John 19:12a), however, will be examined in order to demonstrate the insightfulness of the Roman perspectives that the Gospels, despite their strong apologetic intent, still manage to retain in their narratives. It will be argued that the commonalities of the Gospel narratives, when assessed against the material and literary evidence, do in fact provide a credible Roman portrait of Pilate as a Roman prefect. However, the irony underlying each of the Gospel narratives, strategically employed by the evangelists, provides their readers with a cautionary evaluation of the operations and limitations of first-century AD provincial power of Rome in the eastern Mediterranean basin.

1. Christ and Pontius Pilate: Rome Encounters the Founder of a New Movement

1.1 Prolegomenon

We know nothing concrete about Pontius Pilate before his prefecture of Judea (AD 26–36). Like all the twelve governors of Judea, Pilate, as the fifth, would have possessed equestrian rank, undoubtedly with military experience as a prefect of an *ala* (cavalry 'squadron') and, prior to that, possibly being a prefect of a cohort or a military tribune somewhere (presumably) in Italy.[3] This is confirmed by the strong likelihood that the prefect's cognomen, 'Pilatus', was derived from the Latin noun *pilum* ('javelin'), the weapon *par excellence* of the Roman legionaries.[4] The very rare adjective *pilatus* means 'javelin-armed', testifying to Pilate's military

---

3   Schiavone, *Pontius Pilate*, 56.
4   See Baudoin, 'Sur les traces de Ponce Pilate', 147. The additional suggestion of Brown, *Death*, 1.694, that the name might also have its origin from *pileus* ('cap', 'helmet') is unlikely, given that there is a Latin adjective *pilatus*.

background. Mark D. Smith, however, proposes the explanation 'that one of his ancestors served as *primus pilus* (literally: 'First Spear') in the Roman military, the highest ranking among all centurions in a legion,' acquiring enough money upon retirement to qualify for equestrian status.[5] The claim of Smith has some merit. It is entirely possible that Pilate, in highlighting *pilatus* as his cognomen, was making a more extravagant claim about the legionary background of his family than just membership of the military corps.

The nomen 'Pontius' goes back to the famous Pontii of the Roman republic,[6] among whom was the celebrated ancestor, Gaius Pontius, who saw his Samnite forces triumph over the Romans in the brilliant victory at the Battle of the Caudine Forks (321 BC). This old Samnite family would later pride itself on its resistance to the dictatorship of Julius Caesar, with L. Pontius Aquillius taking part in his assassination after having been humiliated by Caesar (Suetonius, *Caes*. 98). But, by the time of the early Empire, the family was thoroughly Romanised, providing a consul under Tiberius Caesar (Gaius Petronius Pontius Nigrinus: AD 37).[7] If these links, arising from the evidence of the nomen and cognomen, do in fact indicate that Pilate belonged to a famous Samnite family of impeccable military prestige and also had a famous legionary ancestor, then the Roman prefect of Judea would have sought to equal and surpass the inherited glory of his ancestors, as was the ethos of the Roman nobles and equestrians.[8] It should not surprise us, therefore, that upon his arrival in Judea, Pilate sought to establish his personal authority as quickly as possible and maintain the extension of honour to the ruling Julio-Claudian house in this provincial backwater, with a view to enhancing the glory of his Samnite and equestrian ancestors and that of the Roman ruler. Finally, we know nothing of Pilate's

---

5   Smith, *Final Days*, 45.
6   Ollivier, 'Ponce Pilati et les Pontii'.
7   Blinzler, *The Trial of Jesus*, 180–81. On Gaius Petronius Pontius Nigrinus holding the consulship in AD 37, see *CIL* 10.6774; 14.4535; cf. Suetonius, *Tib*. 73; Cassius Dio 58.27.1.
8   See Bond, *Pontius Pilate*, 9–19. On the Roman elite quest to enhance and surpass ancestral glory, see Harrison, *Paul and the Imperial Authorities*, 201–31. A strong indication of the quest for glory and the rendering of ancestral piety by the equestrian order at a Roman provincial level can be gauged by the honorific epigraphy of the equites at Philippi: see Brélaz, *Corpus des inscriptions grecques et latines de Philippes*, Section 3, §§47–71.

wife's family other than his wife's name in tradition (i.e. Claudia Procla or Procula; cf. Gospel of Nicodemus ['Christ's Descent into Hell'] III.8 [Tischendorf, *Ea*, 449–55]),[9] her possible presence with him in Judea,[10] and her (entirely literary?) role in the Gospel of Matthew (Matt 27:19).

Another important issue to realise at the outset is the mutual dependence of the Judean 'retainer' class—that is, the high priests, the effective rulers of Judea (Josephus, *A.J.* 20.251), and the most notable Pharisees, sometimes allied with the high priests—and the Roman prefect in ensuring stability of political rule in Judea. Warren Carter has helpfully drawn attention to the fact that Josephus depicts the chief priests as advocating submission to and cooperation with Rome (Josephus, *A.J.* 2.197, 230, 410–411, 418; *B.J.* 2.318–320; cf. Matt 2:4–6; 28:11–15).[11] The mutually advantageous nature of this relationship between the retainer class and the prefects and procurators of Judea is summarised thus:

> Both governors and the chief priests needed each other. Governors need cooperative priests and local landowners to maintain the hierarchical social order and ensure compliance with Rome. Pleasing the governor was the main way that the chief priests gained access to power, status, and wealth. The price for this position was to become agents of the Roman governors' interests.[12]

---

9   For the Greek and Latin text of Gospel of Nicodemus ['Paradosis'] III.8, see Tischendorf, *Ea*, 449–55, which is translated in Hennecke, *New Testament Apocrypha Volume One*, 482–84, here 484; cf. Bond, *Pontius Pilate*, 133 n. 49. On Pilate in Christian and apocryphal tradition, see Judd, *Pontius Pilate*; Baudoin, *Ponce Pilate*, not seen by me.

10 Lémonon, *Ponce Pilate*, 253, argues that we cannot confirm the presence of Pilate's wife in Judea, dismissing Matthew 27:19 as a late insertion. Cf. similarly, Davies & Allison, *Matthew*, 3.587: 'this probably fictional interlude'. Note, too, Dodson, 'Reading Dreams', 269–76, here 276, who concludes that the dream of Pilate's wife is a 'literary feature ... that creates a narrative intertexture of contrasting characters, repetitive motifs, and narrative parallels'. On the dream, see the excellent discussion of Brown, *Death*, 803–7. Nevertheless, Lémonon concedes that the republican law forbidding wives to accompany governors during their tenure was repealed under the Empire (Tacitus, *Ann.* 1.40; 2:54–55; 3:33–34), partially in the reign of Augustus (Suetonius, *Aug.* 24) and probably fully in the reign of Tiberius. So the possibility of her presence in Judea with Pilate, in my view, remains open.

11 Carter, *Pontius Pilate*, 38–40, 47–49.

12 Carter, *Pontius Pilate*, 48. On high priests generally, see Vanderkam, *From Joshua to Caiaphas*. On Caiaphas, Jesus and Pilate, see Bond, *Caiaphas*, 50–72; Vanderkam, *From Joshua to Caiaphas*, 426–36.

In sum, it is extremely unlikely that Pilate did not know in advance from his retainers about the proposed arrest and accusation of Christ by the high priestly authorities.[13] Indeed, Pilate as prefect of Judaea would have had his own access to military and intelligence networks that would have periodically informed him, along with the other Roman prefects, about potential anti-Roman resistance in the period from AD 6–41.[14] This information was mediated through the robust chain of fortlets and fortresses in the hinterlands of Palestine,[15] or by means of Roman soldiers acting as spies (cf. the later evidence of Sifre Deuteronomy 344) and undercover agents, as was the case in Pilate's aqueduct funds episode (Josephus, *A.J.* 20.105–112; *B.J.* 2.224–227).[16] An itinerant charismatic figure like Christ, who preached an alternate Kingdom to Caesar, stirring up the general populace in the process and upsetting Rome's retainers in Judea, was a figure to be closely watched. The Gospel of Luke indicates that the appointment of spies was a tactic employed by the priestly retainers in monitoring potentially prosecutable sayings of Christ (20:20–22), undoubtedly with a view to assessing their blasphemous intent and the possibility of referring Christ to Pilate for arraignment (cf. Mark 14:63).

What, then, do we learn about Pontius Pilate from the material remains of first-century AD Palestine?

1.2 Our Knowledge of Pilate from the Material Remains: Epigraphy, Numismatics, and Archaeology

In 1961, during the excavation of the theatre of Caesarea Maritima, a broken inscription was unearthed which had been recycled at a later time 'to form a landing between a flight of steps at one of the entryways

---

13 Légasse, *The Trial of Jesus*, 62–63, concludes: 'we have every reason to accept that his relations with the local hierarchy were of the best: … Caiaphas remained high priest all the time that Pilate was in office, and when Pilate had to leave for Rome, Vitellius speedily nominated a successor to Caiaphas, a sign of connivance between Pilate and the latter'.
14 Bermejo-Rubio and Zeichmann, 'Where Were the Romans?'. More generally on Roman espionage, see Sheldon, *Tinker*; Austin and Rankov, *Exploratio*.
15 Bermejo-Rubio and Zeichmann, 'Where Were the Romans?', 84–88.
16 Bermejo-Rubio and Zeichmann, 'Where Were the Romans?', 88–97.

to the seats of the theatre'.[17] However, the gap at the beginning of line 1, Walter Eck observes, has only space for four to five missing letters 'since the text was symmetrically written'. This crucial observation rules out many of the suggested restorations from the time of Antonio Frova's original 1961 edition onwards.[18] Antonio Frova's Latin text of the inscription, unrestored and restored, is set out below:

Frova's edited Latin text	Frova's restored English text
/	
[- - -]S TIBERIEVM	[Caesarien]'s Tiberium
[- - - PON]TIVS PILATVS	[Po]ntius Pilatus
[- - - PRAEF]ECTVS IVDA[EA]A	[Pref]ect of Juda[ea]
/	[d]e[dicates]
- - - - - - - - - - - - - - -	

Craig Evans has helpfully provided translations for the six restorations suggested for the first line since Frova's original edition,[19] but, like Walter Eck, Evans agrees with Geza Alföldy's 1999 restoration set out below, which meets the required space specifications outlined above:[20]

Alföldy's edited Latin text	Alföldy's restored Latin text
[- - -]S TIBERIÉVM	[Nauti]s Tibérium
[- - -]NTIVS PILATVS	[- - Po]ntius Pilatus
[PRAEF]ECTVS IVDAE[A]E	praef[ectus] Iudae[a]e
[REF]ÉCI[T]	[ref]eci[t]

---

17 Vardaman, 'A New Inscription'. The original edition, Frova, 'L'Inscrizione di Ponzio Pilato a Cesarea', was unavailable to me. The most recent edition, with all the literature on the subsequent re-editions since Frova, as well as discussion, is found in Ameling, *Corpus Inscriptionum Iudaeae/Palestinae*, 2.§1277.

18 Eck, 'Inscription Attesting the Restoration of a Lighthouse', 229. The principle editions are set out in Lémonon's 2007 slightly revised edition of *Ponce Pilate*, adding a discussion of Geza Alföldy's 1999 restoration (Lémonon, *Ponce Pilate*, 28–29), which was not available at the time of publication of his previous edition (*Pilate et le gouvernement de la Judée*). In this chapter I will be referring throughout to the 2007 edition of Lémonon's monograph, in this instance drawing upon his discussion of the Caesarea Maritima Pilate inscription on pages 15–17, 23–33.

19 Evans, 'Excavating Caiaphas', 323–40, here 335–36.

20 Alföldy, 'Pontius Pilatus', 85–108; Alföldy, 'Nochmals', 133–48. For a photo of the inscription, see http://cojs.org/pontius_pilate-s_tiberium_inscription-_26-36_ce/ accessed 26.11.2020. The translation used here is Ameling, *Corpus Inscriptionum Iudaeae/Palestinae*, §1277.

Translation
[For the sailor]s the Tiberium
[Po]ntius Pilatus
[Pref]ect of Jude[a]
had restore[d].

The 'Tiberieum' which Pilate restored, Alföldy argued, is the lighthouse of the harbour of Caesarea Maritima, rebuilt for the safety of the sailors and rededicated in honour of the Roman ruler Tiberius. Alföldy draws a parallel between the Tiberieum and the tower called Druseion in the city of Strato's Tower in Palestine, a structure built by Herod the Great in honour of the young Drusus, the deceased young son of Tiberius

(Josephus, *A.J.* 15.336; *B.J.* 1.412):

> This mole which he built by the sea side was two hundred foot wide: the half of which was opposed to the current of the waves, so as to keep off those waves which were to break upon them: and so was called *Procymatia*, or the first breaker of the waves: but the other half had upon it a wall, with several towers: the largest of which was named *Drusus*: and was a work of very great excellence, and had its name from Drusus, the son-in-law of Caesar, who died young.

Thus, if Alföldy is correct, Pilate's 'Tiberieum' was not, as previous scholarship suggested, an imperial cult temple built and dedicated in honour of Tiberius at Caesarea Maritima, paralleling the Caesareum at Cyrene, or, less likely, a public colonnade or administrative building.[21] Alföldy observes that the absence of any mention of the Tiberieum in Josephus is probably best explained by its early destruction and thus it was not known to the historian.[22] That is entirely possible. I would also add that Josephus' access to the voluminous sources on Herod the Great (*A.J.* 15–17), acquired via the now lost life of Herod by Nicholas of Damascus, rapidly diminishes into cursory accounts from Archelaus onwards, with the result that the Tiberieum may well not have been even mentioned in the much sparser records upon which the Flavian historian was drawing for the careers of the Judean prefects. Astutely, Pilate ensures continuing strong diplomatic relations with the Roman ruler by honouring Tiberius with the Tiberieum lighthouse in Caesarea Maritima: this restoration would further enhance honour of the Julio-Claudian ruler and his family in Roman Palestine, building upon what had already been accorded to the ruler's dead son by Herod's construction of the Druseion at Strato's Tower.

Furthermore, Pilate's Tiberieum is a civic structure built for the benefit of shipping approaching and leaving the harbour of Caesarea Maritima, ensuring the safety of their cargoes and crews. It is consonant with Pilate's building of an aqueduct for Jerusalem (Josephus, *A.J.*

---

21 Lémonon, *Ponce Pilate*, 30–31.
22 Alföldy, 'Nochmals', 139.

18.60; *B.J.* 2.175–177), now identified with the archaeological remains of the Arrub aqueduct in the city.[23] It also aligns with the construction of the monumental 2000 foot-long stepped street from the Siloam Pool to the Temple Mount, which has been identified as having been built by Pilate c. AD 30 by virtue of the 101 coins found beneath street level, the most recent dating to AD 30/31.[24] One would have expected coins from Agrippa I to be present if the street had been constructed subsequently to AD 40/41.[25] In other words, what emerges historically and archeologically is the projected persona of Pontius Pilate as a civic builder at Jerusalem and Caesarea Maritima, fostering urban well-being by means of his projects, and eliciting (he had hoped) good-will from the sea-born merchant classes of Caesarea Maritima and the general populace of Jerusalem. By such projects Pilate not only enhanced his own political stakes but also added to his accrued ancestral glory through this traditional Roman pathway of honour acquisition for the equites.

Additionally, the inscription shows us that the actual magistracy of Pontius Pilate was *praefectus*, not the anachronistic term *procurator* that Tacitus uses of Pilate in *Annals* 15.44. The literary sources employ a confusing variety of terminology for the first governors of Judea: *hegemon* in New Testament documents, *epitropos* in Philo, and a blend of terminology (*epitropos*; *eparchos* [= *praefectus*]) in the case of Josephus.[26] However, as our inscription demonstrates and A. H. M. Jones had long since postulated, the early governors before the reign of Claudius were called *praefectus*, whereas upon the accession of Claudius to power the term *procurator* was then used for Judean governors.[27]

Last, regarding Pilate's numismatic evidence,[28] we have *quadrans* issues spanning three years:

---

23 Silver, 'Pontius Pilate', 459–74, here 471–72.
24 Szanton et al., 'Pontius Pilate in Jerusalem'.
25 Szanton et al., 'Pontius Pilate in Jerusalem', 162–63.
26 For full discussion, see Lémonon, *Ponce Pilate*, 45–54.
27 Lémonon, *Ponce Pilate*, 52–54; Jones, 'Procurators', 115–25.
28 For discussion, see Bammel, 'Syrian Coinage'; Bond, *Pontius Pilate*, 20–23; Bond, 'Coins'; Lémonon, *Ponce Pilate*, 94–98; Taylor, 'Pontius Pilate', 556–63; Evans, 'Excavating Caiaphas', 333–34; Jacobsen, 'Coins', 73–96. For excellent photos of the coins, see https://www.forumancientcoins.com/numiswiki/view.asp?key=Pontius%20Pilate, accessed 29.11.2020.

- The issue of AD 29/30 (Hendin, *Guide to Biblical Coins*, §648) has three ears of barley on the obverse, whereas on the reverse there is a cultic wine vessel (*simpulum* or possibly *culullus*);[29] the legend on the obverse is ΙΟΥΛΙΑ ΚΑΙΣΑΡΟΣ ('Julia, of Caesar'), while the legend on the reverse is ΤΙΒΕΡΙΟΥ ΚΑΙΣΑΡΟΣ ('of Tiberius Caesar').
- The issue of AD 30/31 (Hendin, *Guide to Biblical Coins*, §649) has an augur's wand (*lituus*), whereas on the reverse there is a wreath with berries; the legend on the obverse is ΤΙΒΕΡΙΟΥ ΚΑΙΣΑΡΟΣ, with no legend on the reverse.
- The issue of AD 31/32 (Hendin, *Guide to Biblical Coins*, §650) is the same as AD 30/31.

Several questions have dominated discussions of these coins: (a) To what degree were the coin iconography offensive to Jewish sensibilities? Concomitantly, did it merely reflect motifs from previous coin issues of Roman governors in Judea and were, therefore, inoffensive? (b) Do the coins appropriate motifs from the imperial cult and would this have been provocative to Jewish sensibilities? (c) How do we explain their cessation in AD 30/31? And why did Pilate delay several years from AD 26 before issuing coinage? What theories best explain the demise of any further coin issues? Ultimately, what were Pilate's motives in issuing these coins well into his rule as governor of Judea? We will briefly summarise the fruits of New Testament scholarship and come to a conclusion.

First, in terms of conventional and non-offensive images, the three barley ears, Bond argues, 'symbolised the fertility of the land, plenty and good harvests,'[30] having already been issued by previous Roman prefects of Judea (Coponius, Marcus Ambivulus) and subsequently by Agrippa I.[31] But, correctly in my view, Taylor has noted that, in distinction to previous issues, the three ears of barley have drooping ears and are tied to a frame or tripod on the AD 29/30 obverse. This implicitly links the barley to widespread imperial numismatic issues of Livia (the

---

29 On the design differences of the vessels, see Taylor, 'Pontius Pilate', 559.
30 Bond, 'Coins', 250.
31 Bond, 'Coins', 250; Jacobsen, 'Coins', Table 2, 76–77.

wife of Augustus and mother of Tiberius) wearing the corn crown of Ceres, the link reinforced by the legend of Livia being on the obverse as well (ΙΟΥΛΙΑ ΚΑΙΣΑΡΟΣ).[32] The legend is also replicated on the coins of the previous governor, Gratus, but on that occasion it is placed in an uncontroversial wreath and without the significant addition of ΚΑΙΣΑΡΟΣ found on Pilate's coin.[33] Given that Livia died in AD 29 (Cassius Dio 53.2; Tacitus, *Ann.* 5.1), this must be the occasion for the honorific minting of the coin[34] and consequently her name drops out of subsequent issues. The wreath of berries on the reverse of AD 30/31 and AD 32/33, with the legend ΤΙΒΕΡΙΟΥ ΚΑΙΣΑΡΟΣ inside, is uncontroversial for Jews since the facial image of the Roman ruler is not used and there are numismatic precedents for the legend and motif among the coin issues of the Judean governors (Valerius Gratus).[35]

Second, what is controversial, however, is the addition of the *simpulum* (or *culullus*) on the obverse of the AD 29/30 issue, never used before or after on the coins of Roman governors in Judea. The *simpulum* was the ritual vessel for the tasting of wine by the priests before it was poured over the head of a sacrificial animal, being the peculiar emblem of the Roman priestly colleges.[36] Similarly, the *lituus* was the wooden staff held in the right hand of the augurs and raised towards the sky— extending back in antiquity to Romulus the founder of Rome—as the augurs scanned the sacred space of the heavens for prophetic utterances of the gods.[37] It is not correct to say, as Bond argues,[38] that these

---

32 Taylor, 'Pontius Pilate', 561, cf. 560, speculates that the drooping ears of the barley 'may not only suggest cut corn used in a cereal festival, but also the fact that Julia Augusta was herself cut down by death in the year of the coin's issue'. The nomenclature, ΙΟΥΛΙΑ ΚΑΙΣΑΡΟΣ, is not what one would have expected, i.e. Julia Augusta (ΙΟΥΛΙΑ ΣΕΒΑΣΤΗ), which was the title granted Livia in AD 14 upon the death of Augustus (Taylor, 560). Taylor observes that the genitive ΚΑΙΣΑΡΟΣ could refer to the coin 'of Tiberius', but that that inference 'leaves the name of 'Julia' undefined' (Taylor, 560). In my opinion, the genitive ΚΑΙΣΑΡΟΣ in regards to Livia (ΙΟΥΛΙΑ) is to be understood as '(the house) of Caesar'. This designation is because Livia's husband and son were respectively the *princeps* of the Julian and Julio-Claudian houses and she herself had been adopted into the household of Caesar upon Augustus' death (Taylor, 561).
33 Jacobsen, 'Coins', Table 2, 76–77.
34 Taylor, 'Pontius Pilate', 561, notes the link of Julia's death with the AD 29/30 coin issue, but does not suggest this as the occasion of (as I have proposed) this commemorative coin.
35 Jacobsen, 'Coins', Table 2, 77.
36 Taylor, 'Pontius Pilate', 558–59.
37 Taylor, 'Pontius Pilate', 559.
38 Bond, 'Coins', 260–61.

images are polyvalent, in which wine vessels were equally appropriate for both Roman and Jewish audiences, and where the images operated within the ambit of conventionality and precedent (including the use of 'pagan' symbols on Jewish governors' coins: e.g. the cornucopia, and caduceus of Valerius Gratus).[39] Rather the visual symbols of the *lituus* and *simpulum* belonged exclusively to the revelatory and sacrificial rituals employed by the Roman augurs and priests before the traditional gods. This was now summed up now in the person of the Julio-Claudian ruler as Pontifex Maximus ('High Priest'), the intermediary between the Roman state and its protective gods and, as Pilate's coin effectively demonstrates, the controller of the entire system of auspices.[40] Pilate's numismatic issues—notwithstanding the mutual indebtedness of the priestly retainers and the Roman prefect—were his official reminder to the subjects of Judea that the Roman Empire maintained its victory and continued its prosperity through the rituals of the imperial cult and its Pontifex Maximus over against the high priestly theocracy of Israel.[41] Pilate was not unnecessarily intending to be provocative to Jewish sensibilities, but, unlike his prefect predecessors, he did not baulk at asserting the ideology of Roman rule much more forcefully than previously.[42]

Furthermore, the death of Livia in AD 29 (Julia Augusta [= ΙΟΥΛΙΑ ΚΑΙΣΑΡΟΣ]) became the strategic impetus for Pilate to release the bold commemorative edition honouring the matriarch of the Julio-Claudian house and its reigning Caesar, her son Tiberius, the intermediary between the Roman gods and the state. But this is achieved by

39 Bond, 'Coins', 255–58; Jacobsen, 'Coins', Table 2, 76–77.
40 See Musial, 'Princeps', 99–106, on three cases of Tiberius' intervention as *Pontifex Maximus* recorded in Tacitus. For a togate statue of Tiberius as Pontifex Maximus from the Archaeological Museum of Eleusis, see Vermeule, *Roman Imperial Art*, 384 (Illustration no. 113, p. 184). For inscriptions referring to Tiberius as *Pontifex Maximus*, see Braund, *Augustus to Nero*, §§87 (*EJ* 82: AD 21), 92 (*EJ* 50), 93 (*ILS* 8785: AD 30), 104–105 (*EJ* 85–86: AD 32/33, 33). For legends on coins minted at Rome honouring Tiberius as *Pontifex Maxi*mus, see Braund, *Augustus to Nero*, §§89–89, 91 (respectively, *EJ* 83, 84, 49: AD 22–23). The considerable religious status which the office of *Pontifex Maximus* conferred upon Tiberius (1st June, AD 15) at Rome is revealed in the epigraphic protocols of the priestly college of the Arval brethren: '[Under the same consuls], in the Kalends of June, at the Palatine in the sanctuary of Apollo, [Tiberius Caesar] Augustus, pontifex maximus, president of the Arval brethren, co-opted (as) an Arval brother and [called] to the sacred rites', Schied, COMMENTARII FRATRVM ARVALIVM QVI SVPERSVNT, §3.
41 Brown, *Death*, 700, writes regarding Pilate's choice of numismatic motifs: 'Pilate may have been expecting to follow in the territory of Judea general Roman procedure from elsewhere'.
42 Webb, 'Roman Examination', 669–773, here 713–14.

the *simpulum* iconography alone, without resort to offensive images of the Roman ruler, allusions to the apotheosis of Augustus, or the use of provocative legends in the case of Tiberius (e.g. *divi Augusti filius*).

Why, then, did the coins cease to be issued in AD 32/33, even though they continued to be used in economic interactions throughout Roman Palestine beyond that date?[43] One viable explanation, suggested by E. Bammel,[44] is that the autonomous mint in Judea was suppressed in the first half of AD 32 when governor Pacuvius arrived in the province of Syria early in the same year and the issue of coins began once again in the province. Syria's frequent intervention in Palestinian affairs of the past had begun once again.

The traditional influential explanation is that Pilate's antisemitic patron, Sejanus, the Prefect of the Praetorian who deputised for Tiberius at Rome upon his withdrawal to Capri and who was pro-consul in his final year, had been executed for his conspiracy against the Roman ruler in AD 31.[45] Exposed without the protection of his patron at Rome, Pilate moderated his provocative stance towards the Jews, commencing with the curtailment of further coinage issues in the following year and giving in to the crowd's threat of exposure before Caesar should he release Christ (John 19:12a). However, this interpretation, pioneered by Ethelbert Stauffer and followed by many scholars,[46] has deficits. There is no evidence in the Roman sources that Sejanus was the patron of Pilate,[47]

---

43 This is not to deny that some of Pilate's procurator successors felt uncomfortable with the coins and overprinted some of the offensive motifs with neutral iconography: but whether this points to a general withdrawal of Pilate's coinage, as Stauffer, *Christ and the Caesars*, 119, posits, is impossible to quantify on the basis of the meagre evidence we have. Stauffer, *Christ and the Caesars*, 119–20, here 120, notes that the offensive augur's wand of the AD 30/31 and 31/32 issues is over-stamped with an unoffending palm branch, demonstrated by 'a coin of Pilate's in the British Museum which has been overprinted by Procurator Felix in this way'.

44 Bammel, 'Syrian Coinage', 108–10.

45 On Sejanus, see Bird, 'L. Aelius Seianus'; Hennig, *L. Aelius Seianus*; Champlin, 'Seianus Augustus'; Köstner, 'Genesis'.

46 See Stauffer, 'Zur Münzprägung und Judenpolitik des Pontius Pilatus', not seen by me; Stauffer, *Christ and the Caesars*, 103, 118–20; Stauffer, *Jesus and His Story*, 107–10. For scholars agreeing with Stauffer or espousing views consonant with his, see Blinzler, *Trial*, 181–82; Winter, *On the Trial*, 51–61; Meier, 'Sejanus'; Smallwood, *The Jews Under Roman Rule*, 165–70; Brown, *Death*, 694–94. For criticism of the position of Stauffer, see Hennig, *L. Aelius Seianus*, 172–79; McGing, 'Pontius Pilate', 416–38, here 424–28; Bond, *Pontius Pilate*, xiii–xvi, 21–23, 43–44, 45–46; Bond, 'Coins', 261–62; Taylor, 'Pontius Pilate', 562; Lémonon, *Ponce Pilate*, 257; Webb, 'The Roman Examination', 713 n. 126, 722–23.

47 Lémonon, *Ponce Pilate*, 122.

even though elsewhere his political networks are clearly traceable in the literary evidence.[48] The evidence for the so-called 'antisemitism' of Sejanus and Pilate in Philo is abstracted from its highly polemical rhetorical context (*infra*).[49] The idea of Pilate being politically exposed before Tiberius upon the execution of his 'patron' Sejanus at Rome in AD 31 is also highly doubtful, given the fact that Pilate remained a trusted governor of Tiberius until AD 36.[50] D. A. Carson is also correct in saying that Stauffer's reconstruction 'stalls on the uncertainty as to the date of Christ's trial and death', the possibility still being open that Sejanus was alive at the time.[51] In sum, Bammel's explanation is the preferable option as an explanation of the cessation of Pilate's coinage in AD 32/33.

1.3 Our Knowledge of Pilate from the Literary Sources: Key Events of His Prefecture

These episodes have been extensively discussed in the secondary literature, so we will concentrate on the Roman perspective in regards to Pilate's actions in each case.[52] What intentions can be discerned and what possible strategic light might they throw on Pilate's approach to the trial of Christ from a Roman perspective?

- *The episode of the Roman standards* (Josephus, *B.J.* 2.169–174; *A.J.* 18.55–59)

Josephus depicts Pilate at the beginning of his governorship concealing the arrival of the legionary standards into Jerusalem from Caesarea Maritima by dispatching them under the cover of night in a transfer of the auxiliary units to their winter quarters (Josephus, 18.55). The standards bore images of the Roman ruler on them (Josephus, *A.J.* 18.55)—the *imago* being the object of contention here as opposed to

---

48 Köstner, 'Genesis'.
49 McGing, 'Pontius Pilate', 430–33; Bond, *Pontius Pilate*, 26–48.
50 Schiavone, *Pontius Pilate*, 59. Evans, *Saint Luke*, 845, challenges this construct by highlighting Josephus' observation (*A.J.* 18.176ff) that Tiberius deliberately kept governors in office for a long time in order to prevent them from bleeding provinces dry in 'get rich quick' schemes, with the result that they then exited quickly from their command after a short period of rule.
51 Carson, *John*, 607.
52 For extended discussions, see Smallwood, *The Jews Under Roman Rule*, 160–63, 170–71; Brown, *Death*, 698–705; Lémonon, *Ponce Pilate*, 133–59, 189–222; Bond, *Pontius Pilate*, 24–93; Webb, 'The Roman Examination', 714–22.

the *aquila* (the Roman legionary eagle of Jupiter)—with the result that great rancor was stirred up among the Jewish population. The Flavian historian approaches this episode from a Jewish viewpoint, underscoring the impropriety of the action according the Jewish Old Testament law against images (Josephus, *B.J.* 2.170; *A.J.* 18.55; cf. Exod. 20:3–4; 32:8; 34:1; Lev. 19:4; 26:1; Deut. 4:13, 16; 5:8; 27:15). This action of Pilate violated the strong precedent of the previous Roman prefects of Judea who made their inaugural entry into Jerusalem without any offensive images on their military standards (Josephus, *A.J.* 18.56). As Josephus states, Pilate was the first to bring standards with images into the city (*A.J.* 18.56), having intended from the outset of his governorship 'to abolish the Jewish laws' (*A.J.* 18.55). In the face of the intransigence of the Jewish populace, who petitioned the prefect to remove the images, offering their bared necks to the swords of the Roman soldiers, Pilate succumbed to the determination of the Jews 'to keep their laws inviolable', commanding the return of the images back to Caesarea Maritima (*A.J.* 18.59). From a Jewish viewpoint, therefore, the unprecedented action of the new prefect demanded the same type of uncompromising response that was exhibited by the rabbis who tore down the Roman eagle mounted by Herod over the Temple gate (Josephus, *A.J.* 17.149–157).

Notably, the Roman soldiers who captured Jerusalem in AD 71 brought their standards into the Temple precincts, offered sacrifices to them, and hailed Titus as *imperator* (Josephus, *B.J.* 6.316). Thus the absolute loyalty of the legions and their auxiliary units to the ruler was essential to the continuing survival of the Julio-Claudian ruler, lest there was a renewed descent into the chaos of the civil wars of the late republic, as was the case in the 'Year of Four Emperors' in AD 69. Furthermore, not only is worship of the Roman ruler involved here on the part of the army but also the standards themselves were divinities, being a regular feature of the religion of the army.[53] The shrine of the standards within the legionary fortress was a crucial religious site, best exemplified in Tacitus' story about how the ex-consul Munatius Plancus fled to the shrine of the army head-quarter's building in order to escape

---

53 See Kraeling, 'Episode', 276–76; cf. Hegeland, 'Roman Army Religion', 1470–1505.

soldiers chasing him (AD 15), clasping onto the standards and the eagle there for sanctuary (*Ann.* 1.39).

What light is thrown here on Pilate's clandestine actions in introducing the standards late at night—the focus being on the *imago* as opposed to *aquila*—into Jerusalem? Webb argues that this is a case of Pilate stamping 'more clearly the presence an authority of Rome in Jerusalem', exhibiting more a pro-Roman than an anti-Jewish perspective in orientation.[54] Additionally, it was also Pilate's way of ensuring army loyalty in a difficult backwater of the Empire, both to the Julio-Claudian ruler and indirectly to himself as Rome's prefect. We also have to reckon with Pilate's commitment to traditional Roman army *religio*. His cognomen *Pilatus* emphasises how seriously the Roman prefect took his own ancestral legionary legacy, ensuring here that the military standards were appropriately worshiped by the troops in an imperial context, even if that meant breaking with Judean precedent and operating in clandestine manner.

- *The aqueduct funds affair* (Josephus, *B.J.* 2.175–177; *A.J.* 18.60–62)
It has already been argued above that the acquisition of funds from the Temple treasury for the building of an aqueduct for Jerusalem comprised part of Pilate's public persona as a civic builder in Jerusalem and in Caesarea Maritima. This constituted one traditional approach of glory acquisition, ancestral and personal, for an equestrian in a first-century imperial provincial context.[55] Josephus highlights what was in his perception the violation of Jewish law by Pilate's appropriation of the sacred Temple funds which, being dedicated to God and to be used for sacrificial purposes, were designated *corban* (Josephus, *B.J.* 2.175).

However, the later rabbinic evidence (m. Shek. 4.2) allowed the use of surplus money from the Temple treasury on the various needs of the city.[56] Whether such an understanding existed in the New Testament period is debatable: all we know is that the scope of *corban* extension

---

54 Webb, 'The Roman Examination', 715.
55 For examples of inscriptions honouring Philippian equestrian benefactors, see Brélaz, *Corpus des inscriptions grecques et latines de Philippes*, §§54, 60, 62, 64, 68, including one equestrian priest of the divine Augustus who had constructed the pavement of the Forum at his own expense (§66).
56 Bond, *Pontius Pilate*, 86.

was a matter of debate in some Pharisaic circles (Mark 7:11–12). Clearly, the subtleties of such debates were of no importance to Pilate in this instance.[57] That Pilate must have had the cooperation of the Temple authorities on this occasion, whether by persuasion or intimidation, is not as a secure datum as Bond asserts.[58] We can say minimally in regards to Pilate's concern for Jewish sensitivities that his 'undercover' troops used cudgels on this occasion (Josephus, *B.J.* 18.61–62; *A.J.* 2.176–177), as opposed to swords in subjugating the Jewish populace in the episode of the Roman standards,[59] but a massacre still nevertheless ensued.[60] The violence of the soldiers towards the Jewish populace shows the steely determination of the Roman governor to re-establish public order when it was under threat.[61]

- *The episode of the Galilean sacrifices* (Luke 13:1–2)

A Lukan reference reveals that Pilate mixed the blood of Galileans with their sacrifices (Luke 13:1), though the setting of the event is not specified nor its completeness of account maintained.[62] Christ's reference to the event is allusive rather than exhaustive. Was the murder of the Galilean pilgrims on the way to the Jerusalem Temple or, in an unthinking act of desecration on the part of the Roman troops, were the pilgrims slaughtered within its holy precinct? We can only speculate when in Pilate's governorship this event occurred. F. F. Bruce posits that the pilgrims 'had come to Jerusalem to attend one of the great festivals, and were involved in the Temple court in a riot which was suppressed by Roman soldiers from the neighbouring fortress of Antonia.'[63] Nevertheless, as Paul Winter observes, Luke 13:1 has 'escaped undue

---

57 Note the telling comment of Smallwood (*The Jews Under Roman Rule*, 162; cf. 135–36), Pilate's appropriation of the funds was 'an act of sacrilege even from the Roman point of view, since the Temple tax had been made sacrosanct by law'.
58 Bond, *Pontius Pilate*, 86; in agreement with Bond, see Lémonon, Ponce *Pilate*, 158.
59 Webb, 'The Roman Examination and Crucifixion of Jesus', 717: 'Pilate was attempting a measured response rather than an action that might result in a wholesale massacre'.
60 Brown (*The Death of the Messiah*, 701), 'Pilate had underestimated the brutality of his own soldiers, but on Pilate's part there was no calculated savagery against the innocent'.
61 Lémonon, Ponce *Pilate*, 157–58.
62 Paul Winter, *On the Trial of Jesus* (Berlin: Walter de Gruyter, 1961), 54.
63 F. F. Bruce, *Israel and the Nations from the Exodus to the Fall of the Second Temple* (Eerdmans: Grand Rapids, 1969), 201.

editorial revision' and preserves 'a lively memory of Pontius Pilate's indifference to suffering and of his lordly contempt for the religious susceptibilities of those whom he governed'.[64] This estimate is somewhat overblown in regards to total contempt to Jewish sensitivities alleged of Pilate: rather, as a governor, he would not prioritise these over Roman concerns, even when working with the priestly elites.

F. F. Bruce, in an intriguing suggestion, links Luke 13:1 with the enigmatic reference to the tower of Siloam falling upon eighteen victims (Luke 13:4). He suggests that escapee rioters from the Temple court had sought refuge in the tower in south-east Jerusalem, only to have Pilate's troops undermine its foundations after the tower had been secured from any escape, thereby precipitating its collapse and their sudden death.[65] If this reconstruction of the events behind Luke 13:1 and 4 is viable, the strong enforcement of public order by Pilate when it was threatened by civic disturbance is once again highlighted. Pro-Roman sentiment, not antisemitism, is the driving motivation.

- *The episode of the golden shields* (Philo, *Legat.* 299–305)

It is beyond the boundaries of this chapter to discuss the highly negative rhetoric employed by Philo in framing this episode. Suffice it to say,

  a) the wider literary context of the episode is Philo's letter of appeal—possibly an authentic letter of Agrippa I himself[66]—to Claudius upon his accession to power (AD 41). The letter pleads with Claudius not to adopt the desecrating policy that Gaius Caligula had been intending to implement in the Jerusalem

---

64 Winter, *On the Trial of Jesus*, 54.
65 Bruce, *Israel and the Nations*, 201–2. In his famous portrait of Christ as a revolutionary, Robert Eisler (*ΙΗΣΟΥΣ ΒΑΣΙΛΕΥΣ ΟΥ ΒΑΣΙΛΕΥΣΑΣ. Die messianische Unabhängigkeitsbewegung vom Auftreten Johannes des Täufers bis zum Untergang Jakobs des Gerechten* [2 vols.; Heidelberg: Carl Winters Universitätsbuchhandlung, 1929–1930], Vol. 2, 476–525, not seen by me) proceeds less cautiously than F. F. Bruce. Eisler claims that after his messianic entry into Jerusalem, Christ secured the Temple and parts of the city by force, with the result that Pilate's soldiers slaughtered sacrificing Galilean pilgrims in the Temple precincts and toppled over the tower of Siloam upon other Galileans in the city. For the details of Eisler's arguments, I am indebted to Fernando Bermejo-Rubio, 'Jesus and the Anti-Roman Resistance: A Reassessment of the Arguments', *Journal for the Study of the New Testament* 12 (2014), 1–105, here 43–44.
66 On whether the letter was written by Philo or is an authentic letter of Agrippa I, see Lémonon, *Ponce Pilate*, 190–94.

Temple by placing his statue there: providentially, Gaius' assassination halted his plans. Instead, as the letter argues, Claudius should follow the humane policies espoused by Augustus and Tiberius. Therefore, Pilate's character is rhetorically blackened by Philo as an example of the aggressive and insensitive Roman policy to be avoided at all costs by Claudius.[67]

b) The employment of the stock rhetorical language of venality, robbery, and illegal executions makes it difficult to discern how seriously we ought to regard such venomous polemic in regards to Pilate.[68]

Pilate's introduction of aniconic golden shields into Jerusalem, placing them in the praetorium with the name of Tiberius engraved on them, occurred shortly after the execution of Sejanus (17 October, AD 31). Taylor is probably correct in saying that the inscribed shields, like the Roman coins and inscriptions of Tiberius, also carried the honorific *divi Augusti filius*, infuriating the Jews who in all likelihood inferred its presence on the shields along with the ruler's name.[69] There is no need to assume that this is another deliberately provocative action designed to offend Jewish sensibilities on Pilate's part: rather it is simply a case of Pilate rendering Tiberius appropriate honour in the Roman praetorium, the governor's own sanctuary within the city.[70] But, when Tiberius upheld the Jewish complaints regarding his actions, Pilate had no option other than to withdraw the shields from Jerusalem (Philo, *Legat.*, 303–305). Pilate's reluctance to do so initially, prior to the intervention of Tiberius, is best explained by the dishonour such a removal would have occasioned to Tiberius.

- *The Samaritan prophet episode* (Josephus, *A.J.* 18.85–89)

In AD 35 a Samaritan prophet/false Messiah summoned the populace of Samaria to climb Mount Gerizim, promising that they would

---

67 McGing, 'Pontius Pilate and the Sources', 430–35; Bond, *Pontius Pilate*, 24–48.
68 Webb, 'The Roman Examination and Crucifixion of Jesus', 720; also McGing, 'Pontius Pilate and the Sources', 432–33.
69 Taylor, 'Pontius Pilate and the Imperial Cult', 570; also McGing, 'Pontius Pilate and the Sources', 431.
70 Bond, *Pontius Pilate*, 47–48.

unearth sacred vessels buried there by Moses.[71] Aryeh Kasher proposes that 'he may well have fostered illusions concerning the building of the Temple on Mount Gerizim', previously destroyed by the Maccabean priest/king in 112/111 BC.[72] Gathering in the village of Tirathana, they armed themselves and prepared to ascend the mountain. Pilate, however, met them with both infantry and cavalry, killing many, taking prisoners, and executing the most influential leaders from the refugees who were rounded up. Upon the complaint of the Samaritan council to the legate of Syria, Vitellius, regarding Pilate's 'massacre' of innocent refugees, Pilate was ordered by Vitellius to return to Rome in AD 36. He was replaced with a temporary prefect, Marcellus, a 'friend' of the legate, 'perhaps one of his closest aides'.[73] Ironically, however, Tiberius died in March AD 37 before Pilate arrived in Rome. We hear nothing of Pilate's subsequent fate.

Why did Pilate feel compelled to intervene in what was not obviously a rebellion against Roman rule? We must not discount the traditional animosity of the Sadducean priests to the Samaritans, who historically had claimed Mount Gerizim to be an alternative site of worship to the Jerusalem Temple on Mount Zion (cf. John 4:19–20). Another Samaritan claim to legitimation on the basis of doubtful assertions about Moses' activities on Mount Gerizim would have provoked the priestly retainers to pressure Pilate once again to act immediately. Not that Pilate needed much encouragement in that regard: we have seen that the prefect had always reacted swiftly to threats of civic disorder in Judea. The excessive violence of his response is 'further proof of Pilate's familiarity with war' as a praetorian commander previously,[74] but, in this instance, there is a marked military over-reaction in the savage killing of refugees.[75]

---

71 On the rhetoric of Josephus underlying the account and his characterisation of Pilate, see Bond, *Pontius Pilate*, 69–78; Webb, 'The Roman Examination and Crucifixion of Jesus', 721–72. For discussion of the episode, see Smallwood, *The Jews Under Roman Rule*, 170–71; Bond, *Pontius Pilate*, 89–93; Lémonon, *Ponce Pilate*, 215–27; Brown, *Death*, 703–5; Webb, 'The Roman Examination', 721–22.
72 Kasher, 'Josephus on Jewish-Samaritan Relations', 226.
73 Schiavone, *Pontius Pilate*, 178.
74 Schiavone, *Pontius Pilate*, 178.
75 Lémonon, *Ponce Pilate*, 220, concludes regarding Pilate: 'Il croix plus aux vertus de la force armeé qu'à la persuasion'.

1.4 Conclusion: Pilate in the Roman Archaeological and Literary Evidence

The nomenclature of Pontius Pilate points to a member of the equestrian order with prestigious Samnite, consular, and centurion forebears of the highest military prestige. Such an individual would have been deeply imbued as an equestrian with the Roman elite ethos of maintaining and surpassing ancestral honour in his personal quest for glory. In an imperial context, this also meant the priority of provincial magistrates such as Pilate honouring the Julio-Claudian house, the success of whom was predicated on the new pathways opened up by the imperial *cursus honorum* ('course of honour') in provincial administration and army careers. Much of what has been traditionally categorised by New Testament scholars as 'antisemitic' in the case of Pilate was merely pro-Roman and pro-Julio-Claudian, whether it be Pilate's commemorative (AD 29/30) and honorific coinage (AD 30/31, 31/32), or key episodes within his tenure as governor (e.g. the Roman standards and the golden shields episodes).

Other more civic dimensions of Pilate's governorship, such as the building of the aqueduct in Jerusalem and the lighthouse in Caesarea Maritima, belong to the public projection of himself as a builder in urban Judea, confirmed in each case by the archaeological and epigraphic evidence. Another dimension of the historical Pilate that needs to be better appreciated was his commitment to traditional army religion, a devotion amply demonstrated by the Roman standards episode. While Pilate was cautious in some cases to stay within the precedents evinced by previous prefects, the governor nevertheless strengthened pro-Roman commitment in ways that diverged from previous diplomatic practice of the Roman prefects in regard to the Jews. A consistent feature of Pilate's rule was his unswerving commitment to a strong and forthright response to civil unrest, with the result that complaints to the Roman ruler were made, sometimes issuing in strategic withdrawals on the governor's part (the Roman standards and golden shield episodes), but ultimately resulting in his recall to Rome by Tiberius in the case of the Samaritan prophet episode.

Given this inflexibility on Pilate's part, what do we make of the Gospel presentations of the 'weakness' of Pilate? One thing is certain:

Stauffer's argument that the death of Sejanus, Pilate's so-called patron, is the best explanation for the prefect's ultimate decision not to free Christ is no longer as convincing an explanation as it once was. Since space prohibits a full exploration of each Gospel account, we will confine ourselves to discerning the Roman attitudes to the arraignment of Christ that lie behind the common narrative details of the Gospels, notwithstanding the various theological assessments to which each evangelist subjects Pilate.[76]

2. The Roman Perspective on the Arraignment of Christ: Penetrating Behind the Rhetoric and Theology of the Gospels

In this section we will look for what is common in the Gospel traditions regarding the arraignment of Christ before Pilate (Mark 15:1–25; Matt 27:11–26; Luke 23:1–25; John 19:28–19:16) and consider what light this bedrock of tradition throws upon the Roman perspective regarding the threat posed by Christ. This 'minimalist' approach is necessary because Matthew and Luke provide their own theological and historical redaction of the bare bones of the Markan account, whereas John airs his own independent traditions, recounted in seven scenes.[77] The result is that we have multiple scholarly portraits of Pilate emerging from the evidence of the Gospels.[78] Furthermore, the question of the access that believing eyewitnesses had to the conversations of Christ with Pilate, however limited (Matt 27:11–14; Mark 15:2–5a; Luke 23:3) or extended (John 18:33–38; 19:8–11) the interrogations may originally have been, is not able to be answered historically with any

---

76 For discussion of the Gospels' portraits of Pilate's arraignment of Christ, see Bond, *Pontius Pilate*, 94–193; Lémonon, *Ponce Pilate*, 164–88; Brown, *Death*, 723–861; Carter, *Pontius Pilate*, 55–152.
77 Bond, *Pontius Pilate*, 175–92.
78 Carter, *Pontius Pilate*, 3–11.

certainty.⁷⁹ This includes the question whether the arraignment was primarily held inside the *praetorium* (John 18:28–20, 33) or was seated open air on a *bema* outside the *praetorium* on a stone pavement (John 19:13; Matt 27:19; cf. Mark 15:2–5, 8–9), again raising the issue of the access of believing eyewitnesses to the historical traditions of what was actually said.⁸⁰ Moreover, the precise site of the praetorium (the Fortress Antonia or the fortress Palace of Herod the Great on the western side of Jerusalem?) is also disputed.⁸¹

Additionally, an accurate assessment of the motivations of any historical character such as Pilate (e.g. 'fear': John 19:8; frustration and impatience: John 18:28–38; pleasing the crowd: Mark 15:8, 15), including his reactions to Christ's non-response ('amazement': Matt 27:14b; Mark 15:5b) and his own assessments of the motivations of Christ's accusers ('envy': Matt 27:18; Mark 15:10), is notoriously difficult to determine. How does one penetrate what was going on in Pilate's mind? This places us as historians in the awkward position of claiming historical omniscience,⁸² whereas, in reality, we face the inevitable conundrums posed by evidence that is fragmentary in its sources on Pilate in the case of Josephus, riddled with polemic as far as Philo, and

---

79   Keener, *John*, 1088, draws attention as possible sources for the arraignment narrative to the following individuals and groups: Joseph of Arimathea (Mark 15:43; John 19:39), a disciple connected to the high priest's household (John 18:15–16), and later priestly converts (Acts 6:7). These sources, however, would have only provided access to the priestly arraignment of Christ as opposed to the interrogation of Pilate, because the Jews, if John is to be believed (18:28), excluded themselves from Pilate's interaction with the prisoner inside the palace.

80   On the alternating changes of location between the inside and outside of the praetorium in John's Gospel, see Carter, *Pontius Pilate*, 138; Agamben, *Pilate and Jesus*, 15–26. Evans, *Luke*, 844, notes that 'the impression left by the Synoptics is that the whole examination was conducted in the open air, and that after it the soldiers took Jesus inside the palace (*aulē*), which is identified as the *praetorium* (Mark 15:16; Mat 27:27).' If the latter option is accurate, then access of believers to Pilate's final interrogations of the largely non-responsive Christ could have been possible as part of the anonymous crowd assembled before the prefect. By contrast, see Agamben, *Pilate and Jesus*, 2, states: 'The evangelists, who certainly could not have been present at the trial, do not concern themselves with indicating the sources of their narrative'. A similar issue is posed by the access that the first believers would have had to the tradition of Pilate's wife's dream (Matt 27:19). Or is the episode merely a theological creation of the evangelist, expanding upon the significant dream revelations already in his narrative (Matt 2:12, 13, 19, 22)? For discussion, see Brown, *Death*, 803–07.

81   Brown, *Death*, 706–10. On the Herodian Palace and fortress, see Josephus, *B.J.* 2.301 and Philo, *Legat.* 299, 306. Barnett, *Jesus and the Rise*, 144, argues that Herod's Palace was the most likely site for the *praetorium*.

82   On the dangers of presumed 'omniscience', see Martin, 'Response', esp. 342–44.

penetrated by theological and pastoral concerns in terms of the Gospels. We cannot draw, therefore, wide-ranging conclusions about the personal motivations of Pilate in sentencing Christ. At best, we can ask from a Roman viewpoint how Pilate's decisions ensured the continuing stability of Julio-Claudian rule in the provinces, reflects the ethos of his being a member of the equites, and why, in the estimation of the prefect, Christ had a become a destabilising force in Judea. In the case of the Gospels, the comments of evangelists regarding Pilate's motivations are *evaluative*, assessing his character from the providential perspective of salvation history and the biblical understanding of fallen human nature, though it would be wrong to conclude that their observations are not historically insightful in a Roman context.[83]

Two final things. First, the late fourth-century fictitious letter that whitewashes Pilate, purportedly written by the prefect to Tiberius, must be dismissed, along with the wider corpus of apocryphal texts assigned to Pilate.[84] Second, the theological, rhetorical, and literary agendas of each of the Gospel writers, including the audience to which they are writing, predetermine and shape their conclusions to a considerable extent, in the same manner that the prior agendas of any ancient writer (e.g. Tacitus) determines his handling of the evidence.[85]

What then do the commonalities of the Gospel accounts of the arraignment of Christ reveal about the reasons for the decision of Pilate regarding the fate of the arraigned? All the Gospels agree that the fundamental charge brought against Christ was that he had claimed to be the King of the Jews (Mark 15:2: cf. vv. 9, 12; Matt 27:11: cf. vv. 17, 22 ['Christ']; Luke 23:2b–3; John 18: 33–38a: cf. v. 39b; 19:3, 7 ['Son of God': cf. Ps. 2:6–7; 2 Sam 7:13–14a; 4Q246 Col II, 1–8). This is confirmed in each Gospel by the *titulus* on the cross (Mark 15:26; Matt

---

83   For Johannine commentators who helpfully situate Pilate's 'fear' (John 19:8; cf. v. 12) in a Graeco-Roman context, see Carson, *John*, 600; Keener, *John*, 2.1126; Köstenberger, *John*, 534–35.
84   See Winter, 'A Letter from Pontius Pilate'; Baudoin, 'Truth in the Detail'. At a more popular level, see Agamben, *Pilate and Jesus*, 4–8.
35   On the discussion above, see the suggestive comments of Webb, 'The Roman Examination', 733–34, 736.

27:37; Luke 23:36; John 19:19–22),[86] as well by the soldiers' mockery of Christ with a royal scarlet robe and crown of thorns, paying him homage as 'King of the Jews' while holding a staff in his right hand (Matt 27:27–31; Mark 15:16–20).[87] The fact that the charge is initiated by Pilate in his first question to Christ shows the collaboration that Pilate already had with the priestly elites regarding potential trouble makers: the prefect knew beforehand the danger that this ambiguous figure posed to stable Roman rule in Palestine. The Gospel of Mark refers obliquely to the 'many things' of which the chief priests were accusing Christ in addition to being a messianic pretender (Mark 15:3–4), which is expanded by the Gospel of Luke (23:2, 5) in the references to the additional charges of (a) subverting the nation by his provocative teaching to the people of Judea (cf. 23:14) and (b) opposing payment of taxes to Caesar (cf. Mark 12:13–17; Matt 20:20–26). However, whether Luke 23:2 reflects Luke's redactional activity or preserves an authentic historical tradition is an unresolved question in New Testament scholarship.[88]

Having established that Christ was crucified as a messianic pretender in the Gospel tradition, we have to ask what brought Pilate to the conclusion that Christ was a political threat who must be eliminated. What would the charge of being 'King of the Jews' have meant to Pilate? In a Judean context, the charge places Christ amongst a notorious group of Judean messianic pretenders,[89] each claiming to be a king and heading up populist insurrection movements, who had emerged at the time of Herod Archelaus from 4 BC onwards: namely, Judas, son of Hezekiah (Josephus, *A.J.* 17.271–272; *B.J.* 2.256), Simon of Perea (*A.J.* 17.273–277; *B.J.* 2.57–59) and Anthronges the shepherd (*A.J.* 17.278–84; *B.J.* 2.60–65). Additionally, the charge that Christ opposed payment of taxes to Caesar would also have evoked memories of the tax revolt

---

86 See Bammel, 'The *titulus*'. On the historicity of the titulus, see Webb, 'The Roman Examination', 745–49. Mullins, *Luke*, 491, observes that the *titulus* 'may well be the historical bedrock underpinning the accounts of the trial'.
87 One might add to historical consideration here the independent tradition regarding Christ's alternative Kingdom articulated in John 19:35–38, if the pericope is demonstrably historical. For such an attempt, though dependent on Stauffer's 'Sejanus' thesis, see Köstenberger, '"What is Truth?"'.
88 See Webb, 'The Roman Examination', 742–43.
89 For discussion, see Horsley and Hanson, *Bandits*, 88–134.

precipitated by Judas the Galilean during the reign of Archelaus in AD 6 (*A.J.* 18.1–10, 23; *B.J.* 2.433; Acts 5:37).⁹⁰ We have already observed Pilate's intolerance to populist uprisings to Roman rule in the case of the episodes of the military standards, the building of the aqueduct, the golden shields, and the Samaritan prophet: public order was Pilate's priority and military force was used in each case to subdue the eruption of civil unrest. The spectre of Christ fronting a populist movement, claiming to be king, and resisting Roman taxation—assuming that Luke 23:2 is actually historical as opposed to a redactional invention⁹¹—could only be responded to in one way. Furthermore, Pilate's priestly collaborators would likely have long since considered Christ as worthy of the death penalty due to his 'high-handed' violation of Old Testament prohibitions, his critical attitude to key religious institutions and breaches of holiness boundaries during his ministry, as well as provocative logia deemed to be blasphemous in their view.⁹² The pressure placed upon the Roman prefect by the high priests and their colleagues would have been considerable by now, a political inducement to act which Pilate could

---

90 On Judas the Galilean, see Hengel, *The Zealots*, 76–82, though Hengel's claim that Judas inaugurated the 'Zealot' movement must be resisted, since the movement only originated AD 67–68 (Horsley and Hanson, *Bandits*, 217–41). The reference to Simon the Zealot (Ζηλωτήν) among the disciples (Luke 6:15) need not be understood in terms of an incipient Zealot movement but rather that he was the 'zealous one', in the sense of being 'zealous for the Law', as per the Old Testament Phineas and Maccabean traditions (Num 25:1–13; 1 Macc 2:26–27, 58; 4 Macc 18:12; Sir 45:23; Philo, *Spec.* 1:55–56; cf. John 2:17 [Ps 69:10]; Gal 1:13–14; Phil 3:6; Acts 22:4). Notably, Bermejo-Rubio ('Jesus and the Anti-Roman Resistance', 146) posits that Jesus most likely opposed tribute payment to Rome in the same manner as Judas the Galilean. Similarly, Bilde, *Originality of Jesus*, 190–98, here 197. Contra, Bruce, 'Render to Caesar'. A more equivocal stance is taken by Cassidy, *Jesus, Politics and Society*, 65: 'while allowing that tribute might be refused, Jesus did not explicitly commit himself to either tax payment or tax resistance'.

91 Bovon, *Luc 19, 28–24, 53*, 307, argues that while Luke 23:2 is a Lukan redactional creation, the evangelist does not invent the accusations, but rather draws upon the charges made against Christ which he found dispersed in the sources and traditions upon which he had access. Bock, *Luke 9:51–24:53*, 1806–08, argues for the historicity of the sources used in Luke 23:2. In Bock's view, this Lukan deposit was additional to the sources aired elsewhere in the Synoptics and John, each charge rendered here in the evangelists' own words, and not just a literary or theological creation. Either way, these charges are historical, reflecting the deep disturbance created by Christ's ministry amongst his opponents and therefore inexorably arousing the fears of Pilate from a Roman viewpoint.

92 See Horvath, 'Why was Jesus Brought to Pilate?'; Jeremias, *New Testament Theology*, 278–80; Borg, *Conflict, Holiness and Politics*; Betz, 'Jesus and the Purity of the Temple (Mark 11:15–18); Evans, '"Who Touched Me?"'; Evans, 'Jesus' Action in the Temple'; Bock, *Blasphemy and Exaltation*; Kazen, *Jesus and Purity Halakah*; Back, 'Jesus and the Sabbath'; Holmén, 'Jesus and the Holiness Paradigm'; Chilton, 'Jesus and Sinners and Outcasts'.

no longer easily ignore. However, as we will see, this does not mean that Pilate abjectly subjugates Roman *imperium* to their authority: he manipulates the political game to ensure the full exposure of the priestly caste before a watching public as compliant clients of Rome first and foremost, and only then as servants of Israel's god.

Additionally, the fact that Christ claimed to be 'Son of God'—a messianic claim in the estimation of his priestly accusers[93]—would have had significant resonances for imperial auditors.[94] This title collided with the Roman understanding of Augustus as the son of the apotheosised Julius Caesar. Notwithstanding Tiberius' personal disquiet over divine status being ascribed to himself by the city of Gytheum (cf. Tacitus, *Ann.* 4.15),[95] the acclamation of Tiberius as the son of the apotheosised Augustus in the provinces and outside of Rome in the Italian peninsula continued unabated,[96] including the rendering of the same terminology upon his coinage minted at Rome and in the provinces.[97] A Jewish 'Son of God', Pilate would have concluded, could not be allowed become a rival in the minds of his Jewish subjects to the Julio-Claudian house and its two 'sons of God', Augustus and Tiberius, especially when Christ commanded significant popular support among the non-elite classes of Judea. Again, Christ posed a political threat that had to be eliminated.

Several other commonalities in the Gospel narratives provide further insight into why Pilate decided to crucify publicly Christ as a royal pretender, as opposed to whisking him off-stage and executing him privately out of public sight,[98] as had happened with John the Baptist under Herod Antipas. First, the triumphal entry of Christ into Jerusalem on a donkey (with accompanying colt) would have reinforced the sense of imminent

---

93 For the Jewish background, see Hengel, *The Son of God*; Charlesworth, *The Messiah*; Collins, *The Scepter and the Star*.
94 See Peppard, *The Son of God*.
95 For the epigraphic evidence, see SEG 11.923, translated with commentary in Jones and Milns, *The Use of Documentary Evidence*, §24.
96 For inscriptions honouring Tiberius as 'divine', 'son of the divine Augustus', and 'grandson of the divine Julius', see Braund, *Augustus to Nero*, §§92 (EJ 50: Puteoli, AD 30), 93 (ILS 8785: Mostene, Asia, AD 31–32), 100 (EJ 52: Gortyn, Crete), 104 (EJ 85: Via Flaminia, near Capena: AD 31–32), 105 (EJ 86: Oneum, Dalmatia, AD 33), 107 (EJ 88: Myra, Lycia).
97 For legends on coins minted at Rome honouring Tiberius as 'son of the divine Augustus', see Braund, *Augustus to Nero*, §§88–89 (AD 22–23), 91 (AD 22–23), 106 (AD 22–23). For the provinces, see §96 (Bilbilis, Tarraconensis, AD 31).
98 Fredriksen, 'Arms and the Man', 322.

threat posed by this so-called messianic pretender (Matt 21:1–11; Mark 11:1–11; Luke 19:28–40; John 12:12–19).[99] Here the crowd enters as a potent actor in history,[100] acclaiming the Galilean prophet Christ as 'Son of David', though Luke restricts this acclamation to a multitude of disciples (Luke 19:37–39), theologically telescoping the event into a collision between Christ and the Pharisees over the disciples' effusive praise of their Master (19:39–40). Such a spontaneous crowd response to Christ may well have unnerved Pilate, had he reflected on the level of popular support that this ambiguous figure could so quickly muster, let alone his influence throughout Galilee.[101] It was precisely such eruptions of grass-root enthusiasm for nationalistic causes that Pilate had ruthlessly repressed during his prefecture at various stages.

Second, members of the crowd had also spread their cloaks upon the road, along with branches cut from the trees in the fields (Matt 21:8; Mark 11:8; Luke 19:36). In a significant variation on the Synoptic tradition, John presents the crowd as meeting Christ with palm branches, presumably waving them either in royal welcome or as a joyous acknowledgement of Christ's imminent messianic triumph (12:13).[102] If this tradition has a historical basis, then it is reminiscent of the events associated with Simon Maccabeus who, upon purging the Jerusalem Temple of its Seleucid abominations, celebrated its rededication alongside the

---

99 For discussion, see Sheldon, 'Jesus, as Security Risk', 7–10.
100 The role of the crowd is underestimated in modern sociological approaches to history and in the 'great man' paradigm of the ancient historiography. See Miller, *The Crowd in Rome*; Schwab, *The Birth of the Mob*. On the 'great man' approach to historiography in antiquity, see Harrison, *Paul and the Ancient Celebrity Circuit*, passim. Contrast, however, the approach of Schiavone, *Pontius Pilate*, 139, who writes: 'there are solid grounds for arguing that Mark and Matthew introduced the theme of the 'crowd' into their writings [...] Both were greatly concerned to impress upon their readers that the death of Jesus was the responsibility of the whole Jewish people, and not only of a small group of priests and their acolytes'. This seems to me to be another case of where scholars speculatively prioritise the apologetic and theological creativity of the evangelists, which must be acknowledged, at the expense of the more obvious explanations found in the evidence of the historical record. On the proposed Christian antisemitism of Matthew, see Schiavone, ibid., 141–42.
101 Fredriksen, 'Why was Jesus Crucified?', 415–19, notes that the crowds in Jerusalem 'greet Jesus in messianic terms and acclaim the new *basileia* (Mk 11:9–10; Matt 21:9; Luke 19:38; John 12:13–15). It is their mounting enthusiasm in the days before the feast that requires the authorities to arrest Jesus by stealth (Mark 14:2 and parr; John 12:19)'. Contra, see Kinman, 'Jesus' "Triumphal Entry"', 442–48, who argues for a small and atriumphal entry of Christ into Jerusalem, not large enough to attract the attention of Pilate's soldiers.
102 Keener, *John*, 2.869.

city inhabitants. The populace entered the sanctuary 'with praise and palm branches', as well as harps and cymbals (1 Macc 13.50–51; 2 Macc 10.7). This mimicry of Maccabean ritual precedent in John 12:13 underscores that *some* among the crowds expected that Christ, like the Maccabean heroes of the past, would similarly cleanse Jerusalem of its defiling and occupying foreign presence, including the full restoration of its Temple to its former holiness. Christ's subsequent cleansing of the Temple (Matt 21:12–17; Mark 11:12–17; Luke 19:45–47; cf. John 2:12–22) would have heightened messianic expectations in this regard for some, while simultaneously offending the Sadducean aristocracy. Moreover, the fact that Matthew was reminded of the royal 'Zion' text of Zechariah 9:9 upon Christ's triumphal entry into Jerusalem (Matt 21:4–5; John 12:14–15) need not necessarily have been a theological insight exclusive to the evangelist. Others in the crowd may too have recalled this famous messianic text at the time, prompted by the text's mention of the beast of burden upon which Christ rode. These suggestive messianic and Maccabean precedents undergirding Christ's triumphal entry as 'King' to Jerusalem would have disquieted the priestly retainer class and made them all the more determined that Pilate understood the real threat that this messianic pretender posed to Roman rule.

Third, the mention of 'swords' in the Gospel tradition prior and at the time of the arrest of Christ remains a complex and problematic strain of evidence interpretatively and historically.[103] At first glance, we seemingly face contradictory statements on the issue. Christ's logia range from (a) his command to the disciples to buy a sword for their personal protection in the face of his imminent identification with transgressors on the cross as the Isaianic 'Servant' (Luke 22:36–37) to (b) a warning that those who wield the sword would perish by it (Matt 26:52a) and (c) injunctions to put away drawn swords (Matt 26:52b; John 18:11). Furthermore, Christ's retort, 'It is enough' (Luke 22:38), made in response to the disciples' claim that they already had two swords, has been variously interpreted. Was it a case of Christ's frustrated curtailment of the discussion of his disciples who had misunderstood the

---

103 On the historical issues, see the debate between Martin, 'Jesus in Jerusalem', Fredriksen, 'Arms and the Man', and Downing, 'Dale Martin's Swords for Jesus'. For Martin's response, see 'Response'.

real intent of his teaching,[104] an instance of 'grim but playful irony',[105] or a genuine affirmation that armed protection was necessary on the part of the disciples until Christ arrived safely at the Mount of Olives, the mountain of prayer?[106] Certainty regarding the precise intent of Christ's logion remains difficult to discern. Additionally, the impulsive action of Peter slashing off the ear of the servant (Malchus) of the high priest (Matt 26:50–51; Mark 14:47; Luke 22:49–50; John 18:10) at Gethsemane many have initially raised in Roman minds the perception of Christ's disciples as 'revolutionaries' prepared to use armed force when provoked,[107] despite Christ's intervention in defusing tensions by healing the servant, according to Lukan tradition (22:51).[108] At the very least, the fact that some of Christ's disciples were armed in this skirmish attending Christ's arrest must have confirmed in the minds of the priestly retainers their potential danger, if they needed further convincing on the issue. Whether or not this information was passed on to Pilate prior to Christ's arraignment is unknown to us.

This raises the question why Pilate did not seek out and arrest Christ's disciples, in addition to their Master, if a messianic revolution was, in the perception of Rome and its retainer class, a hypothetical possibility through the establishment of a rival king to Caesar (cf. Matt 26: 55–56; Mark 14:48–49; Luke 22:52–53)? Why did Pilate not act more widely and decisively against the rise of another popular movement, as he had in the recent past and would in the future, given the unbridled enthusiasm of the Jerusalem crowds for Christ at his triumphal entry?

104 Bock, *Luke 9:51–24:53*, 1749; Bovon, *Luc 19, 28–24, 53*: 'En disant <<cela sufit>>, Jésus coup court'.; Nolland, *Luke 18:35–24:53*, 1077.
105 Evans, *Luke*, 807.
106 Matson, 'Double Edged'. Similarly, Liefeld, 'Luke', 1029–30.
107 Bermejo-Rubio, 'Jesus and the Anti-Roman Resistance', 103, rightly poses this question, though I do not endorse his portrait of Jesus and the disciples as 'revolutionaries'. See also Bermejo-Rubio, '(Why) Was Jesus the Galilean Crucified Alone?'. For the scholarly tradition of Jesus as Zealot revolutionary, see Eisler, *ΙΗΣΟΥΣ ΒΑΣΙΛΕΥΣ ΟΥ ΒΑΣΙΛΕΥΣΑΣ*; Brandon, *Jesus and the Zealots*; Martin, 'Jesus in Jerusalem', 6–7, 19–20; Aslan, *Zealot*. Contra, see Cullmann, *Jesus and the Revolutionaries*; Hengel, *Was Jesus a Revolutionist?*; Hengel, *Victory over Violence*.
108 Some commentators dismiss this healing miracle as a Lukan 'legendary addition' to the Markan tradition, if Luke is *totally* dependent upon Mark's narrative for this pericope (Evans, *Luke*, 819). However, Bock, *Luke 9:51–24:53*, 1171–72 (cf. Marshall, *Luke*, 837), perceptively notes that if the ear had been left cut off without any healing intervention on Christ's part, it is very hard to explain why there were not mass arrests at this juncture: the unusualness of the episode guarantees its historicity.

One need only remember how the Romans ruthlessly hunted down the followers of Theudas (Josephus, *A.J.* 20.97–98; Acts 5:37–38) and the Egyptian (Josephus, *A.J.* 20.171; *B.W.* 20.171; cf. Acts 21:38), as well as Pilate's own later over-reaction to the episode concerning the Samaritan prophet, noted above.[109] Later, Josephus reports on how the Roman procurator Felix punished both the brigands of Eleazar's group and the common populace that were their supporters (Josephus, *A.J.* 2.253). One answer, proposed by Justin Meggitt,[110] is that Pilate considered Christ a deranged and deluded lunatic and that his followers could be left alone upon his execution. This seems unlikely in my view: deluded followers may well have been just as threatening to the social order as their 'lunatic' leader. Paula Fredriksen argues that Christ had preached his message about the coming Kingdom of God openly, traversing Galilee and Judea, with the result that 'both Pilate and the priests knew perfectly well that his teachings were in no practical way revolutionary'.[111] In his final Passover, Fredriksen proposes, Christ lost control of his audience, but with Pilate's execution of him as the messianic harbinger of Kingdom, the threat subsided and his followers could now be safely ignored.[112] Such a construct underestimates, in my view, the acute concern with which the priestly retainers, along with their occasional collaborators, the Pharisees, would have viewed Christ's provocative teaching and subversive parables, authoritative status claims, Kingdom ministry, unconventional social relations and prophetic critiques of covenantal Israel (cf. John 11:48). Pilate would have felt increasing pressure from his priestly clients in Judea to act.

Rather the disciples' abandonment of Christ at his arrest (Mark 14:51–52, 66–72 et parr.) and their subsequent personal concealment from the authorities (John 20:19) probably convinced Pilate that the movement, although potentially dangerous, was already a spent force and would be effectively terminated by the death of its founder. In sharp contrast to the previous popular movements in Judaea, there was no hint here of any continuing uprising by the closest followers of the

---

109 Meggitt, 'The Madness of King Jesus', 381–82.
110 Meggitt, 'The Madness of King Jesus', passim.
111 Fredriksen, 'Why was Jesus *Crucified*?', 418.
112 Fredriksen, 'Why was Jesus *Crucified*?', 418.

movement. There was no reason, therefore, to press on with hunting down its inner circle of leadership. The greatest problem Pilate had to face was not how to handle the uncommunicative Christ at his arraignment (Matt 27:12–14; Mark 15:3–5; John 19:8–10)—though he was problematic in his dismissive attitude towards Roman authority—but rather how to assess the degree of support that the messianic pretender still retained among the Passover crowds of Jerusalem (Luke 23:14a: 'You brought me this man as one who was inciting *the people* to rebellion'; cf. 23:5: 'He started in Galilee and has come *all the way here*'). Further, Pilate had to satisfy the demands of his elite retainers for a sentence of capital punishment to be imposed on Christ (Mark 16:63–64; cf. Lev 24:16), while at the same time maintain, as prefect of Judea, the primacy of Rome and the honour of the Julio-Claudian house.

Fourth, and finally, the issue of Pilate's interaction with the crowds during Christ's arraignment is highlighted in each Gospel. It allows each evangelist to underscore Christ's innocence of his alleged charges (Matt 27:23a; Mark 15:14; Luke 23:4, 14–15, 22a; John 18:38; 19:4a, 6b) and to expose (in their view at least) the increasing weakness of Pilate during the proceedings (Matt 27:23ab; Mark 15:10, 14–15a; Luke 23:6, 20, 22b–25; John 18:34; 19:7–8, 9a). The prefect was threatened into submission by the relentless demand for crucifixion on the part of the high priests and the shrill crowds (Mark 15:13; Luke 23:21, 23; John 18:39–40; 19:6, 15). This is especially the case if Stauffer's thesis concerning Pilate's *amicitia* ('friendship') with Sejanus is correct.

But how do we explain the evidence if, as has been increasingly argued, the Stauffer hypothesis no longer stands up to scrutiny? Moreover, as I have noted, the Gospel accounts are theologically and pastorally evaluative of Pilate's leadership and fallen human nature more generally (John 18:38a; cf. vv. 37a and 37b), situating the prefect's decisions against the backdrop of the providential denouement of salvation history (Matt 27:25; John 18:32, 36–37; 19:11), and re-evaluating Sadducean and imperial notions of 'power' in light of the sovereignty of Christ (John 18:37b).[113] Notwithstanding, the Gospel accounts

---

113 Referring to John 18:37b, Cassidy, *John's Gospel*, 49, writes: 'And thus does John portray Jesus epitomizing his sovereignty: Jesus, the prisoner whose kingship is not to be evaluated in Roman terms, now moves to invite Pilate, his judge, to acknowledge a kingship defined in Jesus' terms'.

insightfully expose the petty local and imperial politics at work in a provincial backwater during the principate of Tiberius (Matt 27:18, 24; Mark 15:10–11, 15a; Luke 23:11–12; John 18:29–31, 34–35a; 19:12, 15b). So we have to ask how the evidence of the Gospel accounts might be understood from a *Roman* point of view, distinguishing between the events recounted and the interpretations provided by the evangelists. Again, this is not to suggest that the perspectives of the evangelists are somehow misconstrued or deficient: they are simply different in purpose by virtue of their soteriological and Christological focus, but nevertheless they have insightfully accentuated the local rivalries of Christ's elite protagonists as they sought precedence within Israel, and, gratifyingly, sometimes afforded insight from a Roman viewpoint into the political pressures being imposed upon Pilate (John 19:7–8a, 12, 15b). But to misread Pilate as a hapless victim of the crowd's influence or as a puppet of his priestly retainers is naïve.[114] How then do we approach the narrative of Christ's arraignment before the crowds from a Roman viewpoint? How can we penetrate behind the rhetoric of the Gospels and view the actions of Pilate as a provincial prefect in a manner that might intersect profitably our literary evidence?

Warren Carter has helpfully suggested that Pilate's three questions (or interactions in the case of Luke) in the Synoptic Gospels with the assembled multitude regarding the fate of Christ (Matt 27:17 [repeated v. 21], 22, 23; Mark 15:9, 12–13, 14a; Luke 23:14, 20, 22) should be more understood as a case of Pilate polling the crowd.[115] Pilate is adeptly gauging what levels of support the accused still mustered among the general populace after Christ's recent triumphal entry into Jerusalem. As we have seen from the literary sources, Pilate would have had no compunction in viciously clamping down upon the crowd if there was genuine popular support for a messianic pretender or a challenge to Roman social order. Indeed, Pilate's carefully staged and oft-repeated theatrical protestations that he found no substantive charge against Christ could also be understood as a clever manipulation of the crowd designed to harden their resolve in asking for the release of Barabbas as opposed to

---

114 Thompson, *John*, 372.
115 Carter, *Pontius Pilate*, 69–74.

the accused. We cannot conclude from such protestations that Pilate considered Christ innocent: the strong likelihood is that he did not.

According to the Synoptic Gospels, Pilate released Barabbas either in order to satisfy the crowd (Mk 15:15), or because he had washed his hands of the entire affair (Matt 27:26), or, perhaps as part of a formal judicial procedure (Luke 23:24: ἐπέκρινεν), he had substituted Barabbas for Christ according to an agreement struck between the prefect and the people during a brief interlude (Luke 23:18–23).[116] The strategy, nevertheless, was a dangerous one because of the release of an insurrectionist and murderer (Mark 15:7; Luke 23:19; cf. 'notorious prisoner': Matt: 27:16) back into the Judean community.[117] However, should Barabbas have re-offended, Pilate would have immediately executed the insurrectionist, legitimising his prompt delivery of retributive justice because the brigand had already been granted pardon. Pilate, conveniently for his own political purposes, would have appeared to his Jewish contemporaries as if he was astutely responding to the pressure of the people in handing over Christ and defusing any chance of a spontaneous riot, generating thereby their limited and momentary goodwill given his general unpopularity. But, in reality, Pilate was deviously forcing the hand of the general populace to abandon their recent enthusiasm for the messianic pretender. Thus, having secured the loyalty of the Jewish populace to Rome in this instance by manipulating the crowd to abandon a dangerous and ambiguous political figure to his fate—a decision viewed by Matthew 27:25 from a 'bloodguilt' perspective in fulfilment of Christ's prophecy (cf. 23:29–36)[118]—Pilate simultaneously satisfied his elite priestly retainers by handing over Christ to crucifixion.

Finally, an independent tradition from the Gospel of John is worth noting for the insight that it throws upon the 'impact' of the crowd

---

116   Cuany, 'Jesus, Barabbas, and the People', 450.
117   For discussion of the evidence appealed to for the historicity of the release of a prisoner at Passover (Matt 27:17–18; Mark 15:6–10; John 18:39b), see Blinzler, *The Trial of Jesus*, 205–21; Brown, *Death*, 1.793–803, 807–09; Lémonon, *Ponce Pilate*, 173–76.
118   For discussion of potential antisemitic understandings purported for Matt 27:25, see Keener, *Matthew*, 671.

upon Pilate.[119] The Jews threatened that Pilate would no longer be 'friend of Caesar' (φίλος τοῦ Καίσαρος) if the prefect did not accede to their wishes (19:12a).[120] What is the significance of the term in the Gospel of John? A similar title, 'friend of the king', was the designation for loyal supporters of various kings during the Hellenistic Age (1 Macc 2:18; 3:18; 10:65; 3 Macc 6:23; Josephus, *A.J.* 12.298). As Adolf Diessmann notes, in the imperial age φίλος τοῦ Καίσαρος ('friend of Caesar') and φίλος τοῦ Σεβαστοῦ ('friend of Augustus') had emerged in the imperial world from the 'language of the court under the successors of Alexander'.[121] G. H. R. Horsley comments that φιλοκαισαρ in particular was 'one of a cluster of epithets adopted, no doubt with official Roman approval, by individuals from the Greek East, particularly client kings, although by no means them alone'.[122] A few examples will suffice to establish the importance of *amici* ('friends') in the principates of Augustus and Tiberius more generally, before we move onto discussion of φιλοκαισαρ in the Jewish world and at Ephesus.

First, six proconsuls were selected by Augustus for portrait honours and mentions on local coins in Africa and Asia after 7 BC. They were 'without exception *amici principis*, and every one of them was related to him'.[123] Augustus also appointed C. Asinius Gallus, the proconsul of Asia in 5/4 BC and his personal *amicus*, to investigate the murder of Euboulus in 6/5 BC: 'I commissioned my friend Asinius Gallus to examine under torture the slaves who were involved in the case ...'

---

119 Schnackenburg, *John*, 3.262, posits that John did not find this tradition in his independent sources 'but deduced the Jewish accusers' means of pressure from a *general knowledge of the contemporary political situation*' (my emphasis). Schnackenburg's proposal is even more speculative than the proposal he is trying to avoid: how would John, writing late in the late first century AD at Ephesus (?), know authoritatively about late 20s/early 30s Judea other than through his own special sources? Would John's own Flavian context at Ephesus have given him 'general knowledge' about Julio-Claudian Palestine that was in any way convincing?
120 The imperial context of John's Gospel, touching in particular on the kingship of Christ, has been extensively studied: see Reed, 'Rethinking John's Social Setting'; Richey, *Roman Imperial*; Justice, *Competing Visions*; Carter, *John and Empire*; Ripley, '"Behold the Man?"'; Ripley, 'Glorious Death'; Kim, *The Kingship of Jesus*; Wright, *The Governor and the King*.
121 Deissmann, *Light from the Ancient Near East*, 383. For discussion of samples across the eastern Mediterranean basin, see Horsley, 'Minor Philological Notes; 75. Φιλοκαισαρ', 87–88. See also Braund, *Rome and the Friendly King*, 105–08.
122 Horsley, 'Φιλοκαισαρ', 87.
123 Grant, *Aspects of the Principate of Tiberius*, 53.

(IG 12.3 [1898] 174).[124] Second, in the reign of Tiberius, *amicitia princeps* ('friendship of the *princeps*') continued to play an important role in the dynamics of Julio-Claudian rule. We see this pre-eminently in Tiberius' elevation of Sejanus, commander of the praetorian guard from AD 14–31, as an *amicus principis* ('friend of the *princeps*'), linking him to the *domus Augusta* by the betrothal of his daughter to the son of Claudius.[125] An *ara amicitiae* ('altar of friendship') was also set up, flanked by statues of Sejanus and Tiberius (Tacitus, *Ann.* 4.74). Indeed, as the otherwise unknown Marcus Terentius says (Tacitus, *Ann.* 6.8), 'I confess that not only was I the friend of Sejanus, but that I strove for his friendship, and that when I attained it, I rejoiced ... The closer a man's intimacy with Sejanus, the stronger his claim to the emperor's friendship'. Several personal companions of Tiberius, present with him during his withdrawal to Capri, were also chosen as *amici* to be part of the ruler's *consilium* (i.e. state council).[126] Additionally, coin issues with governors' portraits and names on them were also issued by Tiberius in AD 21 in Africa, as well as in Bithynia and Creta-Cyrenaica, following on from the Augustan precedent of 7 BC: this allowed the local cities 'to emphasize his reliance on *amici* as supporters of the dynasty'.[127] Third, even local associations vaunted their friendship with the Julio-Claudian rulers. In the early imperial era, for example, we hear of a priestess from Pergamon setting up an altar 'for Asklepios Soter and for the association of friends of the Augusti' (φιλοσεβαστοι).[128] In sum, *amicitia* represented an important modus operandi in the relationship between Tiberius, Sejanus, his personal companions, and governors during the ruler's principate.

124 See Sherk, 'C. Asinius Gallus', 57–62.
125 Grant, *Aspects of the Principate of Tiberius*, 54.
126 Grant, *Aspects of the Principate of Tiberius*, 54. On the *consilium principis*, see Crook, *CONSILIVM PRINCIPIS*; Millar, *The Emperor in the Roman World*, 110–22.
127 Grant, *Aspects of the Principate of Tiberius*, 58. For full discussion and numismatic evidence, see pp. 50–59.
128 For a translation, see Ascough et al., *Associations*, §120. Bammel, 'Philos tou Kaisaros', 210 n. 2, comments that φιλοκαισαρ and φιλοσεβαστος are titles employed in honorific inscriptions for the high priests of the imperial cult in Asia. For example, see the late first-century/early second century AD Ephesian honorific inscription which eulogises its Ephesian honorand thus: 'the [high priest] loyal to Caesar (φιλοκαίσαρα) both of Asia and [the city], the first man [of the city]' (SEG 46:1524). See also Donner, 'Der "Freund des Königs"'.

Turning to the imperial language of friendship in a Judean context, Jews would have been familiar with the potency of the honorific epithet φιλοκαισαρ ('loyal to Caesar', 'friend of Caesar'). An inscription from a statue base found on the Acropolis of Athens referred to Herod the Great, an internationally known benefactor, as φιλοκαισαρ, eulogising his virtue and good deeds (OGIS 427).[129] A similar but damaged honorific inscription from the Athenian agora also designates Herod as 'a pious king and a friend of Caesar (φιλοκαισαρα)' (SEG 12.150).[130] Later, Herod Agrippa I (AD 37–41), the client-king of Judea, also used the term on the reverse of his coin legends.[131] The importance of these imperial ties of friendship is underscored by Philo (*Flacc.* 40) who speaks of the social danger of insulting 'a king and friend of Caesar'.

However, if we allow for an Ephesian provenance of the Gospel of John,[132] additional φιλοκαισαρ inscriptions from Ephesus can also be drawn upon for consideration, though first-century AD examples are very few, with the vast majority belonging to the second century AD onwards. In terms of the strictly first century AD Ephesian examples, there are only four. In a AD 42/43 inscription honouring a consul and benefactor, there is reference to the *epitropos* ('administrator') of the city who is described as φιλοκαισαρ and φιλοσεβαστος (IEph 3.716).

129 Rocca, *Herod's Judea*, 44 n. 80.
130 See Richardson, *Herod: King of the Jews and Friends of the Romans*, 207–08. Horsley, 'Φιλοκαισαρ', 88, cites the φιλοκαισαρ epigraphic evidence from Dittenberger (OGIS 419, 420, 424, 427) referring to Herod Agrippa I and II, as well as Agrippa I's nephew Herod Eusebes. However, Horsley, 'Φιλοκαισαρ', 88–89, overlooks the two Herod the Great φιλοκαισαρ inscriptions discussed above, claiming that no such inscriptions are extant. First, Horsley accepts Dittenberger's attribution of OGIS 427 to Herod Eusebes, whereas Richardson, *Herod*, 208, rightly dismisses the suggestion, arguing that the inscription honours Herod the Great: 'The location in Athens, the usage "king", and the description of the person honored suggests Herod'. Second, Horsley is also unaware of SEG 12.150, another inscription of Herod the Great.
131 ΒΑΣΙΛΕΩΣ ΑΓΡΙΠΠΑ ΦΙΛΟΚΑΙΣΑΡ ('King Agrippa, friend of Caesar'), Hendin, *Guide to Biblical Coins*, §552 (AD 40/41); ΑΓΡΙΠΠΑΣ ΦΙΛΟΚΑΙΣΑΡ ΒΑΣΙΛΕΥΣ ΜΕΓΑΣ ('Of Agrippa, friend of the great Caesar'), §554 (AD 42/43); ΟΡΚΑΙ ΒΑΣ ΑΓΡΙΠΠΑ ΠΒΣΕΒ ΚΑΙΣΑΡΑ Κ ΣΥΝΚΛΗΤΟΝ Κ ΔΗΜΟ ΡΩΜ ΦΙΛΙ Κ ΣΥΝΜΑΧ ΑΥΤΙΥ ('A vow and treaty of friendship and alliance between the great King Agrippa and Augustus Caesar [i.e. Claudius], the Senate and the People of Rome'), §557 (AD 43/44). See the excellent article of Theophilos, 'John 15:14', who (p.39) lists twelve provincial coins (three from Judea, five from Philadelphia in Lydia, and four from Tripolis in Lydia) employing φιλοκαισαρ during the period AD 14–43.
132 Carter, *John and Empire*, 19–89. For a summary of the arguments, including an Asian provenance of the Gospel (Ephesus? Smyrna?), see Keener, *John*, 1.142–49.

The three other inscriptions are datable to AD 85/96, the reign of Domitian. The clerk (*grammateus*) of the city of Ephesus is also designated φίλοκαισαρ in a dedication to Artemis Ephesia and Domitian (IEph 7.1.3008), as is the clerk of the city in another decree discussing how old buildings at Ephesus should be restored to the grandeur of Domitian's new Temple (IEph 2.499). Finally, another clerk in an honorific inscription eulogising a city benefactor (IEph 3.793) is ascribed the epithet φίλοκαισαρ. What is intriguing about each of these first century AD Ephesian inscriptions, contemporary with the composition of the Gospel of John, is that elite officials (*epitropos, grammateus*) of the city, who are not the focus of the decree, seize the opportunity to vaunt publicly their status as φίλοκαισαρ that they possess with the ruler.[133] Thus this idle threat of the withdrawal of Caesar's friendship, which the crowd did not have the power to effect anyway, would have been a salutary reminder to any Roman prefect to act in ways which fostered Julio-Claudian interests by maintaining civic stability in the provinces, earning thereby the continuing approval of the Roman ruler and manifesting the fidelity and allegiance expected of an imperial client.[134] As Carson rightly comments, the threat would have reminded Pilate that bad reports had already been forwarded to Tiberius at the time of the military standards episode, forcing the prefect on that occasion to reverse his course of action.[135] The threat of Tiberius' potential withdrawal of 'friendship' at an unofficial level, would have been well understood even though there is no evidence that Pilate actually possessed the status of φίλοκαισαρ, unlike his Jewish and Ephesian compatriots who had been formally granted the honour.

Last, the papyrological evidence shows that there were imperial 'friends' among the Roman prefects in Egypt, in the same way that there

---

133 On friendship in the inscriptions and papyri, see Evans, 'Friendship'. Upon a search of the papyrus archive of www.papyri.info, accessed 25.12.2020, there are no cases of φίλοκαισαρ employed in the papyri.

134 Theophilos, 'John 15:14', 38, writes: 'the semantic domain of included clients who were recipients of political favours or privilege from their patron. This political matrix indebted the client to a relationship of obligation, responsibility and commitment to their patron, in what could only be described as fidelity and allegiance'.

135 Carson, *John*, 607.

had been 'first friends' of the Ptolemaic king.[136] 'Friendship', therefore, would undoubtedly have been an important modus operandi for Pilate in securing his power base in Judea, building upon bonds of reciprocity and obligation with elite players in a complex network of relationships. But, as noted, there is no evidence that Pilate had ever acquired the honorific φίλοκαισαρ either from Tiberius or Sejanus.

Notwithstanding, the irony was that 'the Jews', to borrow John's terminology, did not need to remind Pilate about remaining a loyal 'friend of Caesar', even if he did not possess the official status. It is true that the taunt of the Jews in John 19:12a focuses on the obligation of the prefect in a manner that might be mistakenly conceived as a political threat.[137] But the prefect had already demonstrated throughout his prefecture that he was a loyal governor of Tiberius by building the Tiberieum in Jerusalem in honour of the Roman ruler, commemorating the death of Livia (matron of the Julio-Claudian house and mother of Tiberius) with his AD 29/30 *quadrans* issue, and suppressing any hint of civil unrest that had emerged in a troublesome province.

So what are the dynamics of Roman politics in this instance? Again we are witnessing that, by means of his carefully stage-managed vacillations about executing Christ,[138] Pilate has whipped the frenzied crowd into affirming the priority of maintaining Tiberius' good will by crucifying messianic pretenders (John 19:12b) and, remarkably in the case of the chief priests, he elicits from them a confession of the priority of Caesar's kingship over that of Israel's god (John 19:15b). As much as Pilate works with his retainers to ensure a peaceable province by eliminating troublemakers, he also humiliates them before the altar of Rome in the process.

However, when we allow the interpretative overlay of the Gospel narratives to return to our historical consideration and view the

---

136 See the three late first and early second century AD Oxyrhynchus papyri discussed by Evans, 'Friendship', 188–90.
137 Theophilos, 'John 15:14', 41.
138 Wright, 'What is Truth?', 217, concludes regrading Pilate's strategy: 'his repeated statements that he finds "no case" against Jesus come off as feints to release him, which provoke the Jewish authorities and reinforce their dependent status. Pilate does not think Jesus is innocent, and Pilate has no strong concern to release him'.

first-century Roman world from a divine perspective,[139] it emerges that the Gospels subject Pilate to intense theological evaluation, critiquing his personal power base, exposing the duplicitous strategies of his retainers, and revealing the unthinking and vengeful gullibility of the crowd in history. The Gospel narratives, by means of their use of irony, establish that Pilate, along with his collaborators (John 19:11), failed to act justly towards the innocent Christ who was vindicated by God beyond the grave. Pilate was also forced to submit occasionally to the demands that Caesar imposed upon his provincial governors (John 19:12a) which, as we have seen in the case of the golden shields and Samaritan prophet episodes, were instigated by the complaints of his subjects. Furthermore, Pilate refused the offer of Christ's alternate kingdom of truth because of the myopia of the ancestral and imperial honour system to which he, as a praetorian prefect, was deeply committed. Indeed, Pilate's removal from office after the Samaritan prophet episode and his total disappearance from history showed how ephemeral was the Roman quest for glory for its elite competitors. Commitment to ancestral and Julio-Claudian honour was the modus operandi for provincial magistrates such as Pilate, but nothing could compare with the glory and triumph of the crucified, risen, and ascended Lord of all, paradoxically secured through his humiliation and abject weakness. Moreover, the necessity to appease retainers, no matter how much Pilate spotlighted their dependent status in a demeaning manner, was the political reality for provincial prefects if they were to experience longevity of tenure in their post. Last, no matter how large a military detachment (ἡ σπεῖρα) the Roman prefect might potentially dispense to arrest messianic pretenders (John 18:12; cf. v. 3),[140] he still had to gauge how much support from the crowd such figures still commanded in Jerusalem and Judea more widely and what military steps still had to be taken to see off their threat. In sum, the Roman 'strong man' Pilate was ultimately weak, not realising that his power was always derivative and entirely elusive for those who like him, for the sake of personal glory, sought to hold onto it no matter what.

---

139 See the comments of Agamben, *Pilate and Jesus*, 34–35, on the methodological issue.
140 On ἡ σπεῖρα as referring to a large Roman contingent of troops, as opposed to a small Jewish force, see Wright, 'What is Truth?', 215.

3. Conclusion

The archaeological, epigraphic, numismatic and literary evidence pertaining to Pilate provides us with a strong sense of his time as a Roman official in the province of Judea. At the outset, Pilate's nomenclature affords us keen insight into his commitment to his prestigious Samnite and praetorian origins, locating him in the Roman quest to surpass ancestral honour by securing personal glory through the imperial *cursus honorum*, opened up by Augustus to army personnel such as Pilate. An appreciation of this personal quest, well-illustrated by the comparanda of the Philippian praetorian honorific inscriptions, also allows us to see in Pilate's coinage not only a commitment to the imperial cult but also to the enhancement of Julio-Claudian honour (and, similarly, through the Tiberieum). This dimension of Pilate's background has been underestimated by historians, providing us insight into why Pilate was so strongly committed to honouring Tiberius and Livia (Julia Augusta) and in demonstrating his effectiveness as a prefect to the Roman ruler by his ruthless subjugation of any trace of civic disorder in a difficult province. The latter occurred not only by his effective use of military force but also by acting preemptively upon the information received through his priestly retainers and by his access to military and intelligence networks. Furthermore, the prestigious praetorian background of Pilate underscores that smuggling the military standards into the *praetorium* at Jerusalem under the cover of night was not only a strategic statement of Roman strength at the beginning of his prefecture but also an expression of his personal commitment to traditional army *religio* in the form of the worship of the standards, despite the scruples of his Jewish subjects.

Additionally, the independent Johannine tradition of John 19:12a, when viewed against the strong *amicitia* relationships of Augustus and Tiberius with their governors, including client-kings such as the Herods, allows us to appreciate better the *amicitia* networks that Pilate would have exploited as prefect. Notwithstanding, there is no evidence of a formal *amicitia* relationship on Pilate's part with Tiberius or informally with the treasonous prefect Sejanus: the long-established thesis of Ethelbert Stauffer regarding Pilate's links with Sejanus has to be finally abandoned. Last, another underappreciated dimension of Pilate's prefecture is his public projection of himself as a builder, using the funds from the Temple treasury for the erection of an aqueduct at Jerusalem and, with funds from (presumably) siphoned-off or newly imposed taxation, establishing the lighthouse (Tiberieum) at Caesarea Maritima. The construction of a monumental stepped street from the Siloam Pool to the Temple Mount, recently excavated, adds further to Pilate's reputation as a builder. Was Pilate (a) targeting particular groups in Judea as clients by such public beneficence (merchants at Caesarea Maritima and the populace at Jerusalem), (b) surpassing famous Herodian civic projects (e.g. the Druseion tower) with the construction of the Tiberieum, or (c) engaging in the Roman quest for glory by military and civic projects? None of these possible motivations are mutually exclusive.

In grappling with the theological and apologetic overlay of the commonalities in the Gospel narratives regarding Pilate's arraignment of Christ, we have distinguished between the narrative evidence and the evangelists' interpretations, allowing the Roman material and literary evidence to inform our judgements regarding Pilate's motivations. Here we are simply recognising the difficultly of assessing the internal drives of any historical figure in antiquity and, admittedly, the Roman evaluation undertaken in this chapter is but one approach to the issue.[141] But, in taking seriously the mutual interdependence of Pilate and the priestly retainer class in the oversight of Judea, it is highly unlikely from a Roman viewpoint that Pilate considered Christ as 'innocent', as the Gospels predispose us to believe. Because Christ is obviously in the estimation of the retainer class a messianic pretender, having been popularly acclaimed the Davidic King upon his entry into Jerusalem with its disturbing Maccabean and prophetic precedents, his fate should be none other than execution, as per the royal messianic pretenders from the reign of Herod Archelaus. The staged mockery of Christ as 'King' by the Roman soldiers and the titulus on the cross testify to a predetermined decision of crucifixion long since discussed as a hypothetical option, but awaiting a final provocative incident for its implementation, conveniently provided by Christ's royal entry into Jerusalem and the cleansing of the Temple. Moreover, the qualified acceptance of the

---

141 The historiography and sociology of motivation in ancient history is little discussed. See MacMullen, 'Historiens, attention'; MacMullen, *Why Do We Do What We Do?*.

title 'Son of God' on Christ's part (John 19:7–10a; cf. Matt 26: 63–64; Mark 14:60–62; Luke 22:70–71) would have provoked in the Roman prefect a deep sense of unease about the emergence of a rival to the apotheosised 'son of God', Augustus, and—despite Tiberius' personal aversion to divine honours—also to the current reigning 'son of God' who was considered divine in the provinces.

We have argued in agreement with Warren Carter that Pilate's protestations of Christ's innocence in the Gospels are carefully stage-managed and elaborated with high theatre: his repeated questions, his hand-washing ritual, and (speculatively) his possible 'disclosure' of his wife's portentous dream to select Jewish priestly officials as another lever of persuasion (?). This charade on his part is designed to assess how committed the Jewish crowds were to the accused after his arrest, Pilate being well aware of the volatility of the Jewish populace in the military standards and aniconic shields episodes. Ironically, Pilate's charade also makes the crowd even more dependent upon the prefect in their frenzied realization that he had to be threatened or intimidated in acting otherwise if they were to gain their objective: but the crowd's naïve warning to Pilate about abdicating friendship with Caesar only played into what had been Pilate's fundamental motivation all along. To be sure, the role of the crowd in history was not to be underestimated, as anyone familiar with republican history at Rome would be well aware, but Pilate was a skilled manipulator of these dullards. Above all, his manipulation of the priestly retainers into confessing that they had no King but Caesar, demoting Israel's god from his absolute preeminence in Israel's national life, was an exquisite coup for the prefect in establishing in the most humiliating and public way who really controlled the reciprocal relationship between Tiberius' governor and his retainers. But here the irony of the Gospel narratives reasserts itself: Christ's triumph over the grave highlights that cruciform weakness, rather than the Roman strength of Pilate, determines the ultimate course of history and announces that all human power is derivative and ephemeral, inevitably passing away with this current age. A few years after Christ's crucifixion, Pilate too would disappear from history into oblivion and, by contrast, Christ's followers would carry his Gospel of the Kingdom of God from Jerusalem to Rome.

Bibliography

Agamben, Giorgio *Pilate and Jesus* (Stanford: Stanford University Press, 2015).

Alföldy, Geza 'Nochmals: Pontius Pilatus und das Tiberieum von Caesarea Maritima', *Scripta Classica Israelica* 21 (2002), 133–48.

Alföldy, Geza 'Pontius Pilatus und das Tiberieum von Caesarea Maritima', *Scripta Classica Israelica* 18 (1999), 85–108.

Ameling, Walter *Corpus Inscriptionum Iudaeae/Palestinae. Volume II: Caesarea and the Middle Coast 1121–2160* (Berlin/Boston: De Gruyter, 2011).

Ascough, Richard S., Philip A. Harland, John S. Kloppenborg *Associations in the Greco-Roman World. A Sourcebook* (Waco: Baylor University Press, 2012).

Aslan, Reza *Zealot: The Life and Times of Jesus of Nazareth* (New York: Random House, 2013).

Austin, N. J. E., & N. B. Rankov *Exploratio: Military and Political Intelligence in the Roman World from the Second Punic War to the Battle of Adrianople* (London: Routledge, 1995).

Back, Sven-Olav 'Jesus and the Sabbath', in Tom Holmén and Stanley E. Porter (eds.), *Handbook for the Study of the Historical Jesus. Volume 3: The Historical Jesus* (Leiden/Boston: Brill, 2012), 2597–2633.

Bammel, Ernst 'Syrian Coinage and Pilate', *Journal of Jewish Studies* 2 (1950/1), 108–10.

Bammel, Ernst 'Philos tou Kaisaros', *Theologische Literaturzeitung* 77 (1952), 205–10.

Bammel, Ernst 'The *titulus*', in Ernst Bammel and C. F. D. Moule (eds.), *Jesus and the Politics of His Day* (Cambridge: Cambridge University Press, 1984), 353–64.

Barnett, Paul W. *Jesus and the Rise of Early Christianity* (Downers Grove: IVP, 1999).

Baudoin, Anne-Catherine 'Sur les traces de Ponce Pilate', *Le Figaro* (2019), https://www.unige.ch/theologie/files/1315/7554/1207/Ponce_Pilate.pdf; accessed 24.11.2020.

Baudoin, Anne-Catherine 'Truth in the Details: The *Report of Pilate to Tiberius* as an Authentic Forgery', in Edmund P. Cueva and Javier

Martinez (eds.), *Rethinking Fakes and Forgeries in Classical, Late Antique, and Early Christian Literature* (Groningen: Barkhius, 2016), 219–38.

Baudoin, Anne-Catherine — *Ponce Pilate: la construction d'une figure dans la littérature patristique et apocryphe* (PhD diss., École Pratique des Hautes Études, Paris, 2012).

Bermejo-Rubio, Fernando, & Christopher B. Zeichmann, 'Where Were the Romans and What Did They Know? Military and Intelligence Networks as a Probable Factor in Jesus of Nazareth's Fate', *Scripta Classica Israelica* 38 (2019), 83–115.

Bermejo-Rubio, Fernando — 'Jesus and the Anti-Roman Resistance: A Reassessment of the Arguments', *Journal for the Study of the New Testament* 12 (2014), 1–105.

Bermejo-Rubio, Fernando — '(Why) Was Jesus the Galilean Crucified Alone? Solving a False Conundrum', *Journal for the Study of the New Testament* 36.2 (2013), 127–54.

Betz, H. D. — 'Jesus and the Purity of the Temple (Mark 11:15–18), A Comparative Religion Study', *Journal of Biblical Literature* 116.3 (1997), 455–72.

Bilde, Per — *The Originality of Jesus: A Critical Discussion and a Comparative Attempt* (Göttingen: Vandenhoeck & Ruprecht, 2013).

Bird, H. W. — 'L. Aelius Seianus: Further Observations', *Latomus* 29.4. (1970), 1046–50.

Blinzler, Josef — *The Trial of Jesus* (Isabel and Florence McHugh, trans.; Westminster, Maryland: Newman, 1959).

Bock, Darrell L. — *Blasphemy and Exaltation in Judaism: The Charge against Jesus in Mark 14:53–65* (Grand Rapids: Baker, 1998).

Bock, Darrell L. — *Luke 9:51–24:53* (ECNT; Grand Rapids: Baker, 1996).

Bond, Helen K. — 'The Coins of Pontius Pilate: Part of an Attempt to Provoke the People or Integrate Them into the Empire?', *Journal for the Study of Judaism in the Persian, Hellenistic, and Roman Period* 27.3 (1996), 241–62.

Bond, Helen K. — *Caiaphas: Friend of Rome and Judge of Jesus?* (Louisville/London: Westminster/John Knox Press, 2004).

Bond, Helen K. — *Pontius Pilate in History and Interpretation* (SNTSMS 100; Cambridge: Cambridge University Press, 1998).

Borg, Marcus — *Conflict, Holiness and Politics in the Teachings of Jesus* (Lewiston/Queenston: Edwin Mellen, 1984).

Bovon, François — *L'évangile selon Saint Luc 19, 28–24, 53* (Genève: Labor et Fides, 2009).

Brandon, S. G. F. — *Jesus and the Zealots* (New York: Charles Scribner's Sons, 1967).

Braund, D. C. — *Augustus to Nero: A Sourcebook on Roman History 31 BC–AD 68* (Totowa: Barnes & Noble, 1985).

Braund, D. C. — *Rome and the Friendly King: The Character of Client Kingship* (London: 1984).

Brélaz, Cédric — *Corpus des inscriptions grecques et latines de Philippes. Tome II: La colonie romaine. Partie 1: La vie publique de la colonie* (Paris/Athènes: École française d'Athènes, 2014).

Brown, Raymond E. — *The Death of the Messiah: Volume 1* (New York: Doubleday, 1993).

Bruce, F. F. — *Israel and the Nations from the Exodus to the Fall of the Second Temple* (Eerdmans: Grand Rapids, 1969).

Bruce, F. F. — 'Render to Caesar', in Ernst Bammel and C. F. D. Moule (eds.), *Jesus and the Politics of His Day* (Cambridge: Cambridge University Press, 1984), 249–65.

Carson, D. A. — *The Gospel According to John* (Leicester: IVP, 1991).

Carter, Warren — *John and Empire: Initial Explorations* (New York/London: T&T Clark, 2008).

Carter, Warren — *Pontius Pilate: Portraits of a Roman Governor* (Collegeville: Michael Glazier/Liturgical Press, 2003).

Cassidy, Richard J. — *John's Gospel in New Perspective* (Maryknoll: Orbis, 1992).

Cassidy, Richard J. — *Jesus, Politics and Society: A Study of Luke's Gospel* (Maryknoll: Orbis, 1979).

Champlin, Edward — 'Seianus Augustus', *Chiron* 42 (2012), 361–88.

Charlesworth, James H. (ed.) — *The Messiah: Developments in Earliest Judaism and Christianity* (Minneapolis: Fortress, 1992).

Chilton, Bruce — 'Jesus and Sinners and Outcasts', in Tom Holmén and Stanley E. Porter (eds.), *Handbook for the Study of the Historical Jesus. Volume 3: The Historical Jesus* (Leiden/Boston: Brill, 2012), 2801–2833.

Collins, John J.   *The Scepter and the Star: The Messiahs of the Dead Sea Scrolls and Other Ancient Literature* (New York: Doubleday, 1996).

Crook, John A.   *CONSILIVM PRINCIPIS: Imperial Councils and Counsellors from Augustus to Diocletian* (Cambridge: Cambridge University Press, 1955).

Cuany, Monique   'Jesus, Barabbas, and the People: The Climax of Luke's Trial Narrative and Lukan Christology (Luke 23:13–25)', *Journal for the Study of the New Testament* 39.4 (2017), 441–58.

Cullmann, Oscar   *Jesus and the Revolutionaries* (New York: Harper and Row, 1970).

Davies, W. D. & D.C. Allison   *Matthew. Volume III: XIX–XXVIII* (ICC; Edinburgh: T&T Clark, 1997).

Deissmann, Adolf   *Light from the Ancient Near East: The New Testament Illustrated by Recently Discovered Texts from the Graeco-Roman World* (London: Hodder and Stoughton, 2nd ed. 1927; rep. Grand Rapids: Baker, 1978).

Dodson, Derek S.   'Reading Dreams: An Audience-Critical Approach to the Dreams in the Gospel of Matthew (PhD diss. Baylor University, 2006).

Donner, Herbert   'Der "Freund des Königs"', *Zeitschrift für die Altestamentliche Wissenschaft* 73.3 (1961), 269–77.

Downing, F. Gerard   'Dale Martin's Swords for Jesus: Shaky Evidence?', *Journal for the Study of the New Testament* 37.3 (2015), 326–33.

Eck, Walter   'Inscription Attesting the Restoration of a Lighthouse, Called Tiberieum, by the praefectus Iudaeae Pontius Pilatus', in W. Ameling, *Corpus Inscriptionum Iudaeae/Palestinae. Volume II: Caesarea and the Middle Coast 1121–2160* (Berlin/Boston: De Gruyter, 2011), 229.

Eisler, Robert   ΙΗΣΟΥΣ ΒΑΣΙΛΕΥΣ ΟΥ ΒΑΣΙΛΕΥΣΑΣ. *Die messianische Unabhängigkeitsbewegung vom Auftreten Johannes des Täufers bis zum Untergang Jakobs des Gerechten* (2 vols.; Heidelberg: Carl Winters Universitätsbuchhandlung, 1929–1930).

Evans, C. F.   *Saint Luke* (NTC; London: SCM Press, 1990).

Evans, Craig A.   '"Who Touched Me?": Jesus and the Ritually Impure', in Bruce Chilton and Craig A. Evans (eds.), *Jesus in Context: Temple, Purity and Restoration* (Leiden: Brill, 1997), 353–76.

Evans, Craig A.	'Excavating Caiaphas, Pilate, and Simon of Cyrene', in James H. Charlesworth (ed.), *Jesus and Archaeology* (Grand Rapids: Eerdmans, 2006), 323–40.
Evans, Craig A.	'Jesus' Action in the Temple: Cleansing or Portent of Destruction?' in Bruce Chilton and Craig A. Evans (eds.), *Jesus in Context: Temple, Purity and* Restoration (Leiden: Brill, 1997), 395–439.
Evans, Katherine G.	'Friendship in the Greek Documentary Papyri and Inscriptions: A Survey', in John T. Fitzgerald (ed.), *Graeco-Roman Perspectives on Friendship* (SBL Resources for Biblical Study 34; Atlanta: Scholars, 1997), 181–202.
Fredriksen, Paula	'Arms and the Man: A Response to Dale Martin's "Jesus in Jerusalem: Armed and Not Dangerous"', *Journal for the Study of the New Testament* 37.3 (2015), 312–25.
Fredriksen, Paula	'Why was Jesus *Crucified*, But His Followers Were Not?', *Journal for the Study of the New Testament* 29.4 (2007), 415–19.
Frova, Antonio	'L'Inscrizione di Ponzio Pilato a Cesarea', *Rendiconti* 95 (1961), 419–34.
Grant, Michael	*Aspects of the Principate of Tiberius: Historical Comments on the Colonial Coinage Issued Outside of Spain* (New York: The American Numismatic Society, 1950).
Harrison, James R.	*Paul and the Ancient Celebrity Circuit: The Cross and Moral Transformation* (WUNT 430; Tübingen: Mohr Siebeck, 2019).
Harrison, James R.	'The Persecution of Christians from Nero to Hadrian', in Mark Harding and Alanna Nobbs (eds.) *Into All the World: Emergent Christianity in Its Jewish and Greco-Roman Context* (Grand Rapids: Eerdmans, 2017), 266–300.
Harrison, James R.	*Paul and the Imperial Authorities at Thessalonica and Rome: A Study in the Conflict of Ideology* (WUNT 273; Tübingen: Mohr Siebeck, 2011).
Hegeland, J.	'Roman Army Religion', *Aufstieg und Niedergang der römischen Welt* 2.2 (1978), 1470–1505.
Hendin, David	*Guide to Biblical Coins* (New York: Amphora, 3rd ed. 1996).

Hengel, Martin	*The Zealots: Investigations into the Jewish Freedom Movements in the Period from Herod 1 until 70 AD* (Edinburgh: T&T Clark, 1989).
Hengel, Martin	*The Son of God: The Origin of Christology and the History of Jewish-Hellenistic Religion* (London: SCM, 1976).
Hengel, Martin	*Victory over Violence* (David. E. Green, trans.; London: SPCK, 1975).
Hengel, Martin	*Was Jesus a Revolutionist?* (Philadelphia: Fortress, 1971).
Hennecke, E.	*New Testament Apocrypha: Volume 1* (London: SCM Press, 1963).
Hennig, Dieter	*L. Aelius Seianus: Untersuchungen zur Regierung des Tiberius* (München: C. H. Beck, 1975).
Holmén, Tom	'Jesus and the Holiness Paradigm', in Tom Holmén and Stanley E. Porter (eds.), *Handbook for the Study of the Historical Jesus. Volume 3: The Historical Jesus* (Leiden/Boston: Brill, 2012), 2709-44.
Horsley, G. H. R.	'Minor Philological Notes; 75. Φιλοκαισαρ', *New Documents Illustrating Early Christianity* 3 (1983), 87-89.
Horsley, Richard, & John S. Hanson	*Bandits, Prophets, and Messiahs: Popular Movements at the Time of Jesus* (San Franscisco: Harper & Row, 1985).
Horvath, Tibor	'Why was Jesus Brought to Pilate?', *Novum Testamentum* 11.3 (1969), 174-84.
Jacobsen, David M.	'Coins of the First-Century Governors of Judaea and Their Motifs', *Electra* 26 (2019), 73-96.
Jeremias, Joachim	*New Testament Theology. Part 1: The Proclamation of Jesus* (London: SCM, 1970).
Jones, A. H. M.	'Procurators and Prefects in the Early Principate', in A. H. M. Jones (ed.), *Studies in Roman Government and Law* (Oxford: Blackwell, 1960), 115-25.
Jones, B. W., & R. D. Milns	*The Use of Documentary Evidence in the Study of Roman Imperial History* (Sydney: Sydney University Press, 1984).
Judd, Franks K.	*Pontius Pilate in Early Christian Literature* (PhD diss., University of North Carolina, Chapel Hill, 2003).

Justice, David W. *Competing Visions: Kingship in the Gospels and in Roman Ideology* (PhD diss., New Orleans Baptist Theological Seminary, 2008).

Kasher, Aryeh 'Josephus on Jewish-Samaritan Relations', in Alan D. Crown & Lucy A. Davey (eds.), *New Samaritan Studies: Essays in Honour of G. D. Sixdenier* (Sydney: Mandelbaum Publishing, 1995), 217–36.

Kazen, T. *Jesus and Purity Halakah: Was Jesus Indifferent to Impurity?* (ConBNT 38; Stockholm: Almqvist & Wiksell, 2002).

Keener, Craig S. *The Gospel of John: A Commentary* (2 Vols.; Peabody: Hendrickson, 2003).

Keener, Craig S. *A Commentary on the Gospel of Matthew* (Grand Rapids: Eerdmans, 1999).

Kim, Sehyun *The Kingship of Jesus in the Gospel of John* (Eugene: Pickwick, 2018).

Kinman, Brent 'Jesus' "Triumphal Entry" in the Light of Pilate's', *New Testament Studies* 40 (1994), 442–48.

Köstenberger, Andreas J. '"What is Truth?": Pilate's Question in Its Johannine and Larger Biblical Context', *Journal of the Evangelical Theological Society* 48.1 (2005), 33–62.

Köstenberger, Andreas J. *John* (BECNT; Grand Rapids: Eerdmans, 2004), 534–35.

Köstner, Elena 'Genesis and Collapse of a Network: The Rise and Fall of Lucius Aelius Seianus', *Journal of Historical Network Research* 4 (2020), 225–51.

Kraeling, Carl H. 'The Episode of the Roman Standards at Jerusalem', *Harvard Theological Review* 35 (1942), 263–89.

Légasse, Simone *The Trial of Jesus* (London: SCM, 1994).

Lémonon, Jean-Pierre *Ponce Pilate* (Paris: Les Éditions de L'Atelier, rev. ed. 2007).

Lémonon, Jean-Pierre *Pilate et le gouvernement de la Judée: Texts et Monuments* (Paris: Librairie Lecoffre, 1981).

Liefeld, Walter L. 'Luke', in Frank E. Gaebelein (ed.), *The Expositor's Bible Commentary* (Grand Rapids: Zondervan), 797–1059.

MacMullen, Ramsay *Why Do We Do What We Do? Motivation in History and the Social Sciences* (Warsaw and Berlin: De Gruyter, 2014).

MacMullen, Ramsay 'Historiens, attention: motivation = émotion', *Diogène* 3.203 (2003), 23–31.

Marshall, I. Howard *Commentary on Luke* (NIGTC; Grand Rapids: Eerdmans, 1978).

Martin, Dale 'Response to Downing and Fredriksen', *Journal for the Study of the New Testament* 37.3 (2015), 334–45.

Martin, Dale 'Jesus in Jerusalem: Armed and Not Dangerous', *Journal for the Study of the New Testament* 34.1 (2014), 3–24.

Matson, David L. 'Double Edged: The Meaning of the Two Swords in Luke', *Journal of Biblical Literature* 137.2 (2018), 463–80.

McGing, Brian C. 'Pontius Pilate and the Sources', *Catholic Biblical Quarterly* 53 (1991), 416–38.

Meggitt, Justin 'The Madness of King Jesus: Why Was Jesus Put to Death, But His Followers Were Not?', *Journal for the Study of the New Testament* 29.4 (2007), 379–413.

Meier, Paul L. 'Sejanus, Pilate, and the Date of the Crucifixion', *Church History* 37.1. (1968), 3–13.

Miller, Fergus *The Crowd in Rome in the Late Republic* (Michigan: Michigan University Press, 1998).

Miller, Fergus *The Emperor in the Roman World* (London: Duckworth, 1977).

Mullins, Michael *The Gospel of Luke: A Commentary* (Dublin: Columba Press, 2010).

Musial, Danuta 'The Princeps as *Pontifex Maximus*: The Case of Tiberius', *Electrum* 21 (2014), 99–106.

Nolland, John *Luke 18:35–24:53* (WBC 35c; Nashville: Thomas Nelson, 1993).

Ollivier, M. J. 'Ponce Pilatii et les Pontii', *Revue Biblique* 5 (1896), 274–54, 594–600.

Peppard, Michael *The Son of God in the Roman World: Divine Sonship in Its Social and Political Context* (Oxford: Oxford University Press, 2011).

Reed, David	'Rethinking John's Social Setting: Hidden Script, Anti-Language, and the Negotiation of Empire', *Biblical Theology Bulletin* 36 (2005), 93–106.
Richardson, Peter	*Herod: King of the Jews and Friends of the Romans* (Columbia: University of South Carolina Press, 1996).
Richey, L. B.	*Roman Imperial Ideology and the Gospel of John* (CBQMS 43; Washington: Catholic Biblical Association of America, 2007).
Ripley, Jason J.	'Glorious Death, Imperial Rome, and the Death of Jesus', *Journal of Greco-Roman Christianity and Judaism* 15 (2019), 31–76.
Ripley, Jason J.	'"Behold the Man?" Subverting Imperial Masculinity in the Gospel of John', *Journal of the Bible and Its Reception* 2.2 (2015), 219–39.
Rocca, Samuel	*Herod's Judea: A Mediterranean State in the Classical World* (TSAJ 122; Tübingen: Mohr Siebeck, 2008).
Rowe, C. Kavin	*World Upside Down: Reading Acts in the Graeco-Roman Age* (Oxford: Oxford University Press, 2010).
Schiavone, Aldo	*Pontius Pilate: Deciphering a Memory* (Jeremy Carden. trans.; New York and London: Liveright Publishing, 2016).
Schied, John	COMMENTARII FRATRVM ARVALIVM QVI SVPERSVNT: *Les copies épigraphiques des protocols annuels de la confrérie arvale (21 AV.–304 AP. J.-C.)* (Paris and Rome: École française de Rome, 1998).
Schnackenburg, Rudolf	*The Gospel According to St John. Volume 3: Commentary on Chapters 13–21* (Tunbridge Wells: Burns and Oates, 1982).
Schwab, Justin J.	*The Birth of the Mob: Representations of Crowds in Archaic and Classical Greek Literature* (PhD. diss. University of California, Berkeley, 2011).
Sheldon, Rose Mary	'Jesus, as Security Risk: Insurgency in First Century Palestine?', *Small Wars and Insurgencies* 9.2 (1998), 1–37.
Sheldon, Rose Mary	*Tinker, Tailor, Caesar, Spy: Espionage in Ancient Rome* (PhD diss. University of Michigan, 1987).
Sherk, Robert K.	'C. Asinius Gallus and his Governorship of Asia', *Greek, Roman and Byzantine Studies* 7 (1966), 57–62.

Silver, Kenneth K. A. 'Pontius Pilate—An Aqueduct Builder?—Recent Findings and New Suggestions?', *Klio* 82.2 (2000), 459–74.

Smallwood, E. Mary *The Jews Under Roman Rule: From Pompey to Diocletian. A Study in Political Relations* (Leiden: Brill, 1981).

Smith, Mark D. *The Final Days of Jesus: The Thrill of Defeat, the Agony of Victory. A Classical Historian Explores Jesus' Arrest, Trial and Execution* (Cambridge: Lutterworth Press, 2018).

Stauffer, Ethelbert *Christ and the Caesars: Historical Sketches* (London: SCM, 1955).

Stauffer, Ethelbert *Jesus and His Story* (London: SCM, 1955).

Stauffer, Ethelbert 'Zur Münzprägung und Judenpolitik des Pontius Pilatus', *Nouvelle Clio*, I and II (1949–1950), 495–514.

Szanton, Nahshon, et al., 'Pontius Pilate in Jerusalem: The Monumental Street from the Siloam Pool to the Temple Mount', *Journal of the Institute of Archaeology of Tel Aviv University* 46 (2019), 147–66.

Taylor, Joan E. 'Pontius Pilate and the Imperial Cult in Judaea', 52 (2006), 555–82.

Theophilos, Michael P. 'John 15:14 and the ΦΙΛ- Lexeme in Light of Numismatic Evidence: Friendship or Obedience?', *New Testament Studies* 64 (2018), 33–43.

Thompson, Marianne Meye *John: A Commentary* (New Testament Library; Louisville: Westminster John Knox Press, 2015).

Vanderkam, James C. *From Joshua to Caiaphas: High Priests after the Exile* (Minneapolis: Fortress, 2004).

Vardaman, Jerry 'A New Inscription Which Mentions Pilate as "Prefect"', *Journal of Biblical Literature* 81.1 (1962), 70–71.

Vermeule, C. C. *Roman Imperial Art in Greece and Asia Minor* (Cambridge Mass.: Belknap Press of Harvard University Press, 1968).

Webb, Robert L. 'The Roman Examination and Crucifixion of Jesus: Their Historicity and Implications', in Darrell L. Bock and Robert L. Webb (ed.), *Key Events in the Life of the Historical Jesus: A Collaborative Exploration of Context and Coherence* (Eerdmans: Grand Rapids, 2009), 669–773.

Winter, Paul 'A Letter from Pontius Pilate', *Novum Testamentum* 7.1 (1964), 237–43.

Winter, Paul   *On the Trial of Jesus* (Berlin: Walter de Gruyter, 1961).

Wright, Arthur M.   'What is Truth? The Complicated Characterization of Pontius Pilate in the Fourth Gospel', *Review and Expositor* 114.2 (2017), 211–19.

Wright, Arthur M.   *The Governor and the King: Irony, Hidden Transcripts, and Negotiating Empire in the Fourth Gospel* (Eugene: Pickwick, 2019).

Websites:

www. papyri.info

http://cojs.org/pontius_pilate-s_tiberium_inscription-_26-36_ce/

https://www.forumancientcoins.com/numiswiki/view.asp?key=Pontius%20Pilate, accessed 29.11.2020.

CHAPTER 4

Early Christian Reactions to Jesus: Paul as a Paradoxical Test-Case

Joseph D. Fantin

Abstract

Paul's life and ministry is one of the earliest examples of a reaction to Jesus available to us. Some have argued that Paul was not influenced by Jesus and created his own version of Christianity. Others view Paul as a faithful minister of Christ. Paul's life was certainly paradoxical. Prior to his encounter with Christ, he was a zealous persecutor of Jesus' followers. After his encounter, he became one of Christ's most devoted witnesses. This article will explore Paul's reaction to Jesus in two areas. First, I will consider the life of Paul and try to explain his drastic change. Second, I will examine the teaching of Paul and consider whether or not he was influenced by Jesus's life and teaching. Specifically, I will consider Paul's teaching on divorce (1 Cor. 7:10–16). My analysis will suggest that something very real happened to Paul that influenced him and caused his change of direction.

1. Introduction

Paul. Was he a devoted servant and follower of Jesus continuing the work begun by his Lord? Or, was he the second and more influential founder of Christianity? Paul's teaching. Was it in harmony with and dependent upon the teaching of his Lord? Or, was it something new and foreign to the mind and ideas of Jesus? Paul is a controversial figure. This is nothing new. From the beginning of his Christian ministry until today, he has caused fierce debate. This debate is both scholarly and, maybe more significantly, practical. The practical involves the realm of personal religious conviction and Christians' relationships with others. Assuming Acts accurately reflects Paul's activities, it reveals that his presence and teaching result in serious disagreements (Acts 13:44–51; 14:4), riots (Acts 17:5–8; 21:27–34; 22:22–23), imprisonment (Acts 16:19–24), and even the need for Roman protection (Acts 21:32–39; 23:12–31). Paul himself is not above contributing to controversy with his own words (Acts 23:6–10). Turning to Paul directly, he was a controversial figure within the church at Corinth, a church that he founded (1 Cor 1:11–13). On a number of occasions, he had to defend his own apostleship (2 Cor. 11:1–33; Gal 1:11–24). Finally, Paul was not afraid to confront even his close ministry partner, Barnabas, and one of the 'pillars' of the early church, Peter (Gal 2:9, 11–21).

Among some, Jesus has been seen as the good guy. He taught love, peace, and moral living. Paul, on the other hand, is the villain. He corrupted the good and simple religion of Jesus and is responsible for all the problems throughout church history. For example, the historian and philosopher Will Durant states that Paul 'replaced conduct with creed as the test of virtue' and he concluded that Paul's impact on Christianity 'was a tragic change'.[1] This is rather ironic. From Paul's perspective, he was devoted only to teaching about Jesus and his salvific act (1 Cor 2:2). Further, Paul believes that Jesus is the figure of controversy whose death is foolishness to Gentiles and a stumbling block to Jews (1 Cor 1:23). Is Paul sincere? Or is he simply using Jesus to further his own agenda?

One reason that so much controversy surrounds Paul is because the biblical data does not always seem consistent. The debate concerning the relationship between Jesus and Paul will not be solved anytime soon. The purpose of this article is to explore two aspects of this

---

1 Durant, *Caesar and Christ*, 592. There are representatives of this sentiment among New Testament scholars and theologians, including: Walter Bauer (1934), concerning the interpretation of the original Jewish Christian perspective, states: 'in Phrygia it was precisely orthodoxy that rejected Paul' and later, 'if one may be allowed to speak rather pointedly, the apostle Paul was the only heresiarch known to the apostolic age—the only one who was so considered in that period, at least from one particular perspective. It could be said that the Jewish Christians in their opposition to Paul introduced the notion of "heresy" into the Christian consciousness' (*Orthodoxy*, 233, 236; see also, 'the arch-heretic Paul', p. 201); and Ernest Renan (1869) who stated, 'True Christianity, which will last forever, comes from the Gospels,—not from the epistles of Paul. The writings of Paul have been a danger and a hidden rock,—the causes of the principal defects of Christian theology. Paul is the father of the subtle Augustine, of the unfruitful Thomas Aquinas, of the gloomy Calvinist, of the peevish Jansenist, of the fierce theology which damns and predestinates to damnation' (*Saint Paul*, 330). Further, this negative contrast between a 'good' Jesus and a 'bad' Paul is reflected in fields not associated with biblical studies and theology. Examples include: the third President of the United States, Thomas Jefferson (1820) writes, 'while this Syllabus is meant to place the character of Jesus in it's [apostrophe historically correct] true and high light, as no imposter himself, but a great Reformer of the Hebrew code of religion, ... Paul was the great Coryphaeus, and first corrupter of the doctrines of Jesus' ('From Jefferson to Short'). The early, mid-twentieth century American journalist, critic, and scholar H. L Mencken (1926) states 'What faith? Is it argued by any rational man that the debased Christianity cherished by the mob in all the Christian countries of to-day has any colourable likeness to the body of ideas preached by Christ? ... The plain fact is that this bogus Christianity has no more relation to the system of Christ than it has to the system of Aristotle. It is the invention of Paul and his attendant rabble-rousers—a body of men exactly comparable to the corps of evangelical pastors of to-day, which is to say, a body devoid of sense and lamentably indifferent to common honesty' (*Notes*, 74–75). The noted nonviolent Indian independence advocate Mahatma Ghandi (1928) wrote, 'I draw a great distinction between the Sermon on the Mount and the Letters of Paul. They are a graft on Christ's teaching, his own gloss apart from Christ's own experience' ('Discussion', 464). Pulitzer prize winning poet Robert Frost in his play, *A Masque of Mercy* (1945), has the character Keeper warn the biblical Jonah about Paul, 'Now we are hearing from the Exegete. You don't know Paul. He's in the Bible too. He is the fellow who theologized Christ almost out of Christianity. Look out for him' (*Complete Poems*, 615). Jewish existential philosopher Martin Buber wrote, 'Here not merely the Old Testament belief and the living faith of post-Biblical Judaism are opposed to Paul, but also the Jesus of the Sermon on the Mount'. (*Two Types*, 55). Noted mid-twentieth century author, James Baldwin (1962) suggests, 'the real architect of the Christian church was not the disreputable, sun-baked Hebrew who gave it his name but the mercilessly fanatical and self-righteous St. Paul' ('Letter').

relationship. First, I will briefly consider the man Paul himself. How does one who claimed to have been a devoted Jew and enemy of the Jesus movement (Phil. 3:6) completely change directions and become one of Jesus' most devoted followers (Phil. 3:7–11)? Second, what is the relationship between Jesus' and Paul's teaching? This has two aspects. First, does Paul's teaching in his letters reflect a knowledge and appreciation of Jesus' earthly ministry? Second, do Paul's letters demonstrate a knowledge of Jesus' teaching itself? Although the impact of Jesus on Paul personally is important, this topic will only be discussed briefly. Further, the topic of the specific impact of the life and non-passion related ministry of Jesus on Paul's teaching is also of interest. However, this too can only be given minimal consideration. Most of this article will focus on the influence of Jesus' teaching on Paul's letters. Is Paul aware of Jesus' teaching? And if so, is he dependent upon Jesus' teaching tradition, does he develop it further, and/or is he independent? After considering various options, I will focus on one topic about which both of these great teachers instructed their listeners/readers, namely, divorce.

As we look at the man Paul himself and consider the relationship of his teaching to that of Jesus, I acknowledge that these long-standing debates cannot be solved in a short article. Our treatment here is intended to provide a brief overview of the debate and suggest a plausible solution for one particular issue.

Paul is a controversial figure. He is also a complex and puzzling individual. Some might even say, Paul is a paradoxical figure. Paul's life and teaching provide us an opportunity to consider one of the earliest reactions to Jesus Christ. In Paul, we see a significant reaction to Jesus. This is beyond doubt. The issue remains however, what type of reaction was it?

2. Paul: The Man

Our two most credible sources concerning the life of Paul are Paul's own letters and the book of Acts. Although later books such as the *Acts of Paul* (including *Thecla* and the *Martyrdom*) may contain some helpful information, their late second century date makes them too far removed from Paul's life to be used as authoritative sources here.² The canonical book of Acts provides more detail than Paul's own letters. This is to be expected. Paul never set out to give an autobiography. Paul had other priorities in his letters. Also, it is likely that his readers would have known relevant portions of Paul's story through other means, including Paul's visits.

Although Acts is a secondary source for Paul's life, it is both early and does not seem to contradict anything we know from Paul directly.³ Because it is more detailed, I will begin with some observations here before moving on to Paul's own autobiographical accounts.⁴

The reader of Acts first meets Paul (then named 'Saul') at the stoning of Steven (Act 7:58). Paul himself does not participate in the stoning but is complicit. The ones who kill Steven ἀπέθεντο τὰ ἱμάτια αὐτῶν παρὰ τοὺ πόδας νεανίου καλουμένου Σαύλου ('place their clothing at the feet of a young man called Saul') (Acts 7:58).⁵ If any doubt is in the mind of the reader where Paul stood on this matter, Luke makes it clear, Σαῦλος δὲ ἦν συνευδοκῶν τῇ ἀναιρέσει αὐτοῦ ('Now Saul was in agreement with his killing) (Acts 8:1; see also Acts 22:20). Saul becomes the major figure in the persecution of the church.

The main conflict in the Acts story seems to begin to unfold. The church has experienced some resistance but until now, nothing catastrophic. With Saul, this is about to change. The chief villain has been revealed. Or, at least the reader thinks so. The irony here is that the next time we meet Saul, the villain will become the hero.

Acts chapter 9 begins as expected. Saul gets authority to expand his persecution (9:1–2). To be fair, Saul is not a villain because he enjoys

---

2   On the date of the *Acts of Paul*, see Elliott (ed.), *The Apocrypha New Testament*, 357.
3   Loveday Alexander is optimistic on the historical nature of Acts, she states: 'Within the epistemological space created by Luke's preface, then, there is no real room for doubt as to the broadly factual status of the narrative' (*Acts*, 163; the entire chapter, 'Fact, Fiction and the Genre of Acts' [133–63]).
4   There are many helpful accounts of Paul's background, life, and ministry. These include, Carson and Moo, *An Introduction*, 354–75; Harrill, *Paul*, 23–75; Schnelle, *Apostle Paul*, 23–386. More broadly, see Witherington, *The Paul Quest*.
5   All New Testament Greek passages are from the 28th edition of Nestle-Aland, *Novum Testamentum Graece*, edited by Aland et al (NA28). I have noted places where variant readings were preferred to the editors' text. Words in italics are references from the Greek Old Testament (as presented in NA28). All Old Testament Greek (LXX) passages are from Rahlfs and Hanhart (eds.), *Septuaginta*. All English translations are my own.

evil. Rather, he is strongly committed to his Jewish faith and to God. He desires to keep his nation pure.[6] He is a villain from the perspective of the author and his Christian readers.

Then something significant happens. Saul is knocked to the ground and hears the voice of the resurrected Jesus (9:3–9). The event leaves Paul blind and unwilling to eat for three days (9:8). Paul's 'pitiful' state is not punishment but the 'natural consequence of his beholding the heavenly light'.[7] After the help of a Christian named Ananias, Paul regains his sight, begins preaching Jesus, and meets the leaders of the church (Acts 9:10–31).

Debate exists over whether this event was a 'conversion' or 'call'.[8] For my purposes, the label is not important. I am concerned with the results, which are significant. A devoted Jew, a persecutor of the church, becomes one of its chief advocates. Paul preaches (beginning in Acts 9:10–22 and throughout Acts) and is persecuted (beginning in Acts 9:23–25 and throughout Acts).

One further unexpected change occurs. The devoted Jew, now a believer in Jesus as Messiah and preacher to his Jewish people, with Barnabas begins to preach to the Gentiles (ἰδοὺ στρεφόμεθα εἰς τὰ ἔθνη, 'behold, we are turning to the Gentiles'; Acts 13:46). It was just prior to this that Acts begins to refer to Saul as 'Paul' (Acts 13:9).

Interestingly, Acts has two other accounts of Paul's conversion. First, to the people in Jerusalem (Acts 22:1–21) and then later to Agrippa II and Festus (Acts 26:1–20). The accounts differ slightly. This is likely due to their different audiences.[9] Although it is likely that Paul told his story on a number of occasions, the inclusion of three accounts is likely more due to Luke's purpose than anything Paul has done.

---

6   See N. T. Wright's discussion of first-century Pharisees in an attempt to better understand Paul (*Paul*, 75–196; the summary at the end of this section is particularly informative). See the footnote below on 'zeal' in Phil 3:6.
7   Haenchen, *Acts*, 323.
8   Bock, *Acts*, 349, 'consciously' chooses the term 'conversion' because 'Saul after his encounter with the Lord is not the same person'. Koester, *Introduction*, 108, disagrees, 'The use of the term "conversion" for Paul's experience obscures what was in fact essential to him in this event. Paul never understood his experience as a conversion but always as a call'. For further discussion on this issue, see Bock, *Acts*, 349–50; Everts, 'Conversion and Call'; Keener, *Acts*, 2.1614–17; and the literature cited in these sections.
9   Bruce, *Acts*, 461. For a helpful comparison of the three accounts, see Barrett, *Acts*, 1.439–45.

How does this account compare with Paul's own story? Although Paul does not go into depth about his life, he mentions it when it can contribute to the purpose of his letters. Philippians 3:4b–6 is the most important example.[10] Here Paul confronts some attempting to demand Jewish obligations from the Philippians.[11] Paul give his own Jewish credentials:

3:4b Εἴ τις δοκεῖ ἄλλος πεποιθέναι ἐν σαρκί, ἐγὼ μᾶλλον· 5 περιτομῇ ὀκταήμερος, ἐκ γένους Ἰσραήλ, φυλῆς Βενιαμίν, Ἑβραῖος ἐξ Ἑβραίων, κατὰ νόμον Φαρισαῖος,[12] 6 κατὰ ζῆλος διώκων τὴν ἐκκλησίαν, κατὰ δικαιοσύνην τὴν ἐν νόμῳ γενόμενος ἄμεμπτος.

3:4b If anyone thinks that they have confidence in the flesh, I have more reason ⁵ I was circumcised on the eighth day, I am from the nation of Israel, I am from the tribe of Benjamin, I am a Hebrew born of Hebrews,[13] in relation to the Law, I am a Pharisee, ⁶ in relation to zeal, I was a persecutor of the church,[14] [and] in relation to the righteousness that is in the Law, I am blameless.

This description of Paul's life prior to his encounter with Jesus harmonizes well with the accounts in Acts. Paul, from a Jewish perspective, had it all. However, just like the Acts account, Paul goes on to describe that this has all been given up (Phil 3:7–8):

3:7 [Ἀλλ'] ἅτινα ἦν μοι κέρδη, ταῦτα ἥγημαι διὰ τὸν Χριστὸν ζημίαν. ⁸ ἀλλὰ μενοῦνγε καὶ ἡγοῦμαι πάντα ζημίαν εἶναι διὰ τὸ ὑπερέχον τῆς γνώσεως Χριστοῦ Ἰησοῦ τοῦ κυρίου μου, δι' ὃν τὰ πάντα ἐζημιώθην, καὶ ἡγοῦμαι σκύβαλα, ἵνα Χριστὸν κερδήσω

---

10 See also 2 Cor 11:22–33.
11 Philippians provides us some idea of what Paul's opponents were teaching but it gives us little information about who they are; it is impossible to be specific (Holloway, *Philippians*, 148–49).
12 Paul's Pharisaic background and its strict nature is recorded by Luke in Acts 26:5.
13 Fee, *Philippians*, 307, translates Ἑβραῖος ἐξ Ἑβραίων as 'Hebrew, born of pure Hebrew stock'.
14 Holloway, *Philippians*, 158–59, suggests that 'zeal' in its Second Temple and Early Christian context draws on the tradition of Phinehas (Num 25:6–13) and potentially involves 'religious violence'. See also, Bockmuehl, *Philippians*, 198–201.

> ³:⁷ But whatever things were gain for me, these things I consider a loss because of Christ ⁸ but even more than this I even consider all things to be a loss because of the better value of the knowledge of Christ Jesus, my Lord, through whom I forfeited all things and I consider [these things] rubbish, in order that I may gain Christ.

Although it is only implied here, as recorded in Acts, Paul mentions elsewhere that he suffered persecution for the cause of Christ (e.g. 2 Cor 11:23–33). Paul's decision to follow Jesus resulted in loss of everything he had worked for until then (position, status, etc.).

Modern (especially Western) Christians do not always understand or appreciate what Paul did here. In a community-oriented society based on honour and kinship relations, Paul is not simply changing religions.[15] He is reorienting his life. Old ties are broken. New uncertain ones must be pursued. Further, he now had to become part of the very group he had caused to suffer.

At the time of these events, there was nothing external to be gained by doing what Paul did. In fact, it was societal, cultural, reputational, and religious suicide. Paul's choice demands explanation. This is the paradox. How could one committed to destroying the church of Jesus Christ, give up everything and embrace suffering to become one of Jesus' most adherent followers.

The answer to this will not be found in profound psychological analysis of the person of Paul. Such analysis cannot be done on an ancient person anyway. It is rather simple. Concerning the life of Paul, there is no paradox. He simply believed that his encounter with Jesus was real. This resulted in a completely changed life. This change had significant consequences. Paul forfeited any chance of honour among his peers and any success he had hoped to achieve before he met Jesus. Further, his choice would result in alienation, hardship, physical persecution, and possibly death. But for Paul, Jesus, his encounter, and an ongoing relationship with him was real. It was all worth it.

---

15 For understanding the impact of these aspects of ancient life, see Malina, *The New Testament World*, and deSilva, *Honor*.

3. The Teaching of Paul: Dependent, Developed, and/or Independent of Jesus

3.1 Introduction

After exploring Paul's life, there are other aspects of Paul that have puzzled readers. Specifically, his teaching. Paul's influence on Christianity is enormous. All agree on this point. His letters have helped shape the church as we know it. However, the significant impact of Paul's letters demands that we ask the question: what was Paul's relationship to the figure from whom Christianity was allegedly founded, the one from whom Christianity takes its name?

This question is complicated by several factors. First, we have no direct writings from Jesus himself. Our understanding of Jesus is dependent upon writings from his followers. This does not demand that our sources are unreliable. However, direct access would be preferred. Further, a distinction must be made between attributed sayings of Jesus and sayings exclusively from Gospel tradition. 'Attributed sayings' is a broad category and includes sayings found in the Gospel tradition as well as other sayings without Gospel parallels such as those found in Paul, the apocryphal Gospels, and even a saying found in Codex Bezae (D) after Luke 6:4.[16] The purpose of this paper demands that I limit my database for consideration to Pauline sayings as well as allusions and echoes that have parallels in the Gospel tradition and those that do not. Second, because Paul wrote before and around the same time as the four Gospels, it is unclear to what extent and in what form Paul had access to the teaching of Jesus. In other words, even when Paul appears to use tradition found in the Gospels, it is impossible to know how and in what form he had access to this tradition. This is further complicated because the teaching of Jesus in the Gospels is limited. We have little access to other teaching tradition. We do not know how much Jesus tradition was available for Paul to draw upon. Third, there are clearly different emphases in Paul's writing from what is recorded in the Gospels. In some cases, such as divorce, Paul's teaching (1 Cor 7:10–16) seems different from that of Jesus (Mark 10:2–12; Matt 5:31–32; 19:3–9;

---

16 The addition in Codex Bezae could be treated as Gospel tradition; however, it is only found in this manuscript and almost certainly is a later addition that somehow was attached to Luke.

Luke 16:18). Thus, in order to answer our question, we must ask another: are Paul's differences a departure from or in harmony with the teaching of Jesus?

3.2 Towards a Catalogue of References of Jesus' Sayings in Paul

There is no agreement on references to explicit or implicit Jesus' sayings in Paul. Acknowledging this uncertainty, Heinz Hiestermann identifies four possible references in Paul to the Synoptic tradition: 1 Thess 4:15–17; 1 Cor 7:10–11; 9:14; 11:23–25.[17] His study evaluates passages that may be influenced by Jesus' sayings in the Synoptics. For example he concludes that Rom 13:9 (and Gal 5:14) and Gal 1:16 likely have Synoptic parallels (Matt 19:18–19 and 16:16–17 respectively).[18]

Hiestermann also mentions 1 Thess 4:2; 1 Cor 7:25; 14:37; 2 Cor 12:9; and Phlm 8 as suggested explicit quotations but without Synoptic parallels.[19] Hiestermann's focus is on the Synoptic tradition, and these references are not part of his developed argument. However, for my purpose here, any of Jesus' sayings tradition is valuable. Further, Jay Smith identifies at least fifteen allusions and echoes of Jesus' sayings in the Synoptic tradition.[20]

---

17 Hiestermann, *Paul*, 113fn1. Smith has a similar list. He identifies 'six possible quotations' of Jesus in Paul: 1 Cor 7:10(–11) (Mark 10:11–12 // Matt 19:9 // Luke 16:18; Matt 5:32); 1 Cor 9:14 (Matt 10:10; Luke 10:7); 1 Cor 11:24–25 (Luke 22:19–20); 1 Cor 14:37; 2 Cor 12:9; 1 Thess 4:15–17; however, only 1 Cor 11:24–25 is a 'verbatim quotation', 2 Cor 12:9 is 'verbatim' but this is a post-resurrection quotation, 1 Cor 14:37 and 1 Thess 4:15–17 are also likely post-resurrection (likely a 'prophetic oracle' or in the case of 1 Thess 4:15–17, a saying of Jesus not found in the Synoptic tradition), and 1 Cor 7:10; 9:14 are 'best considered allusions' (Smith, 'Discovering the Gospel Tradition', 223–24).
18 Hiestermann, *Paul*, 167–80, 192–216, 218.
19 Hiestermann, *Paul*, 113 n.1. Hiestermann also mentions Acts 20:35 but this is not Pauline so not of interest here. 1 Cor 14:37 and 2 Cor 12:9 were also mentioned by Smith ('Discovering the Gospel Tradition', 223).
20 Rom 8:15 and Gal 4:6 (Mark 14:36); Rom 12:17 (Matt 5:38–41 // Luke 6:29); Rom 13:7 (Mark 12:17 // Matt 22:21 // Luke 20:25); Rom 14:13 (Matt 7:1 //Luke 6:37); Rom 14:14, 20 (Mark 7:15, 18–19 // Matt 15:11, 17–18); 1 Cor 10:27 (Luke 10:7–8); 1 Cor 13:2 (Matt 17:20 and Matt 21:21 // Mark 11:23 // Gospel of Thomas 48 // Luke 17:6); 1 Thess 4:8 (Luke 10:16); 1 Thess 5:2, 4 (Matt 24:42–44// Luke 12:39–40); 1 Thess 5:3 (Luke 21:34–36; Matt 24:37–42 // Luke 17:26–35; Matt 24:8 //Mark 13:8); 1 Thess 5:5–7 (Matt 24:42–44, 48–51 // Luke 12:39–40, 45–46; Luke 21:34, 36 // Mark 13:33); 1 Thess. 5:13 (Mark 9:50 // Luke 6:29); Gal. 1:15–16 (Matt 16:17); Gal 5:14 (Matt 22:39–40 // Mark 12:31) (Smith, 'Discovering the Gospel Tradition', 224–227; n.22 suggests more than these are probable).

3.3 Brief History of the Debate

The question of the relationship between Paul and Jesus goes back almost two hundred years.[21] In 1831, Ferdinand Christian Baur suggested that Paul developed his specific brand of Christian theology in opposition to the earlier, more primitive Jewish Christianity.[22] This approach to the New Testament was foundational for Baur. For him, primitive Jewish Christianity was closer to Jesus and was essentially moral in nature.[23] Paul, however, gives Christian history a 'new beginning'[24] (*neuen Anfangspunkt*[25]). He takes a Jewish-focused religion (Jewish particularism) and initiates a religion that has a much more universal focus, namely a religion that involves 'the general principle of salvation for all people'.[26]

More accessible than Baur is William Wrede's provocative little book, *Paulus* published in 1904 with an English translation appearing in 1907.[27] In this volume, Wrede argued that Paul was responsible for taking Christianity 'out of the narrowness of Judaism' and transforming it.[28] Both through his missionary journeys and his theology, Paul 'not only lifted the Christian religion out of the narrowness of Judaism, but tore it loose (*felbst losgerissen*) from Judaism itself, and gave the Christian community for the first time the consciousness of being a

---

21 The history of the debate itself is worthy of a detailed monograph. Here I will focus on clear claims and a few major scholars. This is not intended to minimize the history, participants, or the debate itself. The area of study is important. For example, the *Studiorum Novi Testamenti Societas* devoted a seminar to this topic from 1984 to 1988. Some of the papers presented in these meetings have been published in Wedderburn (ed.), *Paul and Jesus*. For a concise and informative history of the debate, see Barclay, 'Jesus and Paul', 492–98. For a more detailed discussion of the period from Baur to Bultmann, see Furnish, 'The Jesus-Paul Debate', 17–50.
22 Baur, 'Die Christuspartie', 61–206. See also more briefly, Baur, *Lectures*, 153–56. The impact of Baur's 'Die Christuspartie' is noted by Albert Schweitzer, *Paul*, 12–13.
23 Baur, *The Church History*, 36–37.
24 Baur, *The Church History*, 46.
25 Baur, *Geschichte*, 44.
26 Baur, *The Church History*, 47.
27 A second edition of Wrede's *Paulus* was published in 1907. The second edition has a brief introductory article by Wilhelm Bousset. The changes to the main text itself are cosmetic. The pagination is the same. References to this work here were originally from the second edition but apply to both. For the impact of Wrede's *Paulus*, see Furnish, 'The Jesus-Paul Debate', 24–33. Also, eighty years after it first appeared, Rollermann devoted an article to Wrede's work (Rollermann, '*Paulus alienus*', 23–45). In addition to his impact, I chose to emphasize Wrede as opposed to the many other contributors in this debate because his claims are clear and the response to him was vigorous.
28 Wrede, *Paul*, 175.

new religion (*neuen Religion*)'.²⁹ Although it was not intentional, Paul created a 'new faith'³⁰ (*neuen Glaubens*³¹). Also, Paul took Christianity from a simple religion to a sophisticated movement and a religion of redemption.³² Although acknowledging 'the idea of redemption glimmers' in the words of Jesus, Wrede make the bold claim that 'No one who set out to describe the religion which lives in the sayings and similitudes of Jesus could hit by any chance on the phrase "religion of redemption"'.³³ Paul was 'the real creator of a Christian theology'.³⁴ He was the '*second founder of Christianity*'³⁵ (*zweite Stifter des Christentums*³⁶). Although similar, this terminology is more forceful (and provocative) than Baur's 'new beginning'. Further, 'This second founder of Christianity has even, compared with the first, exercised beyond all doubt the stronger—not better—influence'.³⁷

This radical and at times violent interpretation of Paul's relationship to Jesus has not gone unchallenged. Among the strongest reactions to Wrede and others with similar views was John Gresham Machen in his detailed article, 'Jesus and Paul' (1912). For Machen, the relationship between Paul and Jesus is crucial. If Wrede is correct about Paul being the second founder of Christianity, 'then Christianity is facing its greatest crisis in its history'.³⁸ Machen continues, 'For—let us not deceive ourselves—if Paul is independent of Jesus, he can no longer be a teacher of the church. Christianity is founded upon Christ and only Christ'.³⁹

Machen argues against an independent Paul on a number of fronts. For example, he suggests that Baur limited his sources to only Galatians and the two Corinthian letters.⁴⁰ This selective use of sources magnifies

---

29 Wrede, *Paul*, 175. Wrede, *Paulus*, 101.
30 Wrede, *Paul*, 175–76 (quoted phrase, p. 175).
31 Wrede, *Paulus*, 101.
32 Wrede, *Paul*, 176–77.
33 Wrede, *Paul*, 178.
34 Wrede, *Paul*, 177. Bultmann's conclusion is similar; acknowledging Paul's dependence on Hellenistic Christianity and limits due to our sources, Bultmann, *Theology*, 1.187, states that Paul 'became the founder of Christian theology'.
35 Wrede, *Paul*, 179–80 (quoted phrase, p. 179; italics original).
36 Wrede, *Paulus*, 104.
37 Wrede, *Paul*, 180.
38 Machen, 'Jesus and Paul', 548.
39 Machen, 'Jesus and Paul', 548.
40 Machen, 'Jesus and Paul', 554.

potential differences, for church conflicts are mentioned primarily in these books. Further, Machen even accuses Baur of 'misinterpreting' Galatians and Corinthians.[41] Baur 'failed to do justice to the "right hand of fellowship" (Gal. 2:9) which the pillars of the Jerusalem church gave to Paul'.[42] Thus, Machen reads Paul's confrontation of Peter as much less significant than Baur. Paul is not in fundamental disagreement over principles but 'rebukes Peter for hypocrisy'.[43] This reveals the main contribution of Machen. He consistently reads Paul from a different perspective than scholars such as Baur and Wrede. This difference of perspective is tied up in the approach to the sources and the sources themselves. Unlike Baur, Machen reads Galatians in light of other Pauline books.[44] Paul states that he received his gospel by revelation (Gal 1:12). If this passage is isolated, one could easily infer that Paul is rejecting other testimony. However, read in light of 1 Cor 15:3–7 in which Paul mentions his reliance on Scripture and the testimony of others, it is clear that such sources of information were important to him.[45] Further, Machen argues that Paul was aware of the earthly Jesus and believed that he was important.[46] In fact, there appears to be no conflict between Paul's view of Jesus and that of earlier primitive Christianity.[47] Even the Judaizers did not seem to have an issue with Paul concerning his view of Jesus.[48]

Machen also believes that the earthly life and teaching of Jesus is reflected in Paul more than often granted. He states, 'Paul displays far greater knowledge than is sometimes supposed, and [...], he possesses far greater knowledge than he displays'.[49] Machen defends this assertion with passages such as 2 Cor 10:1, Αὐτὸς δὲ ἐγὼ Παῦλος παρακαλῶ ὑμᾶς διὰ τῆς πραΰτητος καὶ ἐπιεικείας τοῦ Χριστοῦ ('Now I, Paul, myself, appeal to you through the gentleness and kindness of Christ').[50] Here Paul seems to be recalling the earthly life of Jesus as an example. This

---

41 Machen, 'Jesus and Paul', 554.
42 Machen, 'Jesus and Paul', 554.
43 Machen, 'Jesus and Paul', 554.
44 Machen, 'Jesus and Paul', 563.
45 Machen, 'Jesus and Paul', 563.
46 Machen, 'Jesus and Paul', 561–64.
47 Machen, 'Jesus and Paul', 560, 565.
48 Machen, 'Jesus and Paul', 558.
49 Machen, 'Jesus and Paul', 561.
50 Machen, 'Jesus and Paul', 561.

would not make much sense if an exalted Christ figure is all that Paul was concerned about. Machen also appeals to passages such as Rom 15:3; 1 Cor 7:10, 12, 25; 11:1, 23–26.[51] The latter includes a quotation of Jesus with reference to the Last supper.

I have focused on early participants in this discussion where the debate was rather straight-forward. This is not intended to ignore the many others who have contributed to this debate.[52] This section and article will not solve the debate. Too many presuppositional and methodological differences exist between the positions. The purpose of this section has been threefold. First, it was intended to reveal the main positions in a clear manner. Second, it was to demonstrate the controversial nature of Paul. Third, it served as a starting point for further consideration. My purpose is now to look at one example and see what it reveals about Paul and his reaction to Jesus.

---

51 Machen, 'Jesus and Paul', 561–62.
52 There are many other helpful studies on this topic. Those who see minimal emphasis of Jesus tradition on Paul include Rudolf Bultmann, 'The Significance', who concluded that 'Paul was not influenced *directly* by the historical Jesus' (p.220 [italics original]) and that 'Jesus' teaching is ... irrelevant for Paul' (p.223). However, Jesus himself is very important to Paul, 'The significance [of the historical Jesus] can be expressed in one sentence. *It is the historical person of Jesus that makes Paul's proclamation the Gospel*'. (p.220 [italics original]). More recently, in 1989, Nikolaus Walter concluded, 'that we can detect no hint that Paul knew of the narrative tradition about Jesus' ('Paul', 60; however, his discussion is much more nuanced than this, 'Paul,' 78–80). Walter maintains that 1 Cor 11:23–25 is from 'liturgical and ritual tradition' (p.60), and thus does not reflect a direct connection from Jesus to Paul. Works that believe that Jesus's influence on Paul was significant include A. T. Hanson who after noting Paul's 'invention' concludes that 'Paul was not indifferent to the details of Jesus' historical life; on the contrary, he gave to that life a central place in his account of the significance of Jesus' (*Paul's Understanding of Jesus*, 22). More recently, in 1995, David Wenham acknowledging Paul's 'flexibility' in his interpretations of Jesus tradition (specifically concerning food sacrificed to idols but this can be applied more broadly), believed that Paul 'was ... impressively faithful to the spirit and intention of Jesus' and that 'His interpretation may justifiably be said to be a model in terms of method, and to have maintained the church in the faith of Jesus' (*Paul*, 409; see also Wenham's popular treatment, *Paul and Jesus*, 181–84). Other relevant works include Bultmann, 'Jesus and Paul'; Davies, *Paul*, 136–45; Dunn, 'Jesus Tradition'; Dunn, 'Paul's Knowledge' (looking exclusively at Romans); Holzbrecher, *Paulus*; Lindemann, 'Paulus und die Jesustradition'; Lüdemann, *Paul*, 193–212; Kirk, *Jesus*; Kümmel, 'Jesus und Paulus' (SNTS Presidential address); Ridderbos, *Paul and Jesus*; Schoberg, *Perspectives of Jesus*; Shillington, *Jesus*; Wilson, 'From Jesus to Paul'. Possibly, the most recent substantial monograph that impacts issue is Hiestermann, *Paul*. Although this work is focused on the Synoptic tradition reflected in Paul and specifically attempts to determine which Synoptic tradition Paul is drawing upon, it defines clear methodology and furthers the discussion about which passages are influencing Paul.

3.4 Further Critique

Among the differences between Wrede's and Machen's positions is the willingness to grant the existence of a parallel. Some, like Wrede, are minimalists and are reluctant to acknowledge influence or parallels.[53] Others, such as Machen, are maximalists and recognize many.[54] These positions are unlikely to be reconciled. They are both committed to their understanding of how influence is determined at a presuppositional level. For my purposes, it is worth noting that both positions have weaknesses.

a. Select Critique of the Minimalist Approach

Additional criticism can be brought against Wrede and others. Wrede's position can be understood when one considers his view of the relationship between the Jesus of history and the later developed Christ of faith. For him, the incarnation, salvific death, and resurrection are not history in the sense that they actually occurred. They are, instead, 'acts of salvation' or 'history of salvation'.[55] Thus, they are essentially later interpretations of who Jesus was and now is and the significance of his works.[56] Although Wrede acknowledges that some 'preparative work had already been done', this redemptive Christ and his work is what Paul brings to Christianity.[57]

In addition to the issues of dismissive history, it is worth noting that Wrede is held developmentally captive by the chronology of his sources. His contrast is between the accepted recorded words of Jesus during his lifetime and the post-resurrection message of Paul that expresses a theological reflection on the Christ events such as his death and resurrection. If the salvific acts were as Paul says, the death and resurrection of Jesus (1 Cor 15:3–4; 2 Cor 5:21), it would be difficult for sustained teaching of this subject to be reflected in Jesus' words since the provision for redemption had not yet been accomplished. Nevertheless, even

---

53 Smith, 'Discovering the Gospel Tradition', 222.
54 Smith, 'Discovering the Gospel Tradition', 222.
55 Wrede, *Paul*, 178–79.
56 Wrede, *Paul*, 179.
57 Wrede, *Paul*, 178–82 (quotation, p.180).

in this context when such sayings briefly occur, they are likely dismissed as later additions or not mentioned.[58]

Hiestermann provides support for the conclusion that 'Paul would have possessed a substantial amount of knowledge about Jesus' by considering what we know of Paul's life and the likely spread of Jesus tradition throughout the areas where Paul ministered.[59] Further, he suggests two reasons that account for the lack of Jesus tradition reflected in Paul. First, the letters 'reflect a second stage of communication between Paul and the congregations (with the exception of Romans)'.[60] Thus, the letters were not intended to teach about Jesus (which already has taken place) but rather were written to 'answer questions', 'further explain the sayings of Jesus', and/or to meet needs of the churches.[61] Second, circumstances demanded that Paul defend his apostleship and the excessive use of Jesus' sayings tradition may have been interpreted as dependence upon other Apostles.[62] Hiestermann concludes that 'the letters demonstrate the apostle's authority, independence, and self-awareness. The lack of sayings of Jesus does not indicate that Paul was not interested in the life of Jesus, or that he was not familiar with the words of the Lord'.[63]

b. Select Critique of the Maximalist Approach

Machen's position is not without its weaknesses. First, much is based primarily on arguments from inference or silence. Even Hiestermann's robust defence of Paul's extensive knowledge of Jesus tradition cannot overcome this charge. He may be correct. However, the arguments are not invulnerable. Second, if a strong influence of Jesus' life and ministry on Paul is granted, it seems odd that so little of Paul's life makes this explicit. It is difficult to consider the minimal direct references to Jesus' life and teaching and conclude strong influence. Even among the few

---

58   For example, Mark 10:45 is not mentioned in Wrede's book. Even if it is granted that his treatment is brief and his focus is on Paul, the omission of this passage in light of the claims made above is revealing. Further, it is clear that for Wrede such divine activity is already dismissed as not possible (*Paul*, 179).
59   Hiestermann, *Paul*, 81–112, 211.
60   Hiestermann, *Paul*, 211.
61   Hiestermann, *Paul*, 211.
62   Hiestermann, *Paul*, 211–12.
63   Hiestermann, *Paul*, 212

quotations suggested by Machen, only that in 1 Cor 11:24–25 is clearly identifiable in the Gospels. Other direct appeals to Jesus' teaching must be either paraphrases of Jesus' teaching or non-canonical sayings. Finally, although Machen's understanding of Galatians through other Pauline letters is justifiable, all letters are unique. Moving too quickly to other books for interpretive clues to a passage under consideration must be done with caution. At one level, Schweitzer's commendation of Baur is justified, 'he allowed the texts to speak for themselves, to mean what they said'.[64] A balance must be struck. To appeal to other books at the first instance of confusion would be to risk missing what Paul is saying. On the other hand, other writings of Paul can provide us insight into some implicit information not directly accessible in the text at hand. Exegesis must be nuanced. These weaknesses do not demand that the approach of Machen is wrong, but they demonstrates that there is room here for debate. Some influence of Jesus' life and teaching must be granted (even if it is simply using his name).

c. Summary and Conclusion of the Critique

Considering the amount of emphasis Paul places on Jesus, there is remarkably little evidence of Jesus' sayings tradition in Paul. Reasonable explanations can be suggested to account for this. Nevertheless, scholars will remain divided over this issue. More importantly for the purposes of this article, one point can be agreed upon by all, namely, Paul was a significant force in the formation of early Christianity. Even those who maintain that Paul was heavily influenced by Jesus tradition must grant that Paul was fiercely independent and driven to accomplish his goals. This does not demand, however, that he was independent, for he operated on his own personal agenda and wished to shape Christianity into his own vision. As was described above, Paul's view of Jesus was never a point of contention in the earliest church. It is best to allow Paul to define his own ministry. He maintains that he did all he did for Christ and Christ's church (e.g., Rom 1:1–7; 1 Cor 2:2–3; 2 Cor 11:2; Gal 2:20; Phil 1:12–20). Indeed, Paul is still puzzling to today. He was radical and yet traditional. He was possibly the most paradoxical figure of the earliest Christian movement.

---

64 Schweitzer, *Paul*, 13.

3.5 The Life of Jesus and the Letters of Paul

As has already been noted, some have suggested that Paul was not concerned with the life and ministry of Jesus. For Paul, the death and resurrection was all that mattered. Is this the case?

The brief history above touched upon this aspect of Paul's thought. My critique of the minimalist and maximalist positions included specific arguments relevant to this debate.

It is reasonable to conclude that Jesus' life was of interest to Paul. We do not know what knowledge he had of Jesus' life and ministry but Jesus tradition likely circulated widely. Any emphasis on the passion, death, and resurrection is easily explainable. This was the essential event. Without this event, nothing else mattered. It was here that the new stage of salvation history began. Thus, Paul's work extends Jesus' ministry. It need only look back when necessary.[65]

This discussion has been brief. This is because the next section will shed further light on the answer. If it can be demonstrated that Paul was interested in the earthly teaching tradition of Jesus, it supports the notion that he was interested in the life of Jesus.

3.6 Paul and the Teaching of Jesus: Methodology

There are many topics that can be discussed when attempting to understand Paul's relationship to the teaching of Jesus. These include: Jesus' explicit missional focus on the Jews and exclusion of the Gentiles (Mark 7:27–28 // Matt 15:24; Matt 10:5–6, 23) in contrast to Paul's focus on the Gentiles (Rom 1:5; 11:13; Gal 2:8; principal addressees to all of his letters);[66] and Jesus' emphasis on the 'kingdom of God' (e.g. Matt 12:28; 19:24; 21:31, 43; Mark 1:15; 4:30; 9:47; 10:25; Luke 4:43; 6:20; 7:28; 10:11; John 3:3, 5) which is lacking in Paul.[67]

These are important topics and worth pursuing. However, I will focus on only one issue, namely, the teaching on divorce. This topic was chosen

---

65 See above, 3.4.b 'Select Critique of the Minimalist Position' (final paragraph) for Hiestermann's contribution to this specific issue here ('Paul', 81–112, 211–12).
66 See also, Scobie, 'Jesus or Paul?', 47–60.
67 The phrase 'kingdom of God' does occur in Paul: Rom 14:17; 1 Cor 4:20; 6:9, 10; 15:50 Gal 5:21; also in the disputed letters: Col 4:11; 2 Thess 1:5; however, this is rather incidental compared to the emphasis in the words of Jesus. All Bible searches for this article were done with Logos, version 8.3.

because it provides a clear test case. Both Jesus and Paul discuss this explicitly and in some detail (Matt 5:31–32; 19:3–9; Mark 10:2–12; Luke 16:18; 1 Cor 7:10–16). However, although Paul appeals to the teaching of Jesus, his instruction is not identical to what is found in the Gospels.

My goal is to shed some light on whether or not Paul was aware of Jesus' teaching and, if so, whether or not (and how) he used it. Since, there is no extant non-canonical teaching of Jesus on divorce, I am restricted to the Synoptic tradition. I will examine both the tradition found in the Synoptics and Paul. I will consider potential evidence for influence and then evaluate whether or not that evidence is sufficient to conclude that the tradition found in the Synoptics influenced Paul. Finally, if such a conclusion is made, I will propose a solution to account for differences between the two traditions.

It must be stressed that although the hope here is to provide insight on Jesus' influence on Paul, our topic is but one example. My solution here does not demand that it is the only way Paul approached Jesus' teaching. Other topics need to be explored to get a more complete picture. However, because the topic of divorce is so prominent in the Jesus' teaching tradition reflected in the Gospels, this solution may be much more representative of Paul's approach than a less explicit example. Thus, it may be fair to say that our solution has a strong probability to represent Paul's general approach.

3.7 Paul and the Teaching of Jesus: Divorce as A Test Case

Teaching about divorce occurs both in the Synoptic tradition and Paul. Relevant differences and similarities will be explored. However, it must be noted that differences occur within the Synoptic tradition itself. The Greek texts and translations with words and phrase of significance to this article for Mark 10:2–12 (with select Matthean additions noted) and 1 Cor 7:10–16 are provided in an appendix at the end of this article for reference. I have chosen to use Mark as the base text because it is likely earlier (see below). Although all of these passages have significant exegetical issues that are worth addressing, solutions to most of these issues are unnecessary for my purpose and no attempt is made here to do a thorough exegesis of either the Synoptic passages or 1 Cor 7:10–16.

a. Jesus: The Synoptic Tradition

There are four passages in the Synoptic tradition in which Jesus discusses divorce, the most significant being Mark 10:2–12 and its parallel in Matt 19:3–9. In these passages, Jesus' teaching is in response to some Pharisees' questions about the law. There are slight differences in wording and content. There are also some differences in the arrangement of material. For example, in Mark the Pharisees first appeal to Moses who permitted divorce. Jesus responds by citing portions of Genesis 1:27 and 2:24. However, in Matthew, Jesus first answers the Pharisees' question by citing Genesis 1:27; 2:24 and then the Pharisees bring up Moses in response. This difference is relatively minor and likely due to authorial flexibility with sources.

In addition to these minor differences, there are two significant additions in Matthew. First, in Matt 19:3, there is a phrase added to the end of the Pharisees' question, κατὰ πᾶσαν αἰτίαν, 'for any reason'. Second, Matthew includes an exception to Mark's apparent absolute statement on divorce, namely, that divorce is permissible if the wife[68] is guilty of πορνεία (Matt 19:9). A precise meaning for πορνεία is notoriously difficult to determine in this passage.[69] Davies and Allison list three common meanings: 'fornication', 'incest', and 'adultery'.[70] Common translations include 'unchastity' (RSV, NRSV), 'immorality' (NASB) 'sexual immorality' (ESV, NIV), 'fornication' (KJV), and 'marital unfaithfulness' (NIV84). This debate is ongoing and will not be solved here, but neither is a solution necessary to continue. It seems like the meaning of the word must include some type of sexual sin against the marriage. Thus, as will be suggested below, 'adultery' or 'sexual activity outside of one's marriage' with nuance may be the best translation.[71]

---

68 I mention 'wife' here because that is what is in the text (Matt 19:9). However, it likely applies to both parties in today's context.
69 For a detailed discussion, see Davies and Allison, *Matthew*, 1.529–31. See also options in BDAG, Nolland, *Matthew*, 245–46, and Hagner, *Matthew 1–13*, 124–25. The detailed work in these commentaries takes place in the discussion of Matt 5:32.
70 Davies and Allison, *Matthew*, 1.529. They also suggest a fourth possibility, 'sexual irregularity of any kind' ('unchastity') but they acknowledge that this is essentially the same as adultery (1.531).
71 Davies and Allison, *Matthew*, 1.530–31; 3.16, prefer 'adultery'. Hagner defends 'incest' ('illicit marriage') (*Matthew 1–13*, 124–25; *Matthew 14–28*, 549). Nolland remains generally uncommitted (*Matthew*, 245–46, 774).

This is not the place to suggest and defend which Gospel most accurately represents the teaching of Jesus or the earliest level of Synoptic tradition. Jesus tradition may have included both forms. Nevertheless, it is reasonable to conclude that Matthew had access to Mark and added implicit information that was understood or possibly ambiguous in Mark.[72] It is possible that Mark best reflects Jesus' teaching and that Matthew is simply adding what was implied. Or, Matthew may be closer and Mark omitted this phrase for some purpose (or he was unaware of the exception clause). Or, it is possible that both represent independent traditions. What is likely however is that the 1 Cor 7:10–11 is earlier than either of the written Gospels.[73]

Although I maintain that these words go back to Jesus in some form, the most important factor for this essay is to view these passages as part of the Synoptic sayings tradition of Jesus. Thus, I will consider both the Matthean and Markan forms as Synoptic sayings tradition. It is not necessary to determine whether one form is more precise or reflects Jesus' words most closely. Finally, the sayings tradition in Matt 5:31–32 is similar to Matt 19:3–9 (including the exception clause) and Luke 16:18 is brief and summary-type statement. They will not be directly considered here.

---

72 This is Instone-Brewer's position, who summarizes the relationship between the traditions found in Mark and Matthew: 'Although I will agree that Matthew probably added these phrases to the tradition that he received, I will also argue that he has correctly reinserted something that was present in the original debate. These phrases (or their equivalent) were removed when the debate was summarized for oral or written transmission' (*Divorce*, 164). Instone-Brewer includes a detailed discussion including a comparison of the two passages (pp.133–67). Hiestermann disagrees. Although Mark may have been written down first, following Dungan, he maintains that Matthew contains 'more original' elements than Mark (*Paul*, 129; Dungan, *The Sayings*, 102). Dungan himself states, 'Matthew's version seems more original than Mark's', but then he acknowledges that concerning 'originality', any conclusion must be 'inconclusive' (*The Sayings*, 102, 107; full discussion, 102–07).

73 First Corinthians was likely written in the mid 50s. Carson and Moo, *An Introduction*, 448, suggest AD 55 and Brown, *An Introduction*, 512, AD 56–57 or possibly AD 54/55. Dating the Gospels is difficult. Mark is likely first and beyond that, precision is impossible. Carson and Moo, *An Introduction*, 182, date Mark in the 50s or 60s; Ehrman, *The New Testament*, 240–41, to around AD 70; and Brown, *An Introduction*, 127, 164, to AD 68–73. Time must be granted for Mark to circulate widely enough to be used by Matthew and Luke but it cannot be so late that it runs unreasonably close to the date of the composition of these Gospels. Thus, anytime within the range of AD 50–70 is possible with the middle of this range most likely. This refers only to the written Gospels. The tradition found within them is dated much earlier. In the unlikely event that Mark was written in the early 50s, it would predate 1 Corinthians; however, it is difficult to determine whether Paul had access to the written form by the time he wrote the letter.

Since it is likely that Mark is earlier and likely served as a source for Matthew, I will work mainly from Mark and note Matthew when necessary.

b. Paul: 1 Corinthians 7:10–16

1 Cor 7:10–16 is the ideal test case for examining potential influence of Jesus on Paul.[74] Here, Paul directly appeals to teaching given by the Lord (1 Cor 7:10: παραγγέλλω, οὐκ ἐγὼ ἀλλ' ὁ κύριος, 'I command, not I but the Lord') and also includes instruction that Paul claims is not explicitly from the Lord (1 Cor 7:12: λέγω ἐγὼ οὐχ ὁ κύριος, 'I say, I, not the Lord). Thus, the passage contains reference both to some sort of Jesus tradition as well as explicit Pauline teaching.

For this passage to be considered a test case to determine Jesus' sayings tradition on Paul, it must be proven probable that the tradition reflected here is a saying from the historical Jesus. To do this, I will examine 1 Cor 7:10–16 more closely. First, this passage is part of a section in which Paul is answering questions from the Corinthian community (chapters 5—7). In 1 Cor 7:1, Paul turns his attention to topics that the Corinthians asked through a letter (Περὶ δὲ ὧν ἐγράψατε, 'Now the matters about which you wrote').[75] His discussion on divorce begins at 1 Cor 7:10. Thus, Paul is explicitly referring to Jesus' teaching in some way. Of course, this does not demand that it is from the historical Jesus' sayings tradition. This conclusion will need further support.

Second, as I have just stated, Paul is appealing to some type of Jesus' teaching authority here.[76] However, is he referring to teaching of the earthly Jesus or to something else? Paul refers to teaching of 'the Lord' (κύριος) and not specifically to the teaching of 'Jesus'. A case can be made that this is not the earthly Jesus. Paul often refers to the earthly

---

74 For a detailed discussion of 1 Corinthians 7 in its context, see Deming, *Paul*.
75 Ciampa and Rosner, *First Corinthians*, 290.
76 Conzelmann, *1 Corinthians*, 120, states this is 'one of the words of Jesus so very rarely found in Paul'. He does not mention whether or not he believes that this is a part of the Synoptic tradition.

Jesus with an unqualified or title-less 'Jesus'.[77] Most prominently, in 2 Cor 4:10–14, Paul uses the unmodified name 'Jesus' six times (4:10 [2x]; 11 [2x]; 14 [2x][78]). In this passage Paul writes about the life, death, and resurrection of Jesus as well as Christians' association with him. However, despite this general tendency, Paul does not exclusively use the name 'Jesus' and the titles in this way. There are two uses of the title-less name 'Jesus' referring to the post-resurrection Lord (1 Thess 1:10; 4:14)[79] and Paul also refers to the earthly Jesus as κύριος. This is most relevant in 1 Corinthians 11:23–27 which also records teaching tradition of Jesus. Here Jesus is referred to as Lord five times (1 Cor 11: 23 [2x], 26, 27 [2x]). Further, it is interesting that both 1 Cor 7:10–11 and 1 Cor 11:23–27 refer to teaching that is intended to continue after Jesus departed the earth. Thus, it is reasonable to see Paul referring to teaching of the earthly Jesus reflected here.[80] Further, Paul generally uses titles when he refers to Jesus and he normally refers to Jesus in a post-resurrection state. Thus, Paul's use of κύριος may indicate the lasting intention of the teaching reflected in these passages. Although the case for earthly Jesus teaching in 1 Cor 7:10 is

---

77 In the undisputed letters, the name 'Jesus' without a title such as 'Lord' or 'Christ' occurs 15 times. There are twelve occurrences without titles in the immediate context and all but two (1 Thess 1:10; 4:14 [second of two occurrences]) refer to the earthly Jesus: Rom 3:26 (especially relevant if understood as a subjective genitive which is interpreted as Jesus' faithfulness on earth); 2 Cor 4:10–14 (6x; see below); 2 Cor 11:4; Gal 6:17; 1 Thess 4:14 (first occurrence). Also, In two verses, Rom 8:11 and 2 Cor 4:5, an exclusive Ἰησοῦν has Χριστόν following in the next clause (Rom 8:11) or a modified Ἰησοῦν Χριστόν preceding (2 Cor 4:5). Further, Phil 2:10 has a titleless Ἰησοῦ in the phrase ἐν τῷ ὀνόματι Ἰησοῦ ('in the name of Jesus') but this is leading to the confession κύριος Ἰησοῦς Χριστός (Jesus Christ is Lord) in Phil 2:11. Finally, it is worth noting that in the disputed letters, the unmodified Ἰησοῦς is found in Eph 4:21. Thus, the name 'Jesus' normally but not exclusively refers to the historical Jesus.
78 The editors of NA²⁸ have included the word κύριον before the first mention of Jesus in 2 Cor 4:14. However, it is more likely that this word should be omitted. The external evidence for the omission, including P⁴⁶ (AD 200) and B (fourth century), slightly favours the inclusion of κύριον supported most strongly by ℵ (fourth century). The internal evidence also favours the omission. The tendency of scribes is to add, not remove, a title such as κύριος. Also, the omission seems more stylistically probable given the use of Ἰησοῦς without a modifying title in this passage. The best argument for the inclusion is that Paul is writing about the resurrection. However, again, this suggests the omission is more difficult thus affirming its probability. I admit that my decision here weakens my argument that suggests that Paul's use of titles and terms for 'Jesus' is not entirely consistent. Nevertheless, even granting this passage, others have demonstrated that this conclusion is valid.
79 See above.
80 Dunn, *The Theology*, 652, 695, for context, see 186–89.

strong, one further line of evidence will prove convincing.

Third, the word that Paul uses for divorce is χωρίζω,[81] used four times in 1 Cor 7:10–16, and usually translated 'separate' or 'divide' (BDAG).[82] The word is rather rare in biblical literature. Including the four 1 Corinthians 7 occurrences, it is used only thirteen times in twelve verses in the New Testament. Most importantly, among the nine other occurrences in the New Testament, two are in our Synoptic Jesus' sayings tradition passages, Mark 10:9 and Matt 19:6. Outside of the passages under direct consideration in this essay, it does not have the meaning of 'divorce' or 'absolution of marriage'.[83] It is used more generally of separation from various people, places, or attributes. For example, in Romans Paul uses the word in phrases that enforce the notion that nothing can 'separate' us or we cannot 'be separated' (χωρίσει/χωρίσαι) from God's and Christ's love' (8:35, 39). Also, Paul informs Philemon that there was a reason Onesimus 'was separated' (ἐχωρίσθη) from him (Phlm 15).[84]

In the Greek Old Testament (LXX), χωρίζω is used only 23 times (two of which are in the alternate text of Judges).[85] The usages are similar to those in the New Testament. There is one reference that refers to divorce. After Ezra's strong rebuke of Israel because they married foreign wives (1 Esdras 9:7), he commands the people: καὶ ποιήσατε τὸ θέλημα αὐτοῦ καὶ χωρίσθητε ἀπὸ τῶν ἐθνῶν τῆς γῆς καὶ ἀπὸ τῶν γυναικῶν τῶν ἀλλογενῶν, 'and do his will and separate from the nations of the land

---

[81] Probably the most detailed recent attempt to determine whether or not Paul was using the Synoptic tradition is Hiestermann, *Paul*, 114–29. His purpose is beyond that of mine here. He desires to determine which Synoptic tradition is used by Paul, concluding that it was Matthew (pp. 127–29).

[82] BDAG is Bauer, *A Greek—English Lexicon* throughout. See also, Montanari, *The Brill Dictionary*, 2395.

[83] For a detailed discussion of χωρίζω in 1 Cor 7:10–15, see Hiestermann, *Paul*, 119–20, whose discussion of the usage of this word is similar to mine.

[84] The other New Testament examples are similar. In Acts 1:4, Jesus orders his apostles 'not to leave (μὴ χωρίζεσθαι) Jerusalem'. Luke also notes that Paul 'leaves (χωρισθείς) Athens' (Acts 18:1) and Claudius orders the Jews 'to leave (χωρισθείς) Rome' (Acts 18:2). Hebrews states that Christ as high priest was 'separated (κεχωρισμένος) from sinners'.

[85] Lev 13:46; Judg 4:11; 1 Chron 12:9; 1 Esdr 5:39; 7:13; 8:54, 66; 9:9; 2 Esdr 6:21; 9:1; 10:2; 23:3; 1 Macc 1:1; 2 Macc 5:21; 10:19; 12:12; 3 Macc 2:25; 5:50; Prov 18:1; Wisd of Sol 1:3; Ezek 46:19. The alternate text of Judges has two occurrences of the word. The first is in the same verse as the main text (Judg 4:11) and the other is Judg 6:18.

and from the foreign wives' (1 Esdras 9:90).[86]

The more common word[87] for 'divorce' is ἀπολύω. Like χωρίζω it has a wide range of usages that include more a general 'separation' meaning (BDAG [1–4, 6]). However, it is also more specifically used for 'divorce' (BDAG [5]).[88] This word is used of Joseph who chose not to 'divorce' (ἀπολῦσαι) Mary publicly (Matt 1:19). This is also the word used in 1 Esdras 9:36 that describes what Israel did after Ezra commanded them to χωρίσθητε ... ἀπὸ τῶν γυναικῶν τῶν ἀλλογενῶν, 'separate ... from the foreign wives' (9:9). The people ἀπέλυσαν αὐτὰς σὺν τέκνοις, 'divorced [separated from] them with their children'. It is also the main word used in the four Synoptic divorce passages (Mark 10:2, 4, 11; 12; Matt 5:31, 32 [2x]; 19:3, 7, 8, 9; Luke 16:18 [2x]). By comparison, the word χωρίζω is used only in Mark 10:9 and Matt 19:6).[89] Paul also uses the fairly common, yet wide in meaning, term ἀφίημι three times for divorce (1 Cor 7:11, 12, 13),[90] and is the only New Testament author to do so.[91]

---

86 See also the canonical (Hebrew) Ezra 10:11.
87 Louw and Nida have two semantic domain listings for divorce. The first (§33.41) has only ἀποστάσιον, the word used in Matthew and Mark for 'certificate of divorce' (Mark 10:4; Matt 5:31; 19:7; Mark 10:4 and Matt 19:7 have the word in a phrase, βιβλίον ἀποστασίου). It appears that the single word and phrase have the same meaning. The second semantic domain (§34.78) lists our three words as well as the noun λύσις found only in 1 Cor 7:27. The data in Louw and Nida further supports the notion that divorce is not the main meaning of any of these terms: χωρίζω occurs in four semantic domains, ἀπολύω in five, and ἀφίημι is found in twelve.
88 Montanari, *The Brill Dictionary*, 259. Schneider lists 'divorce' as the second of two sections in his article on ἀπολύω. He states, 'In the Synoptics (13 of the occurrences there) ἀπολύω is a (common) term for the dismissal of a woman from marriage by means of a letter of divorce' ('ἀπολύω', 1.140). See also Silva's discussion of λύω, λύσις, and ἀπολύω for divorce ('λύω' 3.197).
89 These are not the only words for divorce in the Greek Old Testament. For example, the phrase βιβλίος ἀποστασίου ('notice of divorce') is used in the foundational divorce passage in Deuteronomy 24:1, 3. As noted above, it is also used in the Synoptic passages Matt 5:31; 19:7; Mark 10:4 which refer back to Deuteronomy. However, my focus remains on χωρίζω because it is the word used by Paul.
90 Among other meanings, BDAG lists 'release', 'send away', 'give up', 'cancel', 'leave', 'forgive'. Such meanings must be determined from context.
91 'Divorce' is not a common meaning for ἀφίημι. See BDAG, Montanari, *The Brill Dictionary*, 355. Neither Bultmann nor Leroy mention the 'divorce' meaning nor the 1 Corinthians verses (Bultmann, 'ἀφίημι', 1.509–13; Leroy, 'ἀφίημι', 1.181–83). Leroy, 'ἀφίημι', 1.183, states, 'The vb. and subst[antive] do not belong to the theological language of Paul' (I assume Leroy is focusing on the meaning of 'forgiveness' specifically with this comment). Also, in a lengthy article, Silva, 'ἀφίημι', 1.447, mentions the divorce meaning and the 1 Corinthian passage in a single sentence. Elsewhere Silva, 'λύω', 3.197, states 'although the compound ἀπολύω occurs with ref[erence] to divorce in the Gospels ..., Paul in this context uses ἀφίημι and χωρίζω (1 Cor 7:10–15)'. This observation may be correct for ἀφίημι but not for χωρίζω which, as has been pointed out, is used in the Synoptic tradition for divorce.

Too much should not be read into this. Paul may simply be using a common term for 'send away' or 'release' for stylistic reasons. The meaning of 'divorce' is clear from context.[92]

Paul's use of χωρίζω is significant. Because this term in both Matthew and Mark is used only by Jesus to mean divorce (Mark 10:9 and Matt 19:6),[93] this Gospel tradition is his likely source. Given the rarity of the word for divorce and Paul's reference to the Lord's teaching, it is difficult to see what other source Paul could have used in 1 Cor 7:10. One might expect him to use ἀπολύω. This word was more common for divorce and is even the main word used in the Synoptic tradition. Instead Paul uses a word from the Synoptic tradition that one would not expect. It is highly improbable that Paul would simply choose χωρίζω without knowledge of the Synoptic tradition. The word ἀπολύω is used by both Jesus and the Pharisees, but only Jesus uses χωρίζω. It is also possible that Paul did not have the entire Synoptic tradition pericopes. He may have had access to only the words of Jesus (either all or part of what is recorded in Matthew and Mark).

c. Conclusion: Jesus' Influence on Paul's Teaching on Divorce

All things considered as above, it seems clear that Paul in 1 Cor 7:10 is dependent on the Jesus' sayings tradition recorded in the Synoptic Gospels. The verbal link to the uncommon word χωρίζω found in Mark 10:9 (// Matt 19:6) is strong support that Paul was directly referring to Jesus' sayings tradition (reflected in Mark 10:9) in 1 Cor 7:10.[94] When

---

92 Louw and Nida mention that some have argued that in 1 Corinthians 7 ἀφίημι means 'legal divorce' and χωρίζω means only 'separation' (§34.78). They reject this and state, 'Such a distinction, however, seems to be quite artificial'. (§34.78). Louw and Nida are correct here. Unless these terms can be demonstrated to have such 'technical' meanings, context suggests a precise distinction is unwarranted. Also, as I have suggested, Paul's choice of χωρίζω is likely because of its use in the Synoptics.

93 The two Synoptic forms of χωρίζω are active. None of the forms in 1 Cor 7:10–16 is active (7:10, 11, 15 [second occurrence] are passive; 7:15 [first occurrence] is middle/passive form (likely middle meaning). This is an interesting but not necessarily significant observation. Non-divorce occurrences also occur both in active and passive. Interestingly, J. B. Bauer, 'χωρίζω', 3.492, notes the passive use in 1 Cor. 7:10 ('Pass[ive] *be separated (get divorced)* (in marriage contracts...') and does not seem to associate it with Mark 10:9 and Matt 19:6 which he lists in a section introduced by 'Of death rather than divorce' (italics original). For a detailed lexical discussion of χωρίζω used for divorce, see Silva, 'χωρίζω', 4.715–17.

94 Hiestermann, *Paul*, 120.

paired with the explicit reference to the Lord's teaching the evidence is conclusive.

Nevertheless, Paul is not slavishly restricted to Jesus tradition. He goes beyond what Jesus said and applies it to his own circumstances. First Corinthians 7:11 takes the statement made in the previous verse and qualifies it, μενέτω ἄγαμος ἢ τῷ ἀνδρὶ καταλλαγήτω, 'she must remain unmarried or be reconciled with her husband'. This brings him back to his earlier stated preference (not command), that in such cases, the person must remain single (1 Cor 7:7–8).[95] I think it is fair to say that, in the area of divorce, Paul develops Jesus' teaching.

In 1 Cor 7:12, Paul continues his teaching on divorce but begins by stating this is not teaching from Jesus but himself, λέγω ἐγὼ οὐχ ὁ κύριος, 'I say, I, not the Lord'. Indeed, Paul is addressing a completely different context than Jesus. Ciampa and Rosner state, 'Unfortunately for Paul this issue was not addressed by the teaching of Jesus. In some respects Paul's Gentile mission was more complicated than the ministry of Jesus, which was primarily to the Jews'.[96] However, he is not departing from or contradicting Jesus. Rather, he is developing the teaching further. He is applying it to a different situation.

d. Excursus: New Testament and Divorce

This conclusion suggests that the divorce sayings of Jesus found in the Synoptics do not provide the complete New Testament teaching on divorce. At least three reasons support this. First, the Matthean account adds certain details that suggest that Jesus is addressing a specific form of divorce. Instone-Brewer suggests that Matthew's addition of κατὰ πᾶσαν αἰτίαν, 'for any reason' (19:3) reflects a first-century Rabbinic debate between the conservative Shammai Pharisees and the more liberal followers of Hillel, specifically, a type of divorce which needed little or no reason ('any case or reason divorce').[97] The Hillel school permitted divorce for any reason or cause. Matthew's addition then is an attempt by the Pharisees to get Jesus' opinion on this debate. They are asking Jesus whether or not he agrees with the Hillel position that

---

95 See Fee, *First Corinthians*, 326–27.
96 Ciampa and Rosner, *First Corinthians*, 295.
97 Instone-Brewer, *Divorce*, 133–36.

maintains that a man can divorce a woman for any cause at all.[98] Jesus' answer is no in both Mark and Matthew. Instone-Brewer also maintains that early Jewish readers of the Markan version would have assumed the Matthean addition as implied.[99]

Second, it seems likely that Mark 10:2–12 and Matt 5:31–32; 19:3–9 are specifically referencing the Deuteronomy 24:1–4 teaching on divorce. This is supported by the use of [βιβλίος] ἀποστασίου in Mark 10:4; Matt 5:31; 19:7 (the only occurrences of ἀποστάσιον in the New Testament). This word (or phrase) is used only four time in the Greek Old Testament. Most prominently, it is used in the foundational divorce passage, Deut 24:1–4 twice (24:1, 3).[100] Instone-Brewer believes that it is likely that the first-century Jews understood Deut 24:1–4 to permit divorce on grounds of adultery.[101] Thus, since the Matthean exception clause, μὴ ἐπὶ πορνείᾳ (except because of immorality) (Matt 19:9; see also Matt 5:32) is likely referring to Deut 24:1–4, it seems probable that the cause for divorce referred to by πορνεία is adultery. This may be correct. However, other words for adultery existed in the first century and are used in the New Testament, including the Matthean passages.[102] Thus, certainty on the meaning here is not possible. Nevertheless, the use of πορνεία may be explainable given the narrow meaning of adultery in the first century. Generally, in the Roman world (of which Israel was a part), adultery for men only involved having relations with a married woman but for women what constituted adultery was more comprehensive.[103] It may be that Jesus and Matthew wanted to avoid this narrow meaning and wished to communicate the more general notion of 'sexual activity outside of one's marriage'. If this is the case, in modern

---

98 Instone-Brewer, *Divorce*, 134–36.
99 Instone-Brewer, *Divorce*, 135.
100 The other two uses are Isa 50:1 and Jer 3:8, which both likely look back to Deut 24:1–4.
101 Instone-Brewer, *Divorce*, 10.
102 The verb μοιχάω is found only in Mark 10:11, 12; Matt 5:32; 19:9. The verb μοιχεύω is more common and occurs fourteen times in ten verses in the New Testament: Mark 10:19; Matt 5:27, 28, 32; 19:18; Luke 16:18 (2x); 18:20; Rom 2:22 (2x); 13:9; Jas 2:11 (2x); Rev 2:22 (additionally, it occurs in the spurious passage, John 8:4). The noun μοιχεία occurs only twice: Mark 7:22 and Matt 15:19 (plus John 8:3).
103 Treggiari, *Roman Marriage*, 264; Glazebrook and Olsen, 'Greek and Roman Marriage', 79. For a discussion of the 'double standard' for men and women in sexual matters, see Treggiari, *Roman Marriage*, 299–309.

terminology, the word, 'adultery', with nuance from above understood, is appropriate.

Adultery is not the only cause for divorce in the first century. Jews believed that neglect was another potential cause or reason (Exod 21:10–11).[104] It is even possible that divorce was permitted for 'deliberate childlessness'.[105]

Third, Paul, after referring to the authoritative Synoptic tradition, adds or develops a reason for divorce not reflected in the Synoptic tradition. There is no indication that Paul believed that the Synoptic tradition, which he clearly believed was authoritative, was the only teaching on the subject. Paul did not dismiss or contradict it. He likely based his development upon the received Synoptic tradition.

4. Conclusion

In the beginning of this article I conceded that given the minimal direct appeal to Jesus' teaching by Paul, it was not unreasonable to conclude that Paul was not influenced by Jesus' teaching. This conclusion is based on a superficial reading of the text and needs to be revisited. It is not justified.

I have considered two aspects of Jesus' influence on Paul. First, Paul's drastic life change was a result of his encounter with the resurrected Jesus. Paul, who was once an enemy of the followers of Jesus and thus of Jesus himself completely changed course and embraced Jesus in such a way that controlled his entire life. Second, with reference to Paul's teaching, I have explored two aspects of Jesus' influence. First, although Paul emphasized Jesus' death and resurrection, he was also interested in the life of Jesus. The topics of his letters demanded more emphasis

---

104 Instone-Brewer, *Divorce*, 9. Although this passage refers to the treatment of a first wife who was likely a slave, Instone-Brewer notes that some rabbi interpreters believed that such rights must also extend to free women.
105 Instone-Brewer makes the case for this through Gen 1:22, 28 and Ezek 16:21–22; 23:37–39, as well as suggesting that this reason for divorce was assumed by both the schools of Shammai and Hillel (*Divorce*, 46; rabbinic reference *m. Yebamot* 6.6 is given in footnote 39). The passage describes a debate between the two schools regarding how many children one must have before ceasing sexual activity is permitted. It is assumed that divorce is permitted if a child is not born from the union (*m. Yebamot* 6.6.F).

on the death and resurrection, but when opportunity and need presented itself, Paul appealed to the life of Jesus. Second, Paul was aware of Jesus' teaching as found in the Synoptic tradition. For an important topic such as divorce, where Jesus' teaching existed, Paul utilized it. This is only one example but one suspects that it illustrates Paul's approach to available Jesus' teaching material. However, Paul did not see Jesus' words as the only teaching on a subject. Jesus' sayings tradition is limited. This does not mean that it is to be ignored, abandoned, or rejected. It is authoritative. However, it cannot always meet emerging needs. Life and the church continue. Communities have needs not addressed directly in the Jesus' teaching tradition. The Jesus' sayings in the Synoptic tradition must be developed, expanded, and/or serve as the basis of new and relevant teaching. This is what Paul is doing.

Thus, Paul is not guilty of the charge that he ignored or perverted the pure teaching of Jesus, neither was he the founder of Christianity. Nevertheless, he was highly influential in its expansion. He was fully committed to Jesus and he ministered tirelessly on his Lord's behalf. When select aspects of Paul are considered, he can be seen as paradoxical. However, when a more complete picture of Paul is embraced, this paradoxical man is quite consistent and understandable.

Appendix: Mark 10:2–12 (with Matthean additions) and 1 Corinthians 7:10–16

For reference, the Greek text and translations are provided here for the main passages under discussion:

A1 Mark 10:2–12

¹⁰:² Καὶ προσελθόντες Φαρισαῖοι ἐπηρώτων αὐτὸν εἰ ἔξεστιν ἀνδρὶ γυναῖκα **ἀπολῦσαι**, πειράζοντες αὐτόν [Matt. 19:3 adds: **κατὰ πᾶσαν αἰτίαν**]. ³ ὁ δὲ ἀποκριθεὶς εἶπεν αὐτοῖς· τί ὑμῖν ἐνετείλατο Μωϋσῆς; ⁴ οἱ δὲ εἶπαν·ἐπέτρεψεν Μωϋσῆς **βιβλίον ἀποστασίου** γράψαι καὶ **ἀπολῦσαι**. ⁵ ὁ δὲ Ἰησοῦς εἶπεν αὐτοῖς· πρὸς τὴν σκληροκαρδίαν ὑμῶν ἔγραψεν ὑμῖν τὴν ἐντολὴν ταύτην.⁶ ἀπὸ δὲ ἀρχῆς κτίσεως ἄρσεν καὶ θῆλυ ἐποίησεν αὐτούς. ⁷ ἕνεκεν τούτου καταλείψει ἄνθρωπος τὸν πατέρα αὐτοῦ καὶ τὴν

μητέρα,¹⁰⁶ ⁸ καὶ ἔσονται οἱ δύο εἰς σάρκα μίαν· ὥστε οὐκέτι εἰσὶν δύο ἀλλὰ μία σάρξ. ⁹ ὃ οὖν ὁ θεὸς συνέζευξεν ἄνθρωπος **μὴ χωριζέτω**.
    ¹⁰ Καὶ εἰς τὴν οἰκίαν πάλιν οἱ μαθηταὶ περὶ τούτου ἐπηρώτων αὐτόν. ¹¹ καὶ λέγει αὐτοῖς· ὃς ἂν **ἀπολύσῃ** τὴν γυναῖκα αὐτοῦ [Matt. 19:9 adds: **μὴ ἐπὶ πορνείᾳ**] καὶ γαμήσῃ ἄλλην μοιχᾶται ἐπ᾽ αὐτήν. ¹² καὶ ἐὰν αὐτὴ **ἀπολύσασα** τὸν ἄνδρα αὐτῆς γαμήσῃ ἄλλον μοιχᾶται. (Mark 10:2–12)

¹⁰:² and some Pharisees came testing him and they were asking him whether it is lawful for a man **to divorce** his wife [Matt. 19:3 adds: **for any reason**]. ³ And he answered and said to them, 'what did Moses command?' ⁴ and they said 'Moses permitted one to write a **notice of divorce** and **to divorce** [his wife]. ⁵ And Jesus said to them 'it was because of your obstinacy [that] he wrote this instruction. ⁶ but from the beginning of creation *[God] made them male and female.* ⁷ *Because of this, a man will leave his father and mother* ⁸ *and the two will be one flesh*; so that there is no longer two but one flesh. ⁹ Therefore, what God joined together, **no one must separate**'.
    ¹⁰ And in the house, the disciples again were asking him about this. ¹¹ And he said to them 'whoever **divorces** his wife [Matt. 19:9 adds: **except because of immorality**] and marries another commits adultery against her. ¹² And if she marries another after **divorcing** her husband, she commits adultery.

A2 First Corinthians 7:10–16

⁷:¹⁰ Τοῖς δὲ γεγαμηκόσιν παραγγέλλω, **οὐκ ἐγὼ ἀλλ᾽ ὁ κύριος**, γυναῖκα ἀπὸ ἀνδρὸς **μὴ χωρισθῆναι**, ¹¹ — ἐὰν δὲ καὶ **χωρισθῇ**, μενέτω ἄγαμος ἢ τῷ ἀνδρὶ καταλλαγήτω,—καὶ ἄνδρα γυναῖκα **μὴ ἀφιέναι**. ¹² Τοῖς δὲ λοιποῖς **λέγω ἐγὼ οὐχ ὁ κύριος**· εἴ τις ἀδελφὸς γυναῖκα ἔχει ἄπιστον καὶ αὕτη συνευδοκεῖ οἰκεῖν μετ᾽ αὐτοῦ, **μὴ ἀφιέτω** αὐτήν. ¹³ καὶ γυνὴ εἴ τις ἔχει ἄνδρα ἄπιστον καὶ οὗτος συνευδοκεῖ οἰκεῖν μετ᾽ αὐτῆς, **μὴ ἀφιέτω** τὸν ἄνδρα. ¹⁴ ἡγίασται γὰρ ὁ ἀνὴρ ὁ ἄπιστος ἐν τῇ γυναικὶ καὶ ἡγίασται ἡ γυνὴ ἡ ἄπιστος ἐν τῷ

---

106 The majority of manuscripts (the earliest of which is D, fifth century) include the phrase καὶ προσκολληθήσεται πρὸς τὴν γυναῖκα αὐτοῦ, 'and he will be united with his wife' (a portion of Gen 2:24). The earlier manuscripts ℵ and B (4th century) among others omit the phrase. It is likely that the phrase was added to Mark later by a scribe who desired to harmonize it with Matt 19:5 which has the same phrase with slight modification. This fits the tendency of manuscript D.

ἀδελφῷ· ἐπεὶ ἄρα τὰ τέκνα ὑμῶν ἀκάθαρτά ἐστιν, νῦν δὲ ἅγιά ἐστιν. ¹⁵ εἰ δὲ ὁ ἄπιστος **χωρίζεται, χωριζέσθω**· οὐ δεδούλωται ὁ ἀδελφὸς ἢ ἡ ἀδελφὴ ἐν τοῖς τοιούτοις· ἐν δὲ εἰρήνῃ κέκληκεν ὑμᾶς ὁ θεός. ¹⁶ τί γὰρ οἶδας, γύναι, εἰ τὸν ἄνδρα σώσεις; ἢ τί οἶδας, ἄνερ, εἰ τὴν γυναῖκα σώσεις;

⁷:¹⁰ Now to those who are married, **I command, not I but the Lord**, a wife should **not separate** herself from her husband. ¹¹ —but if she **does separate**, she must remain unmarried or be reconciled with her husband—and the husband must **not divorce** his wife. ¹² But to the rest **I say, I, not the Lord**, if any [Christian] brother has an unbelieving wife, and she is willing to live with him, he must **not divorce** her. ¹³ and if any wife has an unbelieving husband and he is willing to live with her, she must **not divorce** her husband. ¹⁴ For the unbelieving husband is made holy by the wife and the unbelieving wife [is made holy] by the [Christian] brother. Otherwise, your children are unclean, but now they are holy. ¹⁵ But if the unbeliever **separates, let him or her separate**; in these cases, the brother or sister is not bound; now God has called you to peace. ¹⁶ For how do you know, O wife, whether you will save your husband? Or, how do you know, O husband, whether you will save your wife?

Bibliography

Aland, B. et al (eds.) *Novum Testamentum Graece* (28th edn; Stuttgart: Deutsche Bibelgesellschaft, 2012).

Alexander, L. C. A. *Acts in its Literary Context: A Classicist Looks at the Acts of the Apostles* (Library of New Testament Studies 298; London: T&T Clark, 2006).

Barclay, J.M.G. 'Jesus and Paul', in Gerald F. Hawthorne, et al (eds.), *Dictionary of Paul and His Letters* (Downers Grove, Illinois: InterVarsity Press, 1993): 492–503.

Baldwin, J. 'Letter from a region in my mind', in *The New Yorker* (17 November 1962) <www.newyorker.com/magazine/1962/11/17/letter-from-a-region-in-my-mind> [accessed 08 April 2019].

Barrett, C. K.	*A Critical and Exegetical Commentary on the Acts of the Apostles, Volume 1, Preliminary Introduction and Commentary on Acts I–XIV* (International Critical Commentary; Edinburgh: T&T Clark, 1994).
Bauer, J. B.	'χωρίζω', in H. Balz and G. Schneider (eds.), *Exegetical Dictionary of the New Testament* (Grand Rapids, Michigan: Eerdmans, 1990 [German, 1978–80]), 3.492.
Bauer, W.	*Orthodoxy and Heresy in Earliest Christianity* (Philadelphia: Fortress, 1971 [German, 1934]).
Bauer, W.	*A Greek—English Lexicon of the New Testament and Other Early Christian Literature* (F. Danker, rev. ed.; Chicago: University of Chicago, ³2000).
Baur, F. C.	'Die Christuspartei in der korinthischen Gemeide, der Gegensatz des petrinischen und paulinischen Christentums in der alten Kirche, der Apostel Petrus in Rom', *Tübinger Zeitschrift für Theologie* (1831 [fourth fascicle]), 61–206.
Baur, F. C.	*Geschichte der christlichen Kirche*, vol. 1: *Kirchengeschichte der drei ersten Jahrhunderte* (Tübingen: Fues, ³1863).
Baur, F. C.	*Lectures on New Testament Theology* (Oxford: Oxford University, 2016 [German, 1864]).
Baur, F. C.	*The Church History of the First Three Centuries*, vol. 1 (3rd edn; London and Edinburgh: Williams and Norgate, ³1878 [German: 1863]).
Bock, D. L.	*Acts* (Baker Exegetical Commentary on the New Testament; Grand Rapids, Michigan: Baker, 2007).
Bockmuehl, M.	*The Epistle to the Philippians* (Black New Testament Commentaries; London: Black, ⁴1997).
Brown, R. E.	*An Introduction to the New Testament* (The Anchor Bible Reference Library; New York: Doubleday, 1997).
Bruce, F. F.	*The Book of Acts* (The New International Commentary on the New Testament; Grand Rapids, Michigan: Eerdmans, rev. 1988).
Buber, M.	*Two Types of Faith* (New York: Macmillan, 1951 [German, n.d.]).

Bultmann, R.   'ἀφίημι, ἄφεσις, παρίημι, πάρεσις', in G. Kittel (ed.), *Theological Dictionary of the New Testament* (Grand Rapids, Michigan: Eerdmans, 1964 [German, n.d.]), 1.509-13.

Bultmann, R.   'Jesus and Paul', in *Existence and Faith: Shorter Writings of Rudolf Bultmann* (Cleveland, Ohio: World, 1960 [German, 1936]), 183-201.

Bultmann, R.   'The Significance of the Historical Jesus for the Theology of Paul', in *Faith and Understanding* 1 (London: SCM, 1969 [German: 1966]), 220-46.

Bultmann, R.   *Theology of the New Testament*, vol. 1 (New York: Charles Scribner's Sons, 1951; [German: n.d.]).

Carson, D.A. & D.J. Moo   *An Introduction to the New Testament* (Grand Rapids, Michigan: Zondervan, ²2005).

Ciampa, R.E. & B. S. Rosner   *The First Letter to the Corinthians* (The Pillar New Testament Commentary; Grand Rapids, Michigan: Eerdmans, 2010).

Conzelmann, H.   *1 Corinthians: A Commentary* (Hermeneia; Philadelphia: Fortress, 1975 [German: 1969]).

Davies, W. D.   *Paul and Rabbinic Judaism: Some Rabbinic Elements in Pauline Theology* (Philadelphia: Fortress, ⁴1980).

Davies, W. D. & D. C. Allison   *A Critical and Exegetical Commentary on the Gospel according to Saint Matthew, Volume 1, Introduction and Commentary on Matthew I—VII* (International Critical Commentary; London: T&T Clark, 1988).

Davies, W. D. & D. C. Allison   *A Critical and Exegetical Commentary on the Gospel according to Saint Matthew, Volume 3, Commentary on Matthew XIX—XXVIII* (International Critical Commentary; London: T&T Clark, 1997).

Deming, W.   *Paul on Marriage and Celibacy: The Hellenistic Background of 1 Corinthians 7* (Grand Rapids, Michigan, ²2004).

deSilva, D. A.   *Honor, Patronage, Kinship, & Purity: Unlocking New Testament Culture* (Downers Grove, Illinois: InterVarsity Press, 2000).

Dungan, D. L.   *The Sayings of Jesus in the Churches of Paul: The Use of the Synoptic Tradition in the Regulation of Early Church Life* (Oxford: Blackwell, 1971).

Dunn, J. D. G.	'Jesus Tradition in Paul', in B. Chilton & C. A. Evans (eds.), *Studying the Historical Jesus: Evaluations of the State of Current Research* (New Testament Tools and Studies 19; Leiden: Brill, 1994), 155–78.
Dunn, J. D. G.	'Paul's Knowledge of the Jesus Tradition: The Evidence of Romans', in K. Kertelge, et al (eds), *Christus Bezeugen: Festschrift für Wolfgang Trilling zum 65. Geburtstag* (Leipzig: St. Benno, 1989), 193–207.
Dunn, J. D. G.	*The Theology of Paul the Apostle* (Grand Rapids, Michigan: Eerdmans, 1998).
Durant, W.	*Caesar and Christ: A History of Roman Civilization and of Christianity from the beginnings to A.D. 325* (The Story of Civilization: Part 3; New York: Simon and Schuster, 1944).
Ehrman, B. D.	*The New Testament: A Historical Introduction to the Early Christian Writings* (Oxford: Oxford University Press, ^{6}2016).
Elliott, J. K. (ed.)	*The Apocryphal New Testament: A Collection of Apocryphal Christian Literature in an English Translation Based on M. R. James* (Oxford: Clarendon, 1993).
Everts, J. M.	'Conversion and Call of Paul', in Gerald F. Hawthorne et al (eds.), *Dictionary of Paul and His Letters* (Downers Grove, Illinois: InterVarsity Press, 1993), 156–63.
Faithlife	*Logos Bible Software* (version 8.3.0.0034; Faithlife: Bellingham, Washington, 2019) [faithlife.com].
Fee, G. D.	*The First Epistle to the Corinthians* (The New International Commentary on the New Testament; Grand Rapids, Michigan: Eerdmans, rev. 2014).
Fee, G. D.	*Paul's Letter to the Philippians* (The New International Commentary on the New Testament; Grand Rapids, Michigan: Eerdmans, 1995).
Frost, R.	*Complete Poems of Robert Frost* (New York, Chicago, and San Francisco: Holt, Rinehart and Winston, 1949).
Funk, R. et al (eds.)	*The Five Gospels: The Search for the Authentic Words of Jesus* (New York: HarperCollins, 1993).

Furnish, V. P.	'The Jesus—Paul Debate: From Baur to Bultmann', in A. J. M. Wedderburn (ed.), *Paul and Jesus: Collected Essays* (JSOTSupp 37; Sheffield: Sheffield Academic, 1989), 17–50.
Gandhi, M.	'Discussion on Fellowship (Before 15-1-1928)', in *The Collected Works of Mahatma Gandhi, vol. 35 (1927–1928)* (Ahmedabad, India: Navajivan, 1969), 461–64.
Glazebrook, A. & K. Olson	'Greek and Roman Marriage', in T. K. Hubbard (ed.), *A Companion to Greek and Roman Sexualities* (Chichester, UK: Wiley-Blackwell, 2014), 69–82.
Haenchen, E.	*The Acts of the Apostle: A Commentary* (Philadelphia: Westminster, 1971 [German: 1965]).
Hagner, D. A.	Matthew 1—13 (Word Biblical Commentary 33A; Dallas: Word, 1993).
Hagner, D. A.	Matthew 14—28 (Word Biblical Commentary 33B; Dallas: Word, 1995).
Hanson, A. T.	*Paul's Understanding of Jesus: Invention or Interpretation?* (Hull: University of Hull, 1963).
Harrill, J. A.	*Paul the Apostle: His Life and Legacy in Their Roman Context* (Cambridge: Cambridge University Press, 2012).
Hiestermann, H.	*Paul and the Synoptic Jesus Tradition* (Arbeiten zur Bibel und ihrer Geschichte; Leipzig: Evangelische Verlagsanstalt, 2017).
Holloway, P. A.	*Philippians: A Commentary* (Hermeneia; Minneapolis: Fortress, 2017).
Holzbrecher, F.	*Paulus un der historische Jesus: Darstellung und Analyse der bisherigen Forschungsgeschichte* (Tezte und Arbeiten zum neutestamentlichen Zeitalter herausgegeben von Klaus Berger 48; Tübingen: Francke, 2007).
Instone-Brewer, D.	*Divorce and Remarriage in the Bible: The Social and Literary Context* (Grand Rapids, Michigan: Eerdmans, 2002).
Jefferson, T.	'From Thomas Jefferson to William Short, 13 April 1820', *Founders Online*, National Archives, version of January 18, 2019, <https://founders.archives.gov/documents/Jefferson/98-01-02-1218> [This is an Early Access document from The Papers of Thomas Jefferson: Retirement Series. It is not an authoritative final version.] [accessed 07 March 2019].

Keener, C. S.   *Acts: An Exegetical Commentary, Volume 2: 3:1—14:28* (Grand Rapids, Michigan: Baker, 2013).

Kirk, J. R. D.   *Jesus Have I Loved, but Paul?: A Narrative Approach to the Problem of Pauline Christianity* (Grand Rapids, Michigan: Baker, 2011).

Koester, H.   *Introduction to the New Testament.* Vol. 2: *History and Literature of Early Christianity* (Berlin: de Gruyter, ²2000).

Kümmel, W.   'Jesus und Paulus', *New Testament Studies* 10 (1964), 163–81.

Leroy, H.   'ἀφίημι, ἄφεσις', in H. Balz & G. Schneider (eds.), *Exegetical Dictionary of the New Testament* (Grand Rapids, Michigan: Eerdmans, 1990 [German: 1978–80]), 1.181–83.

Lindemann, A.   'Paulus und die Jesustradition', in R. Buitenwerf et al (eds.), *Jesus, Paul, and Early Christianity: Studies in Honour of Henk Jan de Jonge* (Supplements to Novum Testamentum 130; Leiden: Brill, 2008), 281–316.

Lüdemann, G.   *Paul. The Founder of Christianity* (Amherst, N.Y.: Prometheus, 2002).

Louw, J. P., & E. A. Nida (eds.)   *Greek-English Lexicon of the New Testament Based on Semantic Domains* (New York: United Bible Societies, 1988).

Machen, J. G.   'Jesus and Paul', in *Biblical and Theological Studies by the Members of the Faculty of Princeton Theological Seminary* (New York: Charles Scribner's Sons, 1912), 547–78.

Malina, B. J.   *The New Testament World: Insights From Cultural Anthropology* (Louisville, Kentucky: Westminster John Knox, ³2001).

Mencken H. L.   *Notes on Democracy* (London: Jonathan Cape, 1926).

Montanari, F.   *The Brill Dictionary of Ancient Greek* (M. Goh & C. Schroeder, revs. & eds.; Leiden: Brill, 2015 [Italian: 2013)).

Nolland, J.   *The Gospel of Matthew: A Commentary on the Greek Text* (New International Greek Testament Commentary; Grand Rapids, Michigan, 2005).

Rahlfs, A. and R. Hanhart (eds)   *Septuaginta* (Stuttgart: Deutsche Bibelgesellschaft, ²2006).

Renan, E.	*Saint Paul* (New York: G. W. Carleton, 1869 [French: n.d.]).
Ridderbos. H.	*Paul and Jesus: Origin and General Character of Paul's Preaching of Christ* (Grand Rapids, Michigan: Baker, 1958 [German: n.d.]).
Rollmann, H.	'*Paulus alienus:* William Wrede on Comparing Jesus and Paul', in P. Richardson & J. C. Hurd (eds.), *From Jesus to Paul: Studies in Honour of Francis Wright Beare* (Waterloo, Ontario: Wilfrid Laurier University Press, 1984), 23–45.
Schneider, G.	'ἀπολύω', in H. Balz and G. Schneider (eds.), *Exegetical Dictionary of the New Testament* (Grand Rapids, Michigan: Eerdmans, 1990 [German: 1978–80]), 1.140.
Schnelle, U.	*Apostle Paul: His Life and Theology* (Grand Rapids, Michigan: Baker, 2005 [German: 2003]).
Schoberg, G.	*Perspectives of Jesus in the Writings of Paul: A Historical Examination of Shared Care Commitments with a View to Determining the Extent of Paul's Dependence on Jesus* (Princeton Theological Monograph Series, 190; Eugene, Oregon: Pickwick, 2013).
Schweitzer, A.	*Paul and His Interpreters: A Critical History* (London: Adam & Charles Black, 1912 [German, n.d.]).
Scobie, C. H. H.	'Jesus or Paul? The Origin of the Universal Mission of the Christian Church', in P. Richardson & J. C. Hurd (eds.), *From Jesus to Paul: Studies in Honour of Francis Wright Beare* (Waterloo, Ontario: Wilfrid Laurier University Press, 1984), 47–60.
Shillington, V. G.	*Jesus and Paul before Christianity: Their World and Work in Retrospect* (Eugene, Oregon: Cascade, 2011).
Silva M. (ed.)	'ἀφίημι, ἄφεσις', in *New International Dictionary of New Testament Theology and Exegesis* (Grand Rapids, Michigan: Zondervan, 2014), 1.444–49.
Silva M. (ed.)	'λύω, λύσις, ἀναλύω, ἀνάλυσις, ἀπολύω, διαλύω, ἐκλύω, καταλύω, κατάλυμα, ἀκατάλυτος, παραλύω, παραλυτικός', in *New International Dictionary of New Testament Theology and Exegesis* (Grand Rapids, Michigan: Zondervan, 2014), 3.193–97.

Silva M. (ed.)	'χωρίζω, ἀποχωρίζω, διαχωρίζω', in *New International Dictionary of New Testament Theology and Exegesis* (Grand Rapids, Michigan: Zondervan, 2014), 4.713–17.
Smith, J. E.	'Discovering the Gospel Tradition in the Pauline Letters', in H. W. Bateman & B. I. Simpson (eds.), *Understanding the Gospels: A Guide for Preaching and Teaching* (Grand Rapids, Michigan: Kregel, 2017), 219–35.
Treggiari, S.	*Roman Marriage: Iusti Coniuges From the Time of Cicero to the Time of Ulpian* (Oxford: Oxford University Press, 1991).
Walter, N.	'Paul and the Early Christian Jesus-Tradition', in A. J. M. Wedderburn (ed.), *Paul and Jesus: Collected Essays* (JSOTSupp 37; Sheffield: Sheffield Academic, 1989), 51–80.
Wedderburn, A. J. M. (ed.)	*Paul and Jesus: Collected Essays* (JSOTSupp 37; Sheffield: Sheffield Academic, 1989).
Wenham, D.	*Paul and Jesus: The True Story* (Grand Rapids: Eerdmans, 2002).
Wenham, D.	*Paul: Follower of Jesus or Founder of Christianity* (Grand Rapids: Eerdmans, 1995).
Wilson, S. G.	'From Jesus to Paul: The Contours and Consequences of a Debate', in P. Richardson & J. C. Hurd (eds.), *From Jesus to Paul: Studies in Honour of Francis Wright Beare* (Waterloo, Ontario: Wilfrid Laurier University Press, 1984), 1–21.
Witherington, B., III	*The Paul Quest. The Renewed Search for the Jew of Tarsus* (Downers Gr.: InterVarsity, 1998).
Wrede, W.	*Paul* (London: Philip Green, ²1907 [German: 1904]).
Wrede, W.	*Paulus* (Halle: Gebauer-Schwetschke, 1904; London: J. C. B. Mohr [Paul Siebeck], ²1907).
Wright, N. T.	*Paul and the Faithfulness of God* (Christian Origins and the Question of God 4; Minneapolis: Fortress, 2013).

PART B:
SOCIAL LEGACY OF JESUS OF NAZARETH

CHAPTER 5

Narrating a New Identity[1]: The Role of Isaiah's Suffering Servant in 1 Peter 2:18–25

David M. Shaw

Abstract

In the not-too-distant past, 1 Peter held the dubious honour of being considered an 'exegetical step-child' of NT research.[2] While this is no longer the case, it is still true that Petrine studies too often remains in the shadow of work(s) relating to the Gospels and Paul's letters. Consequently, scholars in the field have taken advantage of this inattention by approaching the text from various angles.[3] One line of discussion has concerned 1 Peter's use of the OT for the composition of the letter which, in the words of D. A. Carson, appear 'in rich profusion'.[4] The present inquiry considers Peter's use of Isaiah's Suffering Servant motif in 1 Pet. 2:18–25 to shape an identity and missional posture that might

---

1 Material in this essay was presented in an earlier form as, Shaw, 'Isaiah 53 and Social Creativity'; and 'Narrating a New Identity'. Content from both presentations is now also found in my PhD thesis, 'A People Called'. I would like to thank those who attended those early presentations whose questions helped refine my thinking on the issue.
2 Elliott, 'The Rehabilitation of an Exegetical Step-Child'.
3 For an overview, see Dubis, 'Research on 1 Peter'; also, Boring, 'First Peter in Recent Study'.
4 Carson, '1 Peter', 1015. On 1 Peter's use of the OT, see especially, McCartney, 'The Use of the Old Testament'; Schutter, *Hermeneutic and Composition in I Peter*; Chapple, 'Appropriation of Scripture'; Sargent, *Written to Serve*.

best be described as resident-alien-ness.[5] While the core of my argument is substantially exegetical, I approach the text through the dual-lenses of Narrative Transportation and Social Identity theories. Doing so provides a methodological basis by which to discuss the narratological and identity elements within the text that aim to shape the corporate identity of Peter's readers in ways that both surprise and undermine typical social identity processes. What follows is a brief description of each theory before contemplating Peter's use of Isaiah's Suffering Servant and its importance for Christian identity and missional posture.

Narrative Transportation Theory

Narrative Transportation Theory (NTT) is a social-psychological theory advanced by Michelle Green and Timothy Brock who suggest that people may be absorbed into narratives to the degree that they impact on their beliefs in the real world, irrespective of those stories being fictional or factual.[6] Their theory is established on a metaphor found in the work of Richard Gerrig whom they quote in full:

> Someone ('the traveler') is transported, by some means of transportation, as a result of performing certain actions. The traveler goes some distance from his or her world of origin, which makes some aspects of the world of origin inaccessible. The traveler returns to the world of origin, somewhat changed by the journey.[7]

The metaphor implies that a story well-told and subsequently imbibed by its recipient(s) has the power to shape one's whole way of life, from their beliefs through to their actions. It is no overstatement then, when

---

5   Petrine authorship remains a contested issue. The most substantial treatment remains Achtemeier, *1 Peter*, 1–43; more recently, see Williams, *Persecution in 1 Peter*, 22–34, 291–95. Both Achtemeier and Williams settle on 1 Peter being a pseudonymous document. For a defense of 1 Peter's authenticity, see Schreiner, *1, 2 Peter, Jude*, 21–36.
6   Green and Brock, 'The Role of Transportation', 703, 707.
7   Gerrig, *Experiencing Narrative Worlds*, 10–11; cited in, Green and Brock, 'The Role of Transportation', 701; cf. Green and Brock, 'In the Mind's Eye', 324.

Tom Van Laer et al., remark that 'nothing is less innocent than a story'.[8]

For narrative transportation to occur, three aspects prove especially pertinent:[9] (1) stories must be received and interpreted, which assumes a level of engagement on behalf of the recipient(s); (2) transportation is likely to occur when the recipient of the story experiences empathy and/or mental imagery.[10] Concerning empathy, the recipient of the story seeks to embrace the experience of a character, so that they 'know and feel the world in the same way'.[11] Mental imagery, by contrast, incorporates vivid images created in the mind of the recipient to the degree that they feel they are experiencing the event(s) of the story themselves.[12] (3) Finally, the narrative world temporarily becomes 'more real' than the real world for the recipient of the story, such that they lose track of reality.

Narrative transportation may also have persuasive influence by impacting emotional and cognitive responses that catalyse changes in belief, attitude, and intentions, with the potential of leading to life transformation.[13] Such persuasion may appear in two forms: (1) *narrative persuasion*, specifically, 'refers to attitudes and intentions developed from processing narrative messages that are not overtly persuasive, such as novels, movies, or video games' which stands in contrast to (2) *analytical persuasion*, which is the result of processing messages that are more explicitly persuasive, such as news reports or speeches.[14] Two reasons may be offered as to how narrative can have such a lasting impact on people or communities. Firstly, narrative is capable of constructing reality as well as imitating it. Over time, such a narrative has the potential to become increasingly internalised.[15]

---

8   van Laer et al., 'The Extended Transportation-Imagery Model', 798. The outline that follows draws primarily from this article as it is the most thorough review of literature covering two decades of research.
9   See van Laer et al., 'The Extended Transportation-Imagery Model', 799, for the three main points. Additional footnotes within refer to further relevant material.
10   On empathy, see Slater and Rouner, 'Entertainment-Education and Elaboration Likelihood', 185–87; on mental imagery, see Green and Brock, 'In the Mind's Eye', 316–17.
11   van Laer et al., 'The Extended Transportation-Imagery Model', 799.
12   Cf. Green and Brock, 'In the Mind's Eye', 323.
13   van Laer et al., 'The Extended Transportation-Imagery Model', 800; following Phillips and McQuarrie, 'Narrative and Persuasion'.
14   van Laer et al., 'The Extended Transportation-Imagery Model', 800.
15   van Laer et al., 'The Extended Transportation-Imagery Model', 800.

Secondly, narratives are conducive towards bringing about an emotional response, making it more probable that the recipient of the story will be transported, thus leading to narrative persuasion.[16]

Interestingly, 1 Peter appears to blur the lines between these distinctions. On the one hand, 1 Peter is undoubtedly explicit in seeking to persuade its recipients towards a particular way of life in light of their present troubles, bringing analytical persuasion to the fore. Conversely, the frequent use of OT narratives within 1 Peter—sometimes explicitly; sometimes more subtly—lends itself to the process of narrative persuasion. The latter point is noteworthy because it has been shown that repeated acquaintance with a story impacts one's self-efficacy, that is, a person's capacity to live as they believe they should.[17] Indeed, stories often integrate a vital point, or trigger, which recipients may recall in order to exercise control over their conduct so that their life aligns with the story's main thrust.[18] Thus, 1 Peter's deployment of Isaiah's Suffering Servant in order to promote a particular way of life in the face of suffering and opposition, suggests that NTT may be of value in bringing fresh understanding to the epistle.

Finally, proponents of narrative persuasion have determined that three antecedents are particularly pertinent for a storyteller (and for our reading of 1 Pet. 2:18-25), (1) identifiable characters; (2) an imaginable plot; and (3) verisimilitude.[19] An *identifiable character* is one whom the story recipient is able to pinpoint on the basis of what the storyteller provides in any given context.[20] To be 'identifiable', the storyteller must present characters in a way that recipients of the story share in the experiences and feelings of the character, as if they were their own.[21] Thus, the more 'identifiable' a character is, the more likely the

---

16 van Laer et al., 801.
17 van Laer et al., 801; following, Bandura, 'Health Promotion', 151, who observes the impact of story on Tanzanian people exposed to dramatisations concerning the importance of safe sex practices.
18 van Laer et al., 'The Extended Transportation-Imagery Model', 811.
19 van Laer et al., 802-03.
20 van Laer et al., 802; following Küntay, 'Development of the Expression of Indefiniteness'.
21 van Laer et al., 'The Extended Transportation-Imagery Model', 802; drawing on Escalas and Stern, 'Sympathy and Empathy', 575-76; cf. Slater and Rouner, 'Entertainment-Education and Elaboration Likelihood', 178, who show that identifiable characters influence narrative transportation because the recipients vicariously experience that which the characters also experience.

recipient of the story is to embrace that character's bias in relation to the overall narrative being presented.[22]

An *imaginable plot* refers to a story's ability to stimulate mental imagery in the mind of the recipient.[23] In short, the greater the level of mental imagery encouraged by the narrative, the greater the level of narrative transportation and/or persuasion is likely. The final antecedent on the part of the storyteller is *verisimilitude,* which refers to the realism or believability of a story, that is, its 'lifelikeness'.[24] The events described in a story must be likely to happen (or to have happened) in real life. It must also be noted at this point that narratives must also have a storyline in which questions are raised and subsequently answered.[25] Pertinent for our own investigation, J. de Waal Dryden observes that stories or narratives can be used to both communicate and construct worldviews by 'depicting all of reality as a single unfolding meta-narrative – a universal history with a beginning, middle and end'.[26] He goes on to note that a well-constructed narrative worldview provides 'a teleological structure to reality, since it points towards a specific fulfilment/conclusion that embodies the worldview's fundamental values'.[27] In other words, one of the challenges that any story or narrative faces is whether or not it can account for trials and tribulations faced in everyday life. Can it provide meaning, and shape values and actions that will allow one to live fruitfully, not only in prosperous times but also in the face of adversity?

And while Green and Brock go so far as to suggest that a recipient may lose access to 'real-world facts' as a result of their transportation into a given narrative,[28] the value of the theory is not diminished for our purposes: namely, to assist in our exploration of how Peter's use of Isaiah's Suffering Servant acts as a summons to share in both the history of Israel and the person and work of Christ, particularly as a means of

---

22 van Laer et al., 'The Extended Transportation-Imagery Model', 802; following Hoffner, Levine, and Toohey, 'Socialization to Work in Late Adolescence', 'favorite characters [...] to which viewers feel closely connected, can have an influence on values and beliefs' (p. 297).
23 van Laer et al., 'The Extended Transportation-Imagery Model', 802.
24 Van Laer et al., 'The Extended Transportation-Imagery Model', 802; quoting Bruner, *Actual Minds*, 11.
25 Green and Brock, 'In the Mind's Eye', 319.
26 Dryden, *Theology and Ethics in 1 Peter*, 56.
27 Dryden, *Theology and Ethics in 1 Peter*, 56.
28 Green and Brock, 'The Role of Transportation', 702–3.

shaping their identity and mission *without seeking escape* from the 'real-world'. In fact, contrary to Green and Brock, J. R. R. Tolkien pointed out (long before the advent of NTT) that, even in the case of *eucatastrophic* events[29]—such as the Anatolian believers have undergone via their conversion[30]—there is no denial of reality, no matter how perilous life may become. By contrast, the joy that Christians experience resulting from their conversion (1:3–9),

> does not deny the existence of *dyscatastrophe*, of sorrow and failure: the possibility of these is necessary to the joy of deliverance; it denies (in the face of much evidence, if you will) universal final defeat and in so far is *evangelium*, giving a fleeting glimpse of Joy, Joy beyond the walls of the world, poignant as grief.[31]

In utilising NTT, then, our goal is not to deny the 'real-world facts' or the '*dyscatastrophe*' faced by these new Anatolian converts, but rather to show how Peter's use of the Isaiah's Suffering Servant grafts these Christians into the history of Israel and of Christ in such a way as to make sense of their new identity and mission in the world.

Social Identity Theory

Social Identity Theory (SIT) is a branch of social psychology that investigates the impact of group membership on an individual's identity.[32] One's social identity is but one facet of an individual's identity that is

---

29   Tolkien, 'On Fairy-Stories', 153, uses the terms 'eucatastrophe' and 'eucatastrophic' to refer to event(s) that bring about a 'sudden joyous turn' from tragedy to triumph.
30   According to Tolkien, 'On Fairy-Stories', 156, 'The Birth of Christ is the *eucatastrophe* of Man's history. The Resurrection is the *eucatastrophe* of the story of the Incarnation'. This is the account of history that the Anatolian Christians have come to believe in, yet this does not lead to a disconnect with 'real-world facts'. Rather, '[t]he Christian has still to work, with mind as well as body, to suffer, hope, and die; but he may now perceive that all his bents and faculties have a purpose, which can be redeemed. So great is the bounty with which he has been treated that he may now, perhaps, fairly dare to guess that in Fantasy he may actually assist in the effoliation and multiple enrichment of creation'.
31   Tolkien, 'On Fairy-Stories', 153, italics original.
32   Exceptional introductory outlines of SIT for the purpose of biblical studies can be found in Kuecker, *The Spirit and the 'Other'*, 24–35; also, Esler, 'Outline of SIT', 13–39. See also, Shaw, 'A People Called', 41–53.

grounded in 'their knowledge of their membership in a social group (or groups) together with the value of and emotional significance attached to that membership'.[33] According to Michael Hogg, people have a 'repertoire' of social identities that have varying degrees of salience in the self-concept.[34] Another way of putting it is to say that people embrace multiple social identities and that those identities vary in importance according to any given context. To give a simple example, if two Australian travellers meet overseas, they are likely to associate on the basis of their common nationality no matter where they are from, i.e., they will relate as fellow Australians. But if those same people happen to meet in Australia, they are more likely to associate on the basis of local geography, 'I'm from Perth', or 'I'm from Sydney'.

Of course, social identity is not limited to geography. In any given context, I might identify myself as a British-Australian, a Christian, a graduate of the University of Exeter, a West Coast Eagles supporter,[35] or something else. Each of these cases speaks of my social identity, but it is my social context that will determine which identity comes to the forefront and will, in turn, influence how I relate to others. Social Identity Theory, because it stresses the *social* character of modern identities, is important for NT studies. As Aaron Kuecker notes, we in the modern West tend to see the world as individualists and, therefore, need help to see our lives and our world more as collectivists.[36] Given that the world of the NT era was a more collectivist culture than our own, SIT provides a framework by which we can receive the text in a manner that more closely resembles that of the original hearers.

For the present essay two aspects of SIT must be outlined: specifically, the act of *social creativity* and the role of *exemplars/prototypes* for the community. Part of the challenge for in-group members of low-status communities is how to go about developing and gaining a sense of positive social identity. Following Henri Tajfel and John Turner,[37] David Milner provides three options that people in perceived low-status

---

33   Tajfel, *Social Identity and Intergroup Relations*, 2.
34   Hogg, 'Intragroup Process, Group Structure and Social Identity', 66.
35   West Coast Eagles FC is an Australia Rules football club that competes in the Australian Football League (AFL). The club is based in my adopted hometown, Perth, Western Australia.
36   Kuecker, *The Spirit and the 'Other'*, 26.
37   Tajfel and Turner, 'The Social Identity Theory of Intergroup Behaviour'.

positions may follow in an effort to gain a positive sense of social identity:[38] specifically, he refers to individual mobility, social creativity, and social competition. Of the three, *social creativity* is most pertinent for our purposes.

Social creativity involves several strategies in and of itself such as (1) redefining the comparative criteria between the in-group and the out-group; (2) inverting previously negative comparisons and claiming them as positive; or (3) selecting a new out-group with which to compare the in-group.[39] It is the second of the three that we find exercised here in 1 Peter. A name or a label is among the most public statements of identity, so the ability to be able to invert the accepted connotations that go with that name or label is a powerful strategy.[40] A recent and commonly known example may be seen in gay rights activists reclaiming terms such as 'queer', using them positively. Similarly, in 1 Peter, it is acknowledged that believers who suffer for bearing the name of Christ, or being 'Christian', ought not be ashamed but should rather embrace it as an opportunity to give glory to God (see 1 Pet 4:16).[41] As will be seen below, the recognition and acceptance of Jesus as Isaiah's Suffering Servant also falls into this category.

Secondly, group exemplars are an important feature of social identity because they embody the prototypical characteristics of the in-group, i.e., those characteristics that are expected of the whole group, and of everyone who claims allegiance to the group.[42] Importantly, agreement over prototypical characteristics generally builds group cohesion and identity,[43] although prototypicality may be fluid and subject to context, especially when sub-groups within a larger group start pressing claims as to what ought to be considered prototypical.[44]

Keeping these methodological considerations in mind, we may

---

38 Milner, 'Children and Racism', 263–66.
39 Milner, 'Children and Racism', 264–65.
40 Milner, 'Children and Racism', 265.
41 Horrell, *Becoming Christian*, 164–210 (esp. 207–09).
42 Smith and Zárate, 'Exemplar -Based Model'; cited by Eiser, 'Accentuation Revisited', 135; also, Kuecker, *The Spirit and the 'Other'*, 29.
43 Turner et al., *Rediscovering the Social Group*, 60–61.
44 Waldzus, Mummendey, and Wenzel, 'When "Different" Means "Worse"'; see also the brief discussion in Kuecker, *The Spirit and the 'Other'*, 34–35.

direct our attention to 1 Peter 2:18–25. We begin by observing the likely circumstances of bond servants in the Petrine community before moving forward to consider Peter's use of Isaiah's Suffering Servant as the prototype and exemplar on which believers are to model their lives.

Οἰκέται as Exemplars (1 Peter 2:18–20)

It is no secret that the life of a servant/slave was tenuous. Seneca's forty-seventh epistle gives extended insight into the common treatment of slaves and how he thought they ought to be treated. Here, Seneca is worth quoting at length:

> The master eats more than he can hold, and with monstrous greed loads his belly until it is stretched and at length ceases to do the work of a belly; so that he is at greater pains to discharge all the food than he was to stuff it down. All this time the poor slaves may not move their lips, even to speak. The slightest murmur is repressed by the rod; even a chance sound, — a cough, a sneeze, or a hiccup, is visited with the lash. There is a grievous penalty for the slightest breach of silence. All night long they must stand about, hungry and dumb [...] They are not enemies when we acquire them; we make them enemies [...] for we maltreat them, not as if they were men, but as if they were beasts of burden (Seneca, *Ep.* 47.2–5).[45]

Seneca continues to document that slaves may even be subject to sexual abuse:

> Another, who serves the wine, must dress like a woman and wrestle with his advancing years; he cannot get away from his boyhood [...] and though he has already acquired a soldier's figure, he is kept beardless by having his hair smoothed away or plucked out by the roots, and he must remain awake

---

45 Seneca, *Epistles*, IV:303, 305, cf. Suetonius, *Aug.* 67.2; Cal. 32.1–7; Tacitus, *Ann.* 4.54; 16.19; Dio Cassius, 54.23.1–2; Petronius, *Satyr.* 45, 53; Achilles Tatius, *Leuc. Clit.* 4.15.6; the latter references are cited by Williams, *Persecution in 1 Peter*, 301, n. 6. See also, Bradley, *Slaves and Masters in the Roman Empire*, 113–38.

throughout the night, dividing his time between his master's drunkenness and his lust; in the chamber he must be a man, at the feast a boy (Seneca, *Ep.* 47.7).[46]

In contrast to such treatment, Seneca recommends to his friend, Lucilius, that he ought to, 'Treat your inferiors as you would be treated by your betters [...] Associate with your slave on kindly, even affable terms' (47.12). On this point, Seneca was likely in the minority when it came to the humane treatment of slaves. Nevertheless, Harrill notes that the goal of Seneca's admonitions was not the end of slavery, but rather the strengthening of the institution by keeping its abuses in check.[47] He concludes that, 'Despite claims by some NT scholars, ancient slavery was not more humane than modern slavery'.[48] This agrees with Keith Bradley's assessment of the situation, writing that for the average Roman slave it was 'a matter of course, [that they] could become the object of physical abuse or injury at any time';[49] in fact, it was probably the norm.[50]

One would be remiss, however, to conclude that this was *always* the case, for some bondservants were placed in positions of authority and treated with genuine respect (Peter appears to assume as much when he acknowledges that some of the οἰκέται may in fact have good masters). Scott Bartchy also warns the reader against drawing comparisons between the race-based chattel slavery of the European colonial era to that experienced in antiquity.[51] Murray Harris describes the situational difference succinctly:

> In the first century, slaves were not distinguishable from free persons by race, by speech, or by clothing; they were sometimes more highly educated than their owners and held responsible professional positions; some persons sold themselves into

---

46 Seneca, *Epistles*, IV:305.
47 Harrill, 'Slavery', 1125.
48 Harrill, 'Slavery', 1125. For a full treatment of slaves and slavery in the NT era, Harrill, *Slaves in the New Testament*; Glancy, *Slavery in Early Christianity*; cf. Harris, *Slave of Christ*, 25–46; also, Martin, *Slavery as Salvation*, 1–49.
49 Bradley, *Slavery and Society at Rome*, 4.
50 Bradley, *Slaves and Masters in the Roman Empire*, 118.
51 Bartchy, 'Slave, Slavery', 1098.

slavery for economic or social advantage; they could reasonably hope to be emancipated after 10 or 20 years of service or by their 30s at the latest; they were not denied the right of public assembly and were not socially segregated (at least in the cities); they could accumulate savings to buy their freedom; their natural inferiority was not assumed.[52]

The thrust of Peter's argument is that regardless of their master's conduct, slaves were to submit themselves to their masters with all fear. The fear of which Peter speaks is directed not towards their master, but rather towards God.[53] And while there is some contention over the matter, decisive in the context is the reference to being mindful of God (2:19), and the notion of fearing God expressed prior (2:17). In fact, every instance of 'fear' that appears in 1 Peter (1:17; 3:2, 6, 14, 16) carries the implication that it is to be reserved for God alone.[54] Christians are to fear God and honour the emperor. Similarly, Christian οἰκέται are to fear God, and subsequently submit to their master, even if they are abused.

The key to understanding this imperative is twofold. The first is in the paradox expressed in 2:16 where all believers in the church are described as both ἐλεύθερος (free) and as θεοῦ δοῦλοι (servants [or slaves] of God), a description that applies to both οἰκέται and free people of the church. As an act of social creativity, the use of such language creates a sense of unity by reminding free people in the church that, ultimately, they belong to God, that they are his δοῦλοι. The οἰκέται are, likewise, reminded that their social status in the world is no longer their defining feature now that they are in Christ. Ironically, as θεοῦ δοῦλοι they possess a new-found freedom (ἐλεύθερος) that was superior to what the world could ever offer.[55] As Edmund Clowney has stated: '[The servant's]

---

52 Harris, *Slave of Christ*, 44; cf. Bartchy, 'Slave, Slavery', 1098–99.
53 Schreiner, *1, 2 Peter, Jude*, 137; so also, Schelkle, *Die Petrusbriefe—Der Judasbrief*, 142; Beare, *The First Epistle of Peter*, 121; Kelly, *The Epistles of Peter and Jude*, 116; Michaels, *1 Peter*, 138; Achtemeier, *1 Peter*, 195; Davids, *The First Epistle of Peter*, 106; contra Brox, *Der erste Petrusbrief*, 131; also, Clowney, *The Message of 1 Peter*, 114.
54 Schreiner, *1, 2 Peter, Jude*, 137.
55 Jacobs, 'Narrative Integration', 221, notes that irony 'can be extraordinarily effective in subverting the intended and hegemonic meanings of public events' (and, presumably, hegemonic cultural narratives as well).

master cannot enslave him, for he is Christ's slave; he cannot humiliate him, for he has humbled himself in willing subjection'.[56] Consequently, in Christ, both the servant and the free become a people belonging to God (2:9–10).[57]

The second point to be made concerns the example of Christ in whose footsteps the church is to follow (2:21). Church members are, corporately, the suffering servants that follow in the footsteps of their Suffering Servant-King. As Jesus suffered unjustly, so too it is likely that those who follow him will also suffer unjustly, regardless of one's status as slave or free in the world. In this way, the οἰκέται are elevated as exemplars within the community because, again, it is they who most closely embody the prototypical characteristics defined in Christ (2:22–24, see further below). Hence, wives are, *likewise,* to be subject to their husbands regardless of their husband's faith or lack thereof (3:1), and *likewise,* husbands are to show honour to their wives (cf. 2:17).[58] To share in bearing the burdens of the οἰκέται who suffer unjustly is to see an image of Christ whose unjust suffering brought about redemption for the whole Christian community. In other words, when the οἰκέται suffer unjustly, their experience reflects the gospel and it is precisely for this reason that they are mentioned first as exemplars for the whole community in Peter's *Haustafel.*[59] Peter then fleshes out precisely what this looks like by drawing upon Isaiah 52–53, to which attention is now directed.

Walking in the Footsteps of Christ (1 Peter 2:21)

Verse 21 is hermeneutically critical for our understanding of the text because: (1) it is here that Peter establishes a bridge and between the conduct of household servants and the conduct of Christ who serves as their exemplar;[60] and (2) it serves as an interpretive lens through which

---

56 Clowney, *The Message of 1 Peter,* 113, cf. Luke 6:32–35.
57 Cf. 1 Pet. 2:9–10; also, Gal. 3:28.
58 On the notion of wives as being paradigmatic for mission in 1 Peter, see Horrell, 'Fear, Hope, and Doing Good'. Herein, Horrell notes the parallels in the instructions given to both bondservants and wives concerning the need for good conduct and appropriate submission (p. 419).
59 Egan, *Ecclesiology and Scriptural Narrative,* 131, notes that ongoing language of good and evil continues here, in anticipation of Psalm 33 LXX to be quoted later in 1 Pet. 3:10–12.
60 Horrell, 'Jesus Remembered', 130.

1 Peter views Isaiah 53 by linking the suffering servants of 2:18–20 with *the* Suffering Servant in 2:22–25. As Egan well observes, 'The calling of the disciple servants has its basis in the suffering of Christ for his people. The example of Christ, in turn, establishes a pattern by which the disciple servants comport themselves'.[61]

The final clause of v. 21, ἵνα ἐπακολουθήσητε τοῖς ἴχνεσιν αὐτοῦ (so that you might follow in his steps), in particular reveals the expectation that household servants would follow Christ, their Servant-Master, in regard to their gracious endurance of suffering. The verse also recalls 1 Pet. 1:14, 18–19 where Peter speaks of his recipients as being obedient children in relation to the fatherhood of God, and to leave the futile ways of their forefathers based on Christ's blood ransom. Such an exhortation establishes 'competing paternities' for the Christian believer: will one follow God the Father by continuing to walk in the footsteps of Jesus, or will one return to the ways of their forefathers (1:14, 18)? One's response to such a question is no small matter.[62] Cicero captures well the sentiment towards those who showed ignorance or disdain towards one's family history in his berating of Piso, consul in AD 58: 'O darkened eyes! O bemired and dingy soul! O forgetful of your father's line, with scarce a memory even of your mother's!' (*Pis.* 62).[63] The issue for Cicero was that familial ignorance meant one was not capable or even worthy to follow in the footsteps of his forebears who held high status positions in the Empire. As such, Piso brought shame upon himself and his family. For Peter, then, to take the phrase ἐπακολουθήσητε τοῖς ἴχνεσιν αὐτοῦ (follow in his footsteps) and apply it to a crucified man (an alleged *divine* man at that!), and then saying to his readers, '*follow in his steps*' (i.e., not those of your forefathers, 1:17) is nothing short of extraordinary. Indeed, it has ramifications for the whole household, which is why the use of Isaiah 53 appears here!

Thus, while one may grant that there is clearly overlap between Christian and Graeco-Roman household codes on the surface (e.g.,

---

61 Egan, *Ecclesiology and Scriptural Narrative*, 145.
62 On the importance of honouring father's in both Jewish and Graeco-Roman antiquity, see Shaw, 'A People Called', 112–16.
63 Cicero, *Pis.*, 215; also cited in Baroin, 'Remembering One's Ancestors', 31. Her own translation as follows: 'You darkness, you filth, you disgrace, you who are forgetful of your father's origin, and scarcely mindful of your mother's!'

slaves submitting to their masters, wives to husbands), their *foundational* values could not be more starkly opposed.[64] The Graeco-Roman model assumed a posture of honour, power, and authority predicated on the respectability of the father (*paterfamilias*), while Peter's model appropriates the posture of a servant (θεοῦ δοῦλοι). Ordinarily, one would expect the servant to be asked to follow the model laid out by his master,[65] the same way in which a son would be expected to follow the model laid out by his father,[66] yet Peter turns all these expectations on their head by bringing the servant to the forefront as the exemplar for the whole congregation. Contra David Balch, this cannot be an act of assimilation,[67] but rather an act of subversion and social creativity that finds its origin and expression in the 'Suffering Servant' of Isaiah 53.[68] It is to Peter's use of Isaiah in this regard that we now turn our attention.

Christ as Exemplar (1 Peter 2:22–23)

It is generally held that Peter's use of Isaiah 53 quotations and allusions broadly follows the Passion narrative laid out in the Gospels.[69] Goppelt goes so far as to identify specific verses from the Gospel tradition (especially Mark), being alluded to, including the abuse and slander after Jesus's

---

64 Contra Bird, *Abuse, Power and Fearful Obedience*, 107–8, who argues that the author of 1 Peter is guilty of colluding with imperial ideology.
65 Bartchy, 'Slave, Slavery' who notes that most slaves adopted the religion and customs of their master; cf. Osiek and Balch, *Families in the New Testament World*, 184.
66 Although our focus is on the slave here, it is worth noting that husbands or sons may have come under particular scrutiny for it was expected that in order to honour their ancestry that they would make every effort to imitate them, or, follow in their footsteps (*vestigia sequi*). In this light, one sees the offence caused when one chooses to follow in the footsteps of a crucified Messiah rather than follow in the glories of one's forefathers. See Baroin, 'Remembering One's Ancestors', 32–33; cf. Harland, *Dynamics of Identity*, 150, who cites *ISardBR* 221, where Sokrates Pardalas, son of Polemaios, is praised 'for following in his ancestor's footsteps' with regards to his piety towards Zeus and benefaction to Zeus's therapeutists.
67 See Balch's well-known monograph, *Let Wives Be Submissive*.
68 One could well imagine, therefore, any convert, be they a slave, a child, a wife, or even a husband, being perceived as committing a form of apostasy or betrayal against the family to which they belonged by either refusing to serve or worship the gods of the household, or abandoning them in favour of something 'quaint' or 'superstitious.' See Plutarch, *Conj. praec.* 19.
69 Carson, '1 Peter', 1034; cf. Horrell, 'Jesus Remembered', 130; Liebengood, *The Eschatology of 1 Peter*, 91; Feldmeier, *The First Letter of Peter*, 167, 173; Jobes, *1 Peter*, 194–95; Goppelt, *A Commentary on 1 Peter*, 211; Achtemeier, 'Suffering Servant', 180; Schutter, *Hermeneutic and Composition in 1 Peter*, 140.

condemnation before the Sanhedrin (Mark 14:65 par.), the mockery by the guards (Mark 15: 17–20a par.), and the contempt by the crucified thief (Mark 15:29–32 par.).[70] Jesus, furthermore, accepts the injustice of his death in silence and without retaliation (Mark 14:61; 15:5), in stark contrast to the Maccabean martyrs who were outspoken in their calling for God's judgement to be brought against their opponents (2 Macc. 7:17, 19, 31, 35; cf. 4 Macc. 10:1–3).[71] Finally, Jesus leaves judgement in God's hands (Mark 14:62).[72] All this leaves one with the impression that Peter was more than familiar with the Passion Narrative.

Moreover, Peter's use of Isaiah 53 seems to be fluid, moving from quotation to allusion freely as required, all the while following the Passion Narrative. For example, 1 Pet. 2:22 is, for all intents and purposes, a direct quote of Isa. 53:9 LXX, save for substituting ἀνομίαν with ἁμαρτίαν. On the other hand, 1 Pet. 2:23 is more subtle. Schreiner acknowledges that we do not have any specific allusion, although the emphasis on Christ's non-retaliatory behaviour echoes the silence of the servant in Isa 53:7c–d.[73] Thus, while Isaiah 53 may be in the background of v. 23, it is not at all as explicit as is the case in v. 22. Given this fluidity between the near verbatim quotation of Isaiah in 1 Pet 2:22 and the subtle allusions in 2:23, it may be that Peter is dependent on both Isaiah 53 and the Passion narrative for his thinking in 1 Pet. 2:22–25.[74] The reason for this is that if Peter were *solely* dependent on Isaiah 53 for this section, we would expect a greater level of verbatim usage as we see elsewhere in the epistle (e.g., 2:6–8; 3:10–12). But if Peter is also drawing on the Passion Narrative (as the re-ordering of the Isaian text suggests), then the fluidity of movement between quotation and allusion throughout 2:22–25 would more likely be expected.

---

70 Goppelt, *A Commentary on I Peter*, 211.
71 Goppelt, *A Commentary on I Peter*, 211–12. See especially, n. 59. Also, 2 Macc. 7:15 is particularly noteworthy for the threat of God's torture, "Keep on, and see how his mighty power will torture you and your descendants!" (NRSV).
72 Goppelt, *A Commentary on I Peter*, 212.
73 Schreiner, *1, 2 Peter, Jude*, 143; similarly, Horrell, 'Jesus Remembered', 135; Egan, *Ecclesiology and Scriptural Narrative*, 135–36, suggests another verbal association in v. 23 with the verb παραδίδωμι which occurs both in Isa. 53:6 and 12, with the emphasis in v. 6 being that of the Lord giving up his servant, while in v. 12 this changes bringing the servant's self-giving to the fore.
74 For a more in-depth discussion of the Gospel tradition and its relationship to 1 Peter 2:21–25, see Horrell, 'Jesus Remembered'.

With 1 Pet. 2:21 acting as a bridge between the conduct of bondservants and Christ, 2:22–23 describes the prototypical characteristics embodied by Christ, the Suffering Servant, in whose footsteps all church members are expected to follow. The example starts in general terms by informing the recipients that Christ did not sin, followed by the specifics of what kind of sin Christ avoided that are likewise to be avoided by the Petrine communities. Peter begins by quoting Isa. 53:9 LXX almost verbatim.[75]

Peter substitutes the Isaian ἀνομία (lawlessness) for ἁμαρτία (sin), which are virtually synonymous. The substitution could be the result of working from memory, relying on oral tradition, or drawing upon a catena of Christian testimonies.[76] It may also be a deliberate tactic to correspond with the use of ἁμαρτίας in v. 24 where Isaiah 53 is again in view.[77] In either event, there is no loss in meaning and the same point is driven home: Christ was sinless in his suffering in the lead up to his death *and* in his life as a whole.[78] Such a narrative dictates that Christians are likewise to emulate Christ in their suffering, especially in terms of their innocence. Such a way of life embodies the prototypical characteristics modelled in Christ's Passion. As Michaels notes:

> his suffering (vv. 21, 23) was both unprovoked and undeserved. He suffered not because of any sin he had committed but rather for doing good, and therefore "unjustly" (cf. vv. 19, 20). This above all else is what makes Christ the appropriate example for the epistle's readers.[79]

The second half of v. 22 moves from the general (Jesus did not sin) to the specific, (that no deceit was found in his mouth). While this was true of Jesus' whole life and ministry, v. 23 insinuates that the Passion

---

75 See the table in Egan, *Ecclesiology and Scriptural Narrative*, 133.
76 McCartney, 'The Use of the Old Testament', 52–53. McCartney's point is well taken. ἁμαρτίας, or variations thereof, appear seven times in Isaiah 53. Specifically, vv. 4, 5, 6, 10, 11, and 12 (twice). So also, Moyise, 'Isaiah in 1 Peter', 183; Achtemeier, *1 Peter*, 200.
77 Schreiner, *1, 2 Peter, Jude*, 143.
78 A point made by both Schreiner, *1, 2 Peter, Jude*, 135; and Horrell, 'Jesus Remembered', 134–35, respectively. See, for example, Matt. 24:7; John 7:48; 8:29, 46; 18:38; 2 Cor. 5:21; Heb. 4:15; 7:27–28; 9:14; 1 John 3:5.
79 Michaels, *1 Peter*, 145.

narrative is likely in view.[80] Verse 23 continues the emphasis on sins of speech, thus elaborating on v. 22.[81] The claim that Jesus did not sin, nor deceit being found in his mouth, is supported by the appeal to his non-retaliatory response toward those who were the cause of his suffering. Yet, while the idea of verbal non-retaliation appears in Isa. 53:7, Horrell correctly points out more obvious connections with the Gospel tradition both in terms of Jesus' teaching concerning non-retaliation (Matt. 5:38–44; Luke 6:27–31), and the evident living out of his teaching described in the Passion narratives (Mark 14:46–48; Matt. 26:51–55; Luke 22:48–53; John 18:3–11, 36).[82]

We may say, therefore, that Peter's selection of his material in vv. 22–23 is shaped both by the content of Isaiah 53 and by his knowledge of the Passion tradition. This not only corresponds to Jesus' exemplary suffering, but also foreshadows the call to bless in 3:8–17 which draws upon the righteous sufferer of Psalm 33 LXX as the emphasised words in the table below demonstrate:

Table 1: Comparison of 1 Peter 2:22–23 with 1 Peter 3:9–10[83]

1 Pet. 2:22–23	1 Pet. 3:9–10
[22] ὃς **ἁμαρτίαν** οὐκ ἐποίησεν οὐδὲ εὑρέθη δόλος* ἐν τῷ στόματι αὐτοῦ,	[9] μὴ ἀποδιδόντες **κακὸν** ἀντὶ **κακοῦ** ἢ *λοιδορίαν* ἀντὶ *λοιδορίας*, τοὐναντίον δὲ εὐλογοῦντες ὅτι εἰς τοῦτο ἐκλήθητε ἵνα εὐλογίαν κληρονομήσητε.
[23] ὃς *λοιδορούμενος* οὐκ *ἀντελοιδόρει*, πάσχων οὐκ ἠπείλει, παρεδίδου δὲ τῷ κρίνοντι δικαίως·	[10] ὁ γὰρ θέλων ζωὴν ἀγαπᾶν καὶ ἰδεῖν ἡμέρας ἀγαθὰς παυσάτω τὴν γλῶσσαν ἀπὸ **κακοῦ** καὶ χείλη τοῦ μὴ λαλῆσαι δόλον*

---

80 Horrell, 'Jesus Remembered', 135.
81 Michaels, *1 Peter*, 145; cf. Horrell, 'Jesus Remembered', 135.
82 Horrell, 'Jesus Remembered', 137.
83 The bolded **ἁμαρτίαν** (2:22) corresponds to **κακὸν** and **κακοῦ** (3:9); δόλος* (2:22) corresponds with δόλον* (3:10); while the underlined/italicised *λοιδορούμενος οὐκ ἀντελοιδόρει* (2:23) corresponds with *λοιδορίαν ἀντὶ λοιδορίας* (3:9).

Liebengood has suggested that Isa. 53:9 was selected because it corresponds both to the way Jesus suffered and responded, and because it matches the description of the Righteous Sufferer of Psalm 33 LXX which is incorporated in 1 Pet. 3:10–12.[84] Indeed, as Liebengood notes, 1 Pet. 2:22 and 3:10 share the word δόλος; there is no *deceit* (δόλος) in Jesus mouth, while the Righteous Sufferer keeps his lips from *deceit* (δόλον). Yet, we can also see a further connection between 2:23, and 3:9 through the use of the term λοιδορίαν (revile, reviling). In 2:22 Jesus did not return reviling for reviling and in 3:9, believers are exhorted to the same behaviour. Rather, they are to bless, for that is their calling. One could also make the claim that ἁμαρτίαν (sin) in 2:22 corresponds to κακόν (evil) in 3:9–10. Thus, Liebengood's suggestion that Isa. 53:9 was also selected in anticipation of 3:10–12 is corroborated further by ongoing parallels that appear in both 2:22–23 and 3:9–10. These parallels indicate that Christ's sufferings are paradigmatic for all believers.

It is not surprising that such exhortations to non-retaliation and righteousness should appear consistently throughout the *Haustafel*. What is interesting is *who* features at various junctures. The Petrine *Haustafel* features the *household servant* who is to walk in the footsteps of Jesus, the Suffering Servant. But the Righteous Sufferer of Psalm 33 LXX echoes the experience of King David during his sojourn in Gath while on the run from Saul (see 1 Samuel 21). In the Petrine household code, therefore, we have a trajectory that moves from bondservants (2:18–25), to wives (3:1–6), to husbands (3:7), and finally, to a king (3:10–12), with Jesus, the Suffering Servant as the central focus (2:21–25).

From the perspective of NTT, the way an author coordinates characters and events into a story inevitably has an impact on recipients' understanding of their past, their future hopes, and how they ought to live in the present.[85] And though these characters appear to have little in common on the surface, the narrative that connects them is that of their election/rejection. Servants, wives, and even husbands, having been called out of darkness to Christ (1 Pet. 2:9), are now in the

---

84 Liebengood, *The Eschatology of 1 Peter*, 92.
85 Jacobs, 'Narrative Integration', 206.

position of facing rejection by their masters and spouses respectively.[86] Similarly the Psalm that alludes to King David, refers not to his time of glory, but to his time of rejection by King Saul once it was revealed that David would soon ascend the throne on account of God's election.

This trajectory, though it proceeds from a lowly servant to a king, nevertheless presents each person in the honourable position of being elect of God, resulting in their subsequent rejection by another. This narrative has as its central feature, Christ, the Suffering Servant (2:21–25), who was likewise elect of God and rejected by the world (cf. 2:4–8), and it is the sharing of this narrative that binds the individual and social identities of these Anatolian believers to Christ.[87] Consequently, it is not unreasonable to understand, given the hermeneutical lens of 1 Pet. 1:10–12, that Jesus is understood and presented not only as the righteous Suffering Servant, but also as the righteous Suffering King, around whom the church is united. That is to say, as sojourners and servants, the church lives with great humility; yet as children who call on God as Father, they are royalty and heirs with Christ.

Moreover, Christ is not only presented as exemplary in terms of his innocence and response to reviling, but also in terms of his context. In the words of Abson Joseph, 'Christ and believers both suffer at the hands of those who are disobedient to God's will and God's word'.[88] The reason that Peter can draw on Isaiah's Suffering Servant is this shared narrative context. The experience of the Suffering Servant in his mission is, likewise, the experience of the Anatolian believers in their mission.[89] Egan goes so far as to say that 'Isaiah 53 does not merely depict Christ as the suffering servant, but also propels the church to understand its own suffering as part of the mission to the nations'.[90]

To summarise the prototypical characteristics defining the Suffering Servant's conduct that have been brought to attention thus far, the Servant (1) *did not* suffer because of sin; (2) there was *no* deceit in his mouth; (3) he *did not* retaliate; nor (4) threaten to return the favour

---

86 For the understanding of husbands having non-believing wives, see Gross, 'Are the Wives of 1 Peter 3:7 Christians?'
87 Cf. Jacobs, 'Narrative Integration', 206.
88 Joseph, *A Narratological Reading of 1 Peter*, 107.
89 Egan, *Ecclesiology and Scriptural Narrative*, 144–45.
90 Egan, *Ecclesiology and Scriptural Narrative*, 145.

when abused. Each of the four points are portrayed in the negative; that is, in terms of what Jesus *did not do*. In 1 Pet. 2:23b, there is a transition into the positive aspects of what he did do. Specifically, he entrusted himself to him who judges justly.[91] That is, by entrusting *himself* to the Father, he entrusts the vindication of his life's work to the Father; by entrusting *himself* to the Father, he entrusts his enemies to the Father's judgement. Moreover, the Passion Narratives present Jesus as a model of hope committing his Spirit to the Father (Luke 23:46), praying for the forgiveness of his enemies (Luke 23:34), and that his disciples would continue his work (Matt. 28:18–20; John 15:27; Acts 1:8).[92]

It is Jesus' trust in the just Judge that enables his non-retaliation, his willingness to forgive those who know not what they do, and his ability to graciously endure suffering. Reflecting on these issues towards the end of *Exclusion and Embrace,* Miroslav Volf asks: 'Our question must be how to live under the rule of Caesar in the absence of the reign of truth and justice. *Does the crucified Messiah have any bearing on our lives in a world of half-truths and skewed justice?*'[93] His response carries unmistakable echoes of 1 Peter:

> Without entrusting oneself to the God who judges justly, it will hardly be possible to follow the crucified Messiah and refuse to retaliate when abused. The certainty of God's just judgment at the end of history is the presupposition for the renunciation of violence in the middle of it.[94]

For Volf, the only way one can follow Jesus in this way of non-retaliation and absorption of evil is precisely by believing in God's justice. If one does not hold such a belief then one must seek justice of his or her own accord, returning reviling for reviling (or worse), because one has no other recourse.

The call to endure suffering graciously has its foundation in Christ's own life. In a world that valued honour and kinship, the presentation

---

91 Joseph, *A Narratological Reading of 1 Peter*, 108.
92 According to Lim, '"Visiting Strangers and Resident Aliens"', 106, the Suffering Servant is presented as 'the model of hope' for Anatolian believers.
93 Volf, *Exclusion & Embrace*, 277, emphasis added.
94 Volf, *Exclusion & Embrace*, 302.

of a crucified Messiah as an example to follow would have been utterly counter-cultural. Such a way of life would almost certainly lead to ostracism and even persecution, whether by family, friends, or the community at large. Peter's exhortation to turn the other cheek and trust in the judgement of God is, therefore, a remarkable act of faith as it has the potential to put believers of all types in harm's way, yet there can be no doubting that it is also a forceful narrative that has the power to transform lives.

Substitution and New Life (1 Peter 2:24–25)

Following the example of Christ in 2:22–23, vv. 24–25 define the purpose of Christ's gracious endurance. In particular, that Jesus 'bore our sins in his body on the tree [...]', alluding to Isa. 53:4 ; 'This one bears *our* sins'; Isa. 53:11, 'he himself will bear their sins'; and Isa. 53:12, 'he bore the sins of *many*'.[95] First Peter 2:25 concludes the pericope, referring to the straying sheep who have been reconciled to their 'Shepherd'. It has been argued that the language of bearing sin draws on the sacrificial language of Leviticus.[96] The key is in acknowledging both goats presented on the Day of Atonement. In Lev. 16:22, the second goat (the scapegoat) is the one which bears the sins of the people of Israel and is then let loose in the wilderness to Azazel (16:10, 22). The language of Lev. 16:22, 'And the goat shall bear on itself their offences' (*NETS*) is conceptually comparable to that of 1 Pet. 2:24, 'He himself bore our sins', thus, it would make sense to see this as the emphasis presented by Peter.[97] At the same time, however, the other goat—the *sacrificial goat*—*does* die in front of a wooden altar before having its blood sprinkled upon it.[98]

The fact that Peter writes that the sins are borne in Christ's body *on*

---

95 All Isaiah quotations here follow the *NETS* translation.
96 Schelkle, *Die Petrusbriefe—Der Judasbrief*, 85; cf. Egan, *Ecclesiology and Scriptural Narrative*, 145–46.
97 The 'bearing sin(s)/iniquities' and other analogous language also appears several times in Isaiah 53, esp., 11–12, 'he shall *bear their iniquities*'; 'yet he *bore the sins* of many'; cf. vv. 4 '*borne our griefs*'; v. 5, '*crushed for our iniquities*'; v. 6, 'the LORD has *laid on him the iniquity* of us all'; v. 8, '*stricken for the transgressions* of the people'.
98 Galling, 'Altar', 96–97.

the tree (a likely allusion to Deut. 21:23), may suggest that the sacrificial goat is also in view *along with* the scapegoat with respect to Christ's death.[99] The Suffering Servant, therefore, suffers precisely because he both bears the sin of the people *and* dies in their place, much like the scapegoat and sacrificial goat respectively in Leviticus. In this manner, Peter may be seeking to show the distinctiveness of Christ's death by showing how the Day of Atonement reaches its *telos* in Christ, who, as the embodiment of Isaiah's Suffering Servant, bears the sins (and curse) of his people by giving up his life.[100] It is through Christ's giving up his life that one 'die[s] to sin and live[s] to righteousness' and finds 'healing', that is, the forgiveness of sins.

Finally, one must consider the title of 'shepherd' (v. 25) that ties itself to the Suffering Servant imagery of vv. 22–24. The work of Kelly Liebengood is helpful here, drawing the reader's attention to Zechariah 9–14 that is unique among the prophets by presenting the shepherd as one who must suffer and die in order for restoration to be accomplished.[101] This theme is developed in constant reference to Isaiah 40–66 and is also brought to bear on the Passion Narrative tradition.[102] It should, therefore, come as no surprise that when 1 Peter utilises the Suffering Servant motif from Isaiah 53 within the framework of the Passion Narrative, that Zechariah 9–14 is also alluded to. Specifically, Zech. 13:7–9 gives biblical warrant for Christ dying on behalf of Yahweh's wandering sheep and why Christians will also likely suffer.[103]

In summary, then, 1 Pet. 2:21–25 brings together the OT prophetic narratives of the Suffering Servant from Isaiah 53 and conflates it with the Shepherd-King imagery found throughout Zechariah 9–14. For Peter, therefore, Jesus is both the Suffering Servant *and* the suffering Shepherd-King who must die to bring about the restoration of his sheep. By bringing together two apparently contradictory roles, that of the servant and the king, Peter engages in a further audacious act of social creativity by drawing his readers further into the OT prophetic

---

99 McCartney, 'The Use of the Old Testament', 91; also, Carson, '1 Peter', 1035.
100 Schreiner, *1, 2 Peter, Jude*, 144.
101 Liebengood, *The Eschatology of 1 Peter*, 99.
102 Liebengood, *The Eschatology of 1 Peter*, 99. For the extended argument, see pp. 23–78.
103 Liebengood, *The Eschatology of 1 Peter*, 100.

narrative. This is remarkable given that the church, and the household servants especially, are encouraged to walk in the footsteps of their Suffering Servant-Shepherd-King regarding their response to suffering should it encroach upon them.[104]

Conclusion

Usually, a narrative designed for a dominant public space reserves heroic character(s) for members of those dominant groups.[105] But Peter, by drawing on OT prophetic narrative, counter-intuitively presents a crucified messianic figure as his hero—one elect of God and yet rejected by the world—who embodies the prototypical characteristics of a holy life, specifically in the gracious endurance of suffering that leads to the redemption of his people. Either side of Christ, Peter elevates characters such as bondservants, wives and husbands of unbelieving spouses, and a king, as exemplars who embody the same story of Christ and Israel, embracing the tension that comes with God's election of them and their subsequent rejection by the world; a life like Christ that is characterised by the gracious endurance of suffering and resident-alien-ness, during which they live as elect sojourners between God's promise of redemption and the full inheritance of that promise.

Bibliography

Achtemeier, Paul J.   *1 Peter: A Commentary on First Peter* (Hermeneia; Minneapolis: Fortress Press, 1996).

Achtemeier, Paul J.   'Suffering Servant and Suffering Christ in 1 Peter', in Abraham J. Malherbe and Wayne A. Meeks (eds.), *The Future of Christology: Essays in Honor of Leander E. Keck* (Minneapolis: Fortress, 1993), 176–88.

Balch, David L.   *Let Wives Be Submissive: The Domestic Code in 1 Peter* (SBLMS 26; Chico: Scholars Press, 1981).

---

104   Cf. Dunn, *Neither Jew nor Greek*, 727; Dunn, *Beginning from Jerusalem*, 1160–66.
105   Jacobs, 'Narrative Integration', 212.

Bandura, Albert	'Health Promotion by Social Cognitive Means', *Health Education & Behavior* 31.2 (2004), 143–64.
Baroin, Catherine	'Remembering One's Ancestors, Following in Their Footsteps, Being Like Them', in Véronique Dasen and Thomas Späth (eds.), *Children, Memory, and Family Identity in Roman Culture* (Oxford: Oxford University Press, 2010), 19–48. Online ed.
Bartchy, S. Scott	'Slave, Slavery', in *Dictionary of the Later New Testament & its Developments* (Downers Grove: InterVarsity Press, 1997), 1098–1102.
Beare, Francis Wright	*The First Epistle of Peter: The Greek Text with Introduction and Notes* (Oxford: Blackwell and Mott, 1970, 3rd revised ed.).
Bird, Jennifer G.	*Abuse, Power and Fearful Obedience: Reconsidering 1 Peter's Commands to Wives* (LNTS 442; London: T&T Clark, 2011).
Boring, M. Eugene	'First Peter in Recent Study', *Word & World* 24.4 (2004), 358–67.
Bradley, Keith R.	*Slavery and Society at Rome* (KTAH; Cambridge, UK: Cambridge University Press, 1998).
Bradley, Keith R.	*Slaves and Masters in the Roman Empire: A Study in Social Control* (Oxford: Oxford University Press, 1987).
Brox, Norbert	*Der erste Petrusbrief* (EKKNT, Bd. 21; Zürich: Benziger Verlag; Neukichen-Vluyn: Neukirchener Verlag, 1979, 4th ed., 1993).
Bruner, Jerome	*Actual Minds, Possible Worlds* (Cambridge, MA: Harvard University Press, 1986).
Carson, D. A.	'1 Peter', in G. K. Beale and D. A. Carson (eds.), *Commentary on the New Testament Use of the Old Testament* (Grand Rapids: Baker Academic, 2007), 1015–45.
Chapple, Allan	'The Appropriation of Scripture in 1 Peter', in Matthew R. Malcolm (ed.), *All That the Prophets Have Declared: The Appropriation of Scripture in the Emergence of Christianity* (Milton Keynes: Paternoster, 2015), 155–71.
Cicero	*In Pisonem* (N. H. Watts, trans.; LCL 252; Cambridge, MA: Harvard University Press, 1931).

Clowney, Edmund P. *The Message of 1 Peter: The Way of the Cross* (BST; Downers Grove: InterVarsity Press, 1988).

Davids, Peter H. *The First Epistle of Peter* (NICNT; Grand Rapids: Eerdmans, 1990).

Dryden, J. de Waal *Theology and Ethics in 1 Peter: Paraenetic Strategies for Christian Character Formation*)WUNT, 2/209; Tübingen: Mohr Siebeck, 2006).

Dubis, Mark 'Research on 1 Peter: A Survey of Scholarly Literature since 1985', *Currents in Biblical Research* 4.2 (2006), 199–239.

Dunn, James D. G. *Beginning from Jerusalem* (Christianity in the Making 2; Grand Rapids: Eerdmans, 2009).

Dunn, James D. G. *Neither Jew nor Greek: A Contested Identity* (Christianity in the Making 3; Grand Rapids: Eerdmans, 2015).

Egan, Patrick T. *Ecclesiology and the Scriptural Narrative of 1 Peter* (Eugene: Pickwick Publications, 2016).

Eiser, J. Richard 'Accentuation Revisited', in W. Peter Robinson (ed.), *Social Groups and Identities: Developing the Legacy of Henri Tajfel* (International Series in Social Psychology; Oxford: Butterworth-Heinemann, 1996), 121–42.

Elliott, John H. 'The Rehabilitation of an Exegetical Step-Child: 1 Peter in Recent Research', in Charles H. Talbert (ed.), *Perspectives on First Peter* (NABPR Special Studies Series 9; Macon: Mercer University Press, 1986), 3–16.

Escalas, Jennifer Edson, and Barbara B. Stern 'Sympathy and Empathy: Emotional Responses to Advertising Dramas', *Journal of Consumer Research* 29.4 (2003), 566–78.

Esler, Philip F. 'An Outline of Social Identity Theory', in J. Brian Tucker and Coleman A. Baker (eds.), *T&T Clark Handbook to Social Identity in the New Testament* (London: Bloomsbury T&T Clark, 2014), 13–39.

Feldmeier, Reinhard *The First Letter of Peter: A Commentary on the Greek Text* (Peter H. Davids, trans.; Waco: Baylor University Press, 2008).

Galling, K. 'Altar', in George Arthur Buttrick (ed.), *Interpreters Dictionary of the Bible* (Nashville: Abingdon Press, 1982), 1:96–100.

Gerrig, Richard J. *Experiencing Narrative Worlds: On the Psychological Activities of Reading* (New Haven: Yale University Press, 1993).

Glancy, Jennifer A. *Slavery in Early Christianity* (Minneapolis: Fortress Press, 2006).

Goppelt, Leonhard *A Commentary on I Peter* (Ferdinand Hahn, ed.; John E. Alsup, trans.; Grand Rapids: Eerdmans, 1993).

Green, Melanie C., and Timothy C. Brock 'In the Mind's Eye: Transportation-Imagery Model of Narrative Persuasion', in Melanie C. Green, Jeffrey J. Strange, and Timothy C. Brock (eds.), *Narrative Impact: Social and Cognitive Foundations* (Mahwah: Lawrence Erlbaum Associates, 2002), 315–41.

Green, Melanie C., and Timothy C. Brock 'The Role of Transportation in the Persuasiveness of Public Narratives', *Journal of Personality and Social Psychology* 79.5 (2000), 701–21.

Gross, Carl D. 'Are the Wives of 1 Peter 3:7 Christians?', *Journal for the Study of the New Testament* 35 (1989), 89–96.

Harland, Philip A. *Dynamics of Identity in the World of the Early Christians: Associations, Judeans, and Cultural Minorities* (New York: T&T Clark, 2009).

Harrill, J. Albert *Slaves in the New Testament: Literary, Social, and Moral Dimensions*. Minneapolis: Fortress Press, 2009.

Harrill, J. Albert 'Slavery', in Craig A. Evans and Stanley E. Porter (eds.), *Dictionary of New Testament Background* (Downers Grove: InterVarsity Press, 2000), 1124–27.

Harris, Murray J. *Slave of Christ: A New Testament Metaphor for Total Devotion to Christ* (NSBT 8; Downers Grove: IVP Academic, 2001).

Hoffner, Cynthia A., Kenneth J. Levine, and Raiza A. Toohey 'Socialization to Work in Late Adolescence: The Role of Television and Family', *Journal of Broadcasting & Electronic Media* 52.2 (2008), 282–302.

Hogg, Michael A. 'Intragroup Process, Group Structure and Social Identity', in W. Peter Robinson (ed.), *Social Groups and Identities: Developing the Legacy of Henri Tajfel* (International Series in Social Psychology; Oxford: Butterworth-Heinemann, 1996), 65–93.

Horrell, David G.   'Fear, Hope, and Doing Good: Wives as a Paradigm of Mission in 1 Peter', *Estudios Bíblicos* LXXIII 3 (2015), 409–29.

Horrell, David G.   'Jesus Remembered in 1 Peter? Early Jesus Traditions, Isaiah 53, and 1 Peter 2.21–25', in Alicia J. Batten and John S. Kloppenborg (ed.), *James, 1 & 2 Peter, and Early Jesus Traditions* (LNTS 478; London: Bloomsbury, 2014), 123–50.

Horrell, David G.   *Becoming Christian: Essays on 1 Peter and the Making of Christian Identity* (LNTS 482; London: Bloomsbury, 2013).

Jacobs, Ronald N.   'The Narrative Integration of Personal and Collective Identity in Social Movements', in Melanie C. Green, Jeffrey J. Strange, and Timothy C. Brock (eds.), *Narrative Impact: Social and Cognitive Foundations* (Mahwah: Lawrence Erlbaum Associates, 2002), 205–28.

Jobes, Karen H.   *1 Peter* (BECNT; Grand Rapids: Baker Academic, 2005).

Joseph, Abson Prédestin   *A Narratological Reading of 1 Peter* (LNTS 440; London: T&T Clark, 2012).

Kelly, J. N. D.   *A Commentary on the Epistles of Peter and Jude* (BNTC; London: Adam & Charles Black, 1969).

Kuecker, Aaron J.   *The Spirit and the 'Other': Social Identity, Ethnicity and Intergroup Reconciliation in Luke-Acts* (LNTS 444; London: T&T Clark, 2011).

Küntay, Aylin C.   'Development of the Expression of Indefiniteness: Presenting New Referents in Turkish Picture-Series Stories', *Discourse Processes* 33.1 (2002), 77–101.

Liebengood, Kelly D.   *The Eschatology of 1 Peter: Considering the Influence of Zechariah 9–14* (SNTSMS 157; Cambridge, UK: Cambridge University Press, 2013).

Lim, Jason J. F.   '"Visiting Strangers and Resident Aliens" in 1 Peter and the Greco-Roman Context', *Scripture and Interpretation* 4.1 (2010), 92–109.

Martin, Dale B.   *Slavery as Salvation: The Metaphor of Slavery in Pauline Christianity* (New Haven: Yale University Press, 1990).

McCartney, Dan G. 'The Use of the Old Testament in the First Epistle of Peter' (PhD diss., Westminster Theological Seminary, 1989).

Michaels, J. Ramsey *1 Peter* (WBC 49; Waco: Word, 1988).

Milner, David 'Children and Racism: Beyond the Value of Dolls', in W. Peter Robinson (ed.), *Social Groups and Identities: Developing the Legacy of Henri Tajfel* (International Series in Social Psychology; Oxford: Butterworth-Heinemann, 1996), 249–68.

Moyise, Steve 'Isaiah in 1 Peter', in Steve Moyise and Maarten J. J. Menken (eds.), *Isaiah in the New Testament* (NTSI; London: T&T Clark, 2005).

Osiek, Carolyn, and David L. Balch *Families in the New Testament World: Households and House Churches* (The Family, Religion, and Culture; Louisville: Westminster John Knox Press, 1997).

Phillips, Barbara J., and Edward F. McQuarrie 'Narrative and Persuasion in Fashion Advertising', *Journal of Consumer Research* 37.3 (2010), 368–92.

Sargent, Benjamin *Written to Serve: The Use of Scripture in 1 Peter* (LNTS 547; London: Bloomsbury T&T Clark, 2015).

Schelkle, Karl Hermann *Die Petrusbriefe—Der Judasbrief* (HTKNT, XIII, 2; Freiburg im Breisgau: Herder, 1980).

Schreiner, Thomas R. *1, 2 Peter, Jude* (NAC 37; Nashville: Broadman & Holman, 2003).

Schutter, William L. *Hermeneutic and Composition in I Peter* (WUNT, 2/30; Tübingen: J. C. B. Mohr, 1989).

Seneca *Epistles* Vol. IV. (Richard M. Gummere, trans.; LCL 75; Cambridge, MA: Harvard University Press, 1917).

Shaw, David M. 'A People Called: Narrative Transportation and Missional Identity in 1 Peter' (PhD thesis, University of Exeter, 2017). http://hdl.handle.net/10871/29761.

Shaw, David M. 'Isaiah 53 and Social Creativity in 1 Pet 2:18–25', in *Letters of James, Peter, and Jude Seminar Group*, 1–12. Atlanta, 2015.

Shaw, David M. 'Narrating a New Identity: The Role of Isaiah's Suffering Servant in 1 Peter 2:22–23', 1–11. Sydney College of Divinity, 2017.

Slater, Michael D., and Donna Rouner 'Entertainment-Education and Elaboration Likelihood: Understanding the Processing of Narrative Persuasion', *Communication Theory* 12.2 (2002), 173–191.

Smith, Eliot R., and Michael A. Zárate 'Exemplar-Based Model of Social Judgment', *Psychology Review* 99 (1992), 3–21.

Tajfel, H., and J. C. Turner 'The Social Identity Theory of Intergroup Behaviour', in Stephen Worchel and William G. Austin (eds.), *Psychology of Intergroup Relations* (Chicago: Nelson Hall, 1986 2nd ed.).

Tajfel, Henri (ed.) *Social Identity and Intergroup Relations* (European Studies in Social Psychology; Cambridge: Cambridge University Press, 1982, Repr., 2010).

Tolkien, J. R. R. 'On Fairy-Stories', in Christopher Tolkien (ed.), *The Monsters and the Critics and Other Essays* (London: George Allen and Unwin, 1983), 109–61.

Turner, John C., Michael A. Hogg, Penelope J. Oakes, Stephen D. Reicher, and Margaret S. Wetherell *Rediscovering the Social Group: Self-Categorization Theory* (Oxford: Blackwell, 1987).

van Laer, Tom, Ko de Ruyter, Luca M. Visconti, and Martin Wetzels 'The Extended Transportation-Imagery Model: A Meta-Analysis of the Antecedents and Consequences of Consumers' Narrative Transportation', *Journal of Consumer Research* 40.5 (2014), 797–817.

Volf, Miroslav *Exclusion & Embrace: A Theological Exploration of Identity, Otherness, and Reconciliation* (Nashville: Abingdon Press, 1996).

Waldzus, Sven, Amélie Mummendey, and Michael Wenzel 'When "Different" Means "Worse": In-Group Prototypicality in Changing Intergroup Contexts', *Journal of Experimental Social Psychology* 41.1 (2005), 76–83.

Williams, Travis B. *Persecution in 1 Peter: Differentiating and Contextualizing Early Christian Suffering* (NovTSup 145; Leiden: Brill, 2012).

CHAPTER 6

Jesus' Impact on Understandings of Gender: Attending to First-Century Dialogue

Sally Douglas

Abstract

Jesus' impact was immediate, costly and scandalous. In Jesus, understandings of God were deconstructed and understandings of faithful living recalibrated. This is exemplified, across Gospel accounts, in Jesus' choice to repeatedly transgress cultural and religious androcentric expectations in living, dying and rising, by engaging people who were women in theology, in ministry and in evangelism. In post resurrection contexts, the impact of Jesus upon understandings of personhood continued. Extraordinary claims about the nullification of gender boundaries were being made while debates raged about the implications of such understandings. Analysis often remains focused on Pauline and Deutero-Pauline texts. This chapter will investigate claims made in 1 Corinthians and 1 Timothy and examine these in relation to the contrary claims made in the orthodox, first-century text of *1 Clement*. By attending to the evidence of this first-century dialogue the disruptive significance of Jesus' impact on understandings of gender is revealed.

KEY WORDS:
Jesus, gender, women, *1 Clement*, Paul, early church

Jesus' impact on those around him, and on those who later gathered in his name, was immediate, costly and scandalous. Understandings of God were deconstructed and remade in Jesus, the self-giving, crucified, risen one. Understandings of the human person were also recalibrated. An example of this recalibration is found across Gospel accounts in Jesus' choice to repeatedly transgress cultural and religious androcentric expectations by engaging people who were women in theology, in ministry and in evangelism. This occurred not only in Gospel accounts of Jesus' living, but also in Gospel accounts of Jesus' dying and rising. The impact of Jesus' disruption of religious and cultural expectations regarding gender continued to ricochet through earliest Jesus communities. This is exemplified in Paul's claim that categories of gender are subsumed in Christ (Gal. 3:28). Alongside such claims, in the earliest church people who were women were leaders and teachers. This leadership and teaching is (inadvertently) highlighted by the condemnation of this reality (e.g. 1 Cor. 11:2–16; 1 Cor. 14:34–36; 1 Tim. 2:9–15). Often contemporary analysis of understandings of gender in the early church remains focused on these Pauline, or Deutero-Pauline, texts.[1] In doing so, an echo chamber is constructed in which only one side of this debate is given attention. Deeper awareness of the disruptive significance of Jesus' impact on understandings of gender is made possible by attending to the dialogue that was taking place in the first century. Access to this dialogue is provided in the evidence of the ancient, orthodox, and commonly overlooked, letter *1 Clement*. In attending to this text the diversity of views within the first-century church regarding gender becomes apparent, understandings of the earliest church are enriched, and constructions of personhood in the contemporary church are challenged.

---

1   As Frances Gench, *Encountering God*, 37, states in relation to 1 Corinthians 11:2–16: 'as one of the lengthiest discussions of gender in the New Testament, it has garnered inordinate attention, and interpretations of it continue to have significant repercussions, shaping understandings of gender distinctions and roles within both church and home in ways that circumscribe the lives of many women to this day'.

Jesus' Impact on Gender Expectations

Before embarking upon investigation of the text of *1 Clement* it is necessary to contextualise analysis by tracing first-century understandings of gender. Only then is Jesus' disruptive impact able to be recognised. As indicated in various sources, people who were women were not considered equal to people who were men. Karen Jo Torjesen summarises the situation accordingly:

> The cultural value of shame prescribed the feminine personality as discreet, shy, restrained, and timid, those qualities deemed necessary to "protect" female sexuality. In this sexual division of moral labor, honor was considered an aspect of male nature expressed in a natural desire for precedence and an aggressive sexuality. Shame, the defining quality of womanhood, was indicated by passivity, subordination, and seclusion in the household.[2]

Torjesen argues that this worldview had significant impacts upon the every day lives of women, and in particular, women's freedom of movement:

> The good woman stayed at home. A woman who cared for her reputation, who had a sense of shame, reserved her sexuality for her husband alone. She was discreet, withdrawn from public life, and quiet. The woman who left the boundaries of the household and entered public space was no longer a good woman because she had abandoned female space.[3]

While preserved literature from this period indicates that people who were women were expected to conform to the construct of their personhood being inherently shameful, more recent scholarship has demonstrated that women did not always adhere to these cultural scripts. Epigraphical evidence indicates that within Graeco-Roman and Jewish

---

2   Torjesen, *When Women Were Priests*, 137. Torjeson goes on to examine various texts from the Graeco-Roman ancient world that provide evidence of this construction of reality, including the legend of Lucretia (138–140).
3   Torjesen, *When Women Were Priests*, 142–43.

contexts people who were women did have public roles in commerce, politics and religion.[4] When preserved texts are read alongside epigraphical evidence the luxury of generalisations evaporates. Written texts exhibit a desire to construct women as inherently shameful, lesser, and best confined to the private sphere. Epigraphical sources demonstrate that various women, most often those with wealth or status, refused to be constrained by such expectations. In contrast, these women exercised power and influence in the public world and were honoured for this. In light of the complex, contradictory evidence caution must be maintained. It is not accurate to present an image of universal oppression, in which women were only passive victims. Neither is it accurate to suggest that most, or many, women in the first century were able to freely exercise leadership and influence within the public sphere.[5]

The complex, untidy tension between cultural and religious expectations and the choices of various women to contravene such expectations is reflected in New Testament accounts. At various points in the Gospels, authors indicate that women, who were not always wealthy or of high status, were actively involved in theological debate, in ministry, and in evangelism with Jesus. Concurrently, these accounts reveal that men were scandalised by the presence of these women. In John's Gospel, the author tells readers that Jesus' disciples were stunned into silence because Jesus engages in conversation with a non-Jewish woman at a well: 'Just then the disciples came. They were astonished that he was speaking with a woman, but no one said, "what do you want?" or "why are you speaking to her?"' (4:27).[6] The author of John speaks in detail about this theological exchange between the woman and Jesus. Within

---

4   After investigating in detail epigraphical evidence from the ancient world and highlighting the active role of women, Ute Eisen, *Women Officeholders*, 18, summarises: 'we can say that historical research on women and theological research on Judaism have shown in the last several decades that no unified picture of the situation of Greco-Roman women can be garnered, be it of the social, political, economic, or religious'. Susan Mathew, *Women in the Greetings*, 64, states: 'Although wealth and status were assumed as the rationale for taking on leadership, the evidence shows women had the skill and potential to become lawyers, politicians, magistrates, patrons of associations, priestesses of cultic worship, and leaders of synagogues'. Mathew acknowledges that many of the sources for her analysis are from a little after the first century C.E.
5   For further reading see Kraemer, 'Women's Judaism(s)'; Lynn LiDonnici, 'Women's religious lives', 80–102.
6   All biblical quotations are taken from the NRSV translation.

this encounter it is to this woman that Jesus first chooses to reveal his identity as the Messiah (John 4:26). This woman then becomes an apostle to her village (John 4:22–30, 39).[7]

In another encounter, described in both Matthew and Mark, Jesus discusses theology with a woman who is also a non-Jewish outsider. In Matthew's Gospel the male disciples seek to have this woman sent away because she does not conform to their expectations. Not only is she an outsider, this woman refuses to comply with the cultural script of passivity and seclusion, and instead, is loud and demanding (Matt. 15:23). While reticent, in both Matthew and Mark, Jesus chooses to engage this woman in theology and through this encounter it is recorded that Jesus' own mind is changed (Mark 7:24–30; Matt. 15:21–28). This has significant repercussions for Jesus' ministry to both Jews and Gentiles. As emphasised in Mark's Gospel, after this encounter with this non-Jewish woman, it is recorded that Jesus goes on to feed more than 4000 people in a Gentile area.[8] In addition to these non-Jewish women, Gospel accounts detail that Jesus engages in theological discussion with various other women, including Martha and Mary (Luke 10:38–42; John 11:18–32).

Jesus not only transgressed cultural and religious expectations by engaging in theological debate with people who were women, Jesus allowed women, not related to him, to touch him and to minister to him in public settings such as large feasts. The tension is traced in these accounts, as women choose to defy cultural and religious expectations about the ways in which they should behave and men express their displeasure about this (e.g. Luke 7:36–50; Matt. 26:6–13; Mark 14:3–9, John 12:1–8). In each of these accounts, between Jesus and women who touch and minister to him, Jesus actively defends these women and deconstructs the dominant assumption that their behaviour is transgressive. Indeed, rather than being transgressive, Jesus declares that their actions are superior in insight and faithfulness (Luke 7:44–50; Matt. 26:10–13; Mark 14:6–9; John 12:7–8).

---

7   Origen, *Commentary on the Gospel of John*, 104, acknowledges this woman as an apostle: 'He [Jesus the Word] uses this woman as an apostle, as it were, to those in the city'.
8   For further discussion see Byrne, *A Costly Freedom*, 124–130; Boring, *Mark: A Commentary*, 209–214; 218–221.

The discipleship of women: those who 'followed Jesus' (Matt. 27:55; Mark 15:41; Luke 23:49) and the active ministry of these women to Jesus: those who 'provided for him' (Matt. 27:55; Mark 15:41) is a constant throughout Jesus' ministry, from the beginning in Galilee, according to Gospel accounts. However, across these accounts, this reality is only made explicit retrospectively, at the foot of the cross (Matt. 27:55–56; Mark 15:40–41; Luke 23:49). It is curious that within the narrative arc of these texts, Gospel authors choose to only acknowledge the active, faithful discipleship and ministry of people who are women at the conclusion of Jesus' life. While this may indicate the desire to push the active presence of woman disciples to the edges (at least of the narrative) ultimately these authors cannot deny the integral place of these women in Jesus' ministry from the very beginning.

In the resurrection accounts the active presence of women is also integral. Across all four Gospels it is women who are the first to encounter the risen Jesus, or the angel messengers from God. It is these people who are women who are given the apostolic command to tell the good news to the others (Matt. 28:1–10; Mark 16:1–10; Luke 24:1–11; John 20:11–18). In 1 Corinthians 15 a different recount of resurrection appearances is listed in which women are not named as the first to see the risen Lord. However, reading contextually, it is unlikely that the preserved Corinthian text could allow women to be named as the first to encounter the risen Jesus, and to be the ones given the apostolic command to tell the male disciples that Jesus has been raised, as this passage in Corinthians immediately follows the directive that 'women should be silent in the churches. For they are not permitted to speak' (1 Cor. 14:34).[9]

The Gospels preserve accounts of the active and faithful presence of women in Jesus' ministry, death, and resurrection. The Gospels preserve accounts of the reticence of male disciples, and perhaps to some extent the reticence of the Gospel writers themselves, to acknowledge and accept the active role of people who are women. Across these accounts Jesus is consistently imaged as including, valuing and defending people

---

9   Debates continue regarding the place of 1 Cor. 14:34–36 within the original letter. See below for further discussion.

who were women, as these women engage in theology, ministry, and evangelism. Jesus' choice to act in this way disrupted preserved cultural and religious practices and expectations and affirmed those women who dared to defy the status quo.

In post-resurrection contexts, the impact of Jesus upon understandings of personhood and gender continued. As indicated at the outset, extraordinary claims were being made about the nullification of gender divisions for those in Jesus Christ: 'There is no longer Jew or Greek, there is no longer slave or free, there is no longer male and female, for all of you are one in Christ Jesus' (Gal. 3:28). While less dramatic language is used, the reframing of gender construction is also evident in 1 Corinthians 7:2–4, in which both the rights of husbands and the rights of wives are highlighted. As Brendan Byrne states: 'the mutuality expressed here diverges sharply from the ethos of the surrounding culture which tended to see everything solely from the male perspective'.[10]

Jesus' disruption of expectations regarding gender in post-Easter contexts is further evidenced in other early church texts. Despite common misconceptions, the Gospel of Thomas defies genre definition.[11] Clarity regarding the dating of this text is also elusive.[12] However, as a text focused on Jesus, and Jesus' teaching, composed in the first century or second century, it contributes to understandings of the early Jesus movement. In this text, perhaps reflecting something similar to the understanding of Gal. 3:28, the disintegration of gender binaries is spoken of:

> Jesus said to them: "When you make the two into one, and when you make the inside like the outside, and the outside like the inside, and the above like the below and when you make the male and the female into a single being, with the result that that the male is not male nor the female female ... then you will enter [the kingdom]". Gospel of Thomas 22.4–5, 7.[13]

---

10 Byrne, *Paul and the Christian Woman*, 20.
11 The scholarly temptation to label Thomas as 'gnostic' dismisses the reality that the text itself lacks many key features that would denote it as such, see Davies, *The Gospel of Thomas*, 28. For further discussion see my monograph *Early Church Understandings*, 134–143.
12 DeConick, *The Original Gospel of Thomas*, 7.
13 Translation by DeConick, *The Original Gospel of Thomas*.

This gender fluidity in relation to the kingdom is also reflected in *2 Clement*: 'For when the Lord himself was asked by someone when his kingdom would come, he said: "When the two are one, and the outside like the inside, and the male with the female is neither male or female"' (*2 Clement* 12.2).[14]

The sharp impact of Jesus' disruption of constructions of gender is perhaps most clearly illustrated in the preserved condemnation of women's leadership, ministry, and teaching in early Jesus communities (1 Cor. 11:2–16; 1 Cor. 14:34–36; 1 Tim. 2:9–15).[15] However, to assess these censorious assertions about the role of women in Pauline and Deutero-Pauline texts only in light of the internal evidence of these texts themselves, creates a petri dish environment in which arguments from silence can be cultivated. This approach has led to a variety of specific claims being made about the church in Corinth and the women within this community.[16] Such imaginative reconstructions are attractive, not least because they create a context in which seemingly harsh admonitions can be rounded out. However, there is insufficient evidence about the Corinthian church, or other early church communities, to make such claims in specificity. While arguments may be mounted based on what Paul, or the author, states, we do not possess definitive details about the

---

14 Translation by Ehrman, *Lost Scriptures*.
15 It is important to note that despite the condemnation of women's leadership in such texts, early church evidence indicates that women continued to offer leadership teaching and ministry and drew their theology from passages such as Gal. 3:28. The heresy hunter Epiphanius recorded evidence about the second century Christian movement referred to as the Montanists. As Epiphanius states: 'They have women bishops, presbyters and the rest; they say that none of this makes any difference because "In Christ Jesus there is neither male nor female"'; Epiphanius, *Panarion* 49.2.5. For further discussion of the Montanists, see Douglas, *Early Church Understandings*, 113–116.
16 Exemplifying this tendency Ben Witherington, *Conflict and Community*, 276, claims that: 'One must assume that he [Paul] singles these women out for comment because he had heard that some of them were notable violators of these principles'. Witherington offers no evidence for why this must be assumed. Reflecting on 1 Corinthians 14, Witherington expands his claims about the specific situation in Corinthian community: 'During the time of the weighing of the prophecies some women, probably married women, who themselves may have been prophetesses and thus entitled to weigh what was said, were asking questions, perhaps inappropriate questions, and the worship service was being disrupted' (287). Witherington again offers no supporting evidence for this claim, but rather extrapolates from knowledge about pagan prophecy to argue that 'it is very believable that these women assumed that Christian prophets and prophetesses functioned much like the oracle of Delphi, who only prophesied in response to questions, including questions about purely personal matters'. Likewise, but in a more detailed discussion, Antoinette Wire, *The Corinthian Women*, draws from Paul's rhetoric to offer a reconstruction of the Corinthian church.

situation in Corinth, and the women and the men in this community. What we do have is evidence from another faithful and orthodox early church community, who also took the time to write to the community in Corinth in the first century. It is to this evidence that we will now turn.

The Evidence of *1 Clement*

For centuries it was argued that *1 Clement* was authored by Clement, known as the third Bishop of Rome.[17] However, in returning to the evidence over the last century, scholars have rejected this view.[18] The letter itself makes no such attribution. Instead in the opening sentence, speaking in the collective, it is stated that the letter is from the: 'church of God that temporarily resides in Rome, to the church of God that temporarily resides in Corinth'.[19] Adding to this internal claim of shared authorship, more recently it has been underscored that the text itself 'strongly suggests the collective voice of many persons'.[20]

1 Clement is one of the oldest Christian texts outside the New Testament. Writing a century ago, John Gregg argued that it 'is one of the few literary remains of the Church of the first century'.[21] More recently, Bart Ehrman has argued that it is the 'oldest Christian writing outside of the New Testament'.[22] The orthodox nature of *1 Clement* is not questioned and *1 Clement* is listed as canonical in the fifth century

---

17 For discussion of the evolution of this view from the second century, see Gregory, '*1 Clement*: An Introduction', 23–24.
18 While wanting to attribute authorship to Saint Clement, already in the 1870's it was acknowledged by J.B. Lightfoot, *S. Clement of Rome*, 252, that: 'This letter, it must be premised, does not emanate from the bishop of Rome, but from the Church of Rome'. As Barbara Ellen Bowe, *A Church in Crisis*, 2, states: 'There is no indication from the text of *1 Clement* [...] that a monarchical episcopacy was in place in Rome, or that Clement was *the* bishop' (italics original). Supporting Bowe's claim in *1 Clement* 42, bishops are discussed and listed alongside deacons as part of 'the first fruits of their [apostles] ministries'. In this discussion there is no reference to a particular bishop in Rome (or anywhere else) who has singular authority (42:4). Likewise, Clayton Jefford, *The Apostolic Fathers*, 17, argues 'if a single authority such as a bishop had presided over the Roman church, the power of his authority would have been readily accessed for the author's argument'.
19 Translation by Ehrman, *The New Testament and Other Early Christian Writings*.
20 Jefford, *The Apostolic Fathers*, 17. As Bowe, *Church in Crisis*, 37, observes: 'the first person plural style is used throughout, not with a veiled authoritative pretense, but genuinely, it seems, with the intention of reaffirming the Christian solidarity that binds writers and addressees'.
21 Gregg, *Early Church Classics*, iv.
22 Ehrman, *The Apostolic Fathers*, 25.

Codex Alexandrinus. *1 Clement* is quoted by various early church fathers, sometimes as scripture, including by Clement of Alexandria, Origen, Eusebius, Didymus the Blind, and Jerome.[23] If Dionysius of Corinth is to be believed, *1 Clement* was read during worship, possibly as a text of scripture, in Corinth in the mid-second century.[24]

Despite this text's revered place in the early church, a significant proportion of *1 Clement* has been ignored for more than 1000 years. There are various reasons why the contents of this ancient and orthodox letter have received limited scholarly attention. The hermeneutical lens of church conflict has commonly been adopted in analysis of this text.[25] While the letter opens with reference to disputes and factions and the theme of church conflict is returned to in a limited number of chapters, church conflict is not the only focus of this 65 chapter letter.[26] Despite this, and despite the lack of information about the nature of the conflict in the church in Corinth (as perceived by the church in Rome), church conflict has remained the focus of research.[27] One of the consequences of this habitual approach to *1 Clement* is that the overwhelming number of passages that do not deal with church conflict are ignored in plain sight. This myopic tendency is perhaps reinforced by the reality that the contents of this ancient letter do not conform to scholarly expectations about the contours of early church theology in relation to understandings of christology, soteriology, discipleship, as well as understandings of personhood and gender. By attending to the evidence of *1 Clement*, access is gained into first-century dialogue about gender. In paying heed to this text, assumptions are disrupted and understandings are enriched as it is discovered that views in the orthodox early church were not univocal about people who were women and people who were men.

---

23 Ehrman, *The Apostolic Fathers*, 28.
24 Ehrman, *The Apostolic Fathers*, 28.
25 Illustrating this, Bart Ehrman, *The New Testament and Other Early Christian Writings*, 302, claims: 'The purpose of the writing, in any event, is perfectly clear. There has been a division in the church in Corinth'. See also Gregory, '*1 Clement*', 24.
26 As Gregory, '*1 Clement*', 26, n.8, points out: '*1 Clement* alludes to the difficulties in Corinth in chap. 1 and returns to them at the end, in chap. 65, but the majority of information about the nature of the problems in Corinth comes in chaps 42–44 and 47'.
27 See also Bowe, *A Church in Crisis*, 4.

1.1 Creation and Ontological Equality in *1 Clement*

In 1 Corinthians 11 and 1 Timothy 2 the second creation story from Genesis 2 is integral to the argument that women are inherently different to men. In 1 Corinthians it is stated 'for a man ought not have his head veiled, since he is the image and reflection of God, but woman is the reflection of man. Indeed, man was not made from woman, but woman from man. Neither was man created for the sake of woman, but woman for the sake of man...' (1 Cor. 11:7–9). In this text the assertion that women should be veiled is, in part, based on the theological argument that people who are women are ontologically lesser than men. That is, according to this construct, men are made in the image of God and women are not. Similarly, in 1 Timothy the second creation story provides the theological justification for the assertion that women must be silent and submissive: 'Let a woman learn in silence with full submission. I permit no woman to teach or have authority over a man; she is to keep silent. For Adam was formed first, then Eve, and Adam was not deceived, but the woman was deceived and became a transgressor' (1 Tim. 2:11–14). In this text, primacy in the order of creation is argued to equate with superiority. Furthermore, this argument is coupled with an interpretation of the second creation story that designates the woman, Eve, as the only transgressor in the narrative.

In contrast to 1 Corinthians and 1 Timothy, the authors of *1 Clement*, writing from the church in Rome to the church in Corinth, choose to emphasise the first creation story found in Genesis 1. As these authors call the church not to tire of doing good, they celebrate God's faithfulness in shaping and creating humanity:

> And with his [God's] holy and perfect hands he formed the one who was Pre-eminent and superior in intelligence to all, the human, stamped with his own image. For as God says, "Let us make a human according to our own image and likeness. And God made the human; male and female he made them". When he had finished all these things, he praised and blessed them, and said "increase and become numerous". (*1 Clement* 33.4–6)

Here the authors from the church in Rome, writing to the church in Corinth, choose to draw from the first creation story for their theology and, in so doing, they emphasise the equality of people who are women and people who are men, and explicitly underscore that both men and women are made in God's image.

This choice to utilise the first creation story, and to emphasise its understanding of the ontological equality of people who are women and people who are men, both made in God's image, does not emerge within a neutral context. This theology of the human person stands in contrast to the theology of the human person constructed in 1 Corinthians 11 and 1 Timothy 2. This is significant because we know that the authors of *1 Clement* were familiar with 1 Corinthians and assumed that the community in Corinth has also already read this text. In *1 Clement* 47 the church in Rome calls the church in Corinth to read the text again: 'take up the epistle of that blessed apostle Paul ... what did he write to you at first, at the beginning of his proclamation of the gospel? To be sure he sent you a letter in the Spirit concerning himself and Cephas and Apollos...' (*1 Clement* 47.1–3). If the assertion in 1 Corinthians 11 that women are not made in the image of God, like men, is not a later addition to Paul's text, the church in Rome and the church in Corinth have both already received a theology of the human person that renders women ontologically lesser than men. Knowing this theology, the church in Rome now chooses to proclaim and underscore a different theology of the human person in which the ontological equality of people who are women and people who are men, both made in God's image, is proclaimed. This decision made by the church in Rome writing to the church in Corinth begins to provide access to the diversity of theologies of the human person in the first-century church.

1.2 Women and Prophecy in *1 Clement*

In *1 Clement* 12, the faithfulness of Rahab, who worked as a prostitute, is celebrated. Drawing from Joshua 2, the story of Rahab and her faithfulness is told at some length by the church in Rome. Within this recount, Rahab's action of hanging a piece of scarlet cloth from her house, is equated with the blood of the Lord and then the authors state: 'You see, loved ones, not only was faith found in the woman, but prophecy as well' (12.8). It seems rather a stretch to link the draping of fabric with prophecy. Yet this is what the authors from the church in Rome state, as they write to the church in Corinth. This choice to describe Rahab's actions as faithful and to underscore that Rahab's faith-filled actions, as a woman, were also prophetic, is not a choice made in a vacuum. From the evidence of 1 Corinthians, which both the Corinthian and Roman communities had already read, we know that debates about women and about the role of women in teaching and prophecy in the early church were ablaze. It is important to note that in 1 Corinthians 11, Paul (or whoever writes in Paul's name) does not command women to be silent, in contrast he assumes that people who are women will prophesy. The issue in 1 Corinthians 11 is that women dress according to the author's religious and cultural expectations (1 Corinthians 11:16). The reality that in 1 Corinthians 11 the prophetic gifts of women are not censured, contributes to debate about the authenticity of 1 Corinthians 14:34–36 in which women are not permitted to speak. In light of the evidence, many conclude that 1 Corinthians 14:34–36 was a later addition to the text.[28]

The authorship, and dating, of 1 Timothy are contested.[29] The dating of *1 Clement* has traditionally been located in the 90's C.E.[30] However more recent scholarship has questioned this assumption, with some, me among them, highlighting evidence that indicates that the letter may have been composed before the destruction of the temple in 70 C.E.[31] It

---

28 Hans Conzelmann, 1 Corinthians, 246, argues that 1 Corinthians 14:34–36 'interrupts the theme of prophecy'. Conzelman continues, 'In content it is in contradiction with 11:2ff, where the active participation of women in the church is presupposed' and he concludes: 'The section is accordingly to be regarded as an interpolation'. See also Horsley, 1 Corinthians, 188–89; Fee, First Corinthians, 699–705. In contrast, Elisabeth Schüssler Fiorenza, In Memory of Her, 230, argues that: 'Since these verses [1 Cor. 14:33b–36] cannot be excluded on textual-critical grounds but are usually declared inauthentic on theological grounds, it is exegetically more sound to accept them as original Pauline statements and then explain them within their present context'. Schüssler Fiorenza seeks to resolve the contradiction by suggesting that Paul has in mind different expectations for unmarried women compared with married women (231–232).
29 In contemporary scholarship it is commonly argued that Paul was not the author of 1 Timothy. For a detailed discussion see Marshall, *The Pastoral Epistles*, 57–92. After weighing the diverse arguments Marshall concludes that 'the indications are that the PE [Pastoral Epistles] belong to the period shortly after the death of Paul' (92). Raymond Collins, *I & II Timothy*, 8, argues: 'Revering the memory of Paul and intending to actualize his teaching, an anonymous author invoked his authority in composing the Pastoral Epistles'. Deborah Krause, *1 Timothy*, 5, shares the view that 1 Timothy was not composed by Paul and points out that the place of 1 Timothy was also ambiguous within the early church. The question of how long after Paul's death *1 Timothy* was composed continues to be debated.
30 Ehrman, *The New Testament and Other Early Christian Writings*, 302; Koester, *From Jesus to the Gospels*, 5; Gregg, *The Epistle of St Clement*, 9.
31 Douglas, Early Church Understandings, 53–54; Jefford, The Apostolic Fathers, 19.

is therefore possible that *1 Clement* was composed before 1 Timothy.[32] However, because both the dating of *1 Clement* and the dating of 1 Timothy remain ambiguous, it cannot be known whether the authors of either text had access to the other. What is known is that the authors from the first-century church in Rome affirm the ontological equality of people who are women and people who are men, and go to some lengths to explicitly affirm that women may be called to faithfully prophesy. In 1 Timothy 2:13, the opposite is true. Relying upon an interpretation of the second creation story in which the man is made first, the author of 1 Timothy argues that women are ontologically inferior to men. For the author of 1 Timothy women's ontological inferiority is further evidenced in Eve's sinfulness (1 Tim. 2:14). Building upon this theology of the human person, the author demands that women be silent (1 Tim. 2:11–13). In attending to both *1 Clement* and 1 Timothy we are able to overhear the theological debate that was occurring within the early church about the role of women.

1.3 The Call for Women to Speak in *1 Clement*

In *1 Clement* 21 appropriate behaviour in Christian community is discussed. Within this passage, and elsewhere in *1 Clement*, the repeated emphasis is upon living in gentleness and humility (1.2; 2.1,5–8; 13.1–4; 14.3; 16.1–17; 21.8–9; 30.8; 44.3; 49.1–6; 56.1; 57.2; 58.2; 62.1–2). The theological framework for this focus is that, according to this text, Jesus is the 'radiance of his [God's] magnificence' and the 'reflection of his [God's] perfect and superior countenance' (36.2). Jesus embodies humility and gentleness (13.1–4; 16.1–17) and thus embodies who—and how—God is. As these authors state: 'we should treat one another kindly, according to the compassion and sweet character of the one who made us' (14.3).[33]

Within this framework in which gentleness is integral, in chapter 21 wives are called to speak with gentleness: 'let them manifest the gentleness of their tongues through how they speak, let them show their

---

32 Krause, *1 Timothy*, 6–7, summarises the arguments of many scholars who analyse the language, themes and the church structures presented in 1 Timothy, and concludes that 1 Timothy was composed in the 'late first century or early second century'.
33 See also 16.1; 23.1; 56.1.

love not with partiality, but equally to all those who stand in reverential awe of God in a holy way' (21.7). This command for women to speak with gentleness may refer to the private realm or the public realm. The preceding verses address issues in the wider context of the public faith community and its disputes, and include instructions regarding leaders, the elderly and youth. In light of this textual reality, it is more likely that the command for women to speak refers to public contexts. There is further external evidence that reveals that these words were understood to refer to the public realm. This is reflected in divergent manuscripts of this passage in which some texts encourage women's 'voice' and others seek women's 'silence', presumably in public. In the fifth-century Codex Alexandrinus this passage is rendered: 'let them manifest their gentleness of tongues by their voice'. However, in the eleventh-century Codex Hierosolymitanus these words are rendered: 'let them manifest the gentleness of their tongues by their silence'.[34] Kim Haines-Eitzen points out that: 'the Syriac, Latin, and Coptic contain "silence" instead of "voice", and the writing of the second century Clement of Alexandria quotes this passage and does so with "silence"'.[35] Considering the increasingly shrill censure of women's leadership, teaching, and speaking in the early church, it should, perhaps, comes as no surprise that more numerous copies of *1 Clement* that preserve the instruction for women to keep silent are in evidence. Haines-Eitzen also points out that the 'earliest Greek manuscript of *1 Clement* accords it scriptural status [in the Codex Alexandrinus] and at *1 Clement* 21.7 offers wives voice'.[36] The evidence of these diverse manuscripts underscores the persistence of the debates that raged in the church regarding people who were women, and their contribution to the community.

1.4 Women Empowered by God to do 'Manly' Deeds in *1 Clement*

In *1 Clement* 55 the faithfulness of various people is proclaimed including Gentiles and 'many [unnamed] kings'. The authors then proclaim that: 'many women were empowered by the gracious gift of God to perform numerous manly deeds' (55.3). The passage goes on to detail both

---

34   Haines–Eitzen, *The Gendered Palimpsest*, 4–7.
35   Haines–Eitzen, *Gendered Palimpsest*, 4–5.
36   Haines–Eitzen, *Gendered Palimpsest*, 5.

Judith's and Esther's courageous actions (55.3–6). According to the text these faithful people, who were women, save the city (*1 Clement* 55:4–5; Judith 8–16) and rescue the twelve tribes of Israel (*1 Clement* 55.6; Esther 7–8). Within this passage in *1 Clement*, Esther is described as 'a woman perfect in faith' (55.6). Yet again, the context of these words must be underscored. The explicit affirmation of people who are women, and the extended celebration of these women's faithful and courageous 'manly' God-inspired actions, emerges from within a specific rendering of reality. That is, these statements are made within a wider cultural context in which people who were women were constructed as lesser and inherently shameful. Even more poignantly, these extended affirmations of God-inspired women and their faithful and 'manly' saving actions are made within an emerging church, in which some, perhaps including Paul, were claiming that women were ontologically lesser beings than men (1 Cor. 11:7–9; 1 Tim. 2:13), that women were more inherently sinful than men (1 Tim. 2:14) and that women should be denied active leadership within the church.

1.5 The First-Century Church in Rome's Defense of Women

In attending to the evidence, contemporary readers are given access to the diversity of theologies of the human person within first-century Jesus communities. The author of 1 Corinthians 14:34–36 explicitly states that women should be 'subordinate' (1 Cor. 14:34) and the author of 1 Timothy argues that women should 'learn in silence with full submission' (1 Tim. 2:11). The authors of 1 Corinthians 11:7–9 and 1 Timothy 2:11–14 reject the ontological equality of people who are women compared with men, arguing that only men are made in the image of God. Building on this theology of the human person, these authors seek to limit, or disallow, the active role of women within the church (1 Cor. 11:5–6; 1 Tim. 2:11–14, see also 1 Cor. 14:34–36). In contrast, the authors from the church in Rome choose to underscore the ontological equality of people who are women and people who are men (*1 Clement* 33.4–6). The church in Rome celebrates and explicates a woman's faithful prophecy (*1 Clement* 12.8) and, in some preserved manuscripts, affirms women's speech in community (*1 Clement* 21.7). These authors from the church in Rome proclaim in detail the faithful, courageous and saving actions of women (*1 Clement* 55.3–6). According to the church in Rome these actions of women are empowered by God and these 'manly' actions, that defy cultural expectations of womanhood, bring liberation and salvation to God's people. These realities in the text of *1 Clement* are not incidental. The authors from the church in Rome are speaking to the church in Corinth within the context of the denial of women's ontological equality and the increasingly shrill condemnation of women's active leadership in the church. Indeed, if 1 Corinthians 11:7–9 and 1 Corinthians 14:34–36 are original, the community in Corinth has already received this theology of the human person in which women are constructed as inherently lesser (*1 Clement* 47.1–3). The choice of the first-century Roman church to articulate a theology of the ontological equality of women and men, both made in the image of God, and to affirm women's prophetic, active, faithful and salvific roles within the church highlights the diversity of the views regarding gender in the early church.

The Church in Rome

Various questions emerge from the evidence of *1 Clement*. Within the confines of space, only one question will be explored here. Why might the church in Rome emphasise a view of women that proclaims women's ontological equality with men and underscores the active role of women as prophets, speakers, and God-empowered 'manly' leaders? While speculation about the church in Corinth, and the role of women therein, continues, thanks to Paul's letter to the church in Rome access to specific information about this first-century church is made available. From Paul it can be gleaned that he did not found this community.[37] From Paul's agonizing emphasis upon God's inclusion of both Jews and Gentiles (e.g. Rom. 9:1–5) it may be concluded that the Roman church has both Jewish and Gentiles members, for whom this question had

---

37 Paul indicates in the opening of Romans that he has not yet visited this community (Rom. 1:11–13). As C.K. Barrett, *Romans,* 5, states: 'The Roman church fell outside the scope of his [Paul's] own apostolic labour. Its origin is completely obscure'.

become an issue.[38] That said, it is commonly argued that Paul assumes that the Roman church is largely Gentile.[39] This broad contextual backdrop for understanding the early church in Rome is important. However, within Romans there is even more detailed information about the first-century church in Rome who wrote to the church in Corinth.

In the concluding chapter of Romans, information is given about specific members of the Roman Church, in particular, those whom Paul perceived to be the people of significance within this church community. Before proceeding, it must be noted that in the past it has been argued that Romans 16 was not originally part of the letter. In particular the issue of how Paul could know so many people by name, in a church he had not visited, has been raised. However, the assumption that this is problematic has been found to be wanting in more recent scholarship. As C.K. Barrett points out: 'In writing to a strange church Paul might very naturally include as many personal greetings as he could in order to establish as close contact as possible'.[40] Similarly, Susan Mathew states: 'The greetings of Roman 16 function to create bonds between Paul's personal friends and the Roman church, between the Roman church and Paul himself, and between the individual members of the ethnically and socially diverse Roman church'.[41] In contemporary context, scholars commonly accept that Romans 16 is part of the whole text.[42]

In the conclusion to his letter to the Roman church, Paul refers to a multitude of people by name and alludes to others. It is reasonable to assume that Paul seeks to greet those who he perceived to be of key importance in the Roman church.[43] What is striking is that so many of the people named in Romans 16 are women: Phoebe, Prisca, Mary,

---

38 Brendan Byrne, *Romans*, 12, discusses the possible context for this letter, suggesting that as expelled Jewish Christians returned to Rome after the death of Claudius in 54 C.E.: 'It is likely that these returning Jewish Christians would have sought to regain their previous ascendency and restore a life–style based on more traditionally Jewish lines'.
39 Byrne, *Romans*, 10. Barrett, *Romans*, 6.
40 Barrett, *Romans*, 257. Barrett also points out that within the early church 'movement' may well have been an important feature, leading to Paul knowing some leaders within the Roman church, without having visited Rome. Byrne, *Romans*, 29, 446, also argues that Romans 16 was an original part of the letter.
41 Mathew, *Women in the Greetings*, 4. See also Byrne, *Romans*, 29; Barrett, *Romans*, 257.
42 Byrne, *Romans*, 29; Mathew, *Women in the Greetings*, 3–4; Barrett, *Romans*, 257.
43 Mathew, *Women in the Greetings*, 4.

Junia, Tryphoena, Tryphosa, Persis, Julia, Nereus' sister and Rufus' mother.[44] Furthermore, Paul explicitly describes women in key roles within this early church setting. Paul names Phoebe as a deacon (16:1). Paul names Prisca first, and then Aquila, and describes them as those who 'work with me in Christ Jesus' and who 'risked their necks for my life' (16:3–4). Paul honours Mary who 'has worked very hard among you' (16:6). Paul describes Junia, along with Andronicus, as those who are 'prominent among the apostles', who have been 'in prison', and who were 'in Christ' before Paul (16:7).

Reception history reveals that Paul's acknowledgement of these women leaders became problematic over time. Phoebe's role as a deacon has been widely debated, and attempts have been made to reduce her role to a 'deaconess' or helper.[45] In contrast, as Mathew demonstrates the evidence indicates that: 'The correct rendering would be a minister of the church of Cenchreae'.[46] After the 12th century C.E., the name of the female apostle Junia was transitioned to the male name 'Junias' in many translations.[47] This is despite both the manuscript evidence to the contrary, and the contextual reality that there is no evidence of the male version of the name 'Junias' in Greek or Latin speaking communities in the Common Era.[48]

While it may be difficult for some to acknowledge, from Paul's perspective women were significant leaders and important participants in the church in Rome in the first century. This is despite what is written in 1 Corinthians 11 and 14 by Paul, or by others writing in

---

44 Mathew, *Women in the Greetings*, 4.
45 For a detailed discussion of Phoebe see Mathew, *Women in the Greetings*, 65–74. Mathew discusses the tendency of some to interpret Phoebe's role as a deacon in a limited way as: 'informal service or a limited ministry caring for the sick' (72).
46 Mathew, *Women in the Greetings*, 74. While not wishing to assert exactly what Phoebe's role was in the early church, likewise, Barrett, *Romans*, 258, translates *diakonos* as minister in 16:1 and points out that 'Phoebe was not the only woman minister in the New Testament church'. For his full discussion see pp.256–58. For further discussion of deacons and deaconesses in the early church see: Eisen, *Women Officeholders*, 12–15.
47 See Mathew, *Women in the* Greetings, 97; Eisen, *Women Officeholders*, 47–49.
48 Mathew, *Women in the* Greetings, 98–99; Barrett, *Romans*, 260.

Paul's name.[49] Alongside Paul's acknowledgement of various important women within the Roman church, Paul trusts that the church in Rome will welcome and support the deacon/minister Phoebe (16:1–2). Paul explicitly acknowledges the prominent apostle Junia (16:7) and Mary's hard work within the church (16:6). It is Paul's view that the Roman church was a community in which the ministry and leadership of people who were women was prominent and honoured. The contents of *1 Clement*, authored by this church in Rome, adds further weight to this, Paul's conclusion.

There is preserved evidence in 1 Corinthians and 1 Timothy of the growing condemnation of women's leadership, teaching, prophecy and speaking within the early church. This condemnation was, at times, justified by claims about the ontological inferiority of women. The church in Rome in the first century proclaimed a different reality. Within the context of increasing condemnation of women, that the Corinth church had (likely) already received, the church in Rome, which had multiple prominent leaders and members who were women, chose to write to the church in Corinth and underscore a different reality. The Roman church emphasised the ontological equality of women and men, and women's faithfulness as prophets, speakers and pivotal actors within the drama of God's salvific plans. Within the emerging church in Rome whose prominent members included Prisca, Mary, Junia, Tryphoena, Tryphosa, Persis, Julia, Nereus' sister and Rufus' mother, perhaps this should come as no surprise. What is, perhaps, more surprising is that the text of *1 Clement* has been overlooked by the church in Rome, and churches elsewhere, for centuries.

---

49 If Paul is the author of all of these texts, it is intriguing to ponder his apparent contradictions regarding women's leadership. For discussion of the way in which Paul recognises Spirit-infused women leaders and his conflicting cultural expectations of gender roles see: Eisen, *Women Officeholders*, 207–08; Douglas, *Early Church Understandings*, 112–13. As Boring observes in relation to the first-century church: 'In a patriarchal society that influenced the ways in which church life and leadership was conceived, the Spirit overcame the stereotypical male / female roles, and theology found itself attempting to catch up with reality already created by the Spirit'; Boring, *Mark*, 207.

Conclusion

Jesus' disruptive impact on androcentric expectations is evident across Gospel accounts and in post-Easter communities as people who were women engaged in theology, ministry and evangelism. The evidence of 1 Corinthians and 1 Timothy reveals that within this context, the role of women in the early church became increasingly contested and constricted. As a way to gain traction in this movement to censure women, women's ontological equality was discredited. Often analysis of understandings of gender in the first century remains focused on these texts alone, and thus only one side of the dialogue is attended to. In doing so, a theological rendering of the human person in which women are constructed as lesser is able to be maintained. By paying heed to the ancient and orthodox text of *1 Clement*, access to the diversity of voices within the first-century church is gained. The church in Rome, writing to the church in Corinth, underscored the ontological equality of women and men, highlighted women's gifts of prophecy, called for women's speech and proclaimed women's faithful, courageous and God-ordained leadership and saving action. By listening to the first-century church in Rome, we are confronted afresh with evidence of the extent of Jesus' impact upon understandings of gender. By re-engaging with this voice from the first-century Roman church, understandings of theology, gender and ecclesiology within the contemporary world-wide church will continue to be disrupted and enriched.

Bibliography

Barrett, C.K.	*The Epistle to the Romans* (BNTC; London: A&C Black, 1991).
Boring, M.E.	*Mark: A Commentary* (Louisville: Westminster John Knox: 2006).
Bowe, B.E.	*A Church in Crisis* (Harvard Dissertations in Religion; Minneapolis: Fortress Press, 1988).
Byrne, B.	*A Costly Freedom: A Theological Reading of Mark's Gospel* (Strathfield: St Pauls Publications, 2008).

Byrne, B.	*Paul and the Christian Woman* (Homebush, NSW: St Paul Publications, 1988).
Byrne, B.	*Romans* (Sacra Pagina; Daniel Harrington, ed.; Collegeville: Michael Glazier, Liturgical Press, 1996).
Collins, R.	*I & II Timothy and Titus: A Commentary* (Louisville: Westminster John Knox, 2002).
Conzelmann, H.	*1 Corinthians: A Commentary on the First Epistle to the Corinthians* (Hermenia; J.W. Leitch, trans.; Philadelphia: Fortress, 1975).
Davies, S.	*The Gospel of Thomas and Christian Wisdom* (New York: The Seabury Press, 1983).
DeConick, A.	*The Original Gospel of Thomas in Translation: With a Commentary and New English Translation of the Complete Gospel* (Mark Goodacre, ed.; Early Christianity in Context, Library of New Testament Studies, 287; London: T&T Clark, 2006).
Douglas, S.	*Early Church Understandings of Jesus as the Female Divine: The Scandal of the Scandal of Particularity* (Library of New Testament Studies, 557; London: Bloomsbury, T&T Clark, 2016).
Ehrman, B.	*Lost Scriptures: Books that Did not Make it Into the New Testament* (Oxford: Oxford University Press, 2003).
Ehrman, B.	*The Apostolic Fathers: 1 Clement, II Clement, Ignatius, Polycarp, Didache,* (LCL 24, vol. 1.; London: Harvard University Press, 2005).
Ehrman, B.	*The New Testament and Other Early Christian Writings: A Reader* (Oxford: Oxford University Press, 2004).
Eisen, U.	*Women Officeholders in Early Christianity: Epigraphical and Literary Studies* (Collegeville: Michael Glazier, Liturgical Press, 2000).
Epiphanius	*The Panarion of Epiphanius of Salamis: Books II and III* (F. Williams, trans.; Nag Hammadi and Manichean Studies; Leiden: E.J. Brill, 1994).
Fee, G.	*The First Epistle to the Corinthians* (NICNT; Grand Rapids: Eerdmans, 1987).

Gench, F.T.	*Encountering God in Tyrannical Texts: Reflections on Paul, Women, and the Authority of Scripture* (Louisville: Westminster John Knox, 2015).
Gregg, J.	*Early Church Classics: The Epistle of St Clement* (London: SPCK, 1915).
Gregory, A.	'*1 Clement*: An Introduction', in P. Foster (ed.), *The Writings of the Apostolic Fathers* (London: T&T Clark, 2007), 21–31.
Haines-Eitzen, K.	*The Gendered Palimpsest: Women, Writing, and Representation in Early Christianity* (Oxford: Oxford University Press, 2012).
Horsley, R.	*1 Corinthians* (ANTC; Nashville: Abingdon, 1998).
Jefford, C.	*The Apostolic Fathers and The New Testament* (Peabody: Hendrickson, 2006).
Koester, H.	*From Jesus to the Gospels: Interpreting the New Testament in Its Context* (Minneapolis: Fortress, 2007).
Kraemer, R.S.	'Women's Judaism(s) at the Beginning of Christianity', in R.S. Kraemer & M.R. D'Angelo (eds.), *Women and Christian Origins* (Oxford: Oxford University Press, 1999), 50–79.
Krause, D.	*1 Timothy* (Readings: A New Biblical Commentary; London: T&T Clark, 2004).
LiDonnici, L.	'Women's Religious Lives in the Greco-Roman City', in R.S. Kraemer & M.R. D'Angelo (eds.), *Women and Christian Origins* (Oxford: Oxford University Press, 1999), 80–102.
Lightfoot, J.B.	*S. Clement of Rome: An Appendix containing the Newly Recovered Portions* (London: MacMillan, 1877).
Marshall, I.H.	*The Pastoral Epistles* (ICC; London: T&T Clark, 1999).
Mathew, S.	*Women in the Greetings of Romans 16.1–16* (Library of New Testament Studies, 471; London: Bloomsbury, T&T Clark, 2014).
Origen	*Commentary on the Gospel of John Books 13–32* (The Fathers of the Church A New Translation, 89; R.E. Heine, trans.; Washington: The Catholic University of America Press, 1993).

Schüssler Fiorenza, E. *In Memory of Her: A Feminist Theological Reconstruction of Christian Origins* (London: SCM, 1983).

Torjesen, K.J. *When Women Were Priests: Women's Leadership in the Early Church and the Scandal of their Subordination in the Rise of Christianity* (New York: HarperSanFrancisco, 1993).

Wire, A. *The Corinthian Women Prophets: A Reconstruction through Paul's Rhetoric* (Minneapolis: Fortress, 1995).

Witherington, B., III *Conflict and Community in Corinth: A Socio-Rhetorical Commentary on 1 and 2 Corinthians* (Grand Rapids: Eerdmans, 1995).

CHAPTER 7

From Passover to Covenant: Exploring the Symbolic Meaning of the Last Supper

Peter Laughlin

Abstract

Along with the shape of the cross, the Last Supper has become the Christian symbol *par excellence*. Every week throughout the world Christians partake of the 'body' and 'blood' of the Lord in an act that embodies the hope of Christian atonement, forgiveness, peace and reconciliation. Furthermore, this symbol has great significance for it is held to be *the* quintessential carrier of salvific meaning in the life of Jesus. And indeed, the words of the institution in which Jesus is said to have broken the bread and drunk from the cup both for the 'forgiveness of sins' and on behalf of 'many', do provide an apparent salvific inference. Yet the debate over the authenticity of these words suggests that the symbolic meaning of the meal should be given due consideration. The challenge is to discern how the meal itself should be understood and what meaning Jesus intended to create through its symbolic praxis. This paper explores this theme in the light of recent scholarly discussion.

Quickly finding its way into Christian tradition and practice, the last meal that Jesus had with his disciples is now a quintessential symbol of the Christian faith. Symbolically second only to the shape of the cross, the re-enactment of the Last Supper draws the participant into the death of Christ so that they might also share in his resurrected life (Rom. 8:17). At the forefront of the early Christian communities was the desire to eat the meal 'in remembrance of [Christ]' (1 Cor. 11:24), and such participation inevitably invoked a tapestry of meaning, both personally and corporately. Given the richness of the symbolism and the personal spirituality of participation, it didn't take long for the early church to explore that tapestry, interpreting the symbolism of the Last Supper in terms of a final sacrifice (Heb. 10:1–18), a new Passover and therefore a new exodus (1 Cor. 5:7), and an inauguration of a new covenant (Heb. 8). As a symbol, the Last Supper is more than capable of incorporating a range of meanings and in recognition of its true status as *sacramentum*, it somehow embodies the hope of Christian atonement, and the mystery of divine forgiveness, peace and reconciliation.

Herein lies the problem for those engaged in historical Jesus studies, particularly around the thorny issue of Jesus' intention for the Last Supper and its relationship to his impending death. The significant faith-shaped elements to the Last Supper accounts in Corinthians and the later Gospels seem to align very nicely, indeed, perhaps too nicely, with later Christian practice and belief. It can readily be argued that here the faith of the early church is more than likely to have been read back into the historical event and in so doing create a theological portrayal that goes well beyond what Jesus intended.[1] Even so, as Howard Marshall demonstrated almost 40 years ago, the liturgical tradition must be grounded in a historical event of some sort. In other words, there must have been a meal in the first place for stories about a meal to be told and developed.[2] And James Dunn concludes in his *Jesus Remembered*, that the story of the Last Supper was a living oral tradition 'well before it was ever written down in semi-formal or formal documentation'. And such a tradition he goes on to say, was 'remembered as begun by Jesus himself, and remembered thus from as early as we can tell'.[3] Such an argument, while not proving that the tradition aligns with what Jesus intended, nevertheless reliably suggests that there is something in the

---

[1] As Crossan argues, *The Historical Jesus*, 360–67. See also: Funk, *Honest to Jesus*, 226.
[2] Marshall, *Last Supper and Lord's Supper*, 34–35.
[3] Dunn, *Jesus Remembered*, 230.

Last Supper accounts that can be historically investigated.

But the fact that a meal took place does not automatically mean that there was meaning attached to it. Partaking of a meal is a frequent if not everyday activity and so the prior question as to *what* meaning Jesus may have intended that fateful night is whether it is likely that he chose to intend meaning in the first place. Perhaps it was just another meal during Passover week that unfortunately turned out to be Jesus' last. However, here contemporary scholarship displays somewhat of a consensus, accepting that Jesus did intend to leave his disciples with something to think about. Even Marcus Borg, who is quite sceptical of much of the Last Supper narrative, recognises that Jesus' recent actions in the temple had put him in grave danger, and so it is possible that fearing the worst, he 'may have spoken about his death'.[4] Indeed, given the temporal proximity of the meal to his arrest and crucifixion, if Jesus was ever planning to imbue his death with meaning, then one would expect to find it here. Perhaps this is why Luke has Jesus 'eagerly' looking forward to the meal (22:15), an attitude which suggests that he did intend to say, or to symbolise, something of importance. In the Gospel accounts, of course, it is the words of the institution that provide this import. Jesus is said to have broken the bread and to have drunk from the cup both for the 'forgiveness of sins' and on behalf of 'many' (Matt. 26:28; Mark 14:24). But the authenticity of these logia is hotly debated. Which brings us back to our fundamental problem. How much of Christian understanding and interpretation of these accounts was established by Jesus himself and how much was accreted through later Christian reflection? It is a thorny question and scholarship has tended to either assume 'nothing' or 'everything' depending upon where one falls along the hermeneutical and historiographical spectrum.

However, what I would like to take as axiomatic for the present discussion is that symbols and symbolic acts do provide a ready mechanism for the communication of meaning. This shouldn't be contentious inasmuch as we commonly ascribe meaning to symbolic acts as a part of everyday life. Gift-giving is an obvious example. In many ways what is symbolised by the act of giving surpasses the material of the gift itself.

---

4   Borg and Wright, *The Meaning of Jesus*, 87.

For instance, when I buy my wife flowers, is the gift an act of contrition or one of celebration? Both meanings could be true even though the gift is the same in each case. What makes one meaning true in any given situation is therefore not the fact of the gift, but the circumstances and intent that surround the event. This simple example demonstrates that communication of meaning goes beyond the mere data of what happened.

Thus, the fact that Jesus shared a meal with his disciples on the night before he died does not in itself tell us what Jesus meant that meal to mean. However, it does provide a context in which Jesus had an opportunity to intend meaning in his actions and to imbue his words with significance. Of course, we cannot simply assume that any meaning Jesus did intend to create for his last meal would nicely correlate to the faith of the early church. When it comes to Jesus' death we must always keep in mind Albert Schweitzer's conclusion that Jesus could have heroically thrown himself against the wheel of the world only to be unceremoniously crushed when it turned.[5] But what we can do is contend that Jesus did have an opportunity to imbue the Last Supper meal with meaning, whatever that meaning might turn out to be. As Ben Meyer said in his well-respected work *The Aims of Jesus*, 'Jesus did not aim to be repudiated and killed, he aimed to charge with meaning his being repudiated and killed'.[6]

So then, where to begin? What kind of meaning could Jesus have created for this, his last meal? Given that the Last Supper was remembered in the Synoptics as a Passover meal, we would do well to start our reflections there. Immediately, however, we are confronted with the question of the meal itself. Was it actually the Passover celebration? The problem is that in John's Gospel, Jesus dies at the very moment that the Passover lamb is being slaughtered (19:36) so how can the night before be the Passover meal, which is what the Synoptics claim? Traditionally the problem has been overcome with appeals to different calendars or other forms of ecclesiastical gymnastics, but modern scholars have concluded the problem is fundamentally unresolvable. That being the case, it seems to me that the preponderance of scholarly opinion is more

---

5   Schweitzer, *The Quest for the Historical Jesus*, 368–69. Schweitzer removed this image from his second edition.
6   Meyer, *The Aims of Jesus*, 218.

inclined to follow the Johannine chronology than the Synoptics and place the meal the night before Passover rather than on Passover itself. Of course, this goes against the grain of usual practice in which Markan priority is assumed, but the depths of the Johannine evidence here is quite convincing.[7]

In any case, as a week-long festival, there is little doubt that every meal would have been eaten with an awareness of the Passover festivities, and each meal would invoke the events for which the festival was remembered.[8] This is why James Dunn argues that despite recognisable liturgical development in each version of the Last Supper tradition, there is nonetheless a core memory of what Jesus said and did. And that core memory had to do with the Passover and exodus tradition. It is, therefore, not at all difficult to perceive Jesus anticipating the Paschal meal by one night, especially if he sensed that his own end was near.[9]

Particularly intriguing is the fact that there is no reference to the Passover *lamb* at all in the Last Supper accounts. Indeed, if the Passover lamb *was* available to Jesus at the meal then there is enormous significance in the fact that Jesus chose not to refer to it.[10] For example, had lamb been eaten, would not a saying such as 'this lamb is my body' better convey his sacrifice than the mere breaking of bread? Scot McKnight, in his work *Jesus and His Death*, acknowledges that this kind of comment is made from silence but on occasion 'silence is golden'. For McKnight, it is 'nearly incomprehensible' for Jesus to prefer bread over the lamb for his symbolism. Of course, such a concern becomes far less imposing if the meal itself was not the Passover meal and the absence of the lamb from Jesus' symbolic action is simply explained by the fact that it was not there to be utilized in the first place.

---

7   And likewise the copious problems that beset the alternative view. Brown, *Death of the Messiah*, 1350–76, esp. 1371–73. Recognizing this, recent scholarship concludes that Mark and hence both Matthew and Luke, have theologized a Passover week meal into the Passover meal itself. Raymond Brown surmises that Mark would have been well aware of the historical inconsistency this introduced but probably chose not to be concerned about it because the paschal characterization of the meal was already entrenched in liturgical theology.

8   McKnight, *Jesus and His Death*, 275. Chilton acknowledges this even though he argues that Jesus had no intention of invoking a Passover context. Chilton, *The Temple of Jesus*, 150 n.25.

9   According to Theissen and Mertz, the whole Last Supper setting implies 'a consciousness of imminent death' on the part of Jesus. Theissen and Mertz, *The Historical Jesus*, 430–31.

10 McKnight, *Jesus and His Death*, 270. Contra Wright, *Day the Revolution Began*, 185.

But there is a further consideration. For the Passover lamb was not a sacrifice for sins being neither a sacrifice (in the priestly sense) nor, indeed, for sins.[11] The original ritual was focused around the family and the home. As Belousek notes, 'the Passover lamb was slain not by the priest but by the family head; it was not offered on the temple altar but was eaten at the family table; and its blood was not poured out at the base of the temple altar but smeared on the doorposts and lintel of the family home'.[12] There is a stark difference then between the sacrifice of Passover and the Levitical sacrifices for atonement. Why then, did Jesus choose the feast of Passover to take his stand in the temple, the event which no doubt precipitated his death? To put it another way, if Jesus wanted to imbue an atoning significance in his last meal then why not choose a ready-made event such as the Day of Atonement or any of the Levitical sacrifices with all their redemptive symbolism?[13] The answer can only be that in some sense Jesus viewed the Passover as a better fit. This raises some important historical and theological questions that need to be answered if we are to have any hope of coming to grips with what Jesus thought he was doing.

Passover as Deliverance

To begin with, the feast of Passover was always about remembering God's *deliverance* of the nation. In Exodus 2:23–25 we read about the plight of Israel as they languished as slaves in Egypt: 'The people of Israel groaned under their bondage, and cried out for help, and their cry under bondage came up to God. And God heard their groaning, and God remembered his covenant with Abraham, with Isaac, and with Jacob. And God saw the people of Israel, and God knew their condition'. The result of God knowing their 'condition' was that God then acted through Moses to deliver Israel from Pharaoh's hand through 'many signs and wonders' (Deut. 4:34). At the end of his life, Moses reminds the Israelites that the very institution of Passover as a festival

---

11 Belousek, *Atonement, Justice, and Peace*, 160.
12 Belousek, *Atonement, Justice, and Peace*, 161.
13 This question is asked by N.T. Wright, *The Day the Revolution Began*, 170.

of remembrance had at its centre the need to recall God's saving action in delivering them from slavery (Deut. 16:1). Later Jewish reflection in the Psalms (80:8; 81:10; 135:9; 136:15) and Prophets (Jer. 2:6; 32:20; Dan. 9:15; Amos 2:6,10) highlight this deliverance aspect as well.

This remembrance of the exodus story provides a viable context for Jesus' own clashes with the established powers. Whether they are understood to be human forces (Rome or a recalcitrant Israel standing in for Pharaoh) or non-human powers (evil spirits in the place of the gods of Egypt), Jesus had a task that paralleled the work of Israel's God in liberating the nation. The parallels don't need to be typologically forced in order to be evident. There was once again a need for Israel to be delivered, only now that deliverance would take on an entirely new shape.

What changed was that in and through Jesus, the deliverance at hand was to be seen through the lens of the coming *Kingdom of God*. Much to the consternation of the disciples (Acts 1:6), the Kingdom was not a restored physical kingdom, but rather the breaking into the world of Kingdom authority. For John the Baptist that breaking in came with an expectation of judgement—directed primarily at the nation for her failure once again to be the light to the nations (Luke 3:8; c.f. Isa. 49:6), but along with judgement also came the hope of restoration. The Prophets had long announced that God would act to preserve both the covenant and election of Israel, not in order to return to the old ways but as a gateway to something new. The question is, what did restoration in the Kingdom look like, and how did it work to deliver God's people from bondage? For Wright the answer is a threefold taxonomy that encapsulates the story of Israel herself:

> We must stress, again, that this message [about the Kingdom] is part of a story, and only makes sense as such. And there is only one story that will do. Israel would at last 'return from exile'; evil would be defeated; YHWH would at last return to 'visit' his people. Anyone wishing to evoke and affirm all this at once, in first-century Palestine, could not have chosen a more appropriate and ready-made slogan than "kingdom of god".[14]

---

14   Wright, *Jesus and the Victory of God*, 227.

Much (metaphorical) ink has been spilt since Wright first proposed this understanding of the coming of the Kingdom and here is not the place to dissect it.[15] What is important for our present task is that both 'return from exile' and 'defeat of evil' are clearly exodus themes. Even the 'visitation of YHWH' arguably recalls the covenant made at Sinai which directly followed the exodus event. It can be contended then that in preaching the coming of the Kingdom, Jesus was promising something on the same level of Israel's greatest redemptive event. In some sense, deliverance was now at hand.

This is why there is no escaping the fact that in Jesus' preaching and ministry the Kingdom of God was already partially realised. The time had come, the hour was at hand in which the forces of this world would be overcome. Jesus says as much in his opening address at the synagogue in Nazareth. The Spirit of the Lord was on him, he says, because he was anointed to preach good news of liberation—to the poor, the prisoner, the blind and the oppressed. Now was the year of the Lord's favour to all who had ears to hear (Luke 4:18–19). That this message was not just for wayward Israel is make clear by the extension of such blessings to the gentiles (Matt. 8:5–13; Mark 7:24–30) and the proclamation that many from the 'East and West' would gather together to share in the feast with Abraham, Isaac, and Jacob in the Kingdom to come (Matt. 8:11). In other words, Jesus not only announced the kingdom to Israel but embodied it to the world. As Dunn concludes, Jesus was certain that God had a purpose for all of creation, and that his mission was an 'expression of that purpose and a vital agency towards its fulfilment'.[16]

But such a mission would come at a cost. This is ultimately seen in the Last Supper accounts and Jesus' submission to Calvary. But the connection of deliverance with trial was already foreshadowed as early as the Lord's Prayer. In Matthew 6 the invocation to be 'delivered from the evil [one]', firmly connects the coming of the Kingdom 'on earth as in heaven' with the hope of evil's defeat, or at least that one would be rescued from it. This final petition is absent from Luke's account (11:2–4) but the previous request to be spared from the trial of temptation is

---

15 See for example, Newman, *Jesus and the Restoration of Israel*.
16 Dunn, *Jesus Remembered*, 465.

well known to have its own eschatological import. Over fifty years ago, Jeremias argued quite successfully that 'temptation' (*periasmos*) was not just any temptation to befall humanity but the final ordeal in which evil would take its last stand before finally being defeated. But such a stand would severely test the saints:

> [It is] the final great Testing which stands at the door and will extend over the whole earth—the disclosure of the mystery of evil, the revelation of the Antichrist, the abomination of desolation (when Satan stands in God's place), the final persecution and testing of God's saints by pseudo-prophets and false saviours. What is in danger, is not moral integrity, but faith itself. The final trial at the end is—apostasy! Who can escape?[17]

But if the saints could endure then they would see the ultimate end of evil and be finally freed from its clutches. By including this petition in the *Pater Noster* what Jesus intends to communicate is a warning to those following him that such an end would only be preceded by a severe time of testing. A testing from which one was advised to petition for avoidance or escape, which is exactly what happened to the people of God in the exodus.[18]

Therefore, this message of freedom and liberation in the Kingdom closely matches that of the exodus story. As N.T. Wright puts it, 'What matters is that the *entire* Passover context made sense of the *entire* event that Jesus envisaged as he went up to Jerusalem for that final visit. Passover said, "Freedom-now!" and "Kingdom-now!"'.[19] Therefore, in proclaiming that the Kingdom had arrived in and through him, Jesus expected that a new-found freedom, or to put it another way, a new exodus was imminent.

What this means is that any meaning Jesus created for his death through the words of the institution and the symbolic breaking and sharing of the bread and wine must be situated within that wider

---

17 Jeremias, *The Prayers of Jesus*, 105–106.
18 See also, Pitrie, *Jesus, the Tribulation, and the End of Exile*. And Brown, 'The Pater Noster as an Eschatological Prayer', 314–16.
19 Wright, *Day the Revolution Began*, 181.

Passover and Kingdom context. Indeed, it readily allows Jesus to draw upon elements of the great exodus story in the creation of meaning for his own death.

From Exodus to Covenant

In considering the Last Supper from the perspective of Passover, a number of significant points can be made. Firstly, despite not having lamb to draw upon, the use of bread to refer to Jesus' body is not without meaning. In Deuteronomy 16:3 the unleavened bread of the Passover is called the 'bread of affliction' because it reminds the people of their suffering in Egypt. Therefore, by connecting his body with the bread of affliction, Jesus may well find in the suffering of Egypt an analogy of his own suffering soon to be experienced. And such a point links the bread to Jesus' death even if the symbolic act of breaking the bread somehow went unnoticed. But the startling, if not shocking element of the meal, is that the bread (and later the cup representing Jesus' blood) is given to the disciples to eat (and drink).[20] The bread of affliction is not broken in abstract but is to be ingested by the believing community so that they might share in the death of Jesus and thereby gain its benefits. This is constitutively new, for the unleavened bread of the Passover is not consumed for its redemptive benefits even if it acquired some form of redemptive significance by virtue of it being an exodus meal. Hence, McKnight contends that having made the identification between his body and the bread, Jesus creates new meaning by offering himself to his followers in order to further offer them the protection of a sacrificial death.[21] The breaking of the bread represents the slaughter of the lamb and evokes the apotropaic (protective) function of the sacrifice.[22] It is, therefore, by Jesus' death that his disciples will be redeemed from affliction and God will pass over them at the time of judgement. In

---

20 McKnight dismisses any suggestion that the disciples would have understood Jesus' statement literally. Such 'unimaginative cannibalistic interpretation[s]' deny the metaphorical power of the symbol. *Jesus and His Death*, 283.
21 McKnight, *Jesus and His Death*, 281.
22 Sabourin and Lyonnet, *Sin, Redemption and Sacrifice*, 171. Also Young, *The Use of Sacrificial Ideas in Greek Christian Writers*, 44.

such a context then, Jesus' death is not only about forgiveness or even atonement, it is about protection.[23]

The cup, which Jesus likens to his own blood, continues the apotropaic theme (as the disciples in turn identify themselves with it), but the words of the institution also connect the cup to the theme of *covenant*. Care must, however, be exercised in determining what covenant connotations are actually present in the symbolism of the cup. The primary reason for this concern arises from the demonstrable *lack* of overt covenant connections with the paschal tradition in Jewish literature. We cannot simply elide the two images together for the significance of the Passover was not construed in covenantal terms.[24] The blood of the paschal lamb, shed for its protective benefits (Exod. 12), does not directly parallel the blood of the bulls, shed to inaugurate the covenant (Exod. 24). The functions and effects of the blood were not the same.

This does not mean, of course, that a covenant connection is untenable, for all four versions of the meal comment that what Jesus offered that night was indeed the cup of the covenant. In fact, for Luke (22:20) and Paul (1 Cor. 11:25) it is the cup of the *new* covenant, a qualification intended to recall the actions of Moses in establishing the first covenant while simultaneously insisting that God was doing something new. This theme was taken up elsewhere by Paul (Gal. 4:24; 2 Cor. 3) and figured prominently in Hebrews (8:1–13; 9:15). So the question is not whether covenant is an appropriate theme by which to understand Jesus' actions, but whether it was Jesus himself who first constituted the connection.

Contrary to Wright, McKnight takes the view that Jesus did *not* constitute the connection himself.[25] The covenant imagery was certainly appropriated by the early Christian community and it became foundational for its Eucharistic celebration but McKnight argues that the connection did not originate with Jesus.[26] Determinative in this regard is the fact that it is only here, in the Last Supper tradition, that the explicit

---

23 As previously noted, the Passover and Paschal lamb were not considered atoning in the Levitical sense. The closest the events of the Passover come to an atoning interpretation is in connection with the Akedah of Isaac. See *Jub.* 17:15–18:19; 49:15. See also the discussion in Sabourin and Lyonnet, *Sin, Redemption and Sacrifice*, 265.
24 As McKnight successfully demonstrates; *Jesus and His Death*, 306–08.
25 Wright, *Jesus*, 554–63, esp. 561. Dunn, *Jesus Remembered*, 816. Meyer, *The Aims of Jesus*, 219.
26 McKnight, *Jesus and His Death*, 306–12.

concept of covenant emerges. Prior to this point the central theme of Jesus' ministry is the Kingdom of God and there is no direct suggestion in Jesus' teaching that the concept of kingdom is coupled with that of covenant. Indeed, covenant terminology is notably absent from Jesus' preaching,[27] which is why when it suddenly occurs here in the Last Supper accounts it has the appearance of being an 'unexpected innovation'.[28] It simply does not fit within the wider context of his ministry. In a similar vein, McKnight points out that the Last Supper does not take the form of a covenant ceremony, there is no oath taking (*contra* Exod. 24:7), the 'blood' is not sprinkled on the disciples nor is a commitment to the new covenant elicited. Thus, he concludes that if Jesus really was 'setting forth a new covenant, he does so without specifying it as a covenant'.[29] In other words, if Jesus was intending to imbue the Last Supper with a covenantal significance then he went about it in a very subdued way.

One cannot counter this argument with an appeal to the authenticity of the word 'covenant' either. Scholarship displays little consensus in this regard and the authenticity of the term is denied just as often as it is affirmed.[30] Therefore, McKnight is not alone when he contends that we can viably understand Jesus to have said 'this is my blood,' as a simple parallel to 'this is my body'.[31] Accordingly, the addition of 'covenant' to the phrase would have its origins in the understanding of the early church who found in Jesus' death and resurrection the reality of a new corporate existence.

It must be said that McKnight argues his case well, though it seems that the present weight of biblical scholarship contends *for* the authenticity of a covenant connection despite the lack of confidence in the term's exact origin.[32] Predominantly, the question is asked as to whether the early church would have made so much of the covenant typology—especially in its burgeoning liturgy—if it had not first been constituted

---

27 Holmén, 'Jesus, Judaism and the Covenant', 26.
28 McKnight, *Jesus and His Death*, 310.
29 McKnight, *Jesus and His Death*, 310.
30 Holmén, 'Jesus, Judaism and the Covenant', 5.
31 McKnight, *Jesus and His Death*, 310.
32 Aside from Wright, Dunn, and Meyer, one can also note Marshall, *Last Supper and Lord's Supper*, 91–93; Sanders and Davies, *Studying the Synoptic Gospels*, 329; and cautiously, Allison, 'Jesus and the Covenant', 65–66.

by Jesus himself. Also, despite overt connections not being present, there are arguably *implicit* connections between Passover and covenant within Second Temple Judaism. As Wright contends, to invoke the exodus tradition is to imply covenant renewal and not just because the dispensation of the Mosaic covenant occurs immediately following the exodus event.[33] In fact, if we are to bring in Wright's threefold taxonomy at this point, an argument can be made that the concept of return from exile connects with the notion of a new covenant through the lens of 'forgiveness for sins'. The argument depends upon three connections being made. The first is between the concepts of exodus and return from exile; the second between exodus/return and forgiveness of sins; and the third between exodus/return and covenant renewal.

The first is readily demonstrated through an analysis of historical texts such as Ezra and Nehemiah and the prophetic text of Jeremiah 30 in particular. It has long been argued that Ezra-Nehemiah presents a narrative intended to be understood as a second exodus.[34] As when leaving Egypt, the exiles returned bearing gold and goods (Ezra 1:4; Exod. 11:2; 12:35–36); the census of Ezra 2:1–67 recalls the census in Numbers (1:1–54); the free will offerings for the temple in Ezra 2:68–69 mirror those in the desert (Exod. 25:2–9; 35:21–29); and after receiving the law, the people celebrated the feast of booths (Ezra 3:4) in the same way that the Israelites did at Sinai. But the prophecy in Jeremiah 30:8–9 is even more direct, in which it is said that no longer will Israel be enslaved by foreigners. Yokes will be broken from their necks and their bonds will be torn off with the resulting freedom enabling Israel to once again serve the Lord their God. The promised restoration of Israel is here strikingly portrayed in exodus terms.

Two chapters later, Jeremiah also points to the second of these connections, that between return from exile and forgiveness of sins. 'For this is what the Lord, the God of Israel, says ... I will bring Judah and Israel back from captivity and will rebuild them as they were before. I will cleanse them from all the sin they have committed against me and will forgive all their sins of rebellion against me' (Jer. 33:4, 7–8). Likewise,

---

33 For Wright, to invoke the exodus tradition implies covenant renewal. Wright, *Jesus*, 557, 560.
34 Koch, 'Ezra and the Origins of Judaism', 173–97.

in Ezekiel 36:24–26: 'For I will take you out of the nations; I will gather you from all the countries and bring you back into your own land. I will sprinkle clean water on you, and you will be clean. I will cleanse you from all your impurities and from all your idols'. The connection between returning from exile and forgiveness is clear, but what of the exodus itself? Is the redemption in Exodus ever seen in terms of divine forgiveness? Moses suggests as much when he pleads with the Lord to 'forgive the sin of these people, just as you have pardoned them from the time they left Egypt until now' (Num. 14:19). The point being that the exodus signalled the arrival of a divine pardon, a pardon that was now potentially coming under threat because of Israel's wilful disobedience. Moreover, the notion of redemption being linked to forgiveness is commonly seen (e.g. 2 Chr. 6:25; Neh. 9:17; Psalm 130:7–8; Isa. 44:22) so much so that if redemption is taking place, then it can be taken for granted that forgiveness has also occurred. God does not redeem those for whom sins are still being judged (Isa. 40:1–2; Jer. 18:23; Hos. 1:6).

Finally, the connection between exodus/return and covenant renewal is also well attested. Jeremiah 31:31–34 makes the link as clear as it needs to be:

> Behold, the days are coming, declares the LORD, when I will make a new covenant with the house of Israel and the house of Judah, not like the covenant that I made with their fathers on the day when I took them by the hand to bring them out of the land of Egypt, my covenant that they broke, though I was their husband, declares the LORD. For this is the covenant that I will make with the house of Israel after those days, declares the LORD: I will put my law within them, and I will write it on their hearts. And I will be their God, and they shall be my people. [34] And no longer shall each one teach his neighbour and each his brother, saying, 'Know the LORD', for they shall all know me, from the least of them to the greatest, declares the LORD. For I will forgive their iniquity, and I will remember their sin no more.

The connections here between the exodus, forgiveness and new covenant are striking.

If we apply these themes then to the ministry of Jesus, we can see that the exorcisms, the healings, and the prophetic claim to fulfil Isaiah 61, places the entirety of Jesus' ministry within the ongoing framework of God's redemptive activity. And that activity must involve in some way a new exodus, a confirmation of forgiveness and the establishment of a covenant relationship between God and God's people. The Last Supper intriguingly brings all these elements to bear. As Wright notes:

> But the mention of "blood" right beside "covenant" strongly suggests that the primary meaning has to do with the covenant renewal spoken of in Jeremiah 31, which refers to the original covenant ceremony in Exodus 24:3–8. [...] The central meaning ought to be clear. Jesus had spoken and acted throughout his public career as if he believed it was his vocation to be the agent of the great renewal, the great new-covenant moment that had been promised ever since Deuteronomy 30 and referred to one way or another in many prophecies and psalms. It should be no surprise that, as he saw his career drawing to its shocking end, he would speak explicitly about this moment of covenant renewal. What is startling is that he would associate it so directly with his own death, that he would refer to his own blood as if it were like the sacrificial blood of the animals in Exodus 24.[35]

This line of reasoning demonstrates that an invocation of the Passover tradition, when viewed in the context of the coming Kingdom of God, requires a corresponding expectation of covenant renewal. Liberation would not be complete without a renewed relationship with YHWH established. The two events go hand in hand: just as redemption from Egypt was followed by the Mosaic covenant, so now redemption through Jesus' protective sacrifice would be followed by the establishment of a new covenant.[36] Importantly, the impetus of what Jesus constitutes here is not how and why his death would achieve this new covenant, but simply in the reality of its very existence.

---

35 Wright, *The Day the Revolution Began*, 187–188.
36 Tan, 'Community, Kingdom and Cross', 145.

A significant point of issue remains though, for if in the Last Supper Jesus did intend to inaugurate a new covenant through his death, then he does so without recourse to the central means of Jewish atonement—the temple.[37] That is, Jesus offers his disciples membership of the new covenant on an alternative basis to that of the temple cult. This is why Wright is correct to insist that the Last Supper and temple action must mutually interpret each other and are therefore to be taken together in the constitution of meaning.[38] 'What Jesus did in the Temple, interpreted (as seems most likely) as a Jeremiah-like symbolic prediction of its forthcoming destruction, must have had to do in some way with his aim of declaring that Israel's God, returning to his people at last, had found the Temple sadly wanting and was establishing something different instead'.[39]

Here Wright suggests that Jesus not only symbolised the future destruction of the Temple but also, in looking to the Last Supper, intended to establish a new way of coming into the presence of God Most High. Not that Jesus viewed the Mosaic dispensation a failure—after all, it had been a God-ordained order—he was, however, convinced that God was doing something new in, and through, him.[40] And there is little doubt that Jesus considered the Last Supper to be symbolic of what God was doing. The eschatological nature of the meal is well recognized and Jesus' apparent eagerness to eat of it indicates a strong desire for the reign of God to come (Luke 22:15). Therefore, at the forefront of Jesus' mind is not the meal itself but the constituted meaning it signifies. Jesus perceives that his suffering and death, represented by the bread and cup, are elements of the eschatological work of a new exodus and a new covenant that God is inaugurating.[41] What we need to conclude then, is that it is not the *meal* that would ultimately displace the

---

37 Wright, *Jesus*, 557.
38 Wright, *Jesus*, 561.
39 Wright, *Day the Revolution Began*, 181.
40 As Stuhlmacher notes, the problem for Jesus was not that the temple cult had failed, the problem was that salvation was now dependent on 'accepting God's new eschatological act of election, represented by Jesus'. Stuhlmacher, *Jesus of Nazareth*, 31 n.41. See also Meyer, *The Aims of Jesus*, 218.
41 This connection can be inferred from the more widely attested refusal to drink again of the fruit of the vine until the coming of the Kingdom (Matt 26:29; Mark 14:24; Luke 22:18). This was an implicit promise of table fellowship beyond death and demonstrates that Jesus combined his expectation of death with the coming of the Kingdom. Meyer, *The Aims of Jesus*, 218.

temple in the eschatological Kingdom, but *Jesus' own death*.⁴² Anthony Bartlett reads Wright well here:

> With the destruction of the Temple pronounced, Jesus would offer in its place, a new construction of the central rite of the Jewish people, the Passover, together with its governing story, the Exodus. *This construction took the old symbols and recast them around his own anticipated death.* But perhaps because the looked-for result was not simply another religious ritual (and a religion with it), but a new human reality, YHWH's Kingdom, Wright is careful to specify that the Eucharist is a quasi-cultic meal. In other words, the eschatological reality it looks toward comes close to overwhelming the cultic aspects, while still allowing them enough purchase to act as metaphors for this radically new event.⁴³

Therefore, what Jesus is doing in the Last Supper is drawing upon the stories of the Passover, exodus, and covenant and stunningly connecting them to his own body and blood, that is, his own death. This is undoubtedly constitutively new, a creation of meaning for Jesus' death that until this point had not been disclosed. Previously, the promise of releasing people from spiritual and physical bondage had been potently displayed through his ministry practice, but now we find it expressed in terms of Israel's greatest release—the exodus. What God had done before he was now dramatically doing again. But this time participation in the exodus was not on the basis of national identity but was open to all those who participated in partaking of the bread and wine and thereby shared in his suffering and death.

Finally, reference must be made to the salvific significance given to the cup in the Synoptic accounts. As one might expect, the authenticity of the phrases 'forgiveness of sins' and 'poured out for many' is debated with many concluding that they are reflective of the tradition's

---

42   Wright, *Jesus*, 558.
43   Bartlett, *Cross Purposes*, 218. Emphasis mine.

development of understanding rather than the words of Jesus.⁴⁴ But even if they are rejected as the words of Jesus there remains an inherent redemptive symbolism within the Last Supper account that must be recognized. In drawing upon both the exodus and covenant traditions, Jesus symbolically creates redemptive meaning for his suffering and death that includes the concept of divine forgiveness. Because of this, the comments are not alien to Jesus' constituted meaning and the tradition may very well, as Wright suggests, be reflecting the meaning of the meal, even if the words themselves cannot be directly attributable to Jesus.⁴⁵

These reflections on the Last Supper arise out of an appreciation for the transformation of meaning that confronted the disciples on that particular evening. Jesus' actions with the bread and wine and the appropriation of the Passover context on a night which was not actually Passover, challenged the disciples' expectations and their understanding of redemption within the covenant nation. Likewise, they continue to challenge us. In a world in which atonement is often understood as the result of a divine transaction, the climax of the Passover in the life of Jesus provides a needed and welcome point of reflection.

Dr Peter Laughlin
Australian College of Ministries
plaughlin@acom.edu.au

---

44 The Matthean 'forgiveness of sins' (Matt 26:28) is particularly dismissed as a redaction of his Markan reading though Wright is willing to give the phrase some currency because it ties in well with his forgiveness of sins = return from exile theme. *Jesus*, 561. We should note that Wright does not suggest that the words are Jesus', but he does argue that in them Matthew has captured the symbolic meaning of the meal. McKnight dismisses the words as does Dunn, but Meyer is prepared to give them a hearing. McKnight, *Jesus and His Death*, 305. Dunn, *Jesus Remembered*, 231. Meyer, *The Aims of Jesus*, 219.
45 Wright, *Jesus*, 561.

Bibliography

Allison, D.C. — 'Jesus and the Covenant: A Response to E. P. Sanders', *Journal for the Study of the New Testament* 29 (1987), 57–78.

Bartlett, A.W. — *Cross Purposes: The Violent Grammar of Christian Atonement* (Harrisburg: Trinity Press International, 2001).

Belousek, D.W.S. — *Atonement, Justice, and Peace: The Message of the Cross and the Mission of the Church* (Grand Rapids: Eerdmans, 2012).

Borg, M.J., and N.T. Wright. — *The Meaning of Jesus: Two Visions* (San Francisco: HarperSanFrancisco, 1999).

Brown, R.E. — *The Death of the Messiah: From Gethsemane to the Grave*. Vol. 1. (New York: Doubleday, 1994).

———. — 'The Pater Noster as an Eschatological Prayer', in *New Testament Essays* (New York: Image Books, 1968), 275–320.

Chilton, B. — *The Temple of Jesus: His Sacrificial Program within a Cultural History of Sacrifice* (Pennsylvania: Pennsylvania State University Press, 1992).

Crossan, J.D. — *The Historical Jesus: The Life of a Mediterranean Jewish Peasant* (New York: Harper Collins, 1992).

Dunn, J.D.G. — *Jesus Remembered. Christianity in the Making*. Vol. 1 (Grand Rapids: Eerdmans, 2003).

Funk, R. W., and R. W. Hoover. — *The Five Gospels: The Search for the Authentic Words of Jesus* (Sonoma: Polebridge Press, 1993).

Holmén, T. — 'Jesus, Judaism and the Covenant', *Journal for the Study of the Historical Jesus* 2.1 (2004), 3–27.

Jeremias, J. — *The Prayers of Jesus* (London: SCM, 1967).

Koch, K. — 'Ezra and the Origins of Judaism', *Journal of Semitic Studies* 19 (1974), 173–97.

Marshall, I.H. — *Last Supper and Lord's Supper* (Carlisle, UK: Paternoster, 1980).

McKnight, S. — *Jesus and His Death: Historiography, the Historical Jesus, and Atonement Theory* (Waco: Baylor University Press, 2005).

Meyer, B.F. — *The Aims of Jesus* (London: SCM, 1979).

Newman, C.C. (ed.) *Jesus and the Restoration of Israel: A Critical Assessment of N.T. Wright's Jesus and the Victory of God* (Downers Grove: InterVarsity Press, 1999).

Pitre, B. *Jesus, the Tribulation, and the End of Exile: Restoration Eschatology and the Origin of the Atonement* (Grand Rapids: Baker Academic, 2006).

Sabourin, L., and S. Lyonnet. *Sin, Redemption and Sacrifice: A Biblical and Patristic Study* (Rome: Biblical Institute Press, 1970).

Sanders, E. P., and M. Davies. *Studying the Synoptic Gospels* (London: SCM, 1989).

Schweitzer, A. *The Quest of the Historical Jesus: A Critical Study of its Progress from Reimarus to Wrede* (W. Montgomery, trans.; London: Adam & Charles Black, 1948 [1906]).

Stuhlmacher, P. *Jesus of Nazareth—Christ of Faith* (S.S. Schatzmann, trans.; Peabody: Hendrickson, 1988).

Tan, K.H. 'Community, Kingdom and Cross: Jesus' View of Covenant', in J.A. Grant & A.I. Wilson (eds.), *The God of Covenant: Biblical, Theological and Contemporary Perspectives* (Leicester: Apollos, 2005), 122–55.

Theissen, G., and A. Mertz. *The Historical Jesus: A Comprehensive Guide* (London: SCM, 1998).

Wright, N.T. *The Day the Revolution Began: Reconsidering the Meaning of Jesus's Crucifixion* (New York: HarperOne, 2016).

———. *Jesus and the Victory of God. Christian Origins and the Question of God.* Vol. 2 (Minneapolis: Fortress, 1996).

Young, F.M. *The Use of Sacrificial Ideas in Greek Christian Writers from the New Testament to John Chrysostom* (*Patristic Monograph Series* 5; Philadelphia: Philadelphia Patristic Foundation, 1979).

CHAPTER 8

St Cyril of Alexandria on the Eucharistic Context of Humankind's Union with the Divine in *Commentary on John*

Wagdy Samir

Abstract

In his *Commentary on the Gospel of St John*, St Cyril of Alexandria develops his theology of progressive human participation in the divine. I focus on the eucharistic dimension of humankind's union with the divine. I show that for St Cyril communicants partake of the real, vivifying flesh of the Word. Eucharistic participation leads to humankind's dual sanctification, spiritual and corporeal. Sanctification is *sine qua non* for believers' union with Jesus Christ. In turn, union is achieved through the interplay of two aspects, divine action and human response. I will also show that for St Cyril, although the eucharistic union resembles the Christological reality of the hypostatic union, it is not identical. Humankind participates in the divine life, whereas the divine, the participated in, is life by nature. Throughout, I demonstrate that St Cyril's language points to the physicality of the presence of Christ in the eucharist, and of the communicant's participation in it, thus showing the degree of intimacy with the partaker, beyond moral union. Finally, my conclusion will point to the significance of St Cyril's eucharistic theology in his construct of Christ's profile.[1]

1. Introduction

That Cyril acknowledged the sanctifying power of the eucharist in *On John*[2] is indisputable.[3] However, essential for appreciating his eucharistic theology is to understand what, for him, makes the body and blood of Christ vivifying, how do believers who partake of it truly transform, and in what manner they do that. In this paper, I attempt to systematise his eucharistic theology in the context of holy life, thus providing a coherent synthesis of otherwise diverse and varied material. I am quite aware that Cyril is not a systematic theologian by any modern standards, thus, all care is taken to avoid imputing to him what he did not say. Although my focus is on his *On John*, to examine the consistency of his teaching below I refer to some of his other writings as well, against the backdrop of relevant scholarly takes on his eucharistic theology. Above all, I present my findings in the light of his views of what humankind achieves through eucharistic participation.

The flow of my argument is as follows. According to Cyril, what believers partake of at the holy tables is the real, vivifying flesh of the Word. Consequently, the eucharist has a 'realistic' effect on those who partake of it. It produces a dual sanctification, spiritual and corporeal, by which the partakers achieve union with Jesus Christ. This union is similar to but not identical to the hypostatic union. My analysis focuses on three intertwined dimensions. First, I consider the nature of the eucharist and its effects on those who partake of it. This enquiry establishes the foundation for the rest of the analysis. Second, I examine

---

[1] I am very grateful for the generous assistance from my supervisor, Dr Fr Doru Costache, who has reviewed multiple versions of this paper.

[2] When referring to St Cyril's *Commentary on the Gospel of John*, unless otherwise stated, I will use Pusey, *Commentary on the Gospel According to St John*; and Randell, *Commentary on the Gospel According to St John*. I refer to the source as follows: *On John* 11.9$^{II:531-2}$, where *On John* 11.9 means book 11, chapter 9 and the superscript II:531–32 denotes Volume II: pages 531–32. However, at times, I will slightly modify the translation to avoid antiquated terminology. In some cases, I will refer to the critical edition of Pusey in Greek, and will clearly indicate when this is the case by referring to it as follows: (Pusey Volume.Pages.Lines).

[3] See, for example, *On John* 3.4$^{I:347}$ and *On John* 4.2$^{I:418}$.

the aspect of dual sanctification. I address the manner by which the eucharist operates and is received, whether spiritually or corporeally, or both. I specifically examine the interplay between the divine bestowal of holiness and humankind's appropriation of it. Third, I examine the notion of humankind's union with the divine through the partaking of the sacrament, while highlighting the difference between the eucharistic and hypostatic unions. Together, the three dimensions contribute a complex understanding of the role the eucharist plays in partakers' attainment of holy life.

The fact of the matter is that, for Cyril, there is another way of knowing Christ, who is mediated not just by Scripture as such, but by the Word incarnate in his eucharistic body.

2. The Nature and Effects of the Eucharist

If the eucharist leads to union with Christ, then it is important to investigate how did Cyril represent the nature of the eucharist. Of what do believers partake? Is it, as some scholars posited, the virtue and gift of the body and blood as represented by the bread and wine, or, as others have argued, the body and blood of Christ? Once partaken of, what are the efficacies of the eucharist? In tackling this matter, I do not aim to be exhaustive, but rather to provide the foundation upon which I build my argument in sections 2 and 3 of this paper.

a. The Nature of the Eucharist

Mahé classified scholarly research undertaken before 1907 into the nature of the eucharist in Cyril's writings into two groups.[4] The first group consists of Steitz, Michaud, and Harnack, who believed that Cyril did not teach the material presence of the body and blood of Christ in the eucharist, but rather the dynamic or spiritual presence and virtue of the body. The second group consists of Baur, Thomasius, and Batiffol, who argued the substantial transformation of the bread and wine into the real body and blood of Christ. Mahé's own conclusion,

---

4   Mahé, 'L'eucharistie', 677–79.

after analysing texts from Cyril's corpus, agreed with the second group that Cyril's doctrine of the eucharist affirms the real presence of Christ's flesh[5] in the sacrament.

When commenting on the abovementioned debate, McGuckin pointed out that while earlier studies on Cyril's eucharistic theology were influenced by the Roman Catholic-Protestant eucharistic controversy, and, therefore, on the notion of change of elements, to him the debate has been settled in terms of the realism of the eucharist in Cyrilline theology.[6] Gebremedhin in his seminal work on the eucharistic doctrine of Cyril spoke of the physical presence of Christ's body and blood in the eucharist.[7] Louth asserted that in the eucharist the bread and wine become the Word's own flesh and blood.[8] Welch recognised in Cyril's theology the explicit conversion of the bread and wine into the body and blood of Christ.[9] Boulnois was baffled that some scholars had any doubt about the realism of the eucharist in Cyril's teachings.[10] In the same vein, to Keating, Cyril's eucharistic theology is straightforward—what is partaken of in the eucharist is the very flesh of Christ that through the ineffable union with the Word has become life-giving.[11] Concannon concluded that the debate has been settled in favour of the 'substantial, corporeal presence' of the body and blood of Christ in Cyril's eucharistic theology.[12]

Having reviewed the relevant scholarship, hereafter I examine Cyril's own exposition and argue in favour of the scholars who advocate the realism of the bread and wine in his eucharistic theology.[13] My argument

---

5   When using the word "flesh," I mean the whole of the human being or the whole of Christ, depending on the context. See, for example, Cyril's definition in *On John* 5.2[1:564] where he states, "in the word flesh we signify the whole humankind." The Greek original is: ἐν τῷ τῆς σαρκὸς ὀνόματι τὸν πάντα δηλοῦμεν ἄνθρωπον (Pusey 1.713.12).
6   McGuckin, 'Saint Cyril of Alexandria's Theology of the Eucharist', 54, n.6; and McGuckin, *Saint Cyril of Alexandria*, 187, 188.
7   Gerbremedhin, *Life-Giving Blessing*, 36, 65, 69–70, 84.
8   Louth, 'The Use of the Term ἴδιος', 201.
9   Welch, *Christology and Eucharist*, 124–28.
10 Boulnois, 'L'eucharistie', 149–50.
11 Keating, *Appropriation*, 68, 69–71.
12 Concannon, 'Eucharist', 319.
13 The realism of the bread and blood on the holy tables is not unique to Cyril. Athanasius also advocates the same position, highlighting that once the Word descends on the bread and cup, they become Christ's body. See *Or. Ad baptiz* (PG 26, 1325C), cited by Gebremedhin, *Life-Giving Blessing* 62.

draws upon passages from *On John* and from his other writings.

Commenting on the bread-of-life discourse in John 6, Cyril speaks of the bread being the true bread-of-life; namely, the flesh of Christ and thus Jesus himself.[14] He paraphrases Christ's words by stating that 'he that eats of this bread, that is me, or my flesh, shall live forever'.[15] Ultimately, the believers 'receive Jesus'.[16] For Cyril, Christ is life, and if the bread partaken of in the eucharist is the true bread-of-life, it then is Christ himself. The fact that he specifically iterates that this bread 'is me (Christ)' and 'my (Christ's) flesh' is another reason to impute the transformation of the bread and wine to being the body and blood of Christ. However, Cyril, in *On John*, does not explain how the bread and wine are transformed into Christ's body and blood.[17]

Despite the implicit reference to the transformation of the bread and wine in the above passages (and elsewhere in *On John*), one cannot miss the possibility that the abovementioned argument could still be pointing to the virtues of Christ's flesh rather than the flesh itself. Thus, one needs to seek further clarifications concerning the nature of the eucharist. This entails looking outside of *On John*.

Commenting on Luke 22:17-22 (the last supper), Cyril has this to say about the transformation of the bread and wine offerings:

> For lest we should be terrified by seeing (actual) flesh and blood placed upon the holy tables of our churches, God, humbling himself to our infirmities (weaknesses), infuses into the things set before us the power of life, and transforms them into the efficacy of his flesh, that we may have them for a life-giving participation, and that the body of (him who is the) life may be found in us as a life-producing seed.[18]

---

14 *On John* – Book 3.4 till Book 4.4 (pages 312–457).
15 *On John* 4.2$^{1:408}$. See also, *On John* 11.9$^{II:523}$.
16 *On John* 4.2$^{I:418}$. Clarifying these words, Cyril goes on to say "For he is life by nature [...] no less quickening is his body also, being in a manner gathered and ineffably united with the all-quickening World."
17 Keating reaches the same conclusion. See Keating, *Appropriation*, 68.
18 *On Luke* 2.142 (668), in Smith, *Commentary on the Gospel According to S. Luke*. I refer to the source as follows: *On Luke* Part Number.Sermon Number (Page Numbers).

The above passage explicitly describes the transformation of the bread and wine into the actual flesh and blood of Christ. The fact that partakers do not see the actual flesh and blood, he argues, is to protect them from being terrified at the sight of the mystery.[19] Cyril ends his argument by urging believers not to have any doubt since Christ himself said 'this is my body' and 'this is my blood', and he does not lie.[20]

The same affirmation of the bread and wine being 'truly changed' by God into the body and blood of Christ appears in Cyril's Commentary on Matthew.[21] Here, again, he instructs the communicants not to think of the visible offerings on the holy tables as a type. Elsewhere, he is again quoted saying that the vivifying eucharist is the real body of Christ.[22] The fact that after the incarnation Christ ascended with his own flesh to the Father points to the necessity of the flesh for humankind's salvation, and hence he gave participants his own body and his own blood in the eucharist.[23] In his third letter to Nestorius, he reaffirms the same argument by insisting that what participants receive is the personal, truly vivifying flesh of God the Word himself.[24]

Finally, Cyril clearly argues Christ's presence in the eucharist in his discourse against Nestorius. Nestorius maintained that it is the flesh of the Lord not his divinity that participants eat in the sacrament.[25] In response, Cyril points out that this reduces the sacrament to pure cannibalism, while at the same time refuting that participants partake of the divinity as such, rather stressing that what is partaken of is the flesh united to the Word, and hence to the indivisible Word.[26] The eucharist is the 'truly vitalizing flesh of God the Word himself'.[27] By separating

---

19   It is interesting to point out that the same argument appears as a lesson by Abba Daniel in Ward, *The Sayings*, 53. The similarity shows either a common source or a connection between Cyril and the desert father, or both.
20   *On Luke* 2.142 (668).
21   *fr. Mt.* 289. 5–12, 17–19 (Reuss, *Matthaüs–Kommentare*, 255) cited in Davis, *Coptic Christology*, 43. The word for 'changed' quoted in Greek is μεταποιεσθαι.
22   *PG 68*, 501B. Cited in Mahé, 'L'eucharistie', 687.
23   Cyril's commentary on Matthew 26:26–28 (*PG* 72, 452B; Reuss 290, p. 256, l. 3–13). Cited by Boulnois, 'L'eucharistie', 150, n.9.
24   *Third Letter* 7; Wickham p.23.
25   Russell, *Cyril of Alexandria*, 167–68.
26   Russell, *Cyril of Alexandria*, 168–69; Gebremedhin, *Life-Giving Blessing*, 69–70; and McKinion, *Words*, 207.
27   *Third Letter to Nestorius*. Cited by Concannon, 'Eucharist', 322, 326.

Christ into two persons, Nestorius not only misinterpreted the incarnation, he also ridiculed the eucharist.[28] What is present in Christ's own flesh and in the eucharistic body is not just the flesh, but also the person of Christ as God incarnate (this notion is explored further in section 3 below, when I discuss the dual sanctification through the eucharist). As Boulnois noted, to separate the divinity from the humanity of the Word is to destroy the efficacies of the eucharist.[29]

After the examination of various passages from Cyril's writings, one can confidently agree with Mahé and other scholars regarding the real presence of Christ's flesh in the eucharist. What is partaken of in the eucharist is the indivisible Christ. Cyril's eucharistic theology points out that it is through the hypostatic union of the two natures that humankind is vivified. Any deviation from this fact renders the eucharist ineffective. This is because it is through the real presence of Christ in the sacrament that partakers are granted eternal life and become partakers of the divine as discussed below.

b. The Effects of the Eucharist

Cyril discusses the effects of the eucharist on believers who partake of it repeatedly, in *On John* and other writings, which makes the task of listing them very difficult. But one can locate some common themes. Partaking of the eucharist grants believers: eternal life,[30] incorruption,[31] immortality,[32] and union with Christ.[33] The fact that God created all things for immortality[34] answers for the meaning of salvation as restoring immortality for humankind. And since the eucharist is the vehicle of immortality, by abstaining from the holy sacrament believers 'exclude themselves from eternal life'.[35]

Cyril refers to the efficacy of the eucharist, the true bread from

---

28 Davis, *Coptic Christology*, 48.
29 Boulnois, 'L'eucharistie', 157. The same notion is advocated by Gebremedhin, *Life-Giving Blessing*, 22.
30 See *On John* 3.6$^{I:376}$. Cf. *On Luke* 2.142 (667–668).
31 See *On John* 3.6$^{I:376}$ and *On John* 4.2$^{I:421-422}$.
32 See *On John* 4.2$^{I:407-408, 421-422}$.
33 See *On John* 3.6$^{I:376}$, *On John* 4.2$^{I:418, 422}$. Cf. *On Luke* 2.142 (667–668).
34 See *On John* 9.1$^{II:318-9}$ and 12.1$^{II:675}$. Cf. *On Luke* 2.142 (665).
35 *On John* 3.6$^{I:376}$.

heaven, as far superior to the manna of the old testament. The manna was the shadow of the true bread from heaven[36] and a type and image of Christ,[37] whereas Christ is the true and spiritual manna.[38] Those who ate the manna hungered,[39] received bodily satisfaction,[40] had life for a season,[41] and died.[42] While the manna does not proceed from the essence of the Father, the only-begotten Son does.[43]

In summary, the eucharist is Christ's vivifying flesh. It restores life and conditions immortality. It is not a theoretical blessing, it is a 'life-giving blessing', one of the most significant Cyrilline terms to describe the eucharist. The eucharist, therefore, becomes a source of holiness through restoring humankind from corruption and by facilitating communion with God. Not only does it sanctify the participants' body and soul by making them partakers of the immortality and incorruptibility of the flesh of the Word, but it also enables believers to partake of the divine nature as discussed in section 4. The prefiguring of the eucharist in John 6 is, for Cyril, not just an event that took place at a certain point in history, rather it points to the everlasting efficacies that partakers of the very flesh and blood of Christ receive. In participating in the eucharist, communicants experience the Christ of yesterday, today, and tomorrow.

3. The Eucharistic Dual Sanctification – Corporeal and Spiritual

Having established the mode of presence of Christ in the eucharist, I now explore the notion of dual sanctification in Cyril's eucharistic theology. A pertinent question presents itself—how does the eucharist operate in participants, corporeally, spiritually, or both? In what follows I wish to demonstrate the centrality of the dual eucharistic sanctification to the divine bestowal of holiness and humankind's appropriation

---

36 *On John* 3.6$^{1:362}$, *On John* 4.1$^{1:396}$, and *On John* 4.2$^{1:407}$.
37 *On John* 4.2$^{1:406, 407}$.
38 *On John* 3.6$^{1:365}$.
39 *On John* 3.6$^{1:365}$.
40 *On John* 4.1$^{1:396}$.
41 *On John* 4.2$^{1:406}$.
42 *On John* 4.2$^{1:421}$.
43 *On John* 3.6$^{1:363}$.

of it. This, in turn, provides the necessary foundation to understanding Cyril's notion of union with the divine, addressed in section 4.

Gebremedhin highlighted, correctly I believe, that the terms 'spiritually' and 'corporeally'[44] reflect not only the two means of operation of Christ in believers who partake of the eucharist, but also the two means of reception of Christ's vivifying work.[45] There is no debate as to the two means of reception of the eucharistic sanctification by the believers, bodily and spiritually. However, there is certainly a debate over the way the eucharist operates, corporeally, spiritually or both.

I propose that when it comes to the dual sanctification in Cyril's eucharistic exposition, there is certainly ambiguity, rather than inconsistency. He frequently advocates humankind's corporeal and spiritual union with the divine. Yet it is not always clear to what he ascribes each means. Boulnois referred to his interpretation of Zechariah 5:5-11, where he uses the metaphor of lead and silver to highlight humankind's purification through Christ mingling with humankind corporeally and spiritually, without explaining what he means by the two terms.[46] Regarding the direct mention of the eucharist, some of the relevant passages focus on the corporeal sanctification or the physical means of operation, while others speak of the dual sanctification and so both means of operation. As Keating noted, read in isolation the relevant texts emphasise either the primarily corporeal or the dual aspects of sanctification.[47] To clarify any ambiguity, it is necessary to examine the texts carefully and in their totality in order to extract the relevant nuances.

The shape of my examination is as follows. First, I provide a summary of scholarly views of the eucharistic dual sanctification. Second, I explore Cyril's eucharistic dual sanctification and the underlying interplay between the divine activity in bestowing holiness and humankind's response in appropriating it.

---

44 Keating, adding to the work of Meunier, listed the many texts in Cyril's corpus that use one or other set of the paired terms 'spiritually' (πνευματικῶς) and 'corporeally' (σωματικῶς). See Keating, *Appropriation*, 75, n.23.
45 Gebremedhin, *Life–Giving Blessing*, 88, n.56.
46 Boulnois, 'L'eucharistie', 154. Boulnois also examined passages from *Against Nestorius* where Cyril uses the dual participation in Christ without further qualification, see n.30.
47 Keating, *Appropriation*, 103–104.

a. Scholarly Debates

Before examining the ramifications of the dual eucharistic sanctification in terms of bestowal and appropriation of holiness, I begin with a brief account of scholarly debates over the way the eucharist operates, corporeally, spiritually or both. Two positions are discernible, largely corresponding to the standpoints adopted in regard to the nature of the eucharist.

The first group, and by far the largest, attributed both means of operation, corporeally and spiritually, to the eucharist. Meunier asserted that the dual sanctification is a representative of Cyril's thought and is repeated across his corpus, giving more than a dozen citations.[48] He highlighted that many passages in *On Matthew* point to the presence of the Spirit in the eucharist, it is by giving the communicants Christ's body and blood that the Spirit dwells in them.[49] Boulnois acknowledged both means of operation and reception. Taking her cue from the position I discussed about the realism of the eucharist, in section 2 above, she emphasised that in the eucharist believers not only receive Christ's flesh but also Christ himself.[50] She concluded, correctly in my opinion, that it is artificial to separate the two means by assigning the corporeal to the eucharist and the spiritual to baptism. In turn, she advocated the coexistence of the two means in both sacraments. McGuckin, referring to *On Luke*, supported Christ's physical and spiritual presence in the eucharist.[51] Gebremedhin posited that Cyril describes the eucharist as 'spiritual blessing, spiritual worship, spiritual burnt offering and spiritual nourishment,' thus pointing to the spiritual operation.[52] He also asserted that the two means of operation through the eucharist are not exclusive of each other. Concannon argued that in the eucharist the Word comes to believers both divinely and humanly.[53] She advo-

---

48 Meunier, *Le Christ*, 163–213, esp. 166, 168, 169 (and n.10), 172, 177, 178, 181, 192, and 196.
49 Meunier, *Le Christ*, 166 (my translation). Meunier here is commenting on *In* Mt 26:27 (PG 72, 452; Reuss 289, p. 255, l. 5–7). Note that Keating pointed out that Matthew 26:26–28 is a unique reference in Cyril's corpus where he attributes that the Spirit is given through the body and blood of Christ. See Keating, *Appropriation*, 80.
50 Boulnois, 'L'eucharistie', 156.
51 McGuckin, 'Saint Cyril of Alexandria's Theology of the Eucharist', 63, 66.
52 Gebremedhin, *Life-Giving Blessing*, 81–85, and 87–88 n.56.
53 Concannon, 'Eucharist', 329 and 335.

cated that in the eucharist partakers receive life, both spiritually and physically. Becker, in his examination of the *Dialogues*, construed that a dichotomy between the corporeal and the spiritual in Cyril's theology is not what Cyril had in mind and that his theology is much more integrative.[54] Although Welch argued that Cyril does not separate the corporeal and the spiritual unity in Christ, he attributed the corporeal unity to the eucharist and the spiritual unity to the Spirit.[55] Having said so, he did not explore whether the Spirit operated through baptism or the eucharist. Based on my reading of Welch, I would hazard to place his argument within the first group.

The second group attributed the spiritual union to the indwelling of the Holy Spirit in baptism, while attributing the corporeal union to the eucharist. Mahé acknowledged both means of operation, pneumatic and somatic, with the latter being manifested in the eucharist.[56] Du Manoir followed Mahé's arguments.[57] Davis posited that the corporeal sanctification has a more privileged status in Cyril's eucharistic theology, as did the spiritual aspect in his baptismal theology.[58] At the same time, he recognised the two means of reception, bodily and spiritually. Keating certainly confirmed the dual means of reception of the vivifying work of Christ in the eucharist. Although he recognised the ambiguity in Cyril's exposition when it comes to the two means of operation, Keating connected the spiritual mode of sanctification in the eucharist more closely to the gift of the Holy Spirit received in baptism and the corporeal mode to the flesh of Christ.[59]

It is worth noting though that scholars on both side of the debate acknowledged the central role Cyril's eucharistic theology plays in humankind's participation in the divine.

From my viewpoint, the dual sanctification is through the one Spirit who is always present with the Word incarnate and the vivifying flesh of

---

54 Becker, 'The Holy Spirit', 58.
55 Welch, *Christology and Eucharist*, 99–102.
56 Mahé, 'L'eucharistie', esp. 685, n.1. He also acknowledged the two means of reception, body and soul/spirit, of Christ's vivifying body (p. 681).
57 du Manoir, *Dogme et Spiritualité*, 190, 193.
58 Davis, *Coptic Christology*, 39–40.
59 Keating, *Appropriation*, 64–75, 76–78, 80, 81, 82, 85, 86, 87–88, 89, 93–95, 101; and Keating, 'The Twofold Manner', 543–549.

the one Christ. It is through both means of operation in the eucharist, as it is in baptism, that humankind participates in Christ's holiness. It is to this argument that I now turn my attention.

b. Dual Sanctification and the Interplay Between Divine Activity and Human Response

I propose that Cyril, like Athanasius,[60] speaks of sanctification in terms of both the spiritual and the corporeal means of operation. The corporeal means of operation is non-controversial. However, the spiritual means of sanctification entails some ambiguity. Sometimes it is connected with the Holy Spirit received at baptism,[61] which is a prerequisite for the believers to partake of the eucharist.[62] Other passages point out that when communicants receive Christ in the eucharist, they receive the single incarnate subject who is one with the Father, and together with his flesh communicants receive the Holy Spirit who is always with the Word incarnate. The fact of the matter is that Christ dwells in believers in various ways—through the union achieved at his incarnation, through the indwelling of his Spirit he sent to humanity upon his glorification, and through baptism. He is present in believers through the eucharist as well. All these point to the conclusion that, given the consistency between the eucharist and other forms of participation in Christ, by partaking of the eucharist communicants receive him corporeally and spiritually. It is from these assumptions that I construct my approach.

In what follows I explore relevant passages from *On John*. I classify these passages into three categories: 1) those that do not explicitly point to the spiritual indwelling through either the eucharist or baptism, 2) those that associate the spiritual indwelling with the Holy Spirit

---

60 Meunier pointed out the similarity with Athanasius' dual sanctification in the eucharist due to Christ being both man and God. However, Athanasius' interest was in demonstrating that the body and blood are also spiritual to prove that Christ is God and possesses the Spirit. See Meunier, *Le Christ*, 177, n.17.

61 *On John* 3.6[I:376].

62 *On John* 12.Introduction[II:659–660], where Cyril uses John 20:17 (Christ asking Mary not to touch him because he had not ascended to his Father as yet) to highlight the role of baptism as a purifying power before touching the body of Christ. In his exposition, Cyril explains that Mary, while being a believer in the Lord, had not received the Spirit as yet, and hence was not allowed to touch the risen Lord.

received in baptism, and finally 3) those that point to the indwelling of the Holy Spirit who is with Christ through the eucharist.

Although, as mentioned earlier, I concur with the first group that attributes both means of operation to the eucharist, my ultimate aim is to demonstrate that, irrespective of the source of the indwelling, Cyril consistently presents eucharistic sanctification as pivotal for the divine bestowal of holiness and its human appropriation. In doing so, I show that the intertwining of his Christology, pneumatology, trinitarian theology, baptismal theology and eucharistic theology, all at once, provides a clue to the manner by which Christ indwells humankind, and humankind's participation in the divine. Irrespective of the source of the spiritual dwelling, communicants are sanctified and attain union with the divine.

The first category, referring to passages where Cyril does not explicitly discuss the manner of the spiritual indwelling, whether it be through baptism or the eucharist, includes his commentary on John 15:1 (I am the true vine). However, in this instance he begins his exposition by considering the corporeal union, before turning to the spiritual one a few passages later. He points to Christ dwelling in participants corporeally as they partake of his flesh. This is how the Gentiles are 'embodied' in Christ, by 'sharing the holy eucharist.'[63] The union in/with Christ is corporeal by virtue of him being the vine who transmits to humankind, the branches, something of his. Although not necessarily signifying the eucharistic union, the union is also spiritual in the sense that it is achieved through participation in the Holy Spirit and the whole trinity. Repeatedly, Cyril highlights that 'union with,' 'abiding in,' 'being joined to,' and 'being begotten of/in' Christ is through participation in the Holy Spirit.[64] At the same time, he emphasises, referring to Ephesians 2:22, that it is through Christ that believers are 'built up' for a 'habitation of God in the Spirit.'[65] The whole trinity is, therefore, involved in bestowing holiness on humankind,[66] since for Cyril, 'everything

---

63 *On John* 10.2$^{II:370}$ (Pusey 2.542.10–15).
64 *On John* 10.2$^{II:363,364}$.
65 *On John* 10.2$^{II:363}$.
66 *On John* 10.2$^{II:364}$.

proceeds from the Father by the Son in the Spirit'.⁶⁷ He also speaks of spiritual union with Christ in the context of participation through love, uncorrupted faith, virtue and purity of mind.⁶⁸ The spiritual union is manifested through both the divine and the human aspects. The divine aspect refers to the participation of the whole trinity. The human response consists in faith, love and virtue.

The second category of passages refers to spiritual sanctification through the Spirit gained in baptism. When commenting on John 6:35, Cyril focuses on Christ's promise that whoever comes to him shall neither hunger nor thirst. He explains that the promise is nothing but 'the blessing in the participation of his holy flesh and blood'.⁶⁹ Hunger and thirst are quenched by participating in Christ, the true spiritual food partaken of at the eucharist, as opposed to the manna and the water from the rock in the old testament. He then adds 'Here he calls water the sanctification through the Spirit [...]. The holy body of Christ then gives life to those in whom it is [...] being commingled with our body'.⁷⁰ Thus, he connects the participation in the eucharist to the sanctification by water through the Spirit.⁷¹ Ultimately, the aim of partaking of the eucharist is for believers to be made partakers of the divine nature.⁷² This is not the only instance when baptismal and eucharistic images mingle.

Speaking of the blood and water flowing from Christ's body at the cross (John 19:34), Cyril brings to the fore yet another connection between baptism and the eucharist. This time, water, a type of baptism, is mingled with blood, a type of the eucharist.⁷³ Both water and blood, baptism and eucharist, belong to Christ. Furthermore, when commenting on John 9:6 (healing the man born blind by spitting in

---

67 *On John* 10.2^(II:365). This phrase is reminiscent of Athanasius' as it appears, multiple times, in his letters to Serapion. See Shapland, *The Letters of Saint Athanasius Concerning the Holy Spirit*, I:1–31 (Letter I: sections 1–31), especially (I:2, page 64), (I:9, page 83), (I:14, page 94), (I:20, page 116), and (I:30, page 142).
68 *On John* 10.2^(II:369,372).
69 *On John* 3.6^(I:376).
70 *On John* 3.6^(I:376) (Pusey 1.475.20–25).
71 Cyril connects 'water' with the gift of the Spirit. See, for example, *On John* 2.4 (I:207), where he posits 'But He calls the quickening gift of the Spirit living water'. See also *On John* 3.6 (I:376), where he equates water to the Holy Spirit in the Scriptures.
72 *On John* 3.6^(I:379).
73 *On John* 12.Introduction^(II:645).

the clay), Cyril adds that partaking of the divine light and receiving the knowledge of the consubstantial trinity cannot be achieved without the eucharist and baptism.[74] In commenting on John 20:17, Cyril is very clear that partaking of the eucharist requires not only faith, but the indwelling of the Holy Spirit received through baptism.[75] Thus a strong link exists between the two sacraments. Again, the divine activity and the human response are both at work here, leading believers to a 'supernatural' life.[76]

Finally, the third category of passages regarding spiritual sanctification point to Christ himself dwelling in the communicants. Here, I examine three passages from *On John*, where Cyril comments on John 17:21, 17:22-23, and 6:35.

Cyril's comments on John 17:21 focus on the unity of all human beings with each other and with the Father, the Son, and the Holy Spirit. After deploying the Adamic typology, he emphasises that union with God can only be achieved through communion with the Holy Spirit.[77] He also advocates humankind's spiritual union with God in the sense that it entails a bond of love, concord, and peace amongst each other, and piety and virtue towards God.[78] Yet, his focus is on highlighting a 'natural unity' with each other and with God, that resembles[79] the 'natural and essential unity that exists between the Father and the Son'.[80] It is at this point that he introduces the notion of corporeal and spiritual union. He does not explicitly elaborate on the meaning of the two terms, but he still sheds some light as to the depth of the achieved union by connecting Christology, pneumatology, and sacramental theology. Through the ineffable union of divinity and humanity at the incarnation, Christ enables humankind to 'partake of the nature of God' and to

---

74 *On John* 6.1[II:19]. In this passage, Cyril's focus is on the gentiles ridding themselves of their blindness through partaking of the holy body and through baptism.
75 *On John* 12.Introduction[II:660], where he says, 'Holy things to the holy'.
76 Gebremedhin, *Life-Giving Blessing*, 53.
77 *On John* 11.11[II:545].
78 *On John* 11.11[II:546,548,551-552].
79 Note that 'resembles' is an operative word. Cyril in no way is advocating an equality between humankind's union with each other and with God to either the hypostatic union or the trinitarian one.
80 *On John* 11.11[II:546,548] (Pusey 2.731.28–29).

reach 'the abiding presence of the Spirit'.[81] The divine intimacy is then manifested through Christ receiving his own Spirit at baptism, thus granting sanctification to the whole humanity that was in him.

Having explained the intertwining role of the incarnation, the indwelling of the Spirit, and of baptism, Cyril now moves to the role the eucharist plays in humankind's 'physical' union with Christ. He emphasises that communicants receive in their bodies the one and indivisible Christ, both body and soul.[82] The one body—or holy flesh—believers receive unites them to him and with each other. Through the eucharist, believers become 'all part of the one bread,' and therefore, 'all are made one body.' By partaking of his flesh, communicants attain an 'actual physical unity'[83] with Christ. This is because as they partake of the holy flesh, it, in turn, 'exists' in them (pointing to the realism of the eucharist as discussed in section 2 above). At this juncture, Cyril juxtaposes the 'physical union' that is through 'his (Christ's) flesh', with the 'spiritual union of all' who partake.[84] Just as the holy flesh produces actual physical unity, it is the Spirit of God who abides in all that 'binds all together into spiritual unity'. Cyril adds that it is 'Christ (who) causes the Spirit, who is his own and who is from the Father, to dwell in us who are many individually, nevertheless the Spirit is one and indivisible'.[85] Just as Christ's flesh unites those who partake of it, likewise the Spirit leads to spiritual unity, since by Christ's dwelling in the communicants, he dwells with his flesh and his Spirit, highlighting the divine activity in bestowing union with Christ Jesus, both corporeal and spiritual.

Cyril concludes his exposition on John 17:21 by summing up that humankind becomes one with the Father, the Son, and the Holy Spirit through 'conformity to the life of righteousness and in the fellowship

---

81 *On John* 11.11[II:549,551].
82 Welch showed that scholarly opinions with regard to the logos-sarx concept differ. Whereas Wilken, Durand, and Welch himself took the Cyrilline 'flesh' to denote the whole human being, body and soul, Grillmeier and Liébaret believed that it excludes the soul. See Welch, *Christology and Eucharist*, 40–60, esp. 46–47, and n.19.
83 *On John* 11.11[II:550] (κατὰ σῶμα νοουμένην ἕνωσιν; Pusey 2.736.9).
84 *On John* 11.11[II:551] (πρὸς ἑνότητα τὴν πνευματικὴν συνάγει τοὺς πάντας; Pusey 2.737.3–4).
85 I opted to use Maxwell's translation for this passage since Pusey's (*On John* 11.11[II:551]) did not adequately convey the meaning of the original Greek (Pusey II.736.21–30). See Maxwell, *Commentary on St John*, 305.

of the holy body of Christ, and in the fellowship of the Holy Spirit'.[86] Thus, he stresses here that the union is achieved through an interplay between humankind's virtuous response and the divine activity predicated on the fellowship with the body of Christ and the Holy Spirit.

The very same notion re-emerges in Cyril's commentary on John 17:22-23 (that they may be one, even as we are one):

> For the Son dwells in us corporeally[87] as Man, commingled and united with us by the mystery of the eucharist; and also, spiritually[88] as God, by the effectual working and grace of his own Spirit, building up our spirit into newness of life, and making us partakers of his divine nature.[89]

Here Cyril shows that the corporeal union is due to the fact that Christ dwells in humankind 'as Man', and this dwelling takes place because communicants partake of his flesh in the eucharist. Furthermore, because Christ is 'also God', humankind is spiritually united with him through the work of his Spirit in them. Again, he highlights the interplay between the two aspects, divine and human, of the union. The divine activity, signified by the dwelling of the Son as God in humankind, works with humankind's spirit, effecting participation to achieve newness of life. Only a couple of paragraphs later, he repeats that union with God is effected through receiving Christ, both corporeally and spiritually, since he is Son by nature and in ontological union with the Father.[90] Thus communicants receive the one Christ (God-man), who is not separated from his Spirit, as they partake of the eucharist.

Finally, referring back to his commentary on John 6:35 (I am the bread of life), Cyril explains that through the bread from heaven, Christ

---

86 *On John* 11.11[II:552].
87 In Pusey's English translation, he uses 'in a corporeal sense'. I have adapted his translation and used 'corporeally' instead to fit the original Greek (Pusey III.3.27–28) which renders σωματικῶς μὲν ὡς ἄνθρωπος ('physically as a man').
88 In Pusey's English translation, he uses 'in a spiritual sense'. I have adapted his translation and used 'spiritually' instead to fit the original Greek (Pusey III.3.29) which renders πνευματικῶς δὲ ... ὡς θεός ('spiritually as God').
89 *On John* 11.12[II:554].
90 *On John* 11.12[II:555], see also *On John* 10.2[II:453].

grants humankind eternal life through the supply of the Holy Spirit and the participation of his flesh:

> [...] the bread from heaven, i.e., Christ, nourishing us unto eternal life, both through the supply of the Holy Spirit, and the participation of his own flesh, which infuses into us the participation of God, and effaces the darkness that comes from the ancient curse.[91]

Keating proposed that in this instance the 'bread from heaven' refers to Christ himself, as distinct from the eucharistic sacrament.[92] This view corresponds to his earlier attribution of the corporeal indwelling to the eucharist and the spiritual one to the Holy Spirit at baptism. However, I would argue that the divine hypostasis incarnate communicates with humankind through its flesh both directly or personally and eucharistically, and given that the divine hypostasis enfleshed is in the eucharist (as discussed in section 2 above), there is too the Spirit, since the Spirit is ever with Christ as God incarnate. Boulnois found in Cyril's Commentary on Romans evidence which supports my aforementioned argument. She pointed out that Cyril posits that humankind participates in Christ spiritually and corporeally, because when Christ dwells in us, he does so through the Holy Spirit and the mystical eucharist.[93] That is, what is present in the communicants is not only his flesh, but the whole person of the Word, and thus his Spirit. Moreover, receiving Christ's flesh signifies being filled by the Holy Spirit since Christ communicates his proper Spirit.[94]

The above analysis leads to important conclusions.

First, Cyril speaks of a complex union, bodily (natural, physical) and spiritual (mystical), between humankind and the divine. This union is granted because of the incarnation, through partaking of the flesh of Christ and fellowship of the Spirit. The partaking of the Spirit could be attributed to either the indwelling at baptism or through the eucharist. Irrespective of the source of the indwelling, union is achieved. It is the

---

91 *On John* 3.6[1:374].
92 Keating, *Appropriation*, 75.
93 *In Rom* 8, 3, 27M (Pusey V.213.8–12). Cited in Boulnois, 'L'eucharistie', 155 (my translation).
94 Boulnois, 'L'eucharistie', 157 (my translation).

one Christ who is the bond of both the natural (physical) union and the spiritual union. Because the incarnated Word is at once God and Man, he dwells in humankind through the indwelling of the Spirit he sent to humanity upon his glorification, received at baptism, and also through the eucharist. The ineffable character of this experience is due to the fact that communicants participate in the flesh of God incarnate, in which the Holy Spirit is ever present.

Second, spiritual union with the Father, the Son, and the Holy Spirit has two aspects: a divine aspect that entails the indwelling of Christ's Spirit, and a human aspect that involves conformity to a holy life through faith, love and virtue. Through the interplay of the two aspects, communicants, renewed, transformed, become partakers of the divine nature. The depth and breadth of this union in Cyril's eucharistic theology is the topic of the next section.

That is, for Cyril, the sacrament of the eucharist is not only a salvific mode for humankind's participation in Christ, but it also leads to corporeal and spiritual sanctification in Christ. The incarnate Word gives communicants his body and blood that they, by accepting him, might be healed and transformed. The historical event of the incarnation of the only-begotten Son of God, thus, transcends time. By becoming fully human, and giving himself on the holy tables, Christ reconstructs the fallen human nature in himself.

4. Humankind's Union with the Divine

The real presence of the one indivisible Christ in the eucharist presupposes the corporeal and spiritual means of operation in the sacrament. Believers who partake of the body and blood of Christ receive both corporeal and spiritual sanctification. In order to attain sanctification, they have not only to be baptised but also lead a life of faith, love and virtue. The vivifying flesh of the only-begotten Word of God then unites them to one another and to himself. Cyril uses a variety of analogies in

On John to demonstrate the extent of this union.[95] He deploys three analogies, water/heat, wax/wax, and leaven/meal, in order to interpret Christ's bread-of-life discourse (John 6:53-57). He uses another analogy, already familiar, that of the vine/branches, when commenting on John 15:1. Hereafter I explore these four analogies.

Commenting on John 6:53 (except you eat the flesh of the Son of Man and drink his blood, you have no life in you), Cyril uses the water/heat analogy to reveal the extent of humankind's transformation as believers partake of the eucharist.[96] He begins by stating that when it is put on the fire, water, cold by nature, gains the property of the fire (heat) and is changed, becoming hot. Likewise, when participants too, who possess a corruptible flesh, partake of the life-giving flesh of Christ, they gain its properties and their flesh is sanctified through participation. He uses terms such 'immingling/mixing ($μίξει$) of life' and being 'transelemented ($ἀναστοιχειούμεθα$) to its (the life-giving flesh of Christ) properties' to express the depth and the effects of the union. Renewal extends beyond the re-creation of the soul of the communicants in the Holy Spirit, possibly alluding to the role of the Spirit in baptism (an interpretation which relates to his use of the water/heat analogy) and definitely to the dwelling of the Spirit in the eucharist (discussed in section 3 above). This means that the soul is not only renewed in the eucharist, but the 'dense/coarse and earthly body' is likewise infused with incorruption. This aspect corresponds to the physical (corporeal) dimension of participants' transformation, earlier discussed. McKinion referred to the same analogy to illustrate the reality of Christ 'making the body his own' and hence 'empower[ing] it to give life'.[97] Both aspects, the physical dimension of participants' transformation and the reality of Christ empowering his own body are well linked. Without Christ's flesh becoming charged with vivifying power (see section 2),

---

95 As posited by McKinion, *Words, Imagery*, 17, Cyril's Christology is 'not a sacred philosophy' but is based on the Alexandrian interpretation of the Scripture. Thus, one should not take his analogies to denote a philosophical intent. Interestingly, McKinion did not seem to focus much on Cyril's analogies in the context of the eucharist.
96 *On John* 4.2[1:419] (Pusey 1.531.10–12). Cyril used the same water/heat analogy in the context of the twofold sanctifying effect of baptism. This is yet another proof of the integration of his baptismal and eucharistic theologies.
97 McKinion, *Words, Imagery* 75.

communicants' eucharistic transformation is not possible.

Union with Christ through the eucharist is possibly best described in Cyril's interpretation of John 6:56 (abiding in Christ through eating his flesh and blood), where he uses the very suggestive image of melted wax:

> For as if one should join wax with other wax, he will surely see (I suppose) the one in the other; in like manner (I deem) he who receives the flesh of our saviour Christ and drinks his precious blood, as he says, is found one with him, commingled (συνανακιρνάμενος) as it were and immingled (ἀναμιγνύμενος) with him through the participation, so that he is found in Christ, Christ again in him.[98]

Practically speaking, when one mixes two pieces of wax the result is a new piece where it becomes almost impossible to discern the original pieces from one another. The first piece is in the second, just as much as the second is in the first. Likewise, the believer who partakes of the flesh and blood of Christ is found in Christ as Christ is found in the believer. Cyril explains that Christ is 'commingled' and 'immingled' with the partaker.[99] The analogy is repeated elsewhere (when commenting on John 15:1, 'I am the true vine'),[100] where he articulates again the union between the participant in the body and blood of Christ and Christ as person. In this second instance, he refers to the melting of the two pieces to form a single piece. He adds that Christ's union with humankind goes beyond being through 'affections', being also by natural[101] participation. The natural participation is, therefore, attributed to humankind's flesh being mingled with his.

The leaven-bread analogy features straight after the wax analogy.[102] Combining Matthew 13:33 and 1 Corinthians 5:6, Cyril makes the

---

98 On John 4.2[I:422] (Pusey 1.535.5–12).
99 The terms 'commingled' and 'immingled' render the original συνανακιρνάμενος ('comingled/mixed together') and ἀναμιγνύμενος ('mingled/immingled'), respectively (Pusey I.535.10).
100 On John 10.2[II:370].
101 The term 'natural' renders the original μέθεξιν ἤτοι φυσικήν ('true natural/physical participation') (Pusey II.542.24). Note also that Mahé, 'L'eucharistie', 685, renders the term 'natural' in this passage to 'physical'.
102 On John 4.2[I:422–423].

leap of faith as he relates the impact of a little leaven on the whole lump to the 'least portion of the blessings' which 'blends our whole body with itself and fills it with its mighty working'.[103] He combines here the efficacy of the eucharist, its 'mighty working', with the process by which it blends into participants' body. Like with the earlier two analogies, he shows once again that through the partaking of the eucharist 'Christ comes to be in us, and we again in him'. The eucharistic union leads not only to Christ being in the recipients, but also to the latter's presence in him. One cannot separate heat from the hot water, nor two pieces of wax melted together, nor leaven in a lump of bread once mixed.

The vine analogy features in Cyril's interpretation of John 15:1. After using the analogy in the context of the indwelling of the Holy Spirit in humankind, he uses it again to highlight the recipients' corporeal participation in Christ through communion of his holy flesh. In short, they receive 'life out and proceeding from him'.[104] Masterfully, Cyril connects John 15:1 with a battery of other verses to strengthen his position. He uses Romans 12:5 to highlight participants' unity with Christ 'in the one body', and 1 Corinthians 10:17 showing that 'we all partake of the one bread'. They receive in themselves the mystery of the eucharist in order to make Christ corporeally dwell in them by participating in his holy flesh. He extends the efficacies of the eucharist to include the gentiles (in reference to Ephesians 3:6) to becoming fellow-members of the body of Christ because of the embodiment that takes place due to their eucharistic participation. He refers to 1 Corinthians 6:15, 16 to point to the role of the eucharist in making believers members of Christ. The key point in this exposition refers to the necessity of participation of like-nature, a requirement satisfied by the analogy of Christ as the vine and the believers as the branches. Cyril points to the ineffable manner in which participation takes place through the indwelling of Christ in the communicants. As discussed earlier, this focus does not deny the union through 'right faith and sincere love',[105] but rather highlights the dual sanctification through the divine activity and the human response.

Although not focusing on any specific analogy, the same views

---

103   Note that 'blessing' translates the Greek *eulogia* (εὐλογία) in *On John* 4.2[I:423].
104   *On John* 10.2[II:370].
105   *On John* 10.2[II:372].

appear in *Dialogues on the Trinity*. In this early work, he anticipated many aspects discussed in *On John*. He highlights that the union in Christ is through the one body, feeding onto the one flesh, being sealed into oneness by the Holy Spirit, and through faith in Christ.[106] Thus, here, like elsewhere, Cyril points to the fact that in the eucharist Christ is corporeally in the communicants as they partake of his body and spiritually through them being sealed to his own Spirit. Cyril adds that the human response, through faith in Christ, also leads to union with Christ, thus connecting the divine activity with the human response.

The wealth of analogies used by Cyril to express participants' union with Christ through the eucharist is amazingly suggestive. However, he does not let his readers wonder as to the level of similarity between union with Christ achieved in the eucharist and the hypostatic union. He highlights the difference, while not denying that the union in the eucharist is real, amounting to becoming one body with each other and with Christ.[107] When he speaks of human participation in the divine in general, and through the eucharist specifically, he certainly insists on the difference between what Christ is by nature, namely life, and what creation receives through participation.[108] Referring to Christ as the bread-of-life which comes down from heaven to give life to the world, he asserts that by participating in life (through generalisation, by partaking of the bread-of-life, the eucharist), the human being is 'not life by nature', but rather that it 'participates of life'.[109] Unlike the enfleshed Word, the flesh of the participant in the life-giving flesh of the Word is not of itself life-giving.[110] These distinctions confirm my earlier findings about Cyril's take on the relation between the participant and the participated in.

Having said so, the above analogies point to two important facts. First, the eucharist is the most effective means of union with the divine

---

106 Cited in, Becker, 'The Holy Spirit', 40–41, 42–43.
107 The same conclusion is reached by Louth, 'The Use of the Term ἴδιος', 201.
108 Focusing on refuting the heretics who taught that the Son is not consubstantial with the Father, Book 1, chapter 6, is packed with arguments concerning the difference between the participant and the participated in, who is life by nature. See, for example, *On John* $1.6^{1:57-58,60,64}$ as well as *On John* $4.3^{1:435-436}$.
109 *On John* $1.6^{1:61}$.
110 *On John* $4.3^{1:437}$.

because of the kinship between the incarnated Word and the corporeal union of humankind. Second, human nature is always at the receiving end. The first fact points to the notion that, as partakers of the flesh of Christ, communicants are united with him and receive eternal life because of the ineffable union of the Word and his flesh. Thus, Christ's ontological kinship with humankind through the hypostatic union underlines Cyril's eucharistic theology.[111] The second fact points to the very notion that humankind is the participant while the divine is the participated in.

In summary, Cyril used four analogies—water-heat, wax-wax, leaven-meal, and vine-branches—to describe communicants' union with Christ through the eucharist. Given that Christ's flesh is vivified through the hypostatic union, it vivifies partakers of the eucharist. By partaking of the eucharist, Christ is in communicants and they in him. This union is real, not metaphorical. It resembles the hypostatic union, but is not the same. This is because Christ is life by nature, whereas partakers of the eucharist participate in life. Nevertheless, through being united to the life-giving Word, partakers of the eucharist are sanctified and receive eternal life.

5. Conclusion

In this essay, I examined Cyril's eucharistic theology. The texts reviewed show that his account is exegetically coherent and convincing in highlighting humankind's union with the divine. Central to this notion is the real presence of Christ in the eucharist. By partaking of his body and his blood, communicants are corporeally and spiritually sanctified and become one in Christ and him in them.

When referring to the dual sanctification Cyril speaks of two means of operation and two means of reception, corporeally and spiritually. He eloquently connects the physical and spiritual means of operation. The physical means of operation refers to the transformed bread and wine in the eucharist. The Holy Spirit, who is always with Christ, is the

---

111 Gebremedhin, *Life-Giving Blessing*, 22, 69; Davis, *Coptic Christology*, 44, 47; Gross, *Divinization*, 227; and Meunier, *Le Christ*, 185.

sanctifier. Although some scholars argued that the spiritual means of operation points to baptism and the corporeal one to the eucharist, I demonstrated that both means of operation are inseparable. Through the ineffable union of two ontologically different natures, divinity and humanity, Christ dwells in humankind and sanctifies it through both baptism and the eucharist. When addressing the means of reception in the sacrament of the eucharist, Cyril is clear that eucharistic communicants receive Christ in their whole being. Thus, humankind is transformed and 'transelemented' into a divine form. Any separation of the two means of operation is certainly not what Cyril had in mind.

I also examined Cyril's use of analogies to provide a vivid image of the union between the divine and humankind. Four analogies were discussed: water/heat, vine/branches, wax/wax, and leaven/meal. The water/heat analogy refers to the union between two different natures, whereas the other three point to a union between two like-natures.

Just as at the incarnation Christ united two different natures, the same is true in baptism and the eucharist. As water gains heat, the property of fire, so does the corruptible flesh of the recipients become sanctified in baptism and the eucharist. The interconnection between Cyril's baptismal and eucharistic theologies is at play here.

The other three analogies focus on a different and yet complementary aspect. Cyril uses the vine/branches (John 15:1-2) analogy to denote humankind's union with Christ founded in the incarnation and manifested in the eucharist. Through the incarnation, humanity participates in the inherent qualities of the incarnate Word of God—just as the branches share in the vine's nature. Similarly, by receiving the eucharist, communicants corporeally participate in Christ. Cyril's use of the wax/wax and leaven/meal analogies (commenting on John 6:56) accentuate the union due to like-natures. In both cases the result is a union that necessitates an intermingling leading to a 'single', or rather shared, entity: sanctified communicants are in Christ as much as Christ is in them. The only difference in the leaven/meal analogy is that by mixing a little leaven with the meal, the latter receives an immeasurable blessing. He carefully attributes these two analogies to the eucharistic union, and not the hypostatic union, to avoid any suggestion of fusion between the divine and human natures of the incarnate Word. All these analogies, whether used in the context of the incarnation, baptism or eucharist, point to the mystery of the union of humankind with the divine.

Further to the above-mentioned concepts, four tenets of Cyril's articulation of holiness in *On John* were analysed throughout this paper. First, any separation of the Word from his flesh is fundamentally flawed. Second, the role of the trinity is paramount. For Cyril the divine action is always the work of the trinity—from the Father, through the Son and in the Spirit. Furthermore, humankind's union with the divine 'resembles' but is not identical with the trinitarian union. Third, the pre-eminence of the divine action in bestowing holiness on humankind does not exclude humankind's endeavour to appropriate it. In addition to the divine grace received through eucharist, imitation of Christ through faith, piety, practising a virtuous life, and obeying the commandments is of the essence. However, the divine action precedes the human response. Through both aspects, humankind achieves growth into the fullness of divine likeness. Finally, despite the fact that humankind's transformation is real, the union between the divine and the human is not between equals. The participated in (the divine) is always other than the participant (humankind), without diminishing the efficacy of the union.

Bibliography

Becker, Timothy J. 'The Holy Spirit in Cyril of Alexandria's Dialogues on the Trinity' (PhD Dissertation, New York: Union Theological Seminary, 2012).

Boulnois, Marie-Odile 'L'eucharistie, mystère d'union chez Cyrille d'Alexandrie: les modéles d'union trinitaire et christologique', *Revue des Sciences Religieuses* 74:2 (2000), 147–172.

Concannon, Ellen 'The Eucharist as Source of St Cyril of Alexandria's Christology', *Pro Ecclesia* 13.3 (2009), 318–36.

Davis, Stephen J. *Coptic Christology in Practice: Incarnation and Divine Participation in Late Antique and Medieval Egypt* (Oxford: Oxford University Press, 2008).

du Manoir, Hubert *Dogme et Spiritualité chez Saint Cyrille d'Alexandrie* (Paris: Librairie Philosophique J. Vrin, 1944).

Gerbremedhin, Ezra *Life-Giving Blessing: An Inquiry into the Eucharistic Doctrine of Cyril of Alexandria* (Sweden: Uppsala, 1977).

Gross, Jules *The Divinization of the Christian According to the Greek Fathers* (Paul A. Onica, trans.; California: A&C Press, 2002).

Keating, Daniel A. *The Appropriation of Divine Life in Cyril of Alexandria* (New York: Oxford University Press, 2004).

Keating, Daniel A. 'The Twofold Manner of Divine Indwelling in Cyril of Alexandria: Redressing an Imbalance', *Studia Patristica* 37 (Leuven: Peeters, 2001), 543–49.

Louth, Andrew 'The Use of the Term ἴδιος in Alexandrian Theology from Alexander to Cyril', *Studia Patristica* 19 (Leuven: Peeters, 1989), 198–202.

Mahé, Joseph 'L'eucharistie d'après Saint. Cyrille d'Alexandrie', *Revue d'histoire Ecclésiastique* 8 (1907), 677–96.

Maxwell, D. R. *Commentary on St John – Cyril of Alexandria*. Vol II (Ancient Christian Texts; Illinois: IVP Academic, 2015).

McGuckin, John A. 'Saint Cyril of Alexandria's Theology of the Eucharist', in *Studia Universitatis Septentrionis – Theologia Orthodoxa* (Romania: U. T. Press, 2011), 53–70.

McGuckin, John A. *Saint Cyril of Alexandria and the Christological Controversy* (New York: SVS Press, 2004).

McKinion, Steven A. *Words, Imagery, and the Mystery of Christ: A Reconstruction of Cyril of Alexandria's Christology* (Leiden-Boston-Köln: Brill, 2000).

Meunier, Bernard *Le Christ de Cyrille d'Alexandrie: L'Humanité, Le Salut et al Question Monophysite* (Paris: Beauchesne, 1997).

Pusey, P. E. *Commentary on the Gospel According to St John by S. Cyril Archbishop of Alexandria*. Vol I (S John I–VIII) (A Library of the Fathers of the Holy Catholic Church; Oxford: James Parker, 1874).

Randell, T. *Commentary on the Gospel According to St John by S. Cyril Archbishop of Alexandria*. Vol II (S John IX–XXI) (A Library of the Fathers of the Holy Catholic Church; London: Walter Smith, 1885).

Russell, Norman *Cyril of Alexandria* (London: Routledge, 2000).

Shapland, C.R.B. *The Letters of Saint Athanasius Concerning the Holy Spirit* (London: Epworth, 1951).

Smith, R. P. *Commentary on the Gospel According to S. Luke by S. Cyril Patriarch of Alexandria.* Part II (Oxford: The University Press, 1859).

Ward, Benedicta (trans.) *The Sayings of the Desert Fathers: The Alphabetical Collection* (Minnesota: Cistercian Publications, 1975).

Welch, Lawrence J. *Christology and Eucharist in the Early Thought of Cyril of Alexandria* (New York: Catholic Scholars Press, 1994).

Wickham, L.R. (ed. & trans.) *Cyril of Alexandria. Select Letters* (Oxford: The Clarendon Press, 1983).

CHAPTER 9

The Teacher and His School: Philosophical Representations of Jesus and Christianity

Doru Costache

Abstract

The early Christians viewed Jesus, beyond his divine and human identity, as an accomplished philosopher who revealed to his disciples the highest philosophy. Jesus did not found a religion; he founded a school which resembled the philosophical schools of the time. Central to his school was the experience of teaching and learning. The goal of his school was the transformation of the human person, indeed the community of believers, by way of successive stages of initiation. Both as catechetical instruction and through the independent schools, the church manifested its philosophical dimension. No wonder that, against this backdrop, the Gospel writers, the early apologists, and the early monastic writers depicted Jesus in philosophical postures, an image echoed by artistic compositions.

Contrary to the widespread view of Christianity as religion, the early Christians believed that theirs was a philosophical ethos, the church being a school. Moreover, they believed that theirs was the true philosophy.[1] As Frances Young pointed out, religion in the ancient sense was ritualistic, not dogmatic or doctrinal.[2] This was definitely not the case with early Christianity. Christians did not construe themselves as religious people in any ancient, traditional senses. They emulated the philosophical schools, placing teaching and learning at the centre of their concerns. As such, they generated a specific literature and reinterpreted ancient ethics and rituals.[3] This interpretive activity—namely, redrafting old customs and texts in the language of truth, reason, wisdom, and the noble life—was common across the philosophical spectrum of antiquity and late antiquity.[4] But the early Christians also trod the path of their Jewish predecessors, who, long before them, earned esteem as genuine philosophers.[5] What matters is that Christianity emerged in history as a philosophical school, albeit one that construed itself as different,[6] and not a religious movement.

The early Christians were lifelong students, the disciples of a Teacher, Jesus Christ, who led them on the Way (Acts 9:2; 19:9,23) towards the fullness of life (John 10:10; 20:31; Acts 5:20).[7] Matching Pierre Hadot's double description of ancient philosophy as discourse and a way of life,[8] the Teacher himself embodied the Way of truth and life (John 14:6). Accordingly, his disciples viewed Jesus as a holy sage or the perfect philosopher, indeed Wisdom incarnate, considering his

---

1 Chadwick, *The Early Church*, 75. Drobner, 'Christian Philosophy', 675–78. Hadot, *Ancient Philosophy*, 237, 239. Hadot, *Philosophy as a Way of Life*, 107. Young, 'Conclusion', 108.
2 Young, 'Christian Teaching', 91.
3 Sanzo, 'Early Christianity', 198–200, 226–36.
4 Brisson, *How Philosophers Saved Myths*, 5–14, 58–61. Young, 'Christian teaching', 91. Young, 'The Literary Culture of the Third Century', 174.
5 Gavrilyuk, *Histoire du catéchuménat*, 63–68. Norris, 'Articulating Identity', 73–74. Urbano, *The Philosophical Life*, 100–10. Young, 'Christian Teaching', 92.
6 Costache, 'Christianity and the World', 31–32, 34–38. Norris, 'The Apologists', 38. Norris, 'Articulating Identity', 71–72. While the difference was mainly ideological, from the age of Julian onwards Christian philosophers began to adopt a different dress code too. Urbano, 'Sizing up the Philosopher's Cloak', 186–89.
7 Gavrilyuk, *Histoire du catéchuménat*, 22–27. Young, 'Christian Teaching', 103.
8 Hadot, *Philosophy as a Way of Life*, 50–69. Hadot, *What Is Ancient Philosophy*, 6, 64–66, 102–103.

teaching—delivered through words and deeds—the highest, true, and divine philosophy (1 Cor. 1:18-25).[9] This understanding does not necessarily stem from the divine and the human sides of Christ's identity, regardless of how solidly attested these are in the early Christian tradition.[10] Instead, the early Christians depicted Jesus in ways that had more to do with philosophy than with religion. This, precisely, is the main topic of my analysis.

From an internal viewpoint, Jesus' philosophical representations draw upon the experience of the early Christians under his and his disciples' guidance. From an external viewpoint, it depicts him after the philosophical portraits of classical and late antiquity.[11] Thus, his philosophical depiction is anchored in the Christian disciples' experience with their Teacher and his successors, as well as culturally contextualised. Accordingly, the church viewed itself as a philosophical school, having its own curriculum of study and spiritual exercises.[12]

That several schools of Christian philosophy emerged in Rome (Justin Martyr, d. ca 165)[13] and Alexandria (Pantaenus, d. ca 200; Clement, d. ca 215; Origen, d. ca 253)[14] in the second and the early third century therefore is not exceptional. These independent schools confirmed and affirmed the philosophical drive inherent to the church's mindset and ethos. For example, they articulated Christian teaching after the principles of classical *paideia*, central to the philosophical movements of the time.[15] In so doing, they further emphasised

---

9   Urbano, *The Philosophical Life*, 34–37.
10 See, for example, Behr, *The Way to Nicaea*, 17–70, 81–92, etc.
11 Urbano, 'The Philosopher Type', 29–34. See Diogenes Laertius' celebrated *Lives of the Eminent Philosophers* and Plutarch's *Parallel Lives*.
12 Hadot, *Ancient Philosophy*, 241–42, 246.
13 Behr, *The Way to Nicaea*, 93–94. Chadwick, *The Early Church*, 74–79. Edwards, 'Apologetics', 552. Gavrilyuk, *Histoire du catéchuménat*, 80–82. Hoek, 'The "Catechetical" School', 76–77. Nasrallah, 'Mapping the World', 306–12. Norris, 'The Apologists', 38–40. Urbano, 'Images of Teachers', 6.
14 Behr, *The Way to Nicaea*, 163–65. Brakke, 'The East', 346–49. Costache, 'Christian Gnosis', 259. Gavrilyuk, *Histoire du catéchuménat*, 124–34. Heine, 'The Alexandrians', 117–127. Urbano, 'Images of Teachers', 12–14.
15 Azkoul, 'Polis and Paideia', 3–21, 67–86. Costache, 'Being', 57–59. Dawson, 'Christian teaching', 236–37. Gemeinhardt, 'Christian Paideia', 88–98. Heine, 'The Alexandrians', 119, 212. Jaeger, 'Paideia Christi', 1–14, and his *Early Christianity and Greek Paideia*, in its entirety. Nasrallah, 'Mapping the World', 289–93. For paideia as the *alma mater* of both Christians and pagans in late antiquity, Urbano, *The Philosophical Life*, 46–54.

Christianity's resemblance with the established schools of philosophy. But the efforts of the independent schools were not entirely a matter of cultural mimicry, having a foundation in the Christian experience itself. For example, the three parts of their curriculum—discussed below—mirror the three stages of Christian initiation, namely, catechumenal training, sacramental enlightenment, and advancement.

It should not come as a surprise that in the second half of the fourth century the Christian ethos was commonly characterised as philosophical life. The idea, introduced in the second century[16] and iterated by Athanasius (d. 373) in the depiction of Antony (d. 356),[17] became commonplace in the Cappadocian discourse.[18] It penetrated the monastic milieux of Egypt towards the end of the same fourth century, undoubtedly through the writings of a disciple of the Cappadocian fathers, Evagrius Ponticus (d. 399). Drawing upon earlier sources,[19] Evagrius[20] described Christian and monastic philosophy as following a Platonic-sounding, threefold curriculum.[21] In the same vein, in the mid-fifth century Theodoret of Cyrrhus (d. 457) referred to the Syrian monks as philosophers.[22] Against this backdrop, the view of Christianity as philosophical was later restricted to monasticism, alternating with its designation as angelic life.[23]

What prompted the early Christians and monastics to define their life as philosophical was a holistic perception of philosophy which in modern times has become largely unfamiliar—as a way of life founded on theoretical axioms, guided by ethical criteria, and aiming at personal betterment and spiritual transformation. In order to retrieve this

---

16 Costache, 'Being', 56–64.
17 Hadot, *Ancient Philosophy*, 242. Urbano, 'Images of Teachers', 19–20.
18 Alieva, 'Moses in the Wilderness', 133–42. Alieva, 'Philosophie et rhétorique', 191–210. Hadot, *Ancient Philosophy*, 241–42. Urbano, 'Images of Teachers', 19–22.
19 Louth, *Origins*, 56–60. Bucur, *Angelomorphic Pneumatology*, 18–24.
20 'Christianity is the teaching of our saviour, Christ, consisting in the practical (life), the natural (contemplation), and the theological (vision)', *The Monk*, 1.
21 For Evagrius' tripartite curriculum, see Hadot, *Ancient Philosophy*, 249–50. For the Platonic curriculum, see Hadot, 'Les divisions', 206–207, 210–11, 218–20, 222 and Louth, *Origins*, 6–13. For a broader philosophical contextualisation of the tripartite curriculum, see Bénatouïl and Bonazzi, 'θεωρία and βίος θεωρητικός', 3–9.
22 Urbano, *The Philosophical Life*, 3. Urbano, 'Images of Teachers', 10, 22–23.
23 Bucur, 'Hierarchy, Eldership, Isangelia', 27–36. Hadot, *Ancient Philosophy*, 241–42, 247–48. Hadot, *Philosophy as a Way of Life*, 130, 269. Zecher, 'Angelic Life', 111–36.

currently unfamiliar understanding, after a foray into Christianity's representations as school, I review several depictions of Jesus as philosopher and teacher.

Together with retrieving this interpretive strand, I emphasise how preaching Jesus Christ was culturally conditioned from the outset. The early Christians preached him in ways that were contextually relevant. The view of Jesus as philosopher, I propose, does not include a historical portrayal in the first place, instead disclosing something fundamental about the views of the community which considered this image meaningful. In short, my essay examines the mindset of Jesus' followers, a mindset which made possible his representation as philosopher.

1. Catechetical Schools, Schools of Christian Philosophy, and Christianity as a Philosophical School

Up until recently, scholars took for granted the existence of early Christian catechetical schools—such as the Alexandrine and the Antiochian ones—which, they supposed, represented distinct theological and exegetical traditions.[24] As it happens, the catechetical schools were episcopal centres, or programmes, of instruction for converts, which existed in many if not all local Christian churches. We do not know much about their workings. The extant series of relevant lectures or instructions come from the fourth century, thus relatively late and from a time when the catechetical schools were rapidly moving towards an untimely demise. The better known series are by Cyril of Jerusalem (d. 386; *Catechetical Lectures* and *Mystagogical Lectures*), Ambrose of Milan (d. 397, *On the Sacraments*), and John Chrysostom (d. 407, *Instructions to Catechumens*).[25] The last known head of an episcopal school for catechumens is Didymus the Blind (d. 398) in Alexandria,[26] but his surviving works do not illustrate his activity as a catechist. Only scarce information from earlier centuries reached us (such as Irenaeus

---

24 This view is no longer fashionable. Clark, 'Early Christian Studies', 9, 23–24. Hoek, 'The "Catechetical" School', 60–61, 85–87. Young, *Biblical Exegesis*, 161–69.
25 For overviews of these catechetical series, see Gavrilyuk, *Histoire du catéchuménat*, 183–86, 189–94, 228–30, 278–308.
26 Louth, 'Athanasius and Didymus', 280–81.

of Lyon's late second-century *On the Apostolic Preaching*) and not in the format of catechesis. Both older and newer writings share in common an interest in the elements of faith and, given the main issue at hand, in the apostolic interpretation of Hebrew Scripture as a Christian book.[27]

While small variations are noticeable,[28] the surviving material does not document catechetical schools in the sense which modern scholars used to discuss, namely, as different and consistent methods in theology and exegesis. Their view was marred by a confusion perpetuated by Eusebius of Caesarea (d. 339),[29] who, being interested in presenting a unified early Christian landscape, conflated the catechetical schools and the independent schools of Christian philosophy. There was nothing in the catechetical schools to resemble the sophisticated theological and exegetical approaches of the independent teachers. As for the teachers mistaken as heads of catechetical schools—such as Justin, Pantaenus, Clement, and Origen—even though their activity cannot be separated from the church's life,[30] they taught Christian philosophy independently. Their methods might have shared in common certain presuppositions, but that does not corroborate the modern concept of consistent schools of thought. For example, Justin and Pantaenus favoured Stoicism without ignoring Platonic concepts, whereas Clement and Origen preferred Platonism but were in fact eclectic. And although Clement and Origen displayed similar philosophical preferences, their output differs significantly. Thus, while Clement proposed an explicit paideutic programme, Origen's philosophy took almost in its entirety the form of scriptural exegesis. Either way, it is these teachers that refined and developed the early Christian theological and exegetical method, undoubtedly due

---

27 Behr, *The Way to Nicaea*, 17–48. Pentiuc, *The Old Testament*, xiii, 16–21, 39–50. Young, *Biblical Exegesis*, 14–15, 21.
28 Compare, for example, the Jewish Christian *Didache* and the Gentile Christian *Letter of Barnabas*, both from the second century. Norris, 'The apostolic and sub-apostolic writings', 11, 15, 19. Norris, 'Articulating Identity', 81, 83, 86.
29 Behr, *The Way to Nicaea*, 166–67. Brakke, 'The East', 349. Hoek, 'The "Catechetical" School', 61–63.
30 Hoek, 'The "Catechetical" School', 71–79.

to their philosophical training.³¹ Sometimes, they did so in ways that could not be sanctioned by the mainstream church, their contributions being eventually forgotten.³²

I must now turn to the philosophical dimension of the early Christian experience. First, I briefly discuss the nature of the catechetical instruction. Second, I survey the activity of the independent schools of Christian philosophy. I contend that, despite the difference, both educational systems illustrate the same philosophical aspect of the early Christian mindset.

1.1 Catechetical Instruction

As I have already shown, the early Christians construed themselves as a community of disciples. This matter was aptly captured by Georges Florovsky:

> From the very beginning Christianity was not primarily a doctrine, but exactly a community. There was not only a Message to be proclaimed and delivered, and Good News to be declared. There was precisely a New Community, distinct and peculiar, in the process of growth and formation, to which members were called and recruited.³³

Florovsky's assessment complements Young's, earlier mentioned, highlighting the priority of the ecclesial body over its own message and doctrine. What the above excerpt means is that the goal of early Christian preaching was not to establish and defend doctrine, but to inaugurate and develop a community of disciples. The community constituted the framework within which teaching was delivered and interpreted, while teaching established the community of disciples and secured its flourishing. Significant is that, responding to the great commission (Matt. 28:18–20), the early Christian community focused upon conversion,

---

31 As a sign of their philosophical training and profession, some, such as Justin and Tertullian, never relinquished their philosophical garment; third-century visual art confirms that many educated Christians wore this attire. Urbano, 'Sizing up the Philosopher's Cloak', 182–86, 191–93. Urbano, 'The Philosopher's Mantle', 218–22.
32 This is the case of Origen, whose methodology has nothing catechetical about it. See Behr, 'Introduction', xvii–xix. See also Edwards, 'Apologetics', 553.
33 Florovsky, *Christianity and Culture*, 67.

teaching, and learning. Teaching was both at the core of the Christian life and instrumental towards mission. It follows that the Christian church was a teaching and learning community, a fellowship of disciples who shared their wisdom and ethos with whoever was interested in receiving them. And since it focused on handing on doctrine—which, we have seen above, is a philosophical activity—the early Christian church was a philosophical community of disciples, resembling any other philosophical school.[34] In so doing, it joined the family of late antique philosophical schools,[35] a trajectory which its Jewish roots doubtlessly facilitated. Indeed, Philo's activity and the synagogal culture of the time mirrored the philosophical schools of the Hellenistic period.[36]

The documentary evidence shows that, overall, the early Christian teaching was communicated in three forms: exhortations to conversion, catechetical preparation, and advanced instruction.[37] The exhortations, which borrowed from a venerable philosophical genre,[38] called on unbelievers to 'taste and see' the nobility of the Christian way of life, presented as philosophical. Most early apologists of the second and the third century adopted this genre, which they used for criticising pagan religion, for praising the philosophical quest, and for proving the superiority of the Christian teaching and ethos. Invariably, the exhortations ended by warmly calling the readers to join the church and be renewed under Christ's own guidance and grace. The classical example for this early Christian genre is Clement of Alexandria's work, *Exhortation to the Gentiles*, whose content is as follows: Christianity is a new, transformative song (1); critique of pagan beliefs and practices (2–4); overview of the philosophical quest (5–7); scriptural utterances (8–9); the beauty of the Christian ethos (10–11); exhortation (12). As a rule, the exhortations did not introduce major theological topics, which were reserved for church's membership.

---

34 For the philosophical schools, see Hadot, *What Is Ancient Philosophy*, 3, 56–57, 59–60, 156.
35 It is for this reason that the suspicion that the early Christian apologists were not sincere in their siding with the philosophers against popular religion does not hold. For an example of scepticism in this regard, see Norris, 'The Apologists', 36–37, 39, 42–43.
36 Hoek, 'The "Catechetical" School', 79–85.
37 See Hoek, 'The "Catechetical" School', 67–71.
38 Heine, 'The Alexandrians', 120. Norris, 'The apostolic and sub-apostolic writings', 12. Young, 'The literary culture of the third century', 173.

In turn, the available catechetical series provide basic theological, ethical, and generally ecclesial instruction for converts, of which some still trained while others prepared for baptismal enlightenment. For example, Cyril of Jerusalem's *Catechetical Lectures* follow the structure of the Nicene creed considered within the broader framework of the local tradition. Specifically, in preparation of those about to be baptised 'for the delivery of the creed' (4.3), they offer a summary of the faith in the Father as one God, creator of all that is and who transcends all things (4.4–6); the Son as God and man, visible and invisible (4.9), and his salvation economy effected through incarnation, cross, tomb, resurrection, ascension, and the final judgment (4.7–15); the Holy Spirit, who possesses all the divine perfections preached about the Father and the Son, 'sanctifier and deifier of all' (4.16–17); the soul (4.18–21); body, food, decent clothing, and resurrection (4.22–31); baptismal regeneration (4.32); and Scripture (4.33–36). After this synthetic introduction, the next lecture contains the text of the creed presented as a faithful summary of the Scriptures (5.12). In order to make sense of the creed, converts should diligently search the Scriptures for confirmation and details. The rest of the lectures, from the sixth to the eighteenth, deal at length with the statements of the Nicene creed and other topics. The above summary shows the complexity of the teaching handed on in the preparatory stage, a teaching which combines doctrinal and ethical topics.[39]

Finally, early Christian discipleship entailed two more stages of instruction, unequal in length. The first stage focused on explaining the initiation rites—baptism, chrismation (or confirmation), and the eucharist—which the recipients underwent without preparation.[40] The explanation followed immediately after the administration of the sacraments, sometimes spanning across several days. The best illustration of this kind of instruction is Cyril of Jerusalem's collection of *Mystagogical*

---

39 For overviews of this catechetical series, see Gavrilyuk, *Histoire du catéchuménat*, 205–209 and Yarnold, *Cyril of Jerusalem*, 22–23. The same doctrinal and ethical preparation already appeared in the second-century work by Clement of Alexandria, *The Pedagogue*, but not in a typical catechetical format.
40 That the 'enlightened' ones did not know the details of their baptism and first communion is made obvious in Justin's second-century *First Apology* 61, 65–66. See also Day, 'Mystagogical Teacher', 62–63.

Lectures, five in total, whose authorship is disputed.[41] These lectures address the spiritual implications of both conversion and the sacramental enlightenment. It presents the neophytes as renewed persons whose life in Christ receive a new impetus through the Spirit's grace in order to pursue virtue.

The postbaptismal, or mystagogical, instruction led to the last stage, which consisted in a lifelong advancement in faith, understanding, and life. This step is typical for what in contemporary culture is known as a learning society, focused on ongoing study. One of the Byzantine liturgies captures the concept with great clarity: 'Grant also to those who pray with us, O God, progress in life and faith and spiritual understanding'.[42] The repetition of this request every time the liturgy is officiated—as it does throughout most of the year—denotes the idea of ongoing instruction, even an open-ended curriculum. Writings such as Clement's *Miscellanies* and the loftier components of his *Didaskalos*, and Origen's *On the Principles*, *Commentary on the Song of Songs*, and *Commentary on John*, address the specifics of this stage. These writings served the interests of sophisticated readers.

The church did not reserve this superior form of training for the intelligentsia. It established, quite early, an annual instruction cycle in the form of its lectionary, still used by several ecclesial traditions. As certain scriptural passages are read for a given Sunday every year, the memory of the listeners is constantly refreshed with lessons which nurture their spiritual progress. Repetition, it is well known, is the mother of all learning. The annual lectionary is a classical mnemonic technique, but repetition contributes to deepen the understanding. Moving through successive yearly cycles, the disciples advance by pondering the same lessons, again and again. The liturgy mentioned above introduces the Gospel reading with this prayer: 'Make the pure light of your divine knowledge shine within our hearts, loving Master, and open the eyes of our mind to understand the message of your Gospel'.[43] Itself being

---

41 Yarnold, *Cyril of Jerusalem*, 23–32. For an overview of this series, see Gavrilyuk, *Histoire du catéchuménat*, 210–14. For the broader curriculum of mystagogical catechesis in late antiquity, see Day, 'Mystagogical Teacher', 57–71.
42 See the second prayer for the believers in *Divine Liturgy*, 42–45.
43 *Divine Liturgy*, 28–29.

repeated every time the liturgy is officiated, this prayer points to the idea of progress through grasping the gospel message better and better.

1.2 Schools of Christian Philosophy

All the above leads to the conclusion that the early Christian church was a genuine learning society, which promoted the ideal of spiritual progress through ongoing study. Once again, the early church was a philosophical school, not a religious organisation.[44] This became even more obvious with the emergence of several independent schools of Christian philosophy in the second century.

Certain early Christian intellectuals—highly educated, some of them professional philosophers—developed the ecclesial training by founding schools of philosophy. I have already mentioned that the independent schools were not the catechetical programmes of the local churches. However, they followed a somewhat similar curriculum. The ecclesial system offered basic catechism, mystagogical initiation, and encouraged ongoing study. In turn, the independent schools led the students from ethical formation to contemplative exercises to divine perception. This mirror structure should not come as a surprise. The catechetical programmes and the independent schools operated within the cultural parameters of the paideutic training for life[45] and the Platonic curriculum.[46]

But there is more to the relation between the catechetical schools and the independent teachers than the latter mirroring the former. The independent schools, beginning with Justin's and ending with Origen's, served the church's interests by teaching both pagan and Christian students. They were so successful in recruiting educated pagans for the Christian way of life, that, as in the case of Justin and his disciples, they angered their pagan competitors who then denounced them to the authorities. What the ecclesial catechesis could not provide, that is, a refined version of Christian teaching, the independent schools did.

---

44 See also Young, 'Christian teaching', 95.
45 For studies of this classical system of education, see Jaeger, *Paideia*, and Borg, *Paideia*. See also Cribiore, *Gymnastics of the Mind*, 127–29, 238–44.
46 For Clement's integration of paideia and the philosophical curriculum, see Hadot, *Ancient Philosophy*, 254–55, and *Philosophy as a Way of Life*, 128.

Not much is known about Justin's and Pantaenus' schools.[47] In turn, the documentary evidence proves that both Clement and Origen were painfully aware of the competitive market of the time—with the Gnostic sects being very popular among the intelligentsia—and that they therefore consistently endeavoured to cater for educated pagans.[48] Accordingly, they devised tripartite curricula which, while mirroring the catechetical approach, presented the Christian message and ethos in ways that met the intelligentsia's expectations. For example, Clement's pedagogy finds a perfect embodiment in the order of his major writings, *Exhortation* (invitation to conversion), *The Pedagogue* (initiation in the Christian faith and way of life), *Miscellanies* (engaging the more profound aspects of Scripture, doctrine, and the spiritual journey), and the notebooks which supposedly composed *Didaskalos* (addressing the mystical experience and the divine insight into Scripture and reality). Except for *Exhortation*, his works illustrate the Platonic curriculum of ethics (formation), physics (contemplation), and epoptics (transformation).[49] Origen illustrated the same curricular structure in his interpretation of three Old Testament books, Proverbs, Ecclesiastes, and Song of Songs.[50] Curricula of this sort—which Evagrius aptly summarised as the very essence of the Christian teaching, as we have seen above—trained the students to become both deeply spiritual people and defenders of the Christian message. As such, stemming from Christianity as a philosophical school, the independent schools exceeded the purview of basic catechism by providing the church with potential leaders, not merely more members. A number of such leaders are known to have emerged from Origen's schools in both Alexandria and Palestinian Caesarea.

In short, from very early on, Christianity displayed the characteristics of a school—a philosophical school properly speaking, in Hadot's sense—not a religion. It was a community of students, a genuine

---

47 For recent overviews, see Gavrilyuk, *Histoire du catéchuménat*, 80–81, 125–26. See also Heine, 'Articulating Identity', 212. Since these schools mirrored the structure of contemporary pagan schools, what we know about the latter is applicable here, too. See Cribiore, *Gymnastics of the Mind*, 36–44, 50–59.
48 Ashwin-Siejkowski, 'Clement of Alexandria', 85–86. Heine, 'The Alexandrians', 119. Le Boulluec, *Alexandrie antique et chrétienne*, 221–32. Runia, *Philo in Early Christian Literature*, 119–31.
49 Bucur, *Angelomorphic Pneumatology*, 18–24. Bucur, 'The Clementine Corpus', 326–29.
50 Hadot, *Ancient Philosophy*, 239–40. Louth, *Origins*, 56–60.

learning society whose members pursued enlightenment beyond baptismal regeneration. Its conversion protocols included three stages of instruction, theoretical and practical, by which a convert became a lifelong student of Jesus Christ and his disciples. Against this backdrop, several Christian philosophers opened independent schools whose activities iterated the apostolic spirit of transformative learning within the rigorous framework of the classical and late antique schools of philosophy. In so doing, they did more than to replicate catechetical instruction. On the one hand, they presented the Christian message in forms acceptable to the intelligentsia; on the other hand, they trained church's leadership. Both forms of Christian instruction, catechetical and independent, shared in common the philosophical drive which from the outset pertained to the Christian ethos.

The representation of the early Christian church as a philosophical school resonated with the image of Christ as Teacher, indeed a sage or philosopher. To this image I must now turn.

2. Jesus Christ as Philosopher

I have already mentioned that the philosophical representations of Christ and of Christianity draw on internal and external factors. Regarding the internal factor, simply put, that is how the first Christian generations perceived both Christ and his church. As to the external factor, ancient philosophical culture provided the closest analogy for the Christian phenomenon—for want of a better word—thus matching the internal criterion. We have seen above that the early Christian communities displayed features typical for the philosophical tradition, related to both the catechetical programmes and the independent schools. In what follows I consider examples of depicting Jesus Christ as philosopher. These illustrations, chronologically, come from two canonical Gospels, Clement of Alexandria, and Neilus the Ascetic (d. ca 430). I consider them in this very order.

2.1 Matthew and Mark

The canonical Gospels paint an icon of Jesus Christ; they do not provide exact snapshots of the Lord in action. Despite one evangelist's claim (Luke 1:4) and apart from the narratives of the trial and the cross, where they gather minute information, the Gospels show no real interest in historical accuracy. They focus upon the acquisition of life through faith in Jesus (John 20:30–31), a message relevant to both Jews and Gentiles (Luke's genealogy and the whole of Matthew), and to the creation in its entirety (Mark 16:15; John 1:1–5). What they offer, accordingly, is not a realistic portrait. Take for instance the otherwise detailed narratives of Jesus' crucifixion, which, against all evidence (Matt. 27:35; Mark 15:24; Luke 23:34; John 19:23–24), refuse to say that he was naked. It goes the same for the oldest images of the crucifixion, which show the Lord fully dressed or wearing a loincloth. As such, after reading the canonical narratives of the crucifixion one does not know about the 'historical Jesus' more than he or she already learned from, say, Isaiah 53. But I do not mean to walk through the valley of the shadow of this minefield, namely, the many and contradictory 'definitive' hypotheses regarding 'the real Jesus of history'. I am interested in three passages which clearly—at least to my eyes—depict Jesus Christ as philosopher or sage.[51]

The first is at Matt. 5:1–2, where the mountain of revelation—Sinai's replica—becomes the setting of a philosophical scene. There, Jesus sits down, teaching his few disciples and the large crowds. The scene echoes the typical posture, common to a Platonic school in late antiquity,[52] of a seated philosopher, a symbol of wisdom, surrounded by the circles of advanced and less advanced students. We know from Luke 6:17 that the ensuing sermon, which contains the 'Beatitudes', actually took place on a field and that initially Jesus stood up. However, there is indication that just before he uttered the 'Beatitudes' he sat down, 'looking up at his disciples' (Luke 6:20). Here, apart from the different setting, the two narratives converge. But while Luke merely noted the chronology of the scene, Matthew introduced it as he did on purpose. Specifically, from a scriptural vantage point, Jesus is the new Moses, preaching on

---

51 I use sage in the sense of Hadot, *Ancient Philosophy*, 220–23. Interestingly, however, at 237 Hadot referred to Jesus as presenting no philosophical features—features which were later added to his portrait by his disciples. A thorough comparison between Jesus and Socrates can be found in Wenley, *Socrates and Christ*, 236–64.
52 Hadot, *What Is Ancient Philosophy*, 60–61, 99–100. See also Urbano, 'Images of Teachers', 7–10, and the imagery presented at 16–17.

Sinai's replica mountain, but, considered through a cultural lens, he is a philosopher.

The second relevant passage is at Mark 4:1–2,10–11, where Jesus taught while sitting in a boat moored at seashore. The image of the seated philosopher is inescapable, despite his unconventional *cathedra*. The distinction between the few/immediate and the many/distant disciples is even more obvious here. After he told parables to the large audience, Jesus clarified the message only for 'those who were around him together with the twelve' (v. 10), but not for 'outsiders' (v. 11). Should one represent this scene graphically, here we have three circles of disciples: the twelve, those alongside the twelve (perhaps a reference to the seventy), and the many. The aspect of philosophical school is equally inescapable. The third occurrence is at Mark 6:34,41, where Jesus, after teaching the crowds—the many/distant disciples—in a remote place, fed them miraculously through his immediate disciples. Teaching and feeding, or teaching as feeding, became a *leitmotif* in Evagrius' philosophical discourse (see his *The Gnostic* 46).

In all three instances, the Lord appears as a holy sage, the teacher par excellence, the master of the school. All these passages present an inner circle, the twelve, an outer circle, possibly coinciding with the seventy, and the outermost circle of casual listeners. (Other passages [Matt. 4:18–22; 17:1; 26:37; Mark 1:16–20; 9:2; 14:33; Luke 9:28] present an elite group of three or four within the inner circle.) The ranks within the school were clearly demarcated, corresponding to the typical structure of a philosophical school. All this confirms that Jesus' sitting posture is a philosophical stance. This conclusion might cast a different light on similar or related scriptural instances.

If the Gospel accounts merely sketch Jesus and his disciples in philosophical hues, in the second century the philosophical representation of their school was already a given. On this note, I turn to a witness from that time, Clement.

2.2 Clement of Alexandria

Undoubtedly, Clement drew upon the Gospel representations of Christ as philosopher, and also emulated Justin's view that the teachings of Jesus, Logos incarnate, are the origin and the culmination of all philosophical thought.[53] As such, he articulated a solid and coherent image of the Lord as holy sage, or an accomplished philosopher—the perfect representative of what Clement designated as 'barbarous philosophy'.[54] Here is a summary of his relevant contributions.

He presented Jesus Christ as supreme educator and teacher, who, as Saviour, Lord, and Son of God, leads his believers to perfection (*The Educator* 1.1.1-2.4).[55] Jesus is 'true gnosis and light' (*Miscellanies* 6.1.2.4.), who 'offers and reveals' to the diligent searchers the understanding 'of things that are and will be' (*Miscellanies* 6.7.61.1). Without Jesus' guidance it is impossible to draw a comprehensive map of reality (*Miscellanies* 6.7.57.2; 6.7.58.1). Nevertheless, ultimately Jesus is the content and the end of all contemplation (*Miscellanies* 5.10.66.2; 5.11.70.1; 6.7.55.2). During his teaching ministry, he adopted pedagogical protocols which mirrored the ancient schools of philosophy. Thus, he instructed his immediate disciples into 'the hidden traditions of true knowledge' (*Miscellanies* 1.12.56.2), offering the deepest teachings to the very few who were apt to receive them (*Miscellanies* 1.1.13.2-4), but not to the untrained many (*Miscellanies* 1.12.55.1).[56] The success of Christ's pedagogical approach was obvious in the training of 'true gnostics, such as James, Peter, John, and Paul, and the other apostles' (*Miscellanies* 6.8.68.2). Corresponding to the successors of the ancient philosophers, Jesus' disciples followed in his footsteps, advancing through stages of initiation. Clement called Jesus' teaching, which the apostles continued, 'holy gnosis' and 'gnostic tradition' (*Miscellanies* 3.9.67.2; 5.10.63.1).

Except for the initiation vocabulary, which echoes the spiritual and intellectual elitism of the time, Clement's description captures the same view of Christ as philosopher and of the church as a philosophical school, encountered in the Gospels. He actually produced quotations from the Pauline corpus and *Letter of Barnabas* to support this view (*Miscellanies* 5.10.60–65). Against this backdrop, no wonder that in the third century Christians began to represent Jesus in philosophical

---

53 Norris, 'The Apologists', 39.
54 Stroumsa, 'Philosophy of the Barbarians', 343–54. Hadot, *Ancient Philosophy*, 239.
55 Costache, 'Being', 58–60.
56 Costache, 'Christian Gnosis', 260–61.

postures in sculpted compositions.[57] Two centuries after Clement, John Chrysostom still considered the apostles people who, being Christ's disciples, attained the highest philosophy and gnosis (*Homilies on Matthew* 1.10-12).

2.3 Neilus the Ascetic

The final witness I have chosen, representing the monastic tradition, is Neilus, an ascetic from Ancyra (modern Ankara), possibly the abbot of a local monastery and a disciple of John Chrysostom's. From the outset of his *Ascetic Discourse* (whose edition is found in the eighteenth-century Athonite collection of spiritual writings, *The Philokalia*), Neilus considered Christianity the culmination of the search which Greek and Jewish philosophers had begun centuries earlier. In what follows I discuss only matters outlined in the prologue to this work.

The appraisal of the Gospel as supreme philosophy is by no means novel, as we have seen above. Long rehearsed is also Neilus' conviction that the philosophical quest of both Greeks and Jews was unsuccessful because of a disparity between their discourse and lifestyle.[58] In short, possibly following Justin Martyr (*Dialogue with Trypho* 2) and John Chrysostom (*Homilies on Matthew* 1.11), Neilus believed that the earlier failures originated in the incapacity of the seekers to pursue a philosophical way of life that matched their lofty discourses. According to him, indeed, 'philosophy is an ethical state allied with the discourse regarding the true knowledge of reality'. The pagan philosophers especially failed on this count. Nevertheless, a more profound cause of their failure is that 'they rejected the Wisdom from heaven, attempting to philosophise without Christ, who alone exemplified the true philosophy in both deed and word'. This was the main shortcoming of Jewish philosophers. It is against this backdrop that Neilus introduced Christ and his disciples as accomplished philosophers.

Jesus' disciples attained 'true wisdom' primarily due to having

---

57 Urbano, 'Images of Teachers', 17. See also a couple of fourth-century images of Christ as philosopher in Frazer, 'Iconic Representations', 524–25, 527.
58 Hadot, *Ancient Philosophy*, 173–75 pointed out that, while different, discourse and lifestyle are inseparable. That said, Christian authors such as Justin, Tatian, and Neilus plainly accused the ancient and late ancient philosophers of immorality.

'Wisdom as their teacher'. This is not only a reference to Christ as God's Word, Power, and Wisdom (1 Cor. 1:24; John 1:1–2), though Neilus undoubtedly alluded to Jesus' divine status too. Instead, this is another point about Jesus teaching 'by example' his disciples 'the way of life they should follow'. Wisdom finds expression in concrete exemplifications, not in lofty reasoning. In the same vein, the prologue to *Ascetic Discourse* depicts Jesus as the one who

> was the first to set the way of true philosophy, revealing it by the purity of his conduct. He ever maintained his soul above the passions of the body. At the end, when his death was required by his economy for humankind's salvation, he despised it [i.e., death]. In so doing, he taught us that whoever wishes to philosophise correctly must renounce all of life's pleasures, mastering pains and passions, and despising the body. Such a person must not consider life something worthwhile, giving it up willingly when there is a need to surrender it for the sake of virtue. (my translation)

While the above passage gives an accurate summary of the Lord's teaching, Neilus' philosophical rendition is unmistakeable. Throughout the Gospels, he found elements corresponding to the profile of an accomplished philosopher who offered lessons in both word and deed. Jesus is the supreme sage, for he teaches through the example of his own, perfect life. Neilus continued the portrait of Jesus with an equally philosophical summary of the apostles' trajectory. They appropriated Christ's way of life by imitating it, 'renouncing their life when he called them, disregarding their country, their relatives, and their possessions'. Following their conversion, they experienced all kinds of adversity for the gospel, eventually meeting death with courage. Thus did they imitate their Teacher 'faithfully, in all things', 'leaving behind the image of the most distinguished way of life'.

It is obvious that, both in regards to Jesus and his disciples, the highest philosophy was not a discourse; it was an eminent lifestyle. And while Neilus presented his case with great enthusiasm—namely, that Christianity is philosophically superior to any other quests—he was no less realistic. Specifically, after this prologue he turned to a lengthy analysis of Christians' involution after the apostles, a gradual process which reached its climax with the dereliction of monastic life.[59] While Christian philosophy is not the book's main topic, it nevertheless serves as a template for affirming the standards which Christians must uphold. More importantly, the book's outline of Christian philosophy emphasises important elements of the early Christian perception of Christ as philosopher and of the church as a philosophical school. These elements match what we discovered in the Gospels and in Clement.

3. Conclusions

While inspired by the disciples' immediate experience with him, the image of Jesus was from the outset culturally contextualised, for missionary and pastoral reasons. Primarily, contextualisation was demanded by the highly competitive landscape of late antiquity, which shaped the Christian message in ways which satisfied the exigencies of the intelligentsia. One such way of representing Jesus, his ministry, his disciples, and his church was the philosophical one. Through this lens, Jesus appeared as the supreme teacher whose perfect philosophy was embodied in his way of life; his lifestyle, in exchange, inspired his disciples who, furthermore, instructed their own disciples in the highest philosophy both through catechism and via advanced training. As such, the early Christian and monastic representations of Jesus as philosopher and of the church as a philosophical school match the Hadotian criteria of perfect philosophy, irreducible to a discourse. The foregoing analysis brought to the fore that, overall, these representations focused on the ethical accomplishments of both the Teacher and his disciples. All this confirms the initial point of this essay—that from the outset and for several centuries Christianity understood itself as a philosophical school, not a religion.

---

59 While he too identified the object of philosophy with ethics, Wenley, *Socrates and Christ*, 247–48, pointed out similarly the incapacity of Christians to attain the standard.

Bibliography

Alieva, O.   'Moses in the Wilderness: Basil of Caesarea on Formation of the Prophet', *Scrinium* 15 (2019), 133–42.

Alieva, O.   'Philosophie et rhétorique dans l'Observe-toi toi-même de Basile de Césarée', in B. Pouderon and A. Usacheva (eds.), *Dire Dieu: Principes méthodologiques de l'écriture sur Dieu en patristique* (Théologique Historique 124: Paris: Beauchesne, 2017), 191–210.

Ashwin-Siejkowski, P.   'Clement of Alexandria', in K. Parry (ed.), *The Wiley Blackwell Companion to Patristics* (Chichester: Wiley Blackwell, 2015), 84–97.

Azkoul, M.   'The Greek Fathers: Polis and Paideia', *St Vladimir's Theological Quarterly* 23:1–2 (1979), 3–21, 67–86.

Behr, J. (ed. and tr.)   'Introduction', in *Origen: On First Principles*, vol. 1 (Oxford Early Christian Texts; Oxford University Press, 2017), xv–xcviii.

Behr, J.   *The Formation of Christian Theology*, vol. 1: *The Way to Nicaea* (Crestwood, NY: St Vladimir's Seminary Press, 2001).

Bénatouïl, T., and M. Bonazzi,   'θεωρία and βίος θεωρητικός from the Presocratics to the End of Antiquity: An Overview', in T. Bénatouïl and M. Bonazzi (eds.), *Theoria, Praxis and the Contemplative Life after Plato and Aristotle* (Philosophia Antiqua 131; Leiden and Boston: Brill, 2012), 1–14.

Brakke, D.   'The East (2): Egypt and Palestine', in S. Ashbrook Harvey and D. G. Hunter (eds.), *The Oxford Handbook of Early Christian Studies* (New York: Oxford University Press, 2008), 344–64.

Borg, B.E. (ed.)   *Paideia: The World of the Second Sophistic* (Berlin and New York: Walter de Gruyter, 2004).

Brisson, L.   *How Philosophers Saved Myths: Allegorical Interpretation and Classical Mythology* (Trans. C. Tihanyi; Chicago and London: The University of Chicago Press, 2004).

Bucur, B.G.   'Hierarchy, Eldership, Isangelia: Clement of Alexandria and the Ascetic Tradition', in D. Costache, P. Kariatlis, and M. Baghos (eds.), *Alexandrian Legacy: A Critical Appraisal* (Newcastle upon Tyne: Cambridge Scholars Publishing, 2015), 2–45.

Bucur, B.G.	*Angelomorphic Pneumatology: Clement of Alexandria and Other Early Christian Witnesses* (Leiden and Boston: Brill, 2009).
Bucur, B.G.	'The Place of the *Hypotyposeis* in the Clementine Corpus: An Apology for The Other Clement of Alexandria', *Journal of Early Christian Studies* 17:3 (2009), 313–35.
Chadwick, H.	*The Early Church* (The Pelican History of the Church 1; Harmondsworth: Penguin Books, 1973).
Clark, E.A.	'From Patristics to Early Christian Studies', in S. Ashbrook Harvey and D. G. Hunter (eds.), *The Oxford Handbook of Early Christian Studies* (New York: Oxford University Press, 2008), 7–41.
Costache, D.	'Christian Gnosis: From Clement the Alexandrian to John Damascene', in G. W. Trompf, G. B. Mikkelsen, and J. Johnston (eds.), *The Gnostic World* (Routledge Worlds; London and New York: Routledge, 2019), 259–70.
Costache, D.	'Being, Well-being, Being for Ever: Creation's Existential Trajectory in Patristic Tradition', in D. Costache, D. Cronshaw, and J. Harrison (eds), *Well-being, Personal Wholeness and the Social Fabric* (Newcastle upon Tyne: Cambridge Scholars Publishing, 2017), 55–87.
Costache, D.	'Christianity and the World in the *Letter to Diognetus*: Inferences for Contemporary Christian Experience', *Phronema* 27:1 (2012), 29–50.
Cribiore, R.	*Gymnastics of the Mind: Greek Education in Hellenistic and Roman Egypt* (Princeton and Oxford: Princeton University Press, 2001).
Dawson, J.D.	'Christian Teaching', in F.M. Young, L. Ayres, and A. Louth (eds.), *The Cambridge History of Early Christian Literature* (Cambridge University Press, 2004), 222–38.
Day, J.J.	'The Bishop as Mystagogical Teacher', in P. Gemeinhardt, O. Lorgeoux, and M. Munkholt Christensen (eds.), *Teachers in Late Antique Christianity* (SERAPHIM 3; Tübingen: Mohr Siebek, 2018): 56–75.
[Divine Liturgy]	*The Divine Liturgy of Our Father among the Saints John Chrysostom*, bilingual edition (Sydney: St Andrew's Orthodox Press, 2005).

Drobner, H. R.	'Christian Philosophy', in S. Ashbrook Harvey and D. G. Hunter (eds.), *The Oxford Handbook of Early Christian Studies* (New York: Oxford University Press, 2008), 672–90.
Edwards, M.	'Apologetics', in S. Ashbrook Harvey and D. G. Hunter (eds.), *The Oxford Handbook of Early Christian Studies* (New York: Oxford University Press, 2008), 549–64.
Florovsky, G.	*Christianity and Culture* (Collected Works 2; Belmont, MA: Nordland Publishing Company, 1974).
Frazer, M.E.	'Iconic Representations', in K. Weitzmann (ed.), *Age of Spirituality: Late Antique and Early Christian Art, Third to Seventh Century* (New York: The Metropolitan Museum of Art and Princeton University Press, 1979), 513–55.
Gavrilyuk, P.	*Histoire du catéchuménat dans l'Église ancienne* (Initiations aux Pères de l'Église; Paris: Cerf, 2007).
Gemeinhardt, P.	'In Search of Christian Paideia: Education and Conversion in Early Christian Biography', *Zeitung für antikes Christentum* 16:1 (2012), 88–98.
Hadot, P.	*What Is Ancient Philosophy?* (Trans. M. Chase; Cambridge, MA, & London: Harvard University Press, 2002).
Hadot, P.	*Philosophy as a Way of Life: Spiritual Exercises from Socrates to Foucault* (Trans. M. Chase; Oxford: Blackwell, 1995).
Hadot, P.	'Les divisions des parties de la philosophie dans l'Antiquité', *Museum Helveticum* 36:4 (1979), 201–23. Translation: 'Forms of Life and Forms of Discourse in Ancient Philosophy' (trans. A. I. Davidson and P. Wissing) *Critical Enquiry* 16:3 (1990), 483–505.
Heine, R.E.	'The Alexandrians', in F.M. Young, L. Ayres, and A. Louth (eds.), *The Cambridge History of Early Christian Literature* (Cambridge University Press, 2004), 117–130.
Heine, R.E.	'Articulating Identity', in F.M. Young, L. Ayres, and A. Louth (eds.), *The Cambridge History of Early Christian Literature* (Cambridge University Press, 2004), 200–21.
Hoek, A. van den	'The "Catechetical" School of Early Christian Alexandria and Its Philonic Heritage', *Harvard Theological Review* 90:1 (1997), 59–87.

Jaeger, W.	*Paideia: The Ideals of Greek Culture* (G. Highet, trans.; 3 vols.; Oxford University Press, ²1986 [1944]).
Jaeger, W.	*Early Christianity and Greek Paideia* (Cambridge, MA: Harvard University Press, 1961).
Jaeger, W.	'Paideia Christi', *Zeitschrift für die neutestamentliche Wissenschaft und die Kunde der älteren Kirche* 50:1–2 (1959), 1–14.
Le Boulluec, A.	*Alexandrie antique et chrétienne: Clément et Origène*, ed. Carmelo Giuseppe Conticello (Collection des Études Augustiniennes: Série Antiquité 178; Paris: Institut d'Études Augustiniennes, 2006).
Louth, A.	*The Origins of the Christian Mystical Tradition: From Plato to Denys* (New York: Oxford University Press, ²2007 [1981]).
Louth, A.	'The fourth-century Alexandrians: Athanasius and Didymus', in F.M. Young, L. Ayres, and A. Louth (eds.), *The Cambridge History of Early Christian Literature* (Cambridge University Press, 2004), 272–82.
Nasrallah, L.	'Mapping the World: Justin, Tatian, Lucian, and the Second Sophistic', *Harvard Theological Review* 98:3 (2005), 283–314.
Norris, R.A., Jr.	'The Apostolic and Sub-Apostolic Writings: The New Testament and the Apostolic Fathers', in F.M. Young, L. Ayres, and A. Louth (eds.), *The Cambridge History of Early Christian Literature* (Cambridge University Press, 2004), 11–19.
Norris, R.A., Jr.	'The Apologists', in F.M. Young, L. Ayres, and A. Louth (eds.), *The Cambridge History of Early Christian Literature* (Cambridge University Press, 2004), 36–44.
Norris, R.A., Jr.	'Articulating Identity', in F.M. Young, L. Ayres, and A. Louth (eds.), *The Cambridge History of Early Christian Literature* (Cambridge University Press, 2004), 71–90.
Pentiuc, E.J.	*The Old Testament in Eastern Orthodox Tradition* (New York: Oxford University Press, 2014).
Runia, D.T.	*Philo in Early Christian Literature: A Survey* (Jewish Traditions in Early Christian Literature 3; Assen and Minneapolis: Van Gorcum and Fortress Press, 1993).

Sanzo, J. E.	'Early Christianity', in D. Frankfurter (ed.), *Guide to the Study of Ancient Magic* (Leiden and Boston: Brill: 2019), 198–239.
Stroumsa, G.G.	'Philosophy of the Barbarians: On Early Christian Ethnological Representations', in H. Cancik et al. (eds.), *Geschichte-Tradition-Reflexion: Festschrift Martin Hengel*, vol. 2 (Tübingen: Mohr Siebeck, 1996), 339–68.
Urbano, A.P., Jr.	'Literary and Visual Images of Teachers in Late Antiquity', in P. Gemeinhardt, O. Lorgeoux, and M. Munkholt Christensen (eds.), *Teachers in Late Antique Christianity* (SERAPHIM 3; Tübingen: Mohr Siebek, 2018), 1–31.
Urbano, A.P., Jr.	'The Philosopher Type in Late Roman Art: Problematizing Cultural Appropriation in Light of Cultural Competition', in N. P. DesRosiers and L. C. Vuong (eds.), *Religious Competition in the Greco-Roman World* (Writings from the Greco-Roman World Supplement Series 10; Atlanta: SBL Press, 2016), 27–40.
Urbano, A.P., Jr.	'Sizing up the Philosopher's Cloak: Christian Verbal and Visual Representations of the *Tribōn*', in K. Upson-Saia, C. Daniel-Hughes, and A. J Batten (eds.), *Dressing Judeans and Christians in Antiquity* (Farnham: Ashgate, 2014), 175–94.
Urbano, A.P., Jr.	*The Philosophical Life: Biography and the Crafting of Intellectual Identity in Late Antiquity* (Washington, DC: The Catholic University of America Press, 2013).
Urbano, A.P., Jr.	'"Dressing a Christian": The Philosopher's Mantle as Signifier of Pedagogical and Moral Authority', *Studia Patristica* 62 (2013), 213–29.
Wenley, R.M.	*Socrates and Christ: A Study in the Philosophy of Religion* (Edinburgh and London: William Blackwood and Sons, 1889).
Yarnold, E.	*Cyril of Jerusalem* (The Early Church Fathers; Lonon and New York: Routledge, 2000).
Young, F.M.	'Christian Teaching', in F.M. Young, L. Ayres, and A. Louth (eds.), *The Cambridge History of Early Christian Literature* (Cambridge University Press, 2004), 91–104.

Young, F.M.	'Conclusion: Towards a Hermeneutic of Second-Century Texts', in F.M. Young, L. Ayres, and A. Louth (eds.), *The Cambridge History of Early Christian Literature* (Cambridge University Press, 2004), 105–11.
Young, F.M.	'Concluding Review: The Literary Culture of the Third Century', F.M. Young, L. Ayres, and A. Louth (eds.), *The Cambridge History of Early Christian Literature* (Cambridge University Press, 2004), 172–78.
Young, F.M.	*Biblical Exegesis and the Formation of Christian Culture* (Cambridge University Press, 1997).
Zecher, Jonathan	'The Angelic Life in Desert and Ladder: John Climacus's Re-Formulation of Ascetic Spirituality', *Journal of Early Christian Studies* 21:1 (2013), 111–36.

PART C:
THE PASTORAL AND ECCLESIAL LEGACY OF JESUS OF NAZARETH

CHAPTER 10

Becoming a Merciful High Priest: The New *Ratio Fundamentalis* for Seminary Formation

Norlan Julia

Abstract

In the latest *Ratio Fundamentalis* on priestly formation issued by the Vatican Congregation for the Clergy, emphasis is placed on two key areas: human accompaniment and discernment in the training of future priests. The *Ratio* envisions 'priests with friendly traits, who are authentic, loyal, interiorly free, affectively stable, capable of weaving together peaceful interpersonal relationships and living the evangelical counsels without rigidity, hypocrisy or loopholes'. This chapter explores how the portrait of Jesus as the High Priest is helpful in the reception and implementation of the *Ratio* in seminary formation in the Philippines and in Asia more generally. An appreciation that the priesthood of Christ is characterised by humanity, solidarity in suffering, and mercy towards humanity is crucial for a more comprehensive understanding of the role of priests today and in drawing up a formation program that can better prepare young men to embrace the vocation of being 'ministers of mercy'.

Introduction: Context, Content, Method

I write this paper in the context of the major seminary where I serve as Rector and Professor of Theology. This seminary, St. John Vianney Theological Seminary (SJVTS), is one three seminaries in Mindanao, Southern Philippines. SJVTS is 36-year old interdiocesan seminary owned by the bishops of Northern Mindanao, but is administered by a mixed team of Jesuits, diocesan priests, and a lay counsellor. SJVTS started with 37 seminarians in 1985. Over the next five years, when all year levels had been filled, SJVTS had 120 seminarians.[1] The number of seminarians steadily increased until around 2012 when the numbers began to decline slowly to about half of what it was in 1995. From 2013 to the present, the average number of seminarians in SJVTS is only between 55–60. Nonetheless, as of May 2021, SJVTS has graduated 601 alumni, including laymen and women who registered in the Graduate Theology Program. Of these, 440 have been ordained priests and six have been named bishops. They come from sixteen dioceses in Mindanao, three dioceses in the Visayas, an island in Central Philippines, one diocese in Myanmar, the military ordinariate and five religious congregations.

One of SJVTS' unique features is its mixed formation team of Jesuits, diocesan priests, and a laywoman counsellor. When SJVTS opened in 1985, there were no available diocesan priests in the area trained and equipped to run a seminary. Hence, the local ordinary at that time asked the Jesuit Provincial to assign men for this task. The Society of Jesus willingly obliged to the bishop's request and sent three Jesuits to begin the seminary. From 1985 to 2000, SJVTS had been run by an all-Jesuit formation team. In 2000, some of the Jesuits in SJVTS were re-assigned and the Provincial could not replace them. Hence, diocesan priests started to serve in SJVTS as resident formators-professors. Since then, the formation team of SJVTS had always been a mix of Jesuits and diocesan priests. The Rector, however, remains a Jesuit. In 2005, a former Columban laywoman missionary joined the formation team as the vocational growth counsellor. While not a resident in the seminary, she is fully involved in the formation program, particularly in the human

---

1   For a brief history of SJVTS, see Julia, 'Vianney Seminary', 83–87.

formation of the seminarians.²

The arrival of a female counsellor was a landmark event in the history of SJVTS. It has never happened that a woman was a member of the formation team. In most seminaries in the Philippines, women are invited for occasional lectures or as visiting professors, but are not considered full time members of the formation team. Previously, too, only seminarians 'with problems' were referred to a counsellor. This created a stigma against confronting one's psychological and developmental issues. Furthermore, the human formation component of seminary formation did not receive as much attention as it did until our lady counsellor came. Again, at best, we had occasional lectures on topics pertaining to human development. If problems of psychological nature arise, the seminarians are asked to see their spiritual director who may not necessarily be equipped to handle the problem brought before them by the seminarians.

The new *Ratio Fundamentalis Institutionis Sacerdotalis* (*Ratio*) which underlines the importance of human formation in the seminary affirms our efforts in SJVTS to implement and continuously improve the human formation as 'the necessary solid foundation of the entire priestly formation'.³ Hence, we are grateful for this document and would like to appropriate it in our context as a seminary in Mindanao. Despite the decrease in numbers of seminarians, we believe that the Lord will continue to call young men to the priesthood. We believe, too, that with humble and magnanimous cooperation on the part of the *formandus*, the Holy Spirit can work through the intricate web of human development concerns that young men carry with them to the seminary. The *Ratio*, therefore, serves as an inspiration and a compass as we seek to make our formation program contextualized and inculturated as well as integrated and interactive.⁴ It is with this objective in mind that I decided to write this chapter. First and foremost, it bears on me as seminary rector to be familiar with this document if I am to effectively fulfil my duties as overseer of the formation program for our seminarians.

---

2 Julia, 'Vianney Seminary', 85–86.
3 Catholic Bishops' Conference of the Philippines (CBCP), *Updated Philippine Program for Priestly Formation* (UPPPF) (Manila: CBCP, 2006), xxiii.
4 *UPPPF*, xxiii.

This chapter has three parts. The first is a review of the portrait of Jesus as High Priest in the Letter to the Hebrews. This is crucial since a deeper understanding of the image of Jesus as High Priest in Hebrews leads to a more vibrant reception and implementation of the *Ratio* in our seminary formation here in the Philippines, even in Asia. The second part takes an in-depth look at the *Ratio*. It examines the *Ratio's* presuppositions regarding formation and its image of the seminarian who undergoes formation. It looks at the qualities desired of priests and the privileged means by which to form seminarians into shepherds. The third part describes the priest as imaged in the Letter to the Hebrews and the *Ratio*. It elaborates on the thesis that the priest, patterned after Jesus the High Priest, is a minister of mercy. He is one deeply in touch with his own humanity and in true solidarity with his fellow human beings. His ministry of shepherding consists primarily in being a companion to his people. Finally, the last part of the chapter enumerates some of the ways in which we in SJVTS are responding to the *Ratio*.

I. Jesus the High Priest in Hebrews

Nowhere else in Scriptures except in the Letter to the Hebrews is Jesus referred to as High Priest. Some passages in Paul's letters speak of the sacrificial nature of Jesus' death (Rom. 3.25; Gal. 2.20), but these passages do not explicitly name Jesus a priest. Although some scholars attribute priestly character to the life and ministry of Jesus, still these do not designate Jesus as a priest. We focus, therefore, on the Letter to the Hebrews in our study of the priesthood of Jesus, especially because of its uniqueness and excellence. Contrasting the priesthood of Jesus with the priesthood in the Old Testament, we highlight the key characteristics of Jesus' priesthood: specifically, that it is a priesthood of solidarity, mercy, and suffering unto glory.

Priests in the Ancient Israel: Tasks and Traits

Tom Greggs enumerates some identifiers of priesthood in the Old Testament, namely, mediation, pointing to God, sacrifice, oblation, bearing iniquity, proclaiming of blessing. Of these, the priest's primary task is that of direct mediation and intercession with God.[5] Roland de Vaux argues that in ancient Israel, 'the priest was a mediator, like the king and the prophet. But kings and prophets were mediators by reason of a personal charisma, because they were individually chosen by God; the priest was *ipso facto* a mediator, for priesthood is an institution of mediation'.[6] De Vaux also argues that all other priestly functions stem from this primary function. Secondly, priests witness to God's covenant with his people. The cultic activity of the priest points to the mercy and forgiveness of God. This is the core meaning of third identifier of priesthood—sacrifice, which is central to the understanding of priesthood in ancient Israel. The sacrifice offered by the priest is efficacious not in themselves, but in their value as signs of God's forgiveness.[7]

A key characteristic of priesthood in the Old Testament is its emphasis on the separation of the priest from the people through the rituals of sanctification (Deut. 18.1–2; Lev. 8.21). Hence, the high priests appeared to be elevated above common mortals (Sir. 45.6). Sirach describes the priest in celestial or heavenly similes:

> How glorious he was when the people gathered round him
> as he came out of the inner sanctuary!
> Like the morning star among the clouds,
> like the moon when it is full;
> like the sun shining upon the temple of the Most High,
> and like the rainbow gleaming in glorious clouds.[8]

Such is the required ritual separation to maintain the purity of the priesthood that all contact with death is prohibited because it is incompatible with the holiness of God. Not even mourning is allowed (Lev. 21:11) because it implies contact with death.[9] The unfortunate consequences of this exalted status accorded to the priest were the ambitions, rivalries, jealousies, corruption, political manipulation and maneuvering, homicidal treachery among the priests themselves (Num. 16; 2 Mac. 4).[10]

---

5   Greggs, 'The Priesthood of No Believer', 378–79.
6   De Vaux, *Ancient Israel: Its Life and Institutions*, 357.
7   Greggs, 'Priesthood of No Believer', 378.
8   Vanhoye, Christ Our High Priest, 32. Cf. Healy, 'Christ's Priesthood and Christian Priesthood', 398.
9   Vanhoye, *Christ our High Priest*, 33.
10 Vanhoye, *Christ our High Priest*, 32.

Priesthood of Christ: Solidarity, Mercy, Suffering

Ole Filtvedt and Martin Wessbrandt see an intimate link between worship and the idea that Jesus is high priest. For them, liturgy exerted a big influence in early Christian imagination and practice and this led to the development of the theology of Jesus as High Priest. They infer that the absence of thorough explanation of Jesus' High Priesthood may point to the fact that people took it for granted that Jesus is High Priest.[11] The priesthood of Jesus as portrayed by the Letter to the Hebrews appears as the fulfilment of the Old Testament priesthood which had been in search for its ultimate and definitive meaning. Benedict XVI proposes this as the hermeneutical key in understanding the meaning of Christ's priesthood. He asserts that "the religious law abolished after the destruction of the Temple was actually moving towards Christ. Hence it was not really abolished but renewed, transformed, so that in Christ all things might find their meaning. The priesthood thus appears in its purity and in its profound depth".[12]

In summarising the elements of the OT priesthood vis-à-vis the priesthood of Christ, Gerald O'Collins identifies three main 'qualifications' of Jesus as High Priest: (1) that he is taken from among human beings; (2) that he is appointed (by God) on behalf of human beings in relation to God; (3) that he is to offer sacrifices and gifts.[13] We shall focus on the first qualification, the priest's being taken from among human beings to underline Jesus' solidarity with humanity. This is the basis for his merciful intercession and interaction with his people. His solidarity with humanity made him into a merciful high priest. "Therefore, he had to be made like his brethren in every respect, so that he might become a merciful and faithful High Priest" (Heb 2.17).

In contrast to the OT priesthood which privileged separation, the newness of Christ's priesthood lies in his solidarity with his brothers and sisters. He renounced all privileges and made himself like them in every way. He allowed himself to be subjected to treachery and humiliation in his passion and death. Not only did he take up a human form. Instead, Christ chose the lowest position: a complete solidarity with

---

11 Filtvedt and Wessbrandt, 'Exploring the High Priesthood', 113.
12 Benedict XVI, *Lectio Divina*, Accessed 22 September 2017.
13 O'Collins and Jones, *Jesus Our Priest*, 47–48.

the least of men, that is, with those condemned to death".[14] "Because he himself suffered and was tempted, he is able to help those who are tempted" (v.18). Vanhoye asserts that by his solidarity, Christ 'effectively achieved what the old rites of priestly consecration, by means of separation, sought in vain to obtain, namely: the elevation of man to intimacy with God and the union of human nature with the divine'.[15] This acceptance was, at the same time, an act of priestly mercy. Jesus descended into the depths of human misery which is ultimately experienced in suffering and death. He infused it with divine love and traced a way out for us. He transformed suffering and death into an occasion of extreme love. This was his task as high priest.[16]

Vanhoye asserts that the mercy of Christ is not merely a sentiment felt easily and superficially. Instead, it is a deeply felt sentiment of one who has personally experienced and shared the actual suffering of men and women. 'Christ can have pity because he has been tested in all things, just like us. From his birth, he knew poverty and exclusion; he knew hunger, thirst, tiredness, contradiction, hostility, betrayal, unjust condemnation, even the cross. In this way, he acquired an extraordinary capacity for compassionate understanding'.[17] Hence, O'Collins and Jones argue that the priesthood of Christ started in his incarnation when he took up the human condition. 'Christ's priesthood embraced his whole life—from his coming into the world to do God's will (Heb. 10.5–7) and living a 'holy, blameless and undefiled' life (Heb. 7.26) during 'all his days in the flesh' (Heb 5.7)'.[18] True, his death, resurrection and exaltation in heaven is the high point of his priesthood, but his entire life, from birth to his death are integral part of his priestly ministry.

---

14 Vanhoye, *Christ our High Priest*, 33.
15 Vanhoye, *Christ our High Priest*, 34.
16 Vanhoye, *Christ our High Priest*, 34.
17 Vanhoye, *Christ our High Priest*, 48.
18 O'Collins and Jones, *Jesus Our Priest*, 50, 242–43. 'Christian tradition has always placed the weight of Christ's priesthood (cf. Heb. 2:5–18; 5:1–10) on his humanity'. See Kibbe, 'Is It Finished?, 25–61. For discussions of Christ's priesthood in patristic and medieval eras see O'Collins and Jones, *Jesus our Priest*, 68–127; Robertson, *Christ as* Mediator, 65–66. Some theologians also hold the minority position that Jesus assumed priestly or quasi-priestly roles in his public ministry. See Cullmann, *Die Christologie des Neuen Testaments*, 82–107; Fletcher-Louis, 'Jesus as the High Priestly Messiah; Part One', 155–75; 'Jesus as the High Priestly Messiah: Part Two', 57–79.

A second aspect of Jesus' solidarity with humanity is his mercy towards them. This mercy, as stated above, flows from his identification with the lot of sinners from the beginning of earthly life. Whereas the OT priesthood demanded that the priest be on the side of God, the mercy of Jesus places him on the side of humanity. Whereas the OT priesthood required the priests to deal with the enemies of God severely (Exod. 32:27,29; Num. 25:6–12), Jesus, in contrast, did not impose ruthless judgement on erring sinners. Instead, he showed them boundless mercy. 'Christ has not become a priest who rages against us sinners; on the contrary, by sharing our miserable fate, which is the consequence of our sins, he has acquired priestly mercy.'[19] Hence in his public life, Jesus interacted with sinners. He dealt mercifully with them. He was on the side of those rejected by society (Mt. 11:19; Lk. 7:34). He was deeply moved by their situation and was impelled to act on them (Mk. 1:40; Mt. 20:34; Lk. 7:13; Mt. 15:32).[20]

Mercy, then, is the primary attribute of Jesus' priesthood. Instead of separating him from us, Jesus' priestly office draws him into the most profound identification with us. His solidarity with sinners is manifested at the beginning of his ministry when he submitted to John's baptism of repentance for the forgiveness of sins (Mk 1:4). The same solidarity is seen at the end of his ministry in his crucifixion as a common criminal between two other criminals (Mk 15:27; cf. Is 53:9). He shows his zeal for God's holiness (Mk 11:15–17; Jn 2:17), not by imposing on sinners the punishment they deserve, but by submitting himself to the death that they deserve. "In Christ, faithfulness to God and solidarity with sinners are perfectly united, thus revealing the infinite mercy of the Father. His priestly consecration, that is, his separation for sanctification, involved, not separating himself by sinners, but by separating sinners from sin".[21]

---

19 Vanhoye, *Christ our High Priest*, 49.
20 For this reason, O'Collins and Jones assert that Jesus exercised priestly ministry in his public ministry and teaching, for example in his healing and teaching. 'By preaching, healing and forgiving sins, Jesus built up a "community of the faithful", those who accepted his message of God's kingdom that was already breaking into the world". O'Collins also see in Jesus' feeding of the hungry an image of a priest feeding the people from the table of the Scriptures and of the Eucharist. See O'Collins, *Jesus our Priest*, 244. See also Wenkel, 'Jesus at Age 30', 195–201.
21 Healy, 'Christ's Priesthood', 395–410.

A third aspect of Jesus' solidarity is his obedient acceptance of suffering by which he was made perfect (Heb. 5.7–10) and glorified. It is worth noting that the verb 'to make perfect' (*teleioo*) is used in the Greek translation of Pentateuch to translate the phrase 'consecrated priest' (Exod. 29:9,29,33,35). In this context, it literally means 'to fill the hand' of a priest—that is, to *ordain* him (Exod. 29:9; Lev. 8.33; Num.3:3). Hence, it was by being made perfect through his suffering that Jesus had been ordained the great high priest (Heb. 4:14). The *locus* and moment of his ordination was the cross. 'Through his passion and resurrection, his human nature was perfected and made infinitely worthy to be offered in sacrifice to God. Simultaneously he was ordained as the high priest who is able to "bring many sons to glory" (Heb. 2:10)'.[22] Hence, 'the perfection acquired by Jesus in his passion was effectively a priestly perfection, a perfection that came from being a mediator between God and men'.[23]

O'Collins notes that in his glorified status as high priest, Jesus intercedes for his people (Heb. 7:25; Rom. 8:34): 'The priesthood of Christ continues forever, since he eternally intercedes for the world and blesses the world, offers himself through the Holy Spirit to the Father, continues to pour out the Holy Spirit upon the Church and the world... Christ's priestly intercession as eternal self-offering'.[24] Jesus performs his high priestly office of eternal self-offering to the Father through the Holy Spirit. In his eternal priestly ministry, Christ continually pours out the Spirit on the world and the Church (Jn. 15:26), to teach the truth and bear witness to Christ (14:16–17,26; 16:13–15), to give new birth and life (Jn. 3:5–8; 4:10,14), to bring about forgiveness and reconciliation (Jn. 20:22–23). These ongoing activities of the Spirit involve a constant sending by the eternal High Priest.[25]

In summary, Jesus' solidarity with humanity in all aspects is the first of several key elements of his priesthood. His priesthood does not separate him from human beings. On the contrary, it unites him most intimately with them, from his being born in the flesh up until

---

22 Healy, 'Christ's Priesthood', 402–03.
23 Vanhoye, *Christ our High Priest*, 62. See also O'Collins and Jones, *Christ our Priest*, 261–62.
24 O'Collins and Jones, *Christ our Priest*, 265.
25 O'Collins and Jones, *Christ our Priest*, 266.

his crucifixion and death on the cross. Having a personal experience of the human lot, he is able to deal with humanity mercifully. His solidarity and his mercy culminate in his loving obedience to the Father. These are the same qualities we hope to see in our priests today: deeply united with people in their humanity, merciful towards their weakness and limitations, intimately united with God in his loving obedience. We now turn to the *Ratio* for a discussion of how to form these qualities in young men training to be priests.

II. Images of Priest and Priestly Formation in the *Ratio*

Key notions regarding formation

The *Ratio* begins with the thesis that formation is a journey of discipleship. It therefore speaks of a 'formation itinerary', a 'pedagogical journey', as well as a 'journey of transformation'.[26] Formation is 'one unbroken missionary journey of discipleship divided into two principal moments: initial formation in the seminary, and ongoing formation in priestly life'.[27] Hence, 'one is always a disciple throughout the whole of life, constantly aspiring to configure oneself to Christ, by exercising pastoral ministry'.[28] Formation is a single and integrated path. It is one journey that begins in the seminary and continues into priestly life, there taking the form of ongoing formation.[29] Pope Francis emphasizes that formation is not a unilateral act of someone transmitting theological or spiritual notions. 'Jesus did not say to those he called: "Come, let me explain", "follow me, I will teach you": No! The formation offered by Christ to his disciples came rather as a "come, and follow me", "do as I do"'. Formation, for Pope Francis, is 'a discipular experience which draws one to Christ and conforms one ever more to Him'.[30] This single

---

26 The Gift of Priestly Vocation: *Ratio Fundamentalis Institutiones Sacerdotalis*, no. 10, 43. See http://www.clerus.va/content/dam/clerus/Ratio%20Fundamentalis/The%20Gift%20of%20the%20Priestly%20Vocation.pdf. Accessed 20 September 2017. Henceforth referred to as *Ratio*.
27 *Ratio*, no. 54–56.
28 *Ratio*, no. 57.
29 *Ratio*, no. 53.
30 Pope Francis' Address to the Congregation for the Clergy (2014). See http://w2.vatican.va/content/francesco/en/speeches/2014/october/documents/papa-francesco_20141003_plenaria-congregazione-clero.html. Accessed 20 September 2017.

journey of discipleship is wholistic and integrative which aims to help the person integrate his graced self and his sinful self, under the guidance of the Holy Spirit, towards gradual and harmonious maturity. In this way, he is freed from fragmentation, polarization, excesses, superficiality, or partiality.[31]

Another key notion in the *Ratio* is the communitarian character of priestly formation. The community envisaged by the *Ratio* is the Church which is responsible for the birth, discernment, and fostering of vocations.[32] The Church as an experience of community is mediated to the seminarian by the seminary community in which he finds himself. The community is not just an accidental grouping of men, but a privileged locus of communion and source of accompaniment. Hence, for the *Ratio*, community life 'must make an impact on each individual, purifying his intentions and transforming the conduct of his life as he gradually conforms himself to Christ'.[33] Furthermore, 'formation comes about everyday through interpersonal relationships, moments of exchange and discussion which result in the development of that fertile soil in which a vocation matures concretely'.[34] The importance of the community, notwithstanding, the person journeying—the seminarian on formation remains the 'necessary and irreplaceable agent in his own formation'.[35]

A third key notion of formation is its missionary character.[36] Pope Francis asserts that missionary zeal 'frees ordained ministers from the comfortable temptation of being over anxious about the opinion of others and of their own well-being, than inspired by pastoral love—in order to proclaim the Gospel, to the remotest peripheries'.[37]

Portrait of a Priest

For the *Ratio*, seminarians are to be formed into whole and integrated persons who possess a 'serene and creative interior synthesis between

---

31 *Ratio*, no. 28.
32 *Ratio*, no. 13–15, 30–31; John Paul II, *Pastores Dabo Vobis*, no. 34.
33 *Ratio*, no. 50.
34 *Ratio*, no. 50.
35 *Pastores Dabo Vobis*, no. 66.
36 *Ratio*, no. 15.
37 Pope Francis' Address to the Congregation for the Clergy (2014).

strength and weaknesses' and who could bring all aspects of their personality to Christ. In addition, they enjoy great interior freedom which means that they have a balanced and mature capacity to enter into relationship with others. Indeed, 'he is called, above all, to a basic human and spiritual serenity that, by overcoming every from of self-promotion or emotional dependency, allows him to be a man of communion of mission and of dialogue'.[38] Pope Francis, in *Evangelii Gaudium,* enumerates the elements of spiritual worldliness which hinder a person from rendering joyful service in the Church: 'obsession with personal appearances, a presumed theological or disciplinary certainty, narcissism and authoritarianism, attempt to dominate others, a merely external and ostentatious preoccupation with the liturgy, vainglory, individualism, inability to listen to others, and every form of careerism'.[39]

The *Ratio* also underlines the priest's closeness to both God and humanity. As Christ showed closeness to the people through his compassionate disposition and his works of mercy, so also the priest must be close to the people. At the same time, he should also be close to God as Christ was. Christ maintained intimate union with the Father throughout his life and intimate union with all that is human as he 'offered himself with loud cries and tears' (Heb. 5.7). In his intimate union with God and with humanity, the priest experiences his priesthood as essentially Eucharistic in the offering of his own person, body and blood as Christ did (Heb. 10.5). In this way does he give meaning to the words he utters: 'This is my body...this is my blood...of the new and everlasting covenant....'[40]

In this self-giving, the priest truly becomes a shepherd who gathers together the scattered sheep of the house of Israel and leads them into the sheepfold (Mt 9.36; Mk 6.34). Thus, he manifests in himself God 'who gathers, accompanies, follows and cares for His own flock and shares our own life to the point of taking upon himself our suffering and our death'.[41] He also shows how Christ as the Spouse of the Church

---

38 *Ratio,* no. 41.
39 *Ratio,* no. 42; *Evangelii Gaudium,* no. 93–97.
40 *Ratio,* no. 36.
41 *Spe Salvi,* no. 6; *Ratio,* no. 37.

gives of himself to His Church as the fruit of his love.[42] Living out this spousal love entails the capacity to love people 'with a heart which is new, generous and pure—with genuine self-detachment, with full, constant and faithful dedication and at the same time with a kind of 'divine jealousy' (cf. 2 Cor. 11:2) and even with a kind of maternal tenderness'.[43] Through this total and genuine self-giving, he is configured more and more to Christ, united with him more closely, and made an instrument of God's mercy.[44]

Configuration through Accompaniment and Discernment

Formation, then, is a process of gradual configuration to Christ, the Merciful High Priest, Head and Shepherd, Servant and Spouse in such a way that the priest becomes a visible sign of the merciful love of the Father in the Church and in the world.[45] The seminarians' years in formation is the time to discern and form the qualities enumerated above. Hence, formation journey is a journey of transformation, a 'gradual inner growth along the journey of transformation principally aimed at making the future priest "a man of discernment", able to read the reality of human life in the light of the Spirit. In this way, he will be able to choose, decide and act according to the will of God'.[46]

Towards the formation of these qualities of the Good Shepherd in seminarians, the *Ratio* proposes accompaniment and discernment, or accompaniment in discernment. These are the two key elements of in the vocational journey. Accordingly, priestly vocation is a gift of divine grace initially received in the Church, nourished over time, and sealed in sacramental ordination. Similarly, the person's response develops through a process which begins with an awareness of the gift received and matures gradually in the years of formation until it becomes a stable way of life".[47] Hence, personal accompaniment at various stages of their journey by their formators is an indispensable means of formation. The

---

42 *Ratio*, no. 39; *Pastores Dabo Vobis*, no. 22.
43 *Ratio*, no. 39; *Pastores Dabo Vobis*, no. 22.
44 *Ratio*, 40.
45 *Presbyterorum Ordinis*, no. 2; *Pasotres Dabo Vobis*, no. 3; *Ratio*, no. 35.
46 *Ratio*, no. 43.
47 *Ratio*, no. 34.

Ratio suggests regular and frequent conversations with formators. In these conversations, all aspects of the seminarians' life must be brought together, so that he is trained in listening, in dialogue, in the true meaning of obedience, and in interior freedom. 'In the process of formation, (through the accompaniment), it is necessary that the seminarian should know himself and let himself be known, relating to the formation with sincerity and transparency'.[48] Through this accompaniment, the seminarian is assisted in becoming aware of his condition, of the talents he has received, and of his frailties so that he can become ever more receptive to the action of grace. Hence, the end goal of accompaniment is docility to the Holy Spirit. Furthermore, the *Ratio* emphasizes that accompaniment must be given from the beginning of the vocational journey and extends throughout life, but taking on different approach after ordination.[49]

The *Ratio* also underlines the importance of community life as a means of accompaniment in the vocational journey. Community life 'must make an impact on each individual, purifying his intentions and transforming the conduct of his life as he gradually conforms himself to Christ'. This is built on the conviction that 'formation comes about everyday through interpersonal relationships, moments of exchange and discussion which result in the development of that fertile soil in which a vocation matures concretely'.[50] Furthermore, community life is a crucial element in the formation of priests because they will exercise 'spiritual fatherhood' in communities and will join the community of priests, the *presbyterium*. 'United among themselves in an intimate sacramental brotherhood' and 'in individual dioceses, priests form one priesthood under their own bishop'.[51] 'The bonds that are created in the Seminary between formators and seminarians, and between the seminarians themselves must be marked by a sense of fatherhood and fraternity'.[52]

---

48 *Ratio*, no. 45.
49 *Ratio*, nos. 44, 46.
50 *Ratio*, no. 50.
51 *Presbyterorum Ordinis*, no. 8.
52 Pope Francis' Address to Seminarians and Novices (July 6, 2013). See http://w2.vatican.va/content/francesco/en/speeches/2013/july/documents/papa-francesco_20130706_incontro-seminaristi.html. Accessed 22 September 2017.

The second element in the vocational journey is discernment. Formation seeks to form the seminarian into a man of discernment, one who can 'read the reality of human life in the light of the Holy Spirit. In this way, he will be able to choose, decide, and act according to the will of God'.[53] The seminarian begins his discernment, first, by looking into his personal life. His aim is the integration of his personal history and current circumstances into his spiritual life, so that his vocation 'does not become either imprisoned in abstract ideals or reduced to a merely practical and organizational activism'.[54] The seminarian in formation can practise discernment in at least two ways: (1) by 'cultivating everyday a deep spiritual life, so as to receive it and interpret it with full responsibility and a growing trust in God, directing the heart towards him everyday'[55]; and (2) by 'working humbly and ceaselessly on oneself, listening to his conscience that judges his movements and the interior urges that motivate his actions'.[56] More than simple introspection, discernment is 'looking within' in a holistic spiritual outlook in view of achieving full and responsible humanity with the capacity to live in the freedom of the children of God (Rom. 8.15; Gal. 4.6).

As a result of discernment, the seminarian is able to do key tasks necessary for someone preparing for the pastoral leadership in the Church. First, he grasps the sense of what can be done and what it would be better not to do. This is the virtue of prudence. Secondly, he organizes his energies, his plans, and duties, with a balanced self-discipline and an honest awareness of his own limit and abilities. This is the virtue of wise judgement. Thirdly, he recognises that these things cannot be done on his own. Hence, he welcomes the gift of divine grace that enables him to transcend himself and to go beyond his own needs and his external conditioning.

---

53 *Ratio*, no. 43.
54 *Ratio*, no. 43.
55 *Ratio*, no. 43.
56 *Ratio*, no. 43.

III. Priesthood: Configuration to Christ, the Minister of Mercy

This part integrates the insights from the preceding sections. The main argument is that the priest who undergoes the vocational journey of discipleship called formation emerges as a man in deep solidarity with humanity as he has achieved his own personal integration. At the same time, he is in intimate communion with God as he has discerned the active and transformative presence of God in his life. His experience of being accompanied by the mercy of God impels him to be an agent of the same mercy to others. His priestly ministry is characterised mainly by mercy as it is the case in his personal life history.

Ministry of Mercy as Accompaniment of People

The primary ministry, therefore, of a priest is the ministry of mercy. As it was in the ministry of Christ the High Priest, so it must be in the ministry of those configured to him. As Christ was in solidarity with his people and with God, in his humanity, and in suffering and death, so must the priest be in solidarity with the people he is called to serve. Mercy is the fruit of this solidarity. Being in merciful solidarity with people especially the poor and the suffering means accompanying them in their misery, in their cries and tears, in their joys and pains. Benedict XVI asserts that the reference to Jesus offering prayers and supplications, with loud cries and tears (Heb. 5.7) does not only point his mortal anguish in the Mount Olives. Instead, 'it sums up the whole history of the Passion that embraces Jesus' entire life. It refers to the tears Jesus wept by the tomb of Lazarus … (where he is) put to the test and he confronts this mystery (of death) in the very depths of his soul'.[57] Jesus' solidarity with the cries and tears of humanity reaches its climax in his cry of abandonment on the cross: 'My God, my God, why have you forsaken me?' (Mk 15:34; cf. Mt 27:46). In this, 'he transforms the whole of suffering humanity, taking it to himself in a cry to God to hear him. Thus we see that in this very way he brings about the priesthood, the function of mediator, bearing in himself, taking on in himself the

---

[57] Benedict XVI, *Lectio Divina* with the Parish Priests of Rome (Feb. 18, 2010). Cf. http://w2.vatican.va/content/benedict-xvi/en/speeches/2010/february/documents/hf_ben-xvi_spe_20100218_parroci-roma.html. Accessed 22 September 2017.

sufferings and passion of the world, transforming it into a cry to God, bringing it before the eyes and to the hands of God and thus truly bringing it to the moment of redemption'.[58] Thus, we can say that Jesus, the Minister of Mercy, accompanies crying and weeping humanity in his own cries and tears throughout his life until his death on the cross.

For his part, Pope Francis uses the image of the journey to Emmaus as the pattern of priestly ministry of accompaniment. First he speaks of a Church that is 'capable of walking at people's side, of doing more than simply listening to them; a Church which accompanies them on their journey; a Church able to make sense of the 'night' contained in the flight of so many of our brothers and sisters from Jerusalem…'.[59] This was what Jesus did on the road: he walked with them, listened to them, opened the Scriptures to them, and fed them at the table. Throughout the journey, he warmed the hearts of the down-trodden disciples (Lk. 24.13–35).

In view of this, he insists on the need to 'train ministers capable of warming people's hearts, of walking with them in the night, of dialoguing with their hopes and disappointments, of mending their brokenness…'.[60] This type of formation which prepares ministers of mercy to accompany people in their miseries and sufferings equips ministers 'to step into the night without being overcome by the darkness and losing their bearings; able to listen to people's dreams without being seduced and to share their disappointments without losing hope and becoming bitter; able to sympathize with the brokenness of others without losing their own strength and identity'.[61] In other words, it is a formation that trains them in the art of accompaniment and discernment.

Primacy of the Humanity of the Priest

In the formation of ministers of mercy who can warm the hearts of fellow disciples on the journey, the person of the minister is of utmost and primary importance. More than his skills and abilities, talents

---

58   Benedict XVI, *Lectio Divina* (2010).
59   Pope Francis' Address to the Bishops of Brazil (July 28, 2013). See https://w2.vatican.va/content/francesco/en/speeches/2013/july/documents/papa-francesco_20130727_gmg-episcopato-brasile.html. Accessed 22 September 2017.
60   Pope Francis' Address to the Bishops of Brazil (28 July 2013).
61   Pope Francis' Address to the Bishops of Brazil (28 July 2013).

and capacities, it is his person, his humanity that matters the most. Humanity precedes piety. Holiness presupposes humanity. Holiness is wholeness. Hence, human formation serves as 'the necessary solid foundation of the entire priestly formation'[62] so that the seminarian's authentic humanity may emerge in the process. 'It is not a vague abstract goal of being human that seminarians aspire for. It is rather the acquisition of the concrete values and attitudes of the human Jesus of the Gospels and living out these values and attitudes in the priest's pastoral service.'[63]

For Pope Benedict, the essential element of being a man, of true humanity is compassionate suffering with the other. 'He can deal gently with the ignorant and wayward, since he himself is beset with weakness' (Heb. 5.2). 'True humanity is real participation in the suffering of human beings. It means being a compassionate person, *metriopathèin*, being at the core of human passion, really bearing with others the burden of their suffering'.[64] In *Fratelli Tutti*, Pope Francis calls attention to the urgency of acting in the manner of the Good Samaritan who turned aside and attended to the wounded person on the roadside. "In the face of so much pain and suffering, our only course is to imitate the Good Samaritan... The parable shows us how a community can be rebuilt by men and women who identify with the vulnerability of others..."[65] Hence, the primary goal of the pastoral formation in the seminary is not to develop the leadership or management skills of seminarians. Instead, it seeks to prepare the seminarians 'to enter into communion with the charity of Christ the Good Shepherd' 'whose intimate knowledge of the flock and sacrificial love for them remains the norm for priests.'[66]

The humanity of the priest, however, finds its perfection in the conformity of his will to the will of the Father. This was the case of Jesus, the Son, who learned obedience in his suffering, and was thus perfected by it by being made High Priest (Heb. 5.7-9). In other words, following the pattern of Jesus' obedience, the priest's humanity is perfected by his obedience to the will of the Father. Pope Benedict affirms that Christ's obedience consists in the conformity of his will with the will of

---

62 *UPPPF*, xxiii.
63 *UPPPF*, no. 26.
64 Benedict XVI, *Lectio Divina* (2010).
65 Francis, *Fratelli Tutti*, 67.
66 *UPPPF*, no. 147; *Pastores Dabo Vobis*, no. 57.

the Father. 'Jesus, in bearing the human being, being human in himself and with himself, in conformity with God, in perfect obedience, that is, in the perfect conformation between the two wills, has redeemed us and redemption is always this process of leading the human will to communion with the divine will'.[67] The attainment of this conformity between the human and the divine will is the attainment of freedom. It is the great paradox in a priest's life: he is most free when he is most obedient to the will of God, as Jesus was. Formation, then, is the process of attaining interior freedom, of growing more and more in docility to the movement of the Spirit in one's life.

The formation towards docility requires the seminarian 'to review his own life constantly, and to be open to fraternal correction, so as to respond ever more fully to the workings of grace'.[68] As Pope Francis says: 'The priest is a man who is born into a certain human context ... Priests too have a history; they are not 'mushrooms' that suddenly spring in a Cathedral on the day of their ordination. It is important that formators and the priests themselves remember this and are able to take account of this personal history along the path of formation'.[69] Hence, as emphasized by the *Ratio*, the first area of discernment in formation is the personal life history of the seminarian himself. There he seeks to find the hand of God leading him throughout his life from the discovery to the nourishment up until the sacramental recognition of this gift by the Church in ordination.

Mercy Embodied in the Priest's Self-Offering

The merciful solidarity which characterizes the ministry of the priest finds its concrete expression in the offering of his very self in the pattern of Jesus Christ. As High Priest, Jesus had to offer sacrifices too. But his sacrifice is one that surpasses all those performed by the Old Testament priests because he offered not a helpless animal but *himself* (Heb. 7.27). He 'entered once for all into the Holy Place, taking not the blood of goats and calves but his own blood' (Heb. 9.12) and this he did through the 'eternal Spirit' (Heb. 9.14). For Vanhoye, this eternal Spirit is an allusion

---

67 Benedict XVI, *Lectio Divina* (2010).
68 *Ratio*, no. 58.
69 Pope Francis' Address to the Bishops of Brazil (28 July 2013).

to the fire that is perpetually kept aflame on the altar of sacrifice in the temple (Lev. 6.12–13). As explained earlier, Jesus was in merciful solidarity with humanity all throughout his life. In his solidarity with the sufferings of people he encountered, he felt their pain in his own body, causing him to shed tears and weep. 'Like a holocaust—the kind of sacrifice in which the victim is completely burnt on the altar—Jesus was entirely consumed in his self-offering. His suffering was the kindling that perfected his obedient love for the Father, and so made his humanity—and thus the humanity of "all who obey him" (Heb. 5.9)—capable of divine life'.[70]

Pope Benedict insists that just as Jesus did not offer God some 'thing', but his own body, so does the priest offers his own body which bears with it all the pains entailed in his total dedication to his ministry of mercy. In his own body, he bears the suffering of the world and offers them to God in union with the sacrifice of Christ's own body and blood. This communion with the mystery of Christ is totally real and essential, existential, and sacramental.[71] For Geerhardus Vos, Christ's solidarity with humanity extends unto eternal life. 'Although removed physically from His people for a time, yet the spiritual identification and bond remains inviolable and His intercession prevails continually for them on this account.... The invisibleness, the remoteness of the present activity of Jesus, far from interfering with its efficacious character, is precisely the ground of the latter'.[72]

Christ crucified and glorified continues his merciful solidarity with his suffering people through the Eucharist. The Eucharist is Jesus perpetually making the oblation of his body to the Father, and with his body, all the pains and sufferings of the humanity and of the earth. Thus, 'the Eucharist which the priest celebrates with and among his people thrusts him right into the middle of their pains and sufferings, their diversity and differences, their searching and longing. Together and never above nor apart from them, he undergoes the same suffering that they are subjected to, and that very suffering is his mission'.[73] The self-offering of the

70 Healy, 'Christ's Priesthood', 406.
71 Benedict XVI, *Lectio Divina* (2010).
72 Vos, *Redemptive History*, 131.
73 Julia, *Man of the Word*, 198–99.

priest, just as Jesus Christ's was, is thoroughly incarnate, that is, felt in his very own body as he pours his own sweat and sheds his own tears, and possibly, even his blood, if needed, for the sake of his flock. In this way, the Eucharist which he celebrates truly becomes the *memoria passionis* of Christ's liberative passion, death, and resurrection.[74]

IV. Implementing the *Ratio* in Seminary Formation

In this final part of the paper, some proposals for the implementation of the *Ratio* in seminary formation will be discussed. Some of these suggestions are given by the *Ratio* itself. Some have already been identified by the Catholic Bishops' Conference on the Philippines and incorporated in the *Updated Philippine Program for Priestly Formation* (2006) prepared by the CBCP Commission on Seminaries. Here, we shall illustrate how St. John Vianney Theological Seminary has responded to the *UPPPF* as well as the *Ratio* through the various programs constituting our seminary formation. Here, we are guided by the *UPPPF*'s key principle of integration and interaction as well as continuity and interrelatedness of the various stages and areas of formation.[75]

Priority of Human Formation

The UPPPF underlines the crucial role of human formation in seminary formation by acknowledging it as the necessary solid foundation of the entire priestly formation. When this foundation has been built, then formation can proceed to deepen the spiritual life of the seminarian. It is spiritual formation that unifies all the other aspects of formation. The intellectual formation ensures the competence of the future priest in handling the responsibilities of his office like teaching, leading the community, and administering the sacraments. Hence, all the aspects of formation are geared towards pastoral formation. All these elements of formation integrate and interact in the context of community living.[76]

---

74 Julia, *Man of the Word*, 199.
75 *UPPPF*, xxii.
76 *UPPPF*, xxiii.

In our seminary, the importance of human formation is manifested in the presence of a full-time female vocational growth counsellor amongst us since 2005. Prior to her arrival, there had never been a woman-member the formation team. As is the case in most seminaries, all formation staff members were men. If there were women, they were mostly guest professors or occasional resource speakers. The presence of a competent and well-trained counsellor in our seminary is a milestone in the history of SJVTS. In the past, only seminarians 'with problems' were referred to a counsellor, thus creating a stigma against confronting one's psychological and developmental issues. However, with the presence of our lay counsellor, every seminarian is required to see her for counselling. In fact, we prefer to call the sessions with her, not counselling, but 'vocational growth accompaniment'. This term perfectly fits the *Ratio*'s view of formation as a journey in which the seminarian training to be priest must be accompanied along the way.

In addition, we have dedicated a specific time for human formation. On Monday afternoons, no academic classes are held. The time is allotted for sessions and meetings pertaining to human formation. Topics such as human development, psycho-emotional-sexual maturity, dynamics of personal relationships, issues involving authority, community life, maintaining personal and professional boundaries and other similar themes are discussed with the seminarians. Our female counsellor plans and facilitates the human formation sessions in consultation with the Rector and the Director for Human-Spiritual Formation. On some occasions, we hold separate sessions for the different year levels since we feel that the various topics are best introduced on a gradually deeper way for each level. This is true for themes related to sexuality, spirituality, and psycho-emotional development.

One element in our formation program which has become quite common in many seminaries in the Philippines is the insertion of an additional year of formation called 'Human-Spiritual-Pastoral Formation Year' or in SJVTS, we call it 'Galilee Year'. The Galilee Year normally takes place on the fourth year of the seminarian in SJVTS. It is a period of 'broadening and deepening of the seminarian's perspective and appreciation of their priestly vocation. More importantly, it is a time for a more personal appropriation, internalization, and a greater integration of the human, spiritual, and pastoral pillars of formation towards an authentic priestly life and fruitful ministry'.[77] In the Galilee Year, intensive focus is given to the human-spiritual and pastoral aspects of formation. There are no academic courses taken. The seminarians undergo modules on personality styles vis-à-vis human relationships. Through a facilitator, they process their personal, family, and sexual histories. They also undergo Clinical Pastoral Education, where they encounter patients in hospital settings and reflect on their experiences through intensive processing with a supervisor. After these human dynamic seminar-workshops, they make the 30-day Ignatian retreat where they deepen their relationship with Christ and make an election as regards their vocation. The last module of the GY is the Integrated Socio-Pastoral Engagements Program where they are sent to various settings of poverty, social crisis, and marginalization. These engagements give them a chance to engage with real poor people with the aim of developing an affective and transformative love for them.

Structures of Accompaniment and Discernment

In SJVTS, our formation program provides for accompaniment of seminarians and training in discernment. We are cognisant of Pope Francis' caution: 'One must carefully study the evolution of a vocation! See whether it comes from the Lord, whether the man is healthy, well-balanced, capable of giving life, of evangelizing, capable of forming a family and renouncing this in order to follow Jesus'.[78] As mentioned above, each seminarian is required to see the lay counsellor at least once a month for counselling/growth accompaniment. This is the venue for processing their human psycho-dynamics as these emerge in their daily life in the seminary. In addition, each seminarian is also assigned a spiritual director whom he is supposed to see once a month. This is where he reflects on his spiritual experiences in prayer and where he tries to make sense of God's movements in his heart. Both the growth accompaniment and the spiritual direction are in the internal forum. In addition to these, each seminarian is also required to see the Rector once a

---

77 *SJVTS Handbook*, 73.
78 Pope Francis' Address to the Congregation for the Clergy (2014).

semester (usually at the beginning of the semester) and the subcommunity moderator also once a semester (usually at the end of the semester. Both colloquia (with Rector and Subcommmunity Moderator) are in the external forum. All these conversations are means to accompany the seminarian in their vocation journey and to help them articulate their growth in responding to the call of Christ. These are also opportunities for training in discernment as they are challenged to read the data from their daily experiences and examine them in the light of the priestly vocation.

Another structure which provides for training in discernment is the periodic evaluation or appraisal of seminarians. This is done usually at the end of the formation year. The *Ratio* insists that at the conclusion of each stage, it is the actual progress in overall integral maturity that has to be determined. In SJVTS, each seminarian is asked to make a self-appraisal/evaluation based on specific points taken from each area of formation (human, spiritual, intellectual, and pastoral). He also has to accomplish an appraisal/evaluation for two other seminarians. This is called 'peer appraisal/evaluation.' The Subcommunity moderators then collate and summarize the three appraisals (self and peer) and add their own appraisal for each seminarian concerned. Each of the formators is also asked to add their appraisal for each seminarian. The summary of all the appraisals is then given to the seminarian concerned by the Rector in an individual colloquium.

This appraisal exercise has been very helpful in training the seminarians to make an honest and objective examination of themselves and of their peers vis-à-vis the goals of each area of formation. This is an annual exercise which the seminarian undertakes up until he is presented for ordination. Hence, we subscribe to the *Ratio*'s view that ordination is 'the goal of a genuinely completed spiritual journey that has gradually helped the seminarian become aware of the call he has received and the characteristics that pertain to priestly identity, allowing him to reach the necessary human, Christian, and priestly maturity.'[79]

Since vocation is a personal call heard from within the depths of the man called to a vocational journey of discipleship, SJVTS provides

---

79 *Ratio*, no. 58.

for structures of personal prayerful encounter with God. The Ignatian examen is built into the daily routine of the seminarians. Weekly exposition and benediction of the Blessed Sacrament is also included in the schedule. A monthly overnight recollection in silence is also part of the schedule. A unique feature of our spiritual formation in SJVTS is the annual silent 5-day retreat done by our seminarians. The first year theology seminarians are asked to undergo a prayer workshop during this week long silent retreat. They are introduced to methods of prayer, principles of Ignatian retreat, and fundamentals of discernment. The other seminarians (second, third, and fourth year) are given individual directors to guide them throughout the week. This has been a very helpful and fruitful formation structure that has taught the seminarians to listen to the voice of God within them and to be sensitive to the movements of the Spirit in their lives. The deep sense of God's love experienced in the retreat has encouraged them to face up to their multi-layered human development issues and take the necessary steps to address them. In this, they begin to understand that their formators are simply guides and they, the seminarians, guided by the Spirit, are the primary agents of their formation.

Formation of Formators

Although the seminarian guided by the Spirit is the primary agent of his formation, the *Ratio* recognizes the crucial role of formators. Hence, it insists that 'each formator should possess human, spiritual, pastoral and professional abilities and resources, so as to provide the right kind of accompaniment that is balanced and respectful of the freedom and the conscience of each person'.[80] It requires from the formators generous dedication to the task, full time presence, witnessing to love and service of the people of God, and total self-giving to the Church. In other words, they are to model, first of all, Christ's priesthood of merciful solidarity as described above. This is their primary service as formators of seminarians.

Notwithstanding these human-spiritual endowments, the Ratio underlines the need for preparation for those who will undertake the task of formation. Hence, in SJVTS, we make sure that our formators

---

80 *Ratio*, no. 49.

undergo adequate preparation before they join the formation team. If they are to serve as professors, they pursue higher studies in their respective fields as required for seminary professors. Moreover, they also undergo training in other tasks of formation such as accompanying seminarians through individual colloquia, spiritual direction, and/or growth accompaniment. They are asked to attend workshops pertaining to these specialized tasks. At the moment, we are also looking into arranging supervision for new spiritual directors and subcommunity moderators. Besides these, we also make provisions for personal renewal of formators in the form of periodic sabbaticals.

Conclusion: Becoming Fully Human to be Fully of God

The Letter to the Hebrews takes pains to emphasize the humanity of Jesus, the High Priest. In his loud cries and weeping, he was fully human. In his full solidarity with humanity in all our pains and sufferings, Jesus was authentically human. And in his total obedience to the Father's will, culminating in his bodily sacrifice of himself on the cross he was perfected in his humanity as well as in his Sonship. His solidarity with humanity and his conformity to God's will established him as eternal High Priest, interceding for us in heaven, out of his mercy for our miserable lot as human beings. Such is the image of Jesus the High Priest that priests are supposed to be conformed to. This is the aim of seminary formation: to form priests who are authentically human and yet fully united with God in their obedience to his will.

Seminary formation is the vocation journey of discipleship whereby the seminarian is gradually configured to Christ, the High Priest, the Shepherd who lays down his life for the sheep. Imbued with a priestly spirituality founded on and animated by his intimate relationship with Christ, he is able to overcome tendencies towards 'spiritual worldliness' manifested in, among others, narcissism and authoritarianism, vainglory, individualism, and careerism.[81] Accompanied throughout his formation journey and taught to discern the ways of God, the seminarian

---

81 *Ratio*, no. 42.

manifests in his person, his words and action the image of Christ, the High Priest.

Norlan Julia, SJ
rector@vianneycdo.ph
St John Vianney Theological Seminary
Camaman-an Hill, Cagayan de Oro City, Philippines

Bibliography

Catholic Bishops' Conference of the Philippines (CBCP), *Updated Philippine Program for Priestly Formation* (UPPPF) (Manila: CBCP, 2006).

Cullmann, O. *Die Christologie des Neuen Testaments* (Tübingen: Mohr Siebeck, 1957).

De Vaux, Roland *Ancient Israel: Its Life and Institutions* (London: Darton, Longman and Todd, 1961).

Filtvedt, Ole Jakob, and Martin Wessbrandt 'Exploring the High Priesthood of Jesus in Early Christian Sources', *Zeitschrift für die Neutestamentliche Wissenschaft* 106.1 (2015), 96–114.

Fletcher-Louis, C. H. T. 'Jesus as the High Priestly Messiah: Part One', *Journal for the Study of the Historical Jesus* 4 (2006), 155–75.

Fletcher-Louis, C. H. T. 'Jesus as the High Priestly Messiah: Part Two', *Journal for the Study of the Historical Jesus* 5 (2007), 57–79.

Greggs, Tom 'The Priesthood of No Believer: On the Priesthood of Christ and his Church', *International Journal of Systematic Theology* 17.4 (October 2015), 374–98.

Healy, Mary 'Christ's Priesthood and Christian Priesthood in the Letter to the Hebrews', *Nova et Vetera*, English Edition, 9.2 (2011), 395–410.

Julia, Norlan 'Vianney Seminary and the Mindanao Mission of the Restored Society', *Tambara: A Journal on the Humanities and Social Sciences*, 31.2 (2014), 79–98.

Julia, Norlan *Man of the Word: Rahner and Asian Priesthood* (Quezon City: Claretian Publications, 2016).

Kibbe, Michael — 'Is It Finished? When Did It Start? Hebrews, Priesthood, and Atonement in Biblical, Systematic, and Historical Perspective', *Journal of Theological Studies* 65.1 (2014), 25–61.

O'Collins, Gerald, and Michael Keenan Jones — *Jesus Our Priest: A Christian Approach to the Priesthood of Christ* (Oxford: Oxford University Press, 2010).

Robertson, Jon M. — *Christ as Mediator: A Study in the Theologies of Eusebius of Caesarea, Marcellus of Ancyra, and Athanasius of Alexandria* (Oxford: Oxford University Press, 2007).

Vanhoye, Albert — *Christ Our High Priest: Spiritual Exercises with Pope Benedict XVI* (Joel Wallace, trans.; Herefordshire: Gracewing, 2010).

Vos, Geerhardus — *Redemptive History and Biblical Interpretation: The Shorter Writings of Geerhardus Vos* (Richard B. Gaffin, ed.; Phillipsburg, PA: Presbyterian & Reformed, 1980).

Wenkel, David H. — 'Jesus at Age 30: Further Evidence for Luke's Portrait of a Priestly Jesus?', *Biblical Theology Bulletin*, 44.4 (2014), 195–201.

Websites

Benedict XVI, *Lectio Divina* with the Parish Priests of Rome (Feb. 18, 2010). http://w2.vatican.va/content/benedict-xvi/en/speeches/2010/february/documents/hf_ben-xvi_spe_20100218_parroci-roma.html.

The Gift of Priestly Vocation: *Ratio Fundamentalis Institutiones Sacerdotalis*, no. 10, 43. http://www.clerus.va/content/dam/clerus/Ratio%20Fundamentalis/The%20Gift%20of%20the%20Priestly%20Vocation.pdf.

Pope Francis' Address to the Congregation for the Clergy (2014). https://w2.vatican.va/content/

francesco/en/speeches/2014/october/documents/papa-francesco_20141003_plenaria-congregazione-clero.html.

https://www.vatican.va/content/francesco/en/encyclicals/documents/papa-francesco_20201003_enciclica-fratelli-tutti.html

CHAPTER 11

Jesus and the Art of Parable: Emulating the Teaching Method of Jesus

Greg Forbes

Abstract

There is a clear consensus in New Testament scholarship that Jesus habitually and regularly used parable as his mode of conveying truth regarding God and his kingdom. It is also generally acknowledged in the church today, as it was amongst those who heard him, that Jesus was a master teacher. However, when it comes to emulating Jesus this is normally construed in terms of ethics, patient suffering, or commitment to the mission of God. Not many, at least in the West, seek to emulate Jesus' teaching method.

On the one hand, this is understandable for a post-Enlightenment, literate, and information saturated society. Nevertheless there is something in the nature of story in general, and parable in particular, that the church needs to recapture in the way it passes on its doctrine and ethics. Although to some extent we do think in propositional terms, our lives have an essential narrative flow. So, if we are communicating biblical truth, which for us is sacred story, and if life is essentially narrative in orientation, then the use of narrative to communicate the Christian message is indispensable. Story stimulates curiosity, ties us to reality, evokes images that facilitate a shift in perspective and so confronts us in a nonthreatening manner thereby helping us to reorientate our lives.

It is the contention of this paper that parable as a literary form has untapped potential in communicating the Christian message today. Although thinking in parable, and indeed constructing parables is difficult for Western Christians, a well-considered application of Jesus' teaching method can only enhance the life and ministry of the church.

With respect to Jesus and the parables there are a number of consensus positions held in New Testament scholarship today. First, Jesus regularly and habitually taught in parable. The parables are attested across all the Gospel strata except for John (Mark, Q, M & L), and are found nowhere else in the NT apart from the Synoptics. This indicates that teaching in parable was not a feature of the early Christians, and thus the church did not retroject such teaching back on to Jesus' lips. They transmitted his parables, and his parabolic teaching no doubt formed part of the early church instruction, but they did not appear to emulate his method. Second, the parables are the closest we come to the original voice of Jesus. The stories he told are saturated in Palestinian imagery and idiom, and are evidently crafted by one immersed in rural Palestinian culture. Third, Jesus used the parables to expound his understanding of the nature of the kingdom of God including its value, timing, make up, entry requirements, and ethical response.

It is also reasonably clear why Jesus used this teaching medium. Story was the grist of an oral culture and was used effectively both by the prophets that preceded him (see Isa 5:1–7; 2 Sam 12:1–6), and the Rabbis that post–dated him. Furthermore, teaching in parable enabled Jesus to subtly disarm his opponents and was probably one of the reasons that he was able to avoid arrest for some time. The shocking and confronting elements of the parables—for example the praise of a dishonest manager (Luke 16:8), a Samaritan who cares for a wounded Jew (Luke 10:30–37), and a pious Pharisee who is rejected (Luke 18:9–14)—not only provoked interest but functioned like a pinch of caustic soda for those with any degree of spiritual (or cultural) perception. As N.T. Wright puts it, 'They were ways of breaking open the worldview of

Jesus' hearers, so that it could be remoulded into the worldview which he, Jesus, was commending.'[1]

Of course there are points of contention. The Markan Parable Theory (Mark 4:10–12 and its blunt statement about the design of the parables to conceal truth) has spawned a variety of interpretations.[2] The authenticity of the parable framework continues to be rejected by some and, underlying this, the legacy of Jülicher's allergic reaction to allegory persists down to the present time. Nevertheless, it no longer seems viable to deny the presence of allegory altogether unless, that is, one is content to regard Jesus as telling interesting stories about life on the farm.

But it is not my task here to either challenge the consensus positions or address the points of contention. Rather, I wish to examine the nature of parable and story as a pedagogical device.

Understandably, Jesus is often used as a model for those who seek to follow him. But this model is normally understood in terms of either commitment to the will of God, in patient unjust suffering, or ethics, in particular the love of one's enemies or acceptance of underprivileged people.[3] What is interesting, however, is that although Jesus is revered as a master teacher there is not usually a concerted effort in Christian circles to follow his method of teaching. There are not many books on homiletics that hold Jesus aloft as the model.[4] That is, we recognise that Jesus regularly used parable and storytelling as a didactic method, we hold him aloft as a master teacher, and yet, paradoxically, we continue to teach in (often bland) propositional forms and, apart from the odd anecdote or illustration, struggle to hold the attention of even the most enthusiastic congregation.

> There was a cricket side that dominated the competition for several years in a row. They trained three nights a week, they had a lucrative sponsorship with a sports company, and they worked extremely hard on their fielding, in fact they were

---

1 Wright, *The New Testament and the People of God*, 77. See also Dillon, *Telling the Gospel Through Story*, 29–30.
2 See Stein, *Mark*, 204–12.
3 We see Jesus as a model to follow used in the NT in Acts 7 (implicitly), Phil 2:5–11; Heb 12:1–4; 1 Pet 2:21–25.
4 A point noted by Lewis & Lewis, *Learning to Preach like Jesus*, 13–14.

known as the outstanding fielding side of the competition. One of the lower sides decided that in order to be successful they needed to emulate the successful team. So, they arranged an important sponsorship which significantly increased the funds of the club, and they also began to train three times a week. They appointed specialist batting and bowling coaches but they decided that fielding was not that significant. The next season that team finished last.

Much modern preaching and teaching presupposes that we are speaking to a rationalist mind, a mind that deals in propositions. For the most part that is a correct assumption. But what happens in this context is that biblical narrative is distilled into its essential point and that point transferred directly to the audience in some manner.[5] So for example, the entire narrative of Acts 10:1–11:18 is about the conversion of the Gentiles. Parable interpretation is no exception. Jülicher insisted on the one point of comparison approach to the parables, and so reduced parable to proposition.[6] The problem is, however, that different interpreters saw different main points.[7]

The end of this approach is often reductionism, particularly when dealing with literary genres that are not propositional in form. The narrative is mined for its propositional point then discarded.[8]

Of course, you might say, it is to be expected that our default position is propositional speech. We are part of a literary, information–saturated society. Jesus was in a totally different situation: an oral culture with high degree of illiteracy. Furthermore, he was teaching about himself to a large extent, whereas we are not teaching about ourselves, we

---

5   Eslinger, *Narrative and Imagination*, 12–14.
6   Eslinger, *Narrative and Imagination*, 14.
7   Jülicher understood the point of the Parable of the Dishonest Manager (Luke 16:1–8) to be that one should make the most of present opportunities in order to ensure a future of happiness (Kissinger, *The Parables of Jesus*, 75). Many recent commentators regard the story a call to decision in the face of eschatological crisis (Garland, *Luke*, 650; Nolland, *Luke 9:21–18:34*, 802–3.)
8   The seminal study is Frei, *The Eclipse of Biblical Narrative*.

are teaching about Jesus.[9] Nevertheless, just because something does not come easy or natural to us does not mean that it should be discarded. Let's consider the value of story.

The Value of Story[10]

i) Life has a narrative flow

Although we do think in propositional terms to some extent (e.g. *I am an Australian, the earth revolves around the sun*), life has an essential narrative flow.[11] This is particularly the case with memory. When I recall something it is as part of a sequence of events. If for example I am trying to find my car keys, I try to mentally chronicle my movements after I last exited the car. In fact, human actions are only intelligible in terms of narrative, that is, their place in a larger story. This is what we call *context*.

The sadness occasioned by the premature death of a loved one is caused by a variety of factors, but one such factor is a sense of an untimely completion of narrative. All that has gone into making that person what they were has come to an end. Their particular storyline is finished, even though it necessarily overlaps with the storyline of others.

On a broader scale, of course, life as narrative relates not only to individuals, but also to cultures. This is particularly the case with oral cultures, where sacred story provides legitimisation for the history and existence of a certain group. Even with the Australian aborigines, where story is presented in musical/dance form, it is still essentially narrative.

Yet it is not the case that 'sacred' story is confined purely to oral or tribal cultures. At the Bicentennial celebrations in 1988, white Australia re-enacted the landing of the First Fleet at Sydney Cove, thereby

---

9   A point well noted by Witherington, *New Testament Theology and Ethics. Volume 1*, 78–79. He states, 'We must accept these differences in storytelling that have everything to do with the fact that Jesus operates at a different juncture in history than do his later followers who are part of the early Christian movement, and that also have to do with the fact that Jesus' historical consciousness of himself does not include all the retrospective Christian theologizing done by his followers after the fact and in light of the whole arc of his narrative'.
10 I am indebted, in part, for the following points to Bausch, *Storytelling*, 29–63; Dillon, *Telling the Gospel Through Story*, 17–33; Pennington, *Reading the Gospels Wisely*, 46–48.
11 See Niebuhr, 'The Story of our Life', 21–44; Crites, 'The Narrative Quality of Experience', 65–88; Eslinger, *Narrative and Imagination*, 3–12.

showing the importance of narrative in understanding our origins. On a more sombre note, Anzac Day 2015 saw an 'eerie and terrifying display' as the Gallipoli landing was re-enacted at Tweed Heads.[12] Clearly we understand who we are via story.

It is instructive how the biblical writers use narrative to encourage and reprove the people of God. In the OT, the Psalms and the prophets constantly appeal to the Exodus to remind Israel of God's power and faithfulness (e.g., Isa 43:14–21; Ps 135:8–12), whereas in the NT we see Stephen presenting a selective narrative of Israel's history in his defence before the Sanhedrin (Acts 7:1–53). In this way the writer (and before him the speaker) is able to meet the readers (hearers) on common ground as they reflect on a shared story.

ii) Stimulate curiosity

Stories stimulate curiosity; we want to know how it will end![13] How often have you stayed up much longer then you should have watching a TV show or movie that you had no real interest in because you had to see how it ended. For me, one of the most frustrating TV dramas is '24', an action packed thriller that is set in real time. The problem is, you have to wait for 24 episodes to get plot resolution. At one episode a week, that is bordering on unbearable!

iii) Ties us to reality / our cultural roots/ common humanity

Why is it that when a preacher starts to lose an audience one guaranteed method of re-engaging them is to tell a story? This is because stories connect us to reality—to the whole of which we are part. Consequently, we tend to see ourselves more clearly in story, as faithful followers who doubt (Thomas), or close friends who betray (Judas) or deny (Peter).[14]

Is interesting how stories the world wide share common themes such as lost paradise, injustice put right, true love.[15] Such stories connect with

---

12 News.com.au, April 25, 2015. www.news.com.au/national/anzac-day/watch-tweed-heads-reenacts-gallipoli-landing-in-eerie-and-terrifying-display/news-story/1238ed4ee6acab4da3c17bc3c6cb14. Accessed 20/2/2017.
13 Bausch, *Storytelling*, 30–31, with some good examples and stories.
14 Pennington, *Reading the Gospels Wisely*, 47–48; Bausch, Storytelling, 59.
15 See Bausch, *Storytelling*, 35–36; Cassady, *Storytelling*, 5–8.

our deep hopes and longings. We particularly value stories that preserve traditions that form an integral part of our culture. No doubt this explains the popularity of the movie *The Dish*[16] to many of Australians of my generation.

iv) Help us to reorientate ourselves or change an unhelpful perspective

Stories help correct a distorted perspective, and in this sense can be an avenue for healing and growth. Jesus' parable of the Workers in the Vineyard, where all the workers receive the same pay regardless of their starting time (Matt 20:1–16) is designed to correct a misguided sense of fairness. The Good Samaritan (Luke 10:25–37) is designed to correct a narrow view of one's neighbour. I remember once hearing a story about a parent feeling rejected by their children. This story really connected with me and gave me insight (as a father of three, two of whom did this to me when they were little) into God's hurt at being rejected by his creatures.

v) Help us overcomes self–deception

Prior to Nathan's parable (2 Sam 12:1–15), David had probably rationalised what he had done with Uriah the Hittite. The parable enabled him to see his actions for what they truly were. We are much more likely to entertain personal criticism when it comes through story rather than direct confrontation. If we can reflect on a story and assess our own actions in terms of those of the characters, then we are much less prone to an automatic defensive response.

vi) Leave a lasting effect

Stories linger on in our minds, particularly those that have unexpected outcomes or express concepts in a unique manner. This is also the case for stories where the meaning is not that apparent, such as Jesus' parable of the Dishonest Manager (Luke 16:1–8). I always judge the quality of a movie by whether I'm still thinking about it the next morning!

---

16 *The Dish* is a comedy/drama based on the televising of first moon landing. The Australian country town of Parkes, with its large radio telescope, had a leading role to play in relaying the signal from the moon to NASA.

vii) Capture the power of words

Stories capture the power of words that appear out of place in ordinary speech. So for example:

> *'Space: the final frontier. These are the voyages of the starship "Enterprise." Its continuing mission—to explore strange, new worlds, to seek out new life, new civilisations—to boldly go where no-one has gone before!'*

In the NT the theological point that humility is a prized virtue before God is much better expressed by the parable of the Pharisee and Tax Collector (Luke 18:9–14), than by a bland propositional statement such as 'God values humility'.[17]

The Limitations of Propositional Language

All this raises a challenge: if life is so narratively orientated, we must be careful how we use abstraction, that is, taking a part of a narrative in isolation and stating it in terms of a proposition or generalised statement. For example, the statement Christ died for sin, really only becomes intelligible in terms of the larger biblical narrative, and if we are to dialogue with those who are not familiar with that larger narrative then the proposition may not be readily understood, let alone accepted.

A point of qualification. Abstraction has its place and is necessary in order to conduct many aspects of life. When ordering pizza, I don't need to give the person serving a narrative account of how I left home and the route I took to get the shop. In theological discussion too abstraction plays a vital role and is the way in which the classic creeds of the Christian confession have been formulated. Nevertheless, if we are communicating biblical truth, which for us is sacred story, and if life is essentially narrative in orientation, then the use of narrative to communicate the Christian message is indispensable.

Systematic theology, however, has not generally been construed, or indeed constructed, in terms of narrative. It is a categorising and

---

17 Pennington, *Reading the Gospels Wisely*, 47.

arranging of various data including biblical, historical, and contemporary in order to discuss Christian doctrine in a theoretical and philosophical manner. This is, of course, valid and necessary and has its rightful place. It is well suited to the post–enlightenment, information rich, literate mind. But there is a price that has been paid. Christianity has tended to become more of an argumentative and cognitive community than one that engages in story–telling.[18]

The rise of post–modern thought over the past 50 years or so has resulted in a caution and indeed suspicion of propositional language. This has gone hand in hand with a distrust of metanarrative (which sometimes is less of a 'narrative' and more like a series of propositions), an aversion to authority, and a subjectifying of truth. For a post–modern person the relational and the personal are of prime importance. In communicating the Christian message in this context it is easy to see why systematic theology may very quickly lose an audience. Ditto for propositional style preaching. If we are concerned about articulating the Christian message responsibly in our current milieu then we need to ponder other approaches.

When matters are conveyed purely in propositional terms, the danger of them remaining abstract concepts without integration certainly increases. 'Jesus suffered under Pontius Pilate, died and was buried' lacks a little compared to the hammering of the nails and the cry of forsakenness from the cross.[19] 'Jesus was rejected' is fairly bland'. 'He came to his own and his own received him not' is a little more poetic.[20] The son being sent to collect the owner's share of the produce and tossed out of the vineyard is way more memorable and striking.

In answer to the question, *Why does God allow evil and suffering in the world?*, one of the answers of systematic theology is that bound up with the preservation of free will. But an answer can also be formulated in narrative form, utilising the biblical narrative itself, without even entering into systematics. That might look something like this:

---

18   Metz, 'A Short Apology of Narrative', 255.
19   Bausch, *Storytelling*, 21.
20   Bausch, *Storytelling*, 28.

> *In Jesus, God himself was subjected to rejection, suffering and injustice. The story of Jesus shows that far from being aloof from suffering, God has got his hands dirty and become the victim, by experiencing death on a Roman cross.*

Or, to paint the scene in even more vivid narrative form:

> *On a hill outside of Jerusalem, long, long ago, darkness covers the land. A man hangs on a cross, body slumped, head bowed, given up to death. The sign above him reads 'King of the Jews'. That was his crime; found guilty by a kangaroo court comprised of those whose jealousy and fear far outweighed their concern for truth and justice. Yes the man had made claims, even extravagant claims, but those claims had been backed up by actions that none could rightly deny. Yet deny it they did, and in the very process they kill the one who claimed to be their messiah, even their God. If he was right, then God experiences death at the hands of mankind, and understands first-hand what injustice and suffering are all about. And why does he willingly do this? Great irony– that we might ultimately be free from suffering and death!*

The Parables of Jesus

Jesus did not often begin with propositions. He told parables, entered into dialogue, asked questions, and offered comparisons. He drew on a shared experience with his audience including employment, temptation, death, bribery, joy, kindness. The fact that Jesus was a master storyteller was due in no small part to his ability to tap into such common experience.

Undoubtedly, the parables of Jesus can circumvent many of the roadblocks faced when attempting to communicate the Christian story to the postmodern mind. Consider the following:[21]

---

21 Stiller, *Preaching Parables to Postmoderns*, 25–30. The following examples are based on his analysis.

Parable of the Pharisee and Tax Collector
- God's acceptance is not by the keeping of strict rules and regulations
- the pronouncement of Jesus in favour of the tax collector is not rational

Parable of the Sower
- emphasis falls upon human responsibility
- there is no insistence that the word must be accepted

Parable of the Judge and the Widow
- illustration of how those with powerless voices tend to be abused by the powerful
- God does not act in this way

Parable of the Lost Son
- enables the gospel to be encapsulated in story form rather than in metanarrative

Parable of the Rich Fool
- rejects the idea that identity is to be found in individualistic/autonomous terms (i.e. both the question that prompts the parable, and also the rich man within the parable)

Parable of the Good Samaritan
- exposes cultural and racial prejudice

Parable of the Friend at Midnight
- God wants to assist us in addressing the problems that life raises; he is approachable

I am aware that when attempting to correct an imbalance there is always the danger of overstatement. We do not wish to move from the 'Age of Exposition to the Age of Show Business'.[22] The task is not just to tell story, but to communicate truth via story. It also needs to be stated

---

22 Larsen, *Telling the Old, Old Story*, 30.

clearly that there is a time for story and a time for argument and reason. Jesus did not speak totally in parables, and despite the views of many in the scholarly world, did interpret at least some of his stories. Metz puts it well:

> I do not intend this to be regarded as a reason for excluding argument from theology. There is no question of...obscuring the distinction between narrative memory and theological argument. It is much more a question of acknowledging the relative value of rational argument, *the primary function of which is to protect the narrative memory of salvation in a scientific world,* to allow it to be at stake and to prepare the way for a renewal of this narrative, without which the experience of salvation is silenced (italics mine).[23]

Communicating in Parable

Communicating in parable is, of course, a subset of communicating in story. While I am certainly concerned and interested in the larger world of story, I want to focus now particularly on parable. One option we have here is to 'update' or re-contextualise one of the synoptic parables.[24] So:

> A NT lecturer was on his way to preach at his friend's country church, running a fine line to get there on time. But it was a hot day and the thought of a Coke was too tempting to pass up. So he pulled over at the next milk-bar and headed straight for the fridge. Grabbing the coldest can he could find he headed off to pay and passed a little boy, probably about four, rummaging through the twisties and potato chips. The kid had a complete skinhead, except for the rat-tails at the back. The lecturer was just thinking what kind of parent would give their kid a

---

23 Metz, 'A Short Apology of Narrative', 259.
24 An excellent resource for preaching the parables of Jesus, including some thoughtful modern-day parallels, is Blomberg, *Preaching the Parables*. Also helpful are Stiller, *Preaching the Parables to Moderns*; Hughes, 'Preaching the Parables', 157–70.

hair–cut like that, when my answer came quite abruptly. 'Get your ……. hands out of the ……..twisties'. He looked up to see one of the hardest female faces he had ever seen—something straight out of Mad Max. Then he saw the father: black canvas jeans, black t–shirt, tatts the whole length of the arm, and the mandatory packet of smokes tucked up under the arm of the t–shirt. Never a more stereotypical bogun had he ever laid eyes on. He walked out shaking his head.

Parked next to his car was a black, late 70's V8 statesman, lowered that much that the exhaust pipes were almost touching the gravel. No guessing who owned that! So off he went, lamenting the sad fate of the little fella—what chance did he have in life? As he was about to pull out on to the highway he was shocked out of his contemplation by a car tooting as it passed. It was his friend the pastor, on his way to church, obviously running a little late as well.

Down the road a couple of kilometres he saw a car pulled over in obvious trouble—hood up, lots of steam coming out, and a fairly elderly lady standing by looking eagerly up and down the road. The pangs of guilt struck, but as he was already battling to get to the church on time, he forced them down. He could hardly stop and help when he was the guest speaker—many people were relying on him. After all this was God's work. His friend obviously had the same reasoning, as he was out of sight around the next bend—it was clear he had not stopped either.

Anyway the lecturer got there OK, the service went well and the sermon was well received, and after exchanging pleasantries he said goodbye to all and headed off on the journey home. As he turned a bend in the road he was surprised to notice that the car he had seen over 2 hours ago in trouble was still there, only now help had arrived. Help in the form of a black statesman, with a man bent over the engine with a handful of spanners. He was a little taken aback. This bloke looked like the sort that would attack little old ladies, not help them in their distress!

> So he drove on. He had a fleeting thought that maybe he should see if he could help in anyway. But it was very fleeting. He didn't know much about cars, and the bogun probably had things under control. So he continued on, reflecting upon the message that he had given in church that morning.

Another, and I do say more challenging, option is to construct parables of our own. Anyone courageous enough to venture down this path may benefit from considering a few points.[25] First, a parable needs to do its work on people, that is, it needs to provoke curiosity and reflection. Consequently a parable must walk the tightrope between being too obvious and being too vague. The obvious may come from either the way the story is told, or by adding a final explanation (usually in the form of propositional statement). This tends to defeat the purpose of the story somewhat as the story is left behind and the focus shifts too soon to the proposition. For example:

> A man was given 100 vouchers for free food. Will he keep them for himself? Will he give them to friends? Or will he give them to everyone who is hungry?[26]

Although there is no propositional statement at the end of this short parable, the point of the story is so obvious that it is readily reduced to a proposition such as 'care for the poor'.

At the opposite extreme a parable may be so vague that it leaves the audience with no idea, even after considered reflection. For example:

> There was a woman who went for a haircut while visiting a strange land. While the barber was working, the woman shared all her life problems. The barber finished, she paid him, said 'thank you', and then left.[27]

---

25 Stiller, *Preaching Parables to Postmoderns*, 15–18 summarises some characteristics of Jesus' parables that are helpful to bear in mind when constructing one's own. Although not focussed on parables as such, some helpful resource for constructing stories in general can be found in in Mellon, *Storytelling and the Art of Imagination*; Cassady, *Storytelling Step by Step*.
26 Parable supplied by a member of my New Testament class at MST.
27 Parable supplied by a member of my New Testament class at MST.

So, a well-constructed parable should give the audience cause for contemplation, and enable them to make the referents after some considered reflection. Such a parable might be:

> Three people went to a doctor, each with a form of treatable cancer. Once the doctor went through all possible risks and outcomes of the surgery the first person stated, 'I think I would prefer to try some alternative medicines'. The second replied, 'I hear the urgency, but still need time to process all of this'. The third person said, 'I know you are capable. When can this surgery occur?'

Second, the parable needs to contain concepts and images that are readily understood by the audience. I once told the following parable, based on my own experience, in a class of mixed Australian and Asian students:

> There was a man who regularly went for walks through a new housing estate. The first person he saw was energetically scalping weeds off the ground with a sharp spade. Passing by a few houses he saw another down on her hands and knees pulling each weed separately, but breaking off many at the top. Later he passed by a woman and her son laying newspaper over the weeds and laying down mulch on top of the newspaper. Finally he saw a man spraying weeds. Returning by this latter house after two weeks he noticed that the weeds had died and the man was hoeing the soil ready to plant.

The Australian students readily understood the concepts, and most were able to interpret the story along the lines of getting rid of sin, or problems, at their root cause rather than adopt superficial responses. The Asian students, however, were unfamiliar with gardening concepts in general, and the meaning of 'mulch' in particular. This proved to be a barrier to them understanding the parable.

Third, the parable should ideally draw on contemporary events or knowledge. A parable told about life in the digital age is more likely to resonate with an audience than one about sending a telegraph.[28] Here is one combining the Australian love of cricket with a bit of a hermeneutical theory:

> Three cricket umpires were talking about the game. The first said, 'There are LBWs and caught behinds[29] and I call them as they are'. The second said, 'There are LBWs and caught behinds and I call them as I see them'. The third said, 'There are LBWs and caught behinds and they don't exist until I call them'.[30]

Conclusion

The value of story is largely untapped in the Australian church today. Our default position is proposition and understandably so. But rather than utilise the occasional story to wake the audience from slumber, we need to emulate the model of Jesus and communicate much more in narrative. When used creatively and thoughtfully, parable is a narratival vehicle that can convey the gospel and spiritual truth in interesting, vivid and possibly even confronting ways.

---

28 A telegraph is a method of conveying a message via pulses sent along a wire.
29 These are two means of dismissal in cricket. For those unfamiliar with cricket substitute 'balls' and 'strikes' in baseball.
30 This parable is an adaptation of one I heard about baseball umpires, but I cannot recall the source.

Bibliography

Bausch, William J. — *Storytelling: Imagination and Faith* (Mystic, CT: Twenty-Third Publications, 1996).

Blomberg, Craig L. — *Preaching the Parables: From Responsible Interpretation to Powerful Proclamation* (Grand Rapids: Baker Academic, 2004).

Cassady, Marsh — *Storytelling: Step by Step* (San Jose, CA: Resource Publications, 1990).

Crites, Stephen — 'The Narrative Quality of Experience', in Stanley Hauerwas and L. Gregory Jones (eds.), *Why Narrative? Readings in Narrative Theology* (Grand Rapids: Eerdmans, 1989), 65–88.

Dillon, Christine — *Telling the Gospel Through Story: Evangelism that Keeps Hearers Wanting More* (Downers Grove, IL: IVP, 2012).

Eslinger, Richard L. — *Narrative and Imagination* (Minneapolis: Fortress Press, 1995).

Frei, Hans — *The Eclipse of Biblical Narrative: A Study in Eighteenth and Nineteenth Century Hermeneutics* (New Haven: Yale University Press, 1974).

Garland, David E. — *Luke* (ZECNT; Grand Rapids: Zondervan, 2011).

Hughes, Robert G. — 'Preaching the Parables', in John Reumann (ed.), *The Promise and Practice of Biblical Theology* (Minneapolis: Fortress, 1991), 157–70.

Kissinger, W. S. — *The Parables of Jesus: A History of Interpretation and Bibliography* (New Jersey: Scarecrow, 1979).

Lewis, Ralph L., & Gregg Lewis, — *Learning to Preach like Jesus* (Wheaton, IL: Crossway Books, 1989).

Mellon, Nancy — *Storytelling and the Art of Imagination* (Rockport, MS: Element, 1992).

Metz, Johann Baptist — 'A Short Apology of Narrative', in Stanley Hauerwas and L. Gregory Jones (eds.), *Why Narrative? Readings in Narrative Theology* (Grand Rapids: Eerdmans, 1989), 251–62.

Niebuhr, H. Richard — 'The Story of our Life', in Stanley Hauerwas and L. Gregory Jones (eds.), *Why Narrative? Readings in Narrative Theology* (Grand Rapids: Eerdmans, 1989), 21–44.

Nolland, John   *Luke 9:21–18:34* (WBC; Dallas, TX: Word Books, 1993).

Pennington, Jonathan T.   *Reading the Gospels Wisely: In Narrative and Theological Introduction* (Grand Rapids: Baker Academic, 2012).

Stein, Robert H.   *Mark* (BECNT; Grand Rapids: Baker Academic, 2008).

Stiller, Brian C.   *Preaching Parables to Postmoderns* (Minneapolis: Fortress Press, 2005).

Witherington III, Ben.   *New Testament Theology and Ethics. Volume 1* (Downers Grove, IL: IVP Academic, 2016).

Wright, N. T.   *The New Testament and the People of God* (London: SPCK, 1992).

Websites

News.com.au, April 25, 2015. www.news.com.au/national/anzac-day/watch-tweed-heads-reenacts-gallipoli-landing-in-eerie-and-terrifying-display/news-story/1238ed4ee6acab4da3c17bc3c6cb14

CHAPTER 12

Jesus Christ as a Victim.
A Christological Light on Contemporary Survivors of Sexual Abuse
The Sodalicio Case in Peru

Rocío Figueroa

Abstract

The essay tries to give voices to eight survivors of sexual abuse from Sodalicio movement in Peru. The aim is to explore the spiritual consequences associated with the abuse and the secondary victimization that survivors suffered from the community, as a theological response tries to propose Jesus as a victim of sexual abuse and questions if it could help survivors in their journey.

1. Introduction

"Where is God now?". In the terrifying Elie Wiesel story, this was the question of a man watching the torment of a little Jewish boy who was hung. Pondering this question, Jurgen Moltmann developed his theology after Auschwitz.[1] In the same way, theology today cannot be the

---

1   Moltmann, 'The Passion of Christ and the Suffering of God'.

same following the severe crisis of sexual abuse that has occurred within the Catholic Church. We must rethink many topics within Ecclesiology, Christology and Pastoral Theology.

Clergy perpetrated sexual abuse (CPSA) has become a crisis of worldwide dimensions for the Catholic Church. Three cases have received attention in Latin America: The Legionaries of Christ in Mexico,[2] the Karadima group in Chile,[3] and Sodalitium Christianae Vitae in Peru.[4] I had a particularly close knowledge of the Sodalicio case. A layman Luis Fernando Figari founded the Sodalicio in 1971. All lay consecrated members make vows of obedience, celibacy and a spirit of poverty. Sodalicio has a presence in schools and churches and runs retreat facilities and Youth Centres with communities in Peru, Argentina, Colombia, Brazil, Chile, Ecuador, Italy and the United States.

I was previously a member of the Marian Community of Reconciliation, a Catholic Association of lay consecrated women, which is the female branch of Sodalicio. I served as the MCR General Superior for 9 years (1991–1998) and I belonged to the community for more than 20 years. An abused victim first contacted me in 2006.

More victims reported being abused. I helped these victims and during this time, I developed a relationship of trust with them. In 2010 the Peruvian journalist Pedro Salinas, a former Sodalicio member, accused Figari and other leaders of the community of physical, psychological and sexual abuse. In 2015, after five years of investigation he wrote the book *Mitad Monjes, Mitad Soldados*[5] (*Half monks, half soldiers*) which contained victims' testimonies. Sodalicio have currently recognized 66 victims and set aside a compensation fund of nearly $ 4 million NZD.[6]

---

2   Berry & Renner, *Vows of Silence*.
3   Monkeberg, *Karadima*.
4   Salinas, *Mitad Monjes*.
5   Salinas, *Mitad Monjes*.
6   For further information, see Figueroa & Tombs, *Listening to Male Survivors*, 157–159.

2. Sexual Abuse and Spiritual Impact

In December 2016, the Centre for Theology and Public Issues, University of Otago in New Zealand, published a report drawing on interviews with eight survivors from the Sodalicio case.[7] The interviewees are all now middle-aged but had been involved with Sodalicio when they were younger. The sexual abuse took place when the participants were minors or young adults.

There are many studies about sexual abuse within the Church. However, the spiritual impact of sexual abuse is a largely neglected topic. One lesson from this report is that the spiritual impact of abuse should be included in any full understanding of its impact and consequences. This appreciation is particularly relevant in instances of church-related sexual abuse.

As noted above, the leadership of Sodalicio are laymen, and so it might be misleading to discuss it in relation to 'clergy perpetrated sexual abuse' (CPSA). Nonetheless, many of the institutional elements associated with CPSA, including hierarchies of power and expectations around spiritual authority and obedience, were also significant in Sodalicio. It is not surprising that many of the issues identified in the literature on the impact of CPSA are also expressed in the interviews with Sodalicio members.

CPSA shares many of the same long-term implications as any other sexual abuse, including psychological, sexual, and behavioural problems in adults.[8] These long-term effects can produce various disorders, such as: anxiety, low self-esteem, depression and post-traumatic stress disorder.[9]

At the same time, there are elements that are commonly involved in clergy perpetrated sexual abuse (CPSA): the abuse of spiritual power by the perpetrator is often a key feature of sexual abuse committed by clergy. The priest or the pastor represents the voice and the love of God for the community. As Fogler affirms: 'the community understands that his decisions stem from the depth of his spiritual connection'.[10]

---

7   Figueroa & Tombs, *Listening to Male Survivors*. See also Figueroa & Tombs, 'Lived Religion'.
8   Fater & Mullaney, 'The Lived Experience'.
9   Garnefesky & Arends, 'Sexual Abuse'.
10 Fogler, *et al.*, 'Theoretical Foundation', 307.

Another important feature in CPSA is that many survivors begin to view the institution as a desecrated place: 'Since they feel hurt by the church and they do not want to be re-victimized, they stay away from the church'.[11]

Different studies have found that sexual abuse also damages a survivor's faith in God. The first impact can be that 'a survivor may question God's benevolence'.[12] Some victims not only have a crisis of faith, but even question the existence of God.[13] Rossetti found that Catholic victims of clergy-child sexual abuse experience a profound loss of spirituality.[14] Many survivors transfer their negative feelings towards the perpetrator onto God. Such feelings include anger, mistrust, and alienation.[15]

Pargament affirms that the spiritual consequences can take three different forms:

> struggles with the divine (e.g., feelings of anger, abandonment, or fear in relation to God), interpersonal struggles (e.g. religious tension and conflict with family, church members and leaders, denomination), and intrapsychic struggles (e.g. religious doubts, questions about dogma, conflicts between thoughts, feelings, and behaviours).[16]

In many cases there is a traumatic sense of betrayal.[17] Wells also affirms that 'clergy sexual abuse is a trauma that denudes the soul of the basic sense of trust that is so needed in the quest for spirituality'.[18]

3. Interviews with Former Members of Sodalicio

We developed and conducted structured personal interviews with eight survivors from Sodalicio.[19] We tried to investigate the impact that sexual

---

11 McLaughlin, 'Devastated Spirituality, 157.
12 Fogler, *et al.*, 'The Impact of Clergy-perpetrated Sexual Abuse', 340.
13 McLaughlin, 'Devastated Spirituality, 157.
14 Rosetti, 'The Impact of Child Sexual Abuse'.
15 Ganje-Fling & McCarthy, 'Impact of Childhood Sexual Abuse'.
16 Pargament, *et al.*, 'Problem and Solution', 404.
17 Durà-Vilà *et al.*, 'Integration of Sexual Trauma'.
18 Wells, 'A Needs Assessment', 211.
19 Figueroa & Tombs, *Listening to Male Survivors*. See also Figueroa & Tombs, 'Lived Religion'.

abuse had on the participants and especially on their spirituality and faith. The participants on the report were referred by the pseudonyms Santiago, Tomás, Xavier, Nicolás, Matías, Jeremías, Lalo and Roberto. I will present here some of their responses:

a. Feelings of betrayal and lack of trust

Betrayal trauma is defined as 'a situation in which the individual suffers a violation from a person or institution on which he depends'.[20]

Santiago

Santiago had described his experience of sexual abuse:

> *When Figari tried to sodomize Santiago he had difficulties with the penetration. In that moment, with the coolness of a surgeon, he went to his night table, opened the drawer and took out a Vaseline jar to continue the ritual. 'The strangest thing is that when he was penetrating me he asked me to masturbate. And the weirdest thing: after that he asked me to go to mass'.*[21]
>
> *It was not the only time that it happened. [...] 'It was always in the same room. I remember the night table, the lights, how the bedroom was organized, the pictures, I remember his mother walking in there'. (Figari's mother lived with him)*

The interview allowed us to ask about his feelings after the abuse, and he explained:

> *Consciousness came little by little. I felt like a storm. Everything was moving around me. I was isolated. [...] I realized that I had been cheated. Sexual abuse destroys the most inner part of yourself. [...] If someone rapes you it is totally different. [...] I think that our case is the worst thing that they can do. I think I am at my most traumatic central point: I don't trust people.*

This is a betrayal trauma: the fact that someone who is trusted as a spiritual guide betrays you. For Santiago, the sexual abuse itself was not the

---

20   Durà Villà *et al.*, 'Integration of Sexual Trauma', 38.
21   Salinas, *Mitad Monjes*, 165.

most traumatic point. The most traumatic point was being wounded in his 'most inner part', the most vulnerable dimension.

Tomás

> 'Once he asked me to stay absolutely naked, he hugged me and he began kissing me and he said, "don't worry, I love you in Christ, as a friend, this is absolutely natural". This continued for three months. In another occasion, he asked me to penetrate him. Other times he asked me to masturbate myself till he ejaculated, and he said: "it is not a sin, I am your superior and you have to trust in me. This is a spiritual path. It is just for some who are elected, it is not for all"'.[22]
>
> *I had a sense of loss. Now I feel sorry, sadness. [...] I think that it is so painful to think that the people you trusted betrayed you and that that is why I cannot feel anything against him.*

b. Damage to faith

In the interviews, we asked: *Did the abuse have any impact on your religious faith and your sense of God?*

Tomás answered:

> 'Catastrophic. When I understood that I was cheated, I lost my faith. Now I have left God on stand-by. It is too much for me to handle. [...] At the beginning, I abandoned the faith. [...] Now when I pass near a church and I see the Blessed Sacrament I feel God. He has not left me. But now my relationship with God is on an orange light, on stand-by. It gives me too much pain and sadness to feel that he abandoned me and just to ponder the possibility that he failed me is unbearable'.

Before the abuse Tomás recalls his spiritual experience: *'As a child I had two drivers on my faith: my home and my parish life. I had a very intense experience. I felt God very close to me. I felt like I was protected'.* The experience of abuse made Tomás lose his childhood innocence and

---

22 Salinas, *Mitad Monjes*, 197.

his strong faith and at the same time left him with a profound spiritual struggle that he was not able to handle.

Xavier

Xavier states:

> 'Yes. I'm not religious because of the abuse. And not only because of the abuse, but also because of the cover-up and the corruption of the Church. It has had a huge impact on my religious life.
>
> If God exists, why did he send this trial to a little kid? What kind of psychopath is God that would put a child in a sexual trial at 14 years with a person double his age? It does not make any sense. It has no sense.
>
> Yes. The abuse has had an impact on my religiousness, or on my lack of religiousness.'

The sexual abuse has caused fundamental theological problems for Xavier. How can a good God allow such terrible evil and suffering in his name? Xavier has been abused by a representative of God and makes the association between God and the one who committed the abuse in the name of God: 'what kind of psychopath is God?'.

c. Secondary victimization

To understand CPSA and help survivors, we need to focus not only on the victims, but also on all the relationships that included that violence. Sometimes CPSA is just associated with the victims and the perpetrators and we forget that CPSA also includes many others, besides the perpetrator and the survivor we should think about the bystanders' reactions: the common Catholics, the wider society and the hierarchy of the Catholic Church itself. CPSA is 'an interactive dynamic process between perpetrators, survivors and religious communities'.[23] 'CPSA is not just a clergyperson's inappropriate sexual advances and behavior. Its definition also includes the cultivation of a relationship in which these behaviors occur, the theological and community context surrounding this usually secret and forbidden relationship, and the impact

---

23   Fogler, *et al.*, 'Theoretical Foundation', 303.

and psychological aftershock of abusive behavior on the survivor and community'.[24]

Therefore, it is necessary to study the theological situation of the community and the impact on it. In this sense, some studies show that the survivors not only feel conflicted by the perpetrator but also alienated from their churches.[25] The reaction of the wider church community can also profoundly affect the victims. In the case of CPSA within the Catholic church victims tend to believe that the church has not responded to the problems of child sexual abuse.[26] This lack of community support combined with the trauma of the sexual abuse itself can lead to a situation where the recovery and spiritual growth of the victim is very difficult. Even worse, the victim may become the scapegoat of the community.[27] The survivor may feel victimized by the experience of rumour and scandal. One of the psychological traumas of sexual abuse is stigmatization. A victim of sexual abuse not only feels different, but in many cases, experiences shame and guilt. These feelings can be intensified by the reactions of the community. This victimization by the community makes the survivors feel lonely. Although it is necessary to study the effect on the victims, it is also critical to look at the impact on the bystanders, the ordinary Catholics.

In our study, we asked our participants: *Did you feel the support of the Church or of some of its representatives after revealing what had happened to you?*

Santiago:

> *'Never. After 3 years of the abuse, I talked to several priests. They told me that I had to forgive'.*

Nicolás:

> *'The Peruvian Episcopal Conference delivered an important message, but I have not felt particularly welcomed by the Church.*

---

24 Fogler, *et al.*, 'Theoretical Foundation', 303.
25 Rossetti, 'The Impact of Child Sexual Abuse'.
26 Rossetti, 'The Impact of Child Sexual Abuse', 479.
27 Ganzevoort, 'Violence within the Church'.

Rather there were many detractors. There were many people who insulted me. People from the community made atrocious comments on the internet. For example, when I said on TV that Figari had hit people and beat us, one commented: it is impossible that this has happened, besides that, you were not man enough to take a punch. For him it seemed justifiable that Figari had the right to hit people because Figari was a living saint. I have not felt any relief, trust or attitude of service from the Church. The Cardinal [name withheld] *maintained an incomprehensible silence, and an obvious complicity because of his long friendship with Figari. I have only received a lot of support and a lot of solidarity from the civil society and from the most progressive sectors of the Church. Also, I have to say that many Catholics' comments have surprised me and I have found them very good".*

Matías:

'It is very difficult to find someone in the Church who wants to listen to you. Clerics are more concerned with defending the image of a clerical Church or are not trained well enough to fully understand what sexual abuse means'.

The gravity of these commentaries demonstrates clearly that the bystanders to sexual abuse such as priests, the hierarchy and common Catholics have been affected negatively and they usually don't know how to react. In the case of Sodalicio, the ecclesiastical tribunal in Peru and the Vatican didn't reply to the victims' accusations for six years. They only came out publicly when the scandal was in the media.

On the one hand, we had the silence of the hierarchy of the Church which represented a secondary traumatization for survivors. On the other hand, we had a range of different reactions in the wider Church from common Catholics: solidarity to the survivors; pain and sadness; some gave no importance to the problem; others felt deluded and eventually abandoned the Church in Lima; others defended the perpetrators and finally there were people who didn't know how to help survivors and actually asked them to forgive and forget their rage and anger.

Clearly, from all these different bystanders' reactions, the Church urgently needs to broaden its response to sexual abuse. The current approach has been limited to aiding both survivors and perpetrators while also developing policies to confront the crisis. However, the Church must also recognize the urgency for putting measures in place to address this crisis so that the response of bystanders becomes part of the solution rather than part of the problem.

4. Identification with Christ

If sexual abuse within the Church is such a huge problem and a worldwide crisis involving all the people of God, should it not also be at the core of our theological reflection? Don't we need to think of how to face this crisis creatively, wisely utilizing the resources of our faith?

The passion narratives offer us details about the Crucifixion of Jesus. According to Matthew 27:28 and Mark 15:18–19, after being condemned by Pilate, the guards took Jesus into the governor's headquarters. In front of all the cohort, that likely numbered 600 hundred soldiers, the guards 'stripped him and put a scarlet robe on him … then they stripped him of the robe and put his own clothes on him' (Matt. 27:28,31).[28]

The Gospel of John, well-known for the great details in his descriptions of the facts, affirms that when the 'soldiers had crucified Jesus, they took his clothes and divided them into four parts, one for each soldier. They also took his tunic: now the tunic was seamless, wove in one piece from the top' (John 19:23).

Roman crucifixions included enforced stripping, naked exposure and public humiliation.[29] As Brown affirms: 'John, who gives the greatest attention to the scene, is so specific about every item of clothing that one would have the impression that nothing was left. The normal Roman pattern would have been to crucify criminals naked, as attested

---

28 The replacement of Jesus' own clothes for the walk to Golgotha was probably a concession to Jewish scruples about public nakedness: 'In having the final disrobing of Jesus only at the place of execution (Mark 15:24 and par.), the evangelist may reflect a local concession that the Romans made to the Jewish abhorrence of public nudity'; Brown, *The Death of the Messiah*, 1.870.
29 Tombs & Reaves, 'Lived Religion'.

by Artemidorus Daldianus (*Oneirokritika* 2,53)'.[30] Brown considered that the question is not settled although he affirms that the evidence favours complete despoliation during the crucifixion.

It also clear that Jews used nakedness during their executions. The Mishnah records two opinions held among the Jews about nakedness in an execution.[31] They claim that a man was executed naked even among his own Jewish countrymen. If the Jews even stripped their own countrymen, it seems very likely that the Romans would do the same or worse for Jesus. For the Romans and Jews nakedness during execution was a sign of humiliation and absolute powerlessness, shame and dishonour were an important factor in the punishment.

The Passion was scandalous and violent. It was a horrendous death. Stripping Jesus was a violent act, but usually we don't think of it as sexual abuse. The exposure of Jesus' body was not a voluntary act of undressing but was an enforced act of being stripped against his wishes.[32] According to Tombs: 'A careful reading of the passion narratives shows that stripping and naked exposure of Jesus is explicitly attested as a feature of his crucifixion. Although this has not been named as sexual abuse, there can be little doubt that it should be recognized as such'.[33] Michael Trainor also considers that the honour-shame dynamic in the Gospels confirms the possibility of hearing the passion narratives from the point of view of one shamed. From a culturally specific viewpoint, the Gospels are stories of one abused.[34]

Beyond the Gospels, the Tradition of the early Church has left us a beautiful text written by bishop Melito of Sardis, who died in AD 180. He not only considered Jesus' nakedness as an important characteristic of his passion, but he gave us a clear vision of the shameful meaning of seeing or talking about Jesus' nakedness:

---

30 Brown, *The Death of the Messiah*, II, 953.
31 'When he was four cubits from the place of stoning they stripped off his clothes. A man is kept covered in front and a woman both in front and behind. So R. Judah. But the Sages say: A man is stoned naked but a woman is not stoned naked'; Danby, *The Mishnah*, Nezikin, Sanhedrin, 6,3.
32 Figueroa & Tombs, 'Lived Religion'.
33 Figueroa & Tombs, 'Lived Religion', 168.
34 Trainor, *The Body of Jesus*.

> 'O unheard of murder! O unheard of injustice! The appearance of the Master has been changed, his body stripped naked; he was not even considered worthy of a garment so that he not be seen. This is why the luminaries turned away, and with them the day became dark so as to conceal the naked one upon the cross, thus obscuring not the Lord's body but human eyes'.
> (Melito of Sardis, *Homily on the Passion*, 97)

This text comes from a leader of a Christian community of the 2nd century. It is likely that the actual reference to the nakedness of Jesus on the Cross came from the oral tradition. As Dunn affirms, the oral Jesus tradition was the primary way in which Jesus was remembered.[35] In an oral culture, like that of the early Christians, the theoretical and practical knowledge depended on what the elders had stored in their memories.

Although this text shows the image of Jesus naked and confirms the references of the Gospels, at the same time it expresses how difficult it was to see Jesus in that condition. So why was the naked image of Jesus played down by tradition? Why did Christian art usually cover Jesus on the Cross with a cloth? It seems clear that this depiction of Jesus was a reaction to the shame, or a fact of '*pudore*' as the Italians call it, of depicting the sexual violence of the crucifixion. It could also explain why this 'nakedness' has never been developed theologically.

This Christian shame about Christ's naked body was eclipsed in part thanks to St. Francis and his emphasis upon the naked humanity, even poverty, of Christ. He popularized the saying of St. Jerome '*nudum Christus*' and affirmed '*nudus nudum Christum sequi*' or 'follow naked the naked Christ'. Francis' theology of the naked Christ had a great impact helping to reinforce the value of poverty as a means of following Jesus.[36]

First, we have clear evidence of abuse in the passion narratives. Second, we know that in the tradition of the church a theology has been developed from the image of Jesus' nakedness. What about then recovering this image of Jesus' nakedness and relating it to Jesus as a victim of sexual abuse?

Could this image of Jesus as a victim of sexual abuse help survivors

---

35 Dunn, *The Oral Gospel Tradition*, 232.
36 Mormando, "*Nudus nudum Christum sequi*".

identifying with Jesus and feel solidarity with Him in his suffering, humiliation and his loss of identity?

Could the image of the naked Jesus and his innocent suffering help our Catholic communities to avoid stigmatizing those who have been victims blaming them as if the abuse was their fault?

Could the theology of Christ as a victim, help bystanders, to consider the victims of sexual abuse as a priority for the mission and comprehend that in the victims we can contemplate Jesus' countenance?

I would like to go in depth in these questions with a new research project. David Tombs from Otago University is keen to collaborate with me on a new research project using dialogues with survivors and bystanders to verify whether the theology of Jesus as victim of sexual abuse can be a way for survivors to heal and a way for the wider Church to understand better the victims and commit ourselves in the defence of the most vulnerable.

Bibliography

Berry, J. & Renner, G. *Vows of Silence: The Abuse of Power in the Papacy of John Paul II.* (New York: Free Press, 2004).

Brown, R.E. *The Death of the Messiah. From Gethsemane to the grave,* 2 vols. (New York: Doubleday, 1994).

Danby, H. *The Mishnah* (Norfolk: Oxford University Press, 1993).

Dunn, J. *The Oral Gospel Tradition* (Michigan: Grand Rapids, 2013).

Durà-Vilà, G., R. Littlewood & G. Leavey 'Integration of Sexual Trauma in a Religious Narrative. Transformation, Resolution and Growth among Contemplative Nuns', *Transcultural Psychiatry*, 50.1 (2013), 21–46.

Fater, K., & J.A. Mullaney 'The Lived Experience of Adult Male Survivors who Allege Childhood Sexual Abuse by Clergy', *Issues in Mental Health Nursing* 21 (2000), 281–295.

Figueroa, R. & Tombs D. *Listening to Male Survivors of Church Sexual Abuse. Voices from Survivors of Sodalicio Abuses in Peru.* Centre for Theology and Public Issues, University of Otago, 2016: Available: https://ourarchive.otago.ac.nz/handle/10523/7052. (accessed August 7, 2016).

Figueroa, R., & D. Tombs, D.   'Lived Religion and the Traumatic Impact of Sexual Abuse: The Sodalicio Case in Peru', in R. Ganzaevoort & S. Sremac (eds.), *Lived Religion and Trauma: Transcending the Ordinary* (London: Palgrave Macmillan, 2019), 155–176.

Fogler, J.M., J.C. Shipherd, S. Clarke, J. Jensen & E. Rowe   'The Impact of Clergy-perpetrated Sexual Abuse: The Role of Gender, Development, and Post-traumatic Stress', *Journal of Child Sexual Abuse*, 17.3–4 (2008), 329–358.

Fogler, J., J. Shiperd, E. Rowe, J. Jensen & S. Clarke   'Theoretical Foundation for Understanding Clergy-perpetrated Sexual Abuse', *Journal of Child Sexual Abuse*, 17.3–4 (2008), 301–328.

Ganje-Fling, M. & P. McCarthy   'Impact of Childhood Sexual Abuse on Client Spiritual Development: Counseling Implications', *Journal of Counseling and Development*, 74.3 (1996), 253–259.

Garnefesky, N., & E. Arends   'Sexual Abuse and Adolescent Maladjustment: Differences between Male and Female Victims', *Journal of Adolescence* 21 (1998), 99–107.

Ganzevoort, R.   'Violence within the Church', *Paper for the 2nd International NOSTER Conference.* Soesterberg NL, 21st January 2003.

McLaughlin, B.R.   'Devastated Spirituality: The Impact of Clergy Sexual Abuse on the Survivor's Relationship with God and the Church', *Sexual Addiction & Compulsivity: The Journal of Treatment and Prevention* 1.2 (1994), 145–158.

Melito of Sardis,   *Homily on the Passion.* Cited from L.J. Johnson, *Worship in the Early Church: An Anthology of Historical Sources* (Collegeville, Minn.: Liturgical Press, 2009), I, 90–105.

Moltmann, J.   'The Passion of Christ and the Suffering of God', *Asbury Theological Journal* 48.1 (1993), 19–28.

Monkeberg, M.O.   *Karadima el señor de los infiernos* (Santiago: Random House, Mondadori, 2010).

Mormando, F.   "*Nudus nudum Christum sequi*": The Franciscans and differing interpretations of Male Nakedness in Fifteenth-Century Italy', in E. DuBruck & B. Gusick (eds.), *Fifteenth Century Studies* (New York: Camden House, 2008), 171–197.

Pargament, K.I., N.A. Murray-Swank, & A. Mahoney 'Problem and Solution: The Spiritual Dimension of Clergy Sexual Abuse and its Impact on Survivors', *Journal of Child Sexual Abuse* 17.3–4 (2008), 397–420.

Rossetti, S. 'The Impact of Child Sexual Abuse on Attitudes toward God and the Catholic Church', *Child Abuse & Neglect* 19.12 (1995), 1469–1481.

Salinas, P. *Mitad Monjes, Mitad Soldados: Todo lo que el Sodalicio no quiere que sepas* (Lima: Planeta, 2015).

Tombs, D. 'Crucifixion, State Terror, and Sexual Abuse', *Union Seminary Quarterly Review* 53.1–2 (1999), 89–109. Available at http://hdl.handle.net/10523/6067.

Tombs, D. & Reaves J. 'Lived Religion and the Intolerance of the Cross', in R.R. Ganzevoort & S. Sremac (eds.), *Lived Religion and the Politics of (In)tolerance* (London: Palgrave Macmillan, 2017), 63–83.

Trainor, M. *The Body of Jesus and Sexual Abuse: How the Gospel Passion Narratives Inform a Pastoral Response* (Eugene: Wipf & Stock, 2014).

Wells, K. 'A Needs Assessment Regarding the Nature and Impact of Clergy Sexual Abuse Conducted by the Interfaith Sexual Trauma Institute' *Sexual Addiction & Compulsivity: The Journal of Treatment and Prevention* 10.2–3 (2003), 201–217. DOI:10.1080/10720160390230691.

CHAPTER 13

Nowhere to Lay His Head: An Eco-Theological Reflection on Homelessness

Deborah Guess

Abstract

The theme of 'homelessness' in relation to Jesus and his disciples has often been interpreted eschatologically, thereby endorsing 'cosmic homelessness', which poses a problem for ecological theology. This chapter draws on Halvor Moxnes' discussion of the spatial aspects of the historical Jesus and specifically on three aspects of his thesis: (1) the radical nature of Jesus' leaving of home and the way it was impelled by structural (social, economic and political) factors, (2) the trauma that it would likely have entailed, and (3) the ambiguous question of whether an alternative or new home is indicated in the gospels. 'Developing Moxnes' three aspects, this essay points to several eco-theological resonances with today's context. A radical challenge is posed to contemporary understandings of 'home', especially as places of consumerism; ecological devastation sometimes causes unacknowledged distress; and, last, the question of what any kind of new home might mean is somewhat ambiguous.

Introduction—The Problem of Cosmic Homelessness[1]

The homelessness of Jesus and his disciples is rather often taken as an unremarkable part of the background to the gospels that requires little further examination. When taken at face value the idea that Jesus may have lived and taught a transient way of life is inevitably problematic for Christian followers who have (or want) a more settled existence. A similar question arises in relation to Jesus' behaviour and teaching on wealth and possessions. A number of Christian groups, from the Desert Mothers and Fathers to St Francis to alternative Christian communities today, have taken the question very seriously. But on the whole the rootlessness of Jesus and his disciples has been interpreted as having a predominantly spiritual and eschatological meaning, pointing towards a future existence that is in some sense beyond Earth.[2] Consequently, the contextual and tangible aspects of homelessness in the gospels has been relatively neglected. There may be various reasons for this. Perhaps gospel passages about Jesus and the disciples leaving home are so familiar that we fail to register their significance. Perhaps it is because the idea of a young man leaving home is such a 'natural' rite of passage for western people that we fail to see it as anything else. Perhaps Jesus has been romanticised as a solitary moral hero whose status, when seen through a neoliberal lens, diminishes the real pain and destitution involved in homelessness.[3] Or perhaps reflecting on Jesus' domestic setting evokes an uncomfortably feminine or less-than-heroic side to him. These, and other reasons, might begin to explain why homelessness in the gospels has been primarily interpreted eschatologically. However, an eschatological understanding of homelessness can detract people from their present earthly context in favour of an ultimate and true 'heavenly home'.

This poses a problem for theology that explores Christian thought in relation terms of an ecological ethos. A central concern of eco-theology is to affirm the value of the bio-physical world, claiming that God's creation is an authentic 'home' place for human beings. When homelessness is valorised in the Christian tradition, ecological theologians

---

1   Some of the material in this essay overlaps with my 'Earth as Home-Place', published since the 2017 Impact of Jesus conference.
2   Theissen, *Social Reality*, 43.
3   Myles, 'Homelessness, Neoliberalism, and Jesus' "Decision" to Go Rogue', 219.

are likely to critique it and suggest that it may be associated with indifferent or negative attitudes to Earth that have led to ecological neglect and abuse. For example, Ernst Conradie sees some Christian theologies as 'instigating, reinforcing and legitimising' an alienation between humankind and the natural world in the way they have over-emphasised God's transcendence.[4] Similarly, Sallie McFague is critical of the way that the Christian tradition has at times seen humans as 'sojourners' on Earth and insists we must see Earth as our home.[5]

There can be little doubt that Christianity is among the religious traditions which have at times endorsed an attitude of hostility towards, and disengagement from, the Earth, denying the value of the world and/or promulgating the view that authentic existence is not to be found in it.[6] A lack of attachment to place is a recurring though by no means straightforward or unambiguous theme in the biblical narrative. In the Hebrew Bible the journeying towards, and occupation of, a particular piece of land comprises a major theme: but alongside it is a theme of itinerancy (for example in the story of Abraham) and, as Belden Lane has said, Yahweh 'refuses to be bound by any geographical locale'.[7] The New Testament records the geographical expansion of Christianity through missionary journeys, yet it is also said that for Paul any 'geographical identity' became 'subordinated to that of being in Christ'.[8] In the gospels much of the narrative follows Jesus journeying from his home place through specific named locations, yet at the same time places often have a highly spiritualised meaning, for example in the story of the Woman at the Well, (Jn 4:21–24) where geographical location is specifically de-emphasised in favour of a symbolic meaning.[9] Patristic Christianity is said to have emphasised the doctrine of salvation in a way which placed the human being in 'direct relation to God rather than to the cosmos'.[10] And some recent theologies which have emphasised existential subjectivity, claiming that we are 'forlorn'

---

4 Conradie, *An Ecological Christian Anthropology*, 26, and *Christianity and Ecological Theology*, 54.
5 McFague, *The Body of God*, 100–102.
6 Haught, *The Promise of Nature*, 39.
7 Belden Lane (1992) cited by Inge, *A Christian Theology of Place*, 41.
8 The thought of W.D. Davies summarised by Inge, *A Christian Theology of Place*, 48.
9 Lee, *The Symbolic Narrative of the Fourth Gospel*, 83.
10 Scott, *A Political Theology of Nature*, 11 (citing Louis Dupré).

in the cosmos, or that the origin of religious meaning is found in the human subject, are said to have led to an excessive humanism that devalues the non-human world.[11] John Haught considers that Christianity, along with many other religions, has fostered what he calls the spirit of 'cosmic homelessness', by which he means 'a sense that we do not really belong here in the cosmos or on the earth'.[12] For Haught the idea that we are homeless on earth affects how we regard ourselves in relation to Earth. He says the impression of cosmic homelessness, stamped on human awareness by the theme of homeless exile present in the teachings of the major religions, leads many devout people to regard the natural environment as something from which to disassociate themselves in the name of religious integrity. One of the central aspects of many religions is their teaching that authentic existence is 'homeless', that pilgrimage, sojourning and rootlessness define our lives in this world. It is not entirely unexpected, then, that this feature of religious existence can give rise to carelessness about our natural homeland. The origins of our ecological crisis may lie, in part at least, in a deeply entrenched suspicion that the cosmos is not really our home.[13]

The emphasis that human beings are part of the cosmos and creatures of Earth provides an important corrective to cosmic homelessness, yet at the same time it must be acknowledged that at the heart of religion there is a genuine sense of a fundamental spiritual homelessness, often expressed in metaphor, symbol and myth. Haught acknowledges that a certain sense of *spiritual* homelessness may be indispensable, yet he argues that this need not translate into *cosmic* homelessness: 'It is possible to accept the sojourning, exilic character of religion without interpreting it as an imperative to remove ourselves from the natural world'.[14] Therefore 'We can, at least in principle, preserve the lofty ideal of religious homelessness without requiring the environmentally unhealthy conviction that we do not belong to the universe'.[15]

It would be helpful had Haught provided guidance for distinguishing

11 Haught, *The Promise of Nature*, 54–60.
12 Haught, *The Promise of Nature*, 40.
13 Haught, *The Promise of Nature*, 40.
14 Haught, *The Promise of Nature*, 40–41.
15 Haught, *The Promise of Nature*, 47.

between spiritual and cosmic homelessness in more diverse ways than simple affirming the 'story of the universe'.[16] Nevertheless the spiritual/cosmic distinction he makes does acknowledge the unavoidably spiritual and universal dimension of religion, while also allowing for a greater emphasis on its earthly, material, and tangible aspects and allows for further elaboration.

Even in this introductory discussion there has been an assumption that the words 'home' and 'homelessness' have a straightforward meaning and that they mean the same in the west today as they did in the ancient near east. This is not the case.

Home and Homelessness

'Home' is a complex and ambiguous term with varied connotations.[17] Although the English word itself has an older European etymology, many of the meanings associated with it today are characteristically modern. For example, it is often seen as a place that is essentially private and perhaps inviolate, in contrast to the more public places of work or socialising. It may evoke ideas of relaxation and leisure and be seen as providing stability and respite from the world. The desire for home may be associated with deep desires for companionship, love, intimacy, and family (especially we may think of the nuclear family), and a longing for these aspects of home can be intensified by the accelerated fragmentary pace of life and the social and geographical mobility of a globalised digital culture. A positive understanding of home can also involve nostalgic, at times sentimental, emotions which derive from childhood memories.

There are also darker associations with the notion of home. The solitude and privacy provided by a modern home allow it to function as a highly personal zone which excludes other people and eschews aspects of communal or political reality that are disturbing or distasteful. For the lonely or the ill home may foster and nurture grief, pain or despair.

---

16 The 'Story of the Universe' refers to the scientific account of the evolution of the cosmos, recounted in narrative form in much eco-theological and eco-spiritual literature. See for example much of the work of Thomas Berry, especially Swimme and Berry, *The Universe Story*.

17 A volume that explores contemporary theologies relating to home is Jackson, Cronshaw, and Dewerse, ed., *Reimagining Home*.

For women it may be a place of drudgery, and for women and children it may be a place of oppression, abuse or violence. Terminology such as 'home-land' serves as a reminder that a strong self-identification with home or home place is a significant component in nationalistic and racist ideologies.[18]

An aspect of home that is significant for this essay is the extent to which the meaning of home is influenced by wider social, economic and political factors. Many of our ideas around what a home should be like are strongly stimulated and fabricated by media or marketing (for example TV advertisements, home and lifestyle magazines). At the heart of globalised, neoliberal society is the economic and political system which casts the human being into the role of a consumer, the end-point of the larger production-consumption paradigm. Hence one of the functions of a home today is to function as a place to store possessions—in some western countries such as Australia houses have in recent decades (up until eight years ago) become bigger even while families have become smaller.[19]

In addition to having a wide variety of connotations, it is highly significant that the idea of 'home' as understood today in the ways described above is a rather recent, essentially Modern concept.[20] Prior to the modern period, and especially in relation to places such as the ancient near east, a more likely way to describe a person's dwelling place was to use the more neutral 'house' or 'household', words which have fewer connotations of leisure and privacy and more of an economic and social unit where resources and work are shared, usually within a patriarchal structure and in social interrelationship with other households.[21] In that situation the individual was far more dependent on the group and had a greater sense of being part of the group, not only

---

18 See Moxnes' comments on Heidegger's philosophy of place and Nazi ideology: Moxnes, *Putting Jesus in His Place*, 9.
19 Although houses in Australia have become somewhat smaller in the last eight years, it is still has the second-largest house size in the world. https://www.homestolove.com.au/house-sizes-how-does-australia-compare-3047.
20 Moxnes, *Putting Jesus in His Place*, 25.
21 Moxnes, 'What Is Family?', 20–21, notes that there is no term for 'family' in the modern meaning of the nuclear family in Greek or Latin and that terminology such as *oikos* and *familia* denotes mostly large, prosperous households with slaves.

in practical ways but in the way the household and its group formed one's self-identity, especially given the emphasis in ancient near eastern society on group honour and recognition.[22] Moxnes gives evidence for the semantic shift from 'household' to 'home' in the way that English-language Bibles have, over the last three hundred or so years, increasingly translated phrases such as 'house' and 'household' with 'home'.[23]

The term 'homelessness' is also complex. A western middle-class person today can easily distance themselves from situations of poverty, war, and famine that have in recent decades caused massive displacement leading to a global refugee crisis in which large numbers of people have either no home at all or are living in inadequate temporary housing or camps. In addition, exponential growth has more than doubled global population in the last fifty years causing a shortage of housing even in wealthy countries such as Australia, with rapidly increasing numbers of people living on the streets or in make-shift accommodation such as cars. A common way of responding to homelessness is shown in the way the Australian government has in recent years shown a remarkable lack of compassion for both refugees and homeless people, often relying on a common neoliberal naïve assumption that people largely 'choose' their situation and could more easily pursue different courses of action than is the case.

Homelessness is generally seen as negative, but it can also have positive and even heroic connotations. Positive ancient and medieval examples of itinerancy are found, for example, in mendicant friars and in the literary and mythological hero who embarks on the 'quest'. The image from the Romantic era of the free, wandering aesthete was intensified by Enlightenment values of self-determination and individualism (the 'self-made man'), and in the modern era by the possibility and desirability of high levels of mobility that characterise the ubiquitous culture of globalisation. The self-autonomous, usually male, itinerant who is free of domestic or familial attachments can be a heroic figure in the western imagination. Importantly in relation to the theme of this essay, in the west the leaving of home and family has become a standard, expected and unexamined rite of transition to adulthood.

---

22 Moxnes, 'What Is Family?', 20.
23 Moxnes, *Putting Jesus in His Place*, 26.

Halvor Moxnes on Homelessness and Jesus of Nazareth

It is difficult to know what message about home/lessness was intended in the gospels and what message was heard. Halvor Moxnes discusses the significance of Jesus' homelessness in historical and political terms, asking questions about the kind of household Jesus comes from, why he left household, what the leaving meant, and what impact Jesus' itinerance had on his activity and teaching. Moxnes' work is significant because he avoids and critiques a primarily eschatological interpretation of the meanings of home and homelessness. Therefore, some of Moxnes' ideas are useful for exploring whether the idea of homelessness in the gospels supports or critiques 'cosmic homelessness' and what it might mean today as we enter a time of social, economic and intellectual transition which has been caused, in part at least, by the ecological crisis. Moxnes does not use an ecological lens but his social, economic and political focus has some overlap with the contextual focus of ecological theology.

Subsequent to Jesus' leaving of home and the calling of the disciples, it is often unclear in the gospels where, when and how Jesus and his disciples are housed. The most prominent suggestion that Jesus was homeless during his ministry occurs in the text of Matthew (8:20) and Luke (9:58) where Jesus says: 'Foxes have holes, and birds of the air have nests; but the Son of Man has nowhere to lay his head'.[24] The homelessness of Jesus is supported in other parts of the synoptic gospels (and the Gospel of Thomas) in narratives where Jesus rejects home and family and calls the disciples to leave their households.[25] While it is impossible to know to what extent Jesus and his disciples were literally homeless in the sense that a modern person would understand it, it seems uncontestable that Jesus left his household of origin at the beginning of his ministry, that the leaving entailed conflict, and that the followers were

---

24 NRSV 1989.
25 Space does not allow for discussion of these supporting texts in this essay. This essay deals not with hermeneutics but with the general theme of homelessness. In Moxnes, the calling narratives portray differing situations. Some take for granted Jesus' identity as grounded in house and village, but negate and dislocate it, other texts call Jesus' followers to leave household or predict family crises without a sense of a future place, and a third group of texts speaks of followers leaving household and establishing an alternative 'fictive kinship household'. For analysis of biblical texts, see Moxnes, *Putting Jesus in His Place*, 48.

also called to leave their households.[26] What is more open for discussion is the *meaning* of homelessness that is conveyed in the claim that Jesus had nowhere to lay his head.

Moxnes suggests that Jesus' home-place is an important subject because, given his time and place Jesus' self-identity would have been formed primarily through his house/hold. Not only would the physical location, make-up and social relations that took place in the household have influenced him, but it is also, in Moxnes' view, that the house/hold would have mentally and ideologically influenced him to the extent that he would have experienced his household as 'a microcosm of a people and of the world'.[27] The influence of house/hold on Jesus is supported by the way that household images form a core component to a number of Jesus' sayings and parables.

Although the gospel texts do not indicate what type of house or household Jesus was from, Moxnes argues, from studying types of houses and households of the time and place that Jesus grew up in, that it was a household within a kinship society and beyond that within a broader village society whose values and interactions centred around the honour/shame model.[28] The household was the central institution of ancient Galilee and would have been a patriarchal place with the father at the centre/head and in which the father-son relationship would have been central. In the synoptic gospels where the disciples were urged to leave 'family', the text also mentions 'house' and 'fields' which again suggests a close kinship household of peasant communities.[29] In contrast to the way that leaving home for westerners has become an unremarkable and standard 'rite-of-passage', in ancient and in some non-western cultures today identity was so strongly located in the household and its embedded roles that 'to a Mediterranean mind in the first century, "household" and "self" were not two separate entities, but two aspects

---

26 Moxnes, *Putting Jesus in His Place*, 48, argues that the texts are authentic because they appear in Mark, Q, and the *Gospel of Thomas*, and mostly present three (or at least two) independent witnesses to a saying or story which indicates 'that we are dealing here with a tradition that takes us as close to the historical Jesus as we can possibly get'.
27 Moxnes, *Putting Jesus in His Place*, 47.
28 For more detailed discussion, see Moxnes, *Putting Jesus in His Place*, 52.
29 Moxnes, *Putting Jesus in His Place*, 20; Moxnes, 'What Is Family?', 23.

of the same condition. The self was located in the group.'[30]

Three particular themes in Moxnes' thesis are selected here as fruitful for reflection on the idea of homelessness from the perspective of a person living in ecologically fraught times.

The first is the radical nature of the situation which caused Jesus to leave home as an act of protest and the loss of identity this entailed. Moxnes argues that the peasant household model which formed the social grounding for Jesus and his followers was subjected to social, economic and political pressures which favoured a wealthier, exploitative slave-based household model. Especially during Herodian times, land increasingly fell into the hands of an elite, as a result of which an increasing number of farmers were forced into being tenants or were forced off the land. The crisis this posed for the peasant extended family model, posits Moxnes, made 'young men without property ... especially vulnerable' and led some to leave their patriarchal household and gain employment in new industries such as fish processing.[31] These social changes destabilised the social and economic viability of households and weakened their ties, especially the authority of the father, and made it more likely that young men would join religious and/or political groups.[32] These changes in part at least serve to explain the conflicts that surrounded Jesus. Moxnes suggests that not only did Jesus' household group refuse him the honour associated with household, reject him and move him 'beyond their limits'[33] but Jesus in turn rejects the honor-shame paradigm of his household and community, including its patriarchal order and structure. Jesus was critical, Moxnes suggests, of the (patriarchal) household of his day and the domination and subordination that were part of the way it functioned.[34] Jesus, then, does not passively accept the loss of place but actively dislocates himself from the household and its village community, questioning 'the value of their activity as well as their power to grant or withhold honor.'[35] Moxnes suggests that in doing this Jesus deliberately transgressed and challenged

---

30 Moxnes, *Putting Jesus in His Place*, 47, 57.
31 Moxnes, *Putting Jesus in His Place*, 42–43.
32 Moxnes, *Putting Jesus in His Place*, 64.
33 Moxnes, *Putting Jesus in His Place*, 53.
34 Moxnes, *Putting Jesus in His Place*, 64–67.
35 Moxnes, *Putting Jesus in His Place*, 68.

the usual, taken for granted, understanding of place and that he actually sought conflict within households (his own and possibly those of his followers). The claim that Jesus had nowhere to put his head, then, does not just indicate a vagabond existence. It meant to be in no-place, without any location that could give social identity. Thus, as a saying coming from Jesus, it could also be heard as an expression of transgression, deliberately placing Jesus at the outside, in no-place, to challenge the places that were taken for granted, which had authority.[36]

Jesus is therefore a marginal figure. Not only is his place of origin, Galilee, marginal but his death at Golgotha occurs 'at the absolute margin'.[37] Because of Jesus' marginality, Moxnes describes him as 'queer', not with the intention of delineating him in relation to sexual or any other kind of binary identity but as a means of describing his unsettling quality, his resisting of social norms, of being in opposition to something and of 'questioning of settled or fixed categories of identity, not accepting the given orders or structures of the places that people inhabit'.[38] Queerness in this sense applies also to the people Jesus identifies in his teaching on the kingdom of God—unorthodox persons such as 'eunuchs, barren women, and presexual children'.[39]

Moxnes' thesis that Jesus was in conflict with traditional life in Galilean households and villages is supported by Robert Myles who argues that instead of seeing Jesus' lack of home as a choice, it should be seen, like other displacements in the Gospel such as the flight to Egypt, as having socio-political implications, being a 'symptom of wider structural crises'.[40] Jesus' withdrawal is forced but is also a choice which is made both an act of self-preservation and as a form of inaction which is also a 'subversive political act'.[41] Enforced marginalisation provides Jesus with an awareness of his outsider status, which has occurred not because of individual moral or economic failure, but as a remnant of wider social and political forces and his God-given mission. The text retroactively transforms his abject social reality into a theological locus

---

36 Moxnes, *Putting Jesus in His Place*, 67.
37 Moxnes, *Putting Jesus in His Place*, 3.
38 Moxnes, *Putting Jesus in His Place*, 5, 6.
39 Moxnes, *Putting Jesus in His Place*, 110.
40 Myles, 'Homelessness, Neoliberalism, and Jesus' "Decision" to Go Rogue', 221.
41 Myles, 'Homelessness, Neoliberalism, and Jesus' "Decision" to Go Rogue', 224–25.

for organizing revolutionary power.[42]

A second significant aspect of Moxnes' argument is that the transient status of Jesus and his disciples and the conflict relating to that status is not neutral, inevitable or trivial—on the contrary it entailed great anxiety and distress. Jesus' identity was so strongly grounded in his household of origin therefore, as would not be the case for a young man today, the leaving of household is a more significant and traumatic incident for him than studies have generally acknowledged.

Moxnes' understanding of Jesus' statement that he has nowhere to lay his head is that having a place to dwell is 'natural', being something animals have and that a human being should have. This reading reinforces the claim around emotional trauma. Because Jesus does not have a dwelling, it means that he is 'below' the animals and is therefore dislocated from human civilisation and from the way existence should be, hence the phrase conveys 'an ominous meaning' indicating a loss of identity, a slide from order to disorder.[43] The text presents an unsettling picture of Jesus as 'a transgressor of the boundaries of human society'.[44] Far from being emotionally neutral, Jesus' homeless status entails conflict and involves an underacknowledged level of anxiety or distress. Moxnes' argument is supported by Myles who emphasises that for modern westerners who almost unconsciously ascribe a high value to self and individualism, it is hard to understand that at the time of the gospels the household group and its wider close-knit community was central to its members' sense of self-identity and that leaving house/hold would have been traumatic.[45]

Third is the complex question of the extent to which the gospels posit a new house/hold. It seems that Jesus is creating a new family of fictive kinship, made up of those who do 'what my father wants'.[46] Yet Moxnes sees the gospels as equivocal about new locations or households. On the one hand, in the non-Markan traditions there is little indication of a new place of identity and Jesus is presented as inviting

---

42 Myles, 'Homelessness, Neoliberalism, and Jesus' "Decision" to Go Rogue', 229.
43 Moxnes, *Putting Jesus in His Place*, 50.
44 Moxnes, *Putting Jesus in His Place*, 51.
45 Myles, 'Homelessness, Neoliberalism, and Jesus' "Decision" to Go Rogue', 227.
46 Moxnes, *Putting Jesus in His Place*, 68.

followers (mostly, Moxnes believes, male followers) to occupy an in-between or liminal position.[47] When Jesus calls the disciples to leave their households and set out on the road, 'way' or journey, no clear indication is given of what the new location will be—it is implied that 'the way' leads to Jerusalem, the place where Jesus will die but it is also the place from which his vocation to the whole world will continue.[48] No actual dwelling place is suggested.

On the other hand, Moxnes notes that in Mark a new location for Jesus' fictive kinship group is made possible where Jesus stays in houses and new households are promised to his followers. Not only does Mark present a certain degree of 'domestication' around the new fictive kinship group with a social and spatial location, there is also a suggestion that the disciples did not completely leave their old households.[49] Moxnes thinks that the first set of texts (the 'Q' and *Thomas* narratives) are more likely than Mark to be closer to Jesus' position and that they involve a dislocation of identity being part of a 'stand alone' community.[50]

Moxnes supports his preference for a 'no place' option by suggesting that some of Jesus' sayings about the kingdom echo his calls to leave house/hold and seem to be addressed to displaced or liminal persons outside the social order. The peasant extended family is in the gospels seen as 'a model for human society and for the ideals associated with the Kingdom of God',[51] yet the actual households of Jesus and his followers, their honour codes and patriarchal authority, are rejected. While alternative literal homes or houses are not, in Moxnes' view, on offer, some of Jesus' kingdom sayings do suggest imaginary or, better, 'imagined' ideal places where God is father and plans or visions are presented 'for alternative ways to use and structure places and material practices'.[52] The function of the kingdom sayings is to 'strengthen the followers of Jesus in their critical attitude toward the social order, but also to compensate for some of the losses they have experienced, first of all their dislocation

---

47 Moxnes, *Putting Jesus in His Place*, 70.
48 Moxnes, *Putting Jesus in His Place*, 55.
49 Moxnes, *Putting Jesus in His Place*, 69.
50 Moxnes, *Putting Jesus in His Place*, 69.
51 Moxnes, 'What Is Family?', 25, 24.
52 Moxnes, *Putting Jesus in His Place*, 109.

from house and household'.⁵³ Therefore, even though Jesus deliberately sought to dislocate himself and his disciples from household, the image of house/hold was nevertheless one imagined way of expressing the kingdom. Imagined households provide a new but radically different home for those who had left and experienced conflicts with their own household of origin.⁵⁴ The lack of clarity in relation to the possibility of households in the new order of the kingdom in Jesus' sayings gives rise to a certain openness and ambiguity.

Moxnes' (supported by Myles') political and social approach offers a radically different and ecologically fruitful alternative to scholarship which sees Jesus' transience and his kingdom teaching as eschatological and as oriented towards 'cosmic homelessness'.⁵⁵

Eco-theological Meanings of Home and Homelessness

If cosmic homelessness raises questions for an ecologically oriented theology, how might the three aspects of Moxnes' thesis listed above—that Jesus' leaving of household was influenced by his socio-economic context, that it was traumatic, and that it invites revised understandings of home—help to address those questions?

First, if socio-economic and political factors enforced Jesus' choice to leave home, contemporary questions and choices are similarly impelled by today's wider structural questions.⁵⁶ The present ecological challenges (climate change, over-fishing, deforestation, ocean pollution and loss of biodiversity to name a few) have many dimensions but they are essentially social, economic and political. They are the outcome of human actions that are embedded in the prevailing social and economic structures and they call for substantial policy changes in industry, extraction and agriculture. The importance of changes at this 'macro' level should not be underestimated, yet personal choices also

---

53 Moxnes, *Putting Jesus in His Place*, 108.
54 Moxnes, *Putting Jesus in His Place*, 107.
55 Moxnes, *Putting Jesus in His Place*, 110. For Moxnes' fuller discussion of the kingdom teachings, see pp.108–24.
56 The focus on the ecological context in this essay means leaving aside many important things that might also relate to the topic of homelessness today—for example, in relation to social justice.

matter, including those relating to peoples' homes. The contemporary person and their home are unavoidably embedded in the structures which have during most of the Enlightenment and modern era been committed to growth (in economy and population) and to the valorisation of consumption.

Physically, houses have a large negative ecological impact. The spread of housing has been a major cause in depleting the size and quality of other-than-human habitat and in loss of biodiversity. Additionally, building itself makes extremely heavy use of resource and energy, and this is influencing a recent turn to smaller and more sustainably-built dwellings. The modern home is often ecologically unsustainable because some understandings of home encourage it as the locus for the purchase and storage of consumer items. In contrast to the work and production model of the ancient near eastern household, today's home is only rarely a place of production but is essentially a place of consumption. Despite a fairly strong uptake of renewable energy options, many homes continue to be powered by fossil fuel and serve as a storage place for non-essential luxury and consumer items whose manufacture is very likely to have emitted carbon, caused pollution and depleted resources. A good deal of responsibility for challenging high carbon emissions lies with householders acknowledging that their actions, either explicitly or implicitly, support over-consumption and the waste and pollution that result from it.

The first step is perhaps deep and radical—protesting and rejecting the consumerist social and economic system. This means stepping back from the idea of oneself as an over-consumer and adopting a different identity. It also means seeing our home differently, breaking with the deeply-embedded desire for unnecessary possessions. Relinquishing consumerist understandings of ourselves and our homes might be described as choosing to be 'homeless' in a metaphorical sense, or even in a physical sense where we choose a dwelling (shared community, shack, tiny house) that falls outside of the usual understanding of 'home'.

The viability of the peasant household of Jesus' day was threatened by the taxation of Herod the Great and by Herod Antipas' move towards an economy favouring large estates and the elite. The viability of the modern western home as a locus of consumerism, privacy, comfort, safety, and individual indulgence is today under threat because an ideology of unlimited growth, resource use and consumption has caused a destabilising of Earth systems on which, it is becoming increasingly understood, our biophysical existence relies. So powerful is the ideology of the economic paradigm that opting out of it and rethinking who we are and how we are to live means adopting a 'marginal' position, indicating Moxnes' 'queer' choice of becoming transient. As Theissen notes, itinerancy involves 'extreme living conditions' and can therefore only be practised at the margins of society.[57]

Theologically, a decision to break with consumerist patterns in our home life might be seen as integral to discipleship. The fundamental aspect of discipleship as homeless in the gospels has been noted by Theissen—'Homelessness belonged to the discipleship of Jesus, and not merely during his lifetime.'[58] Discipleship for Christians entails giving something up, leaving something behind and becoming socially displaced. Yet it is not just an option but is pressed upon us. The tragic manifestations of climate disruption—fire, drought, inundation—unsettle the business-as-usual understandings of ourselves and of the world and challenge the identity formed in the modern era. Climate change not only disrupts Earth's life-giving systems, it also disrupts and displaces people—literally through the effects of famine, fire, drought and flood, and symbolically by demonstrating the need to break with one's identity as consumer.

A second aspect of Moxnes' thesis is the claim that leaving a household in the ancient near east would have entailed a generally unacknowledged degree of pain and grief. Today, an increasing number of people affected by the degradations of the natural world, whether it occurs locally and on a small scale or more broadly and globally, experience real and intense emotional distress, trauma and grief.

There is discourse in eco-philosophy about the deep grief caused by ecological destruction by Glenn Albrecht who has coined the term 'solastalgia' to describe the grief, distress and trauma experienced when a particular ecology has been lost or degraded.[59] Solastalgia is a combination of two terms, 'nostalgia' and 'solace'. The nostalgia part refers

---

57 Theissen, *Social Reality and the Early Christians*, 40.
58 Theissen, *Social Reality and the Early Christians*, 37–38.
59 Albrecht, 'Solastalgia', 45.

less to the more usual meaning of looking back to a past time, and more to an older (and more geographical) use of the term. Up to the middle of the twentieth century Albrecht notes that nostalgia was a medically diagnosable psycho-physiological disease experienced by people distant from their home, such as soldiers in war. It was a form of melancholia and the cure was simply to return home. The 'solace' aspect of Albrecht's concept indicates a need for comfort, at a time of distress or desolation caused by ecological degradation. Solastalgia is a type of homesickness that we can experience even while we are still at home.[60] The traumatic pain and despair experienced by people today as they witness the devastation of the natural world and its systems and thereby feel distanced and rejected from Earth itself is perhaps not completely dissimilar to the pain and trauma implied in the leaving of household in the gospel narratives.

Religiously, recognising the systemic and socio-economic aspects of environmental decay along with the extent to which we have explicitly or implicitly supported them in our own choices is essentially the work of repentance which has not only a mental dimension, but also an emotional one which needs to be fully experienced for repentance to be authentic. Repentance, whether individual or communal (liturgical) is an essential part of acknowledging the trauma involved in experiencing the destruction of our wider home-place Earth. Experiencing the pain of solastalgia is necessary in order to move from regret to *metanoia*.

The third significant aspect of Moxnes' thought involves identifying the possibility of a new or alternative 'home' or way of living. Recognising, and rejecting, the problems related to the contemporary home invites the question of what is our true home. Without denying Haught's acknowledgement that there is a certain kind of spiritual home which cannot be physically or geographically located, ecological awareness suggests that at one important level at least, Earth is our true and authentic home-place. Current scientific predictions are not optimistic about the future of Earth as a viable home-place for human beings, but the only course of action available is to do the best we can to mitigate

---

60 Albrecht, 'Solastalgia', 48.

and deeply adapt to the situation.[61]

Jesus' own challenge to the kinship group, its honour system and its patriarchal head led to the creation of a new 'fictive' kinship group in which 'the first Christians regarded and treated each other as "family"'.[62] Today alternative movements such as Transition Towns, Permaculture, and the Eco-Village movement suggests that environmentally aware people also recognise the value of a 'fictive kinship' group which adopts a more intentionally communal way of living using less space, energy and resources and which, like the ancient near eastern household, focuses primarily on producing (rather than consuming) the things it needs. A radical non-consumerist way of living would, like the Christian monastic tradition, share resources and skills and focus on producing what is essential.

Loosening the connection with modern understandings of home and thereby becoming in some sense 'homeless' facilitates the 'adoption' of new local places, for example a marginal or threatened river or forest with the aim of protecting or restoring it.[63] The act of supporting and identifying with a local and specific place positions us in our material context. Not only does this positioning benefit the environment, the Christian tradition too has an ongoing engagement with place and matter not only through the kind of study undertaken by Moxnes into Jesus' actual context but through its sacramental life.

A realistic assessment of the ecological situation today is not hopeful and the different ways of living suggested above are not to be seen as courses of action that will easily or simply correct the present highly complex and apparently insoluble crisis. But they are examples of the few courses of action that seem available at a time whose meaning is not yet fully known. Jesus' own decision to be homeless, and his calling of the disciples to do the same, is not simply about rejecting one home in favour of another one, but is about something more deeply unsettling and disturbing, leaving an old way of being in favour of living a radically new one.

---

61 Bendell, 'Deep Adaptation'.
62 Moxnes, 'Introduction', 1 (citing Neyrey).
63 Mathews, *Reinhabiting Reality*, 68; Plumwood, *Environmental Culture*, 231–33.

Conclusion

The patriarchal peasant household of the ancient near east may seem highly remote in time, place and culture from the homes of contemporary westerners. And the difference should not be underestimated. Following the attempts of the first and second quest for the historical Jesus, it is now appreciated how much an attempt to understand Jesus of Nazareth and his contemporaries will be prejudiced by the (often unconscious) cultural assumptions of one's own place and time and of our lack of understanding of the other place and time. For examples, Moxnes notes that the project of the 'quest for the historical Jesus' has led to an understanding of Jesus as a unique, solitary and 'other' personality, consistent with 'cultural and theological ideals of the heroic male individual from the late nineteenth century and which has led to a tendency to treat religion in an abstract way and to separate it from its spatial and social context'.[64]

It would be anachronistic to seek ecological meaning in an ancient text—'home' as we understand it may be a modern concept, but so is 'ecology'. No simple equation can be made between 'then' and 'now' or between 'here' and 'there'. A contemporary western middle-class person cannot expect to fully apprehend the social and mental make-up of ancient near-eastern people. As Moxnes has noted, the historical Jesus 'was not just an idea, nor was he a modern individualist. If he was a true human being of his time, his identity was based on his being placed in a particular household group and locality'.[65]

Yet as Moxnes also notes, it is the role and responsibility of the reader to create meaning out of the text.[66] That is what has been sought in this chapter. The gospel narratives are rarely straightforward but can often convey a multivalent, complex, rich and deep meaning that can to some extent transcend time, place and culture. Perhaps this is especially so for Christian thought today at a time of significant social challenge and transition. The way Jesus of Nazareth continues to impact the Church is often by destabilising it, including the way each of us understands home

---

64 Moxnes, *Putting Jesus in His Place*, 11.
65 Moxnes, *Putting Jesus in His Place*, 45.
66 Moxnes, *A Short History of the New Testament*, 206.

and home-places. As Moxnes notes, Jesus 'destabilizes places—potentially also those of the present readers'.[67]

The analyses of Moxnes is to some extent ecologically applicable because like eco-theology it is contextual. Moxnes grounds Jesus of Nazareth socially and politically, and relates Jesus' kingdom sayings to Earth rather than Heaven. If an ecological ethos is contradicted by the eschatological orientation of cosmic homelessness, with its underlying assumption of a Heaven-Earth dualism, then Moxnes' thesis, and the eco-theological interpretation of it in this chapter, argues for dismantling that dualism and for seeing homelessness in the gospel narrative not as pointing towards heaven but towards the here-and-now.

In this essay it has been suggested that three aspects of Moxnes' studies on Jesus of Nazareth are ecologically meaningful today. First, Moxnes' argument that social, economic and political questions of Jesus' time impelled the choice for Jesus and the disciples to leave their households resonates with the argument that the Modern understandings of home as consumer driven are ecologically problematic. Second, just as the trauma associated with leaving household in the ancient near east needs to be acknowledged, so does the solastalgic grief and despair that is experienced today. Third, the ambiguity and complexity associated with unravelling the meaning/s of new homes and new communities in Jesus' time echoes with the complex attempts of people today to work out alternative ways of living.

The way that Jesus of Nazareth continues to impact Christian thought is expressed by Moxnes when he notes that the question 'Who was Jesus' is always related to question of who I am and of who we are,[68] a question that is undoubtedly pertinent to the current ecological context.

Deborah Guess, Pilgrim Theological College, University of Divinity
deborahguess@bigpond.com

---

67   Moxnes, *Putting Jesus in His Place*, 6.
68   Moxnes, *Jesus and the Rise of Nationalism*, 1.

Bibliography

Albrecht, Glenn — 'Solastalgia: A New Concept in Health and Identity', *PAN: Philosophy, Activism, Nature* 3 (2005), 44–59.

Bendell, Jem — 'Deep Adaptation: A Map for Navigating Climate Tragedy', *IFLAS Occasional Paper* 2 (2018).

Conradie, Ernst M. — *Christianity and Ecological Theology: Resources for Further Research* (Stellenbosch: Sun Press, 2006).

Conradie, Ernst M. — *An Ecological Christian Anthropology: At Home on Earth?* (Aldershot: Ashgate, 2005).

Guess, D. — 'Earth as Home-Place: Eco-theology and the Incarnation', in D. Jackson, D. Cronshaw, R. Dewerse (eds.), *Reimagining Home: Understanding, Reconciling and Engaging with God's Stories Together* (Macquarie Park, NSW: Morling Press, 2019), 18–33.

Haught, John F. — *The Promise of Nature: Ecology and Cosmic Purpose* (New York/Mahwah, NJ: Paulist Press, 1993).

Inge, John — *A Christian Theology of Place: Explorations in Practical, Pastoral and Empirical Theology* (Farnham: Ashgate, 2003).

Jackson, Darrell, Darren Cronshaw, and Rosemary Dewerse (eds.) — *Reimagining Home: Understanding, Reconciling and Engaging with God's Stories Together. The 5th Conference of the Australian Association for Mission Studies, Whitley College, Melbourne, 2–5 July 2017* (Macquarie Park NSW: Morling Press, 2019).

Lee, Dorothy A. — *The Symbolic Narrative of the Fourth Gospel: The Interplay of Form and Meaning* (Sheffield: Sheffield Academic Press, 1994).

Mathews, Freya — *Reinhabiting Reality: Towards a Recovery of Culture* (Albany, NY: State University of New York Press, 2005).

McFague, Sallie — *The Body of God: An Ecological Theology* (Minneapolis, MN: Fortress, 1993).

Moxnes, Halvor — *A Short History of the New Testament* (London: I.B. Tauris, 2014).

Moxnes, Halvor — *Jesus and the Rise of Nationalism: A New Quest for the Nineteenth-Century Historical Jesus* (London: I.B. Tauris, 2012).

Moxnes, Halvor	*Putting Jesus in His Place: A Radical Vision of Household and Kingdom* (Louisville & London: Westminster John Knox Press, 2003).
Moxnes, Halvor	'Introduction', in Halvor Moxnes (ed.), *Constructing Early Christian Families: Family as Social Reality and Metaphor* (London: Routledge, 1997), 1-9.
Moxnes, Halvor	'What Is Family? Problems in Constructing Early Christian Families', in Halvor Moxnes (ed.), *Constructing Early Christian Families: Family as Social Reality and Metaphor* (London: Routledge, 1997), 13-41.
Myles, Robert J.	'Homelessness, Neoliberalism, and Jesus' "Decision" to Go Rogue: An Analysis of Matthew 4:12-25', in Bruce Worthington (ed.), *Reading the Bible in an Age of Crisis: Political Exegesis for a New Day* (Minneapolis MN: Augsburg Fortress, 2015), 217-43.
Plumwood, Val	*Environmental Culture: The Ecological Crisis of Reason* (London and New York: Routledge, 2002).
Scott, Peter	*A Political Theology of Nature* (Cambridge: Cambridge University Press, 2003).
Swimme, Brian, and Thomas Berry	*The Universe Story: From the Primordial Flaring Forth to the Ecozoic Era—a Celebration of the Unfolding of the Cosmos* (San Francisco: Harper Collins, 1992).
Theissen, Gerd	*Social Reality and the Early Christians* (Minneapolis: Fortress, 1992).

CHAPTER 14

Social Sin and Social Grace: Christ Risen, Healing and Creating in History

John Francis Collins

Abstract

This article is an exercise in pastoral or practical theology. It is an interdisciplinary exercise that draws on insights from a range of disciplines to address a concrete practical concern. The intent of the article is to examine the notion of social grace as understood as the cooperative interaction of the Word and Holy Spirit of God with human agents as the necessary antidote to social sin.

The article has five main parts: Part 1 is an outline of the main contours of relevant insights from neuroscience as related to the psychoanalytically informed Objects Relations theory. The purpose of this outline is to support the argument that social sin is the fruit of the condition theologically understood as original sin, and accumulated personal sin. That is Object Relations theory as interpreted through the light of neuroscience operates as an explanatory schema for understanding original sin as the tendency to psychological splitting followed by conceptual justification of the psychological phenomenon leading to action. Part 2 introduces the notion of Social Grace as developed by Robert Doran as an antidote of the theological category of Social Sin. Part 3 provides some background on the relationship between God and Politics as proposed by the Australian theologian Neil Ormerod. This part investigates the influence of original and personal sin on individuals, the social sphere, and the cultural spheres as manifested under the category of politics. Part 4 draws on both the work of Doran and Ormerod to explore the divinely initiated solution to the problem of evil as systematically developed through an overview of operation of the Scale of Values in history. Part 5 draws on insights from the first four sets of ideas to identify ways to facilitate God's grace to be effective in healing political division and developing creative ways of cooperation.

Part 1: Insights from Neuroscience

Neuroscience provides new insights for understanding and evaluating psychoanalytic theory. The findings of research into brain functioning confirm some aspects of psychoanalytic theory and challenge others. The limbic system contains the brain structures that control affect expression.[1] This system acts as the 'centre for emotional responsiveness, motivation, memory formation and integration, sense of smell, and the mechanisms to keep ourselves safe'.[2] The limbic system includes several sub-systems including the neuro sub-systems of the amygdala, the hippocampus, the thalamus and the hypothalamus. The amygdala is an assembly of neurons about the size and shape of an almond located in the centre of the brain.[3] The role of the amygdala is to be constantly alert to the needs of basic survival including sex and emotional reactions such as anger and fear. The hippocampus is the part of the brain that 'processes new memories for long-term storage'. The thalamus is located at the top of the brain stem and 'acts as a two-way relay station, sorting, processing, and directing signals from the spinal cord

---

1 Kernberg, 'Neurobiological Correlates', 39.
2 Dahlitz, 'The Limbic System'.
3 The information in this paragraph is taken from the summary diagram of Bragdon & Gamon, 'Your Brain and What It Does'.

and mid-brain structures up to the cerebrum[4] and, conversely, from the cerebrum down the spinal cord to the nervous system'. The hypothalamus is located at the base of the brain and its role in the limbic system is to maintain the body's status quo in terms of the regulation of temperature, hunger, thirst, fight-flight reactions, and sexual excitement. It is the hypothalamus that is concerned with the activation of both positive and negative affects.

Positive and negative affect-activating brain structures operate separately from each other and at a basic level of affect activation a simultaneous separation, or split, of positive and negative affect has evolved.[5] The integration of split positive and negative affects occurs at a higher level of limbic structures and involves the limbic system interacting with parts of the brain that are engaged in planning and decision-making—particularly the prefrontal and preorbital cortex.[6]

Research in neuroscience indicates that Freud was correct in proposing that the unconscious mind develops before the conscious mind. The research also confirms the psychoanalytic observation 'that the early development of the unconscious is equivalent to the genesis of a self-regulating system that operates beneath conscious, verbal levels for the rest of the life span'.[7] Challenging one of Freud's foundational

---

4   The cerebrum is the largest brain structure in humans and accounts for about two-thirds of the brain's mass. It is divided into two sides — the left and right hemispheres—that are separated by a deep groove down the centre from the back of the brain to the forehead. These two halves are connected by long neuron branches called the *corpus callosum* which is relatively larger in women's brains than in men's. The cerebrum is positioned over and around most other brain structures, and its four lobes (Frontal, Temporal, Parietal and Occipital) are specialized by function but are richly connected. The outer 3 millimetres of 'grey matter' is the cerebral cortex which consists of closely packed neurons that control most of our body functions, including the mysterious state of consciousness, the senses, the body's motor skills, reasoning and language. The Frontal Lobe is the last to develop in young adulthood. It's dorso-lateral prefrontal circuit (PFC) is the brain's top Executive. It organizes responses to complex problems, plans steps to an Objective, searches memory for relevant experience, adapts strategies to accommodate new data, guides behaviours with verbal skills and houses working memory. Its orbitofrontal circuit manages emotional impulses in socially appropriate ways for productive behaviours including empathy, altruism, and interpretation of facial expressions. The Temporal Lobe controls memory storage area, emotion, hearing, and, on the left side, language. The Parietal Lobe receives and processes sensory information from the body including calculating location and speed of Objects. The Occipital Lobe processes visual data and routes it to other parts of the brain for identification and storage. Bragdon & Gamon, 'Your Brain and What It Does'.
5   Kernberg, 'Neurobiological Correlates', 39.
6   Kernberg, 'Neurobiological Correlates', 39.
7   Quotations in this paragraph from Schore, 'Foreword', xii.

ideas, however, the research has refuted the idea that the unconscious solely represents material that is repressed and banned from consciousness because it is unacceptable. Neuroscience research shows that bodily-based affects are expressed rapidly and spontaneously. The speed at which bodily-based affects are expressed is such that, due to the limited capacity of conscious awareness to process the data, affects are 'recorded' beneath levels of conscious awareness. In short, with regard to origins of the unconscious, neuroscience offers an explanatory framework that differs significantly from Freud's framework. Neuroscience has confirmed, however, that affects can be unconscious, indeed dissociated. That is, an affect can be disconnected from its source or origin.

The psychoanalytic insight that emotions often occur at unconscious levels has, in many ways, been confirmed by neuroscience. The brain research, however, has challenged and extended psychoanalytic understanding as to the reasons why negative and positive emotions often occur at unconscious levels. In classic psychoanalytic theory emotions are repressed because they are unacceptable. In the light of neuroscience research however, the unconscious is no longer viewed to be 'a repository of archaic untamed passions and destructive wishes'. The unconscious is 'now seen as a cohesive, active mental structure that continuously appraises life's experiences and responds according to its scheme of interpretation.'[8]

While research in neuroscience has overturned some of the basic tenets of psychoanalytic theory in relation to an understanding of the unconscious as the fruit of repression of what is unacceptable, it has confirmed the existence of the unconscious *per se*. The research has discovered that much, if not most, of our brain functioning occurs outside of conscious awareness. Brain imaging has also confirmed that, at metaphoric brain 'levels', negative and positive affects are separated at lower levels and are integrated in higher levels of brain function. The fact that positive and negative affects are strictly separated at lower limbic levels and can only be integrated at the higher level confirms the basic principles of psychoanalytic Object Relations theory. Object Relations theory is a field of thought that was developed from Freud's psychodynamic

---

8   Quotations in this paragraph from Schore, 'Foreword', xiii.

theory in the early-mid 20th century by a range of practitioners-theorists including Otto Rank, Sandor Ferenczi, Ronald Fairbairn and Donald Winnicott. A key contributor to Object Relations theory was the Austrian-British psychoanalyst Melanie Klein (1882–1960). Through critical reflection on her therapeutic practice with children, Klein developed her own contribution to psychoanalytic theory. Klein's theory focuses primarily on development within the first year of life and is grounded in the notion of Unconscious Phantasy.[9] For Klein unconscious phantasies are defined as primitive internalized mental images of instincts and drives. The unique mental and emotional capacities of an individual are the fruit of the interaction of these phantasies with actual experience, and the emotions.

According to Klein, in the first six months of life the infant's ego is still in a primitive state and he or she is unable to maintain a unified mental image of the self or of others. During this stage, relationships are maintained with parts of Objects (e.g. breast rather than mother). In terms of a mental image a newborn's sucking reflex will only become a mental image when the newborn finds the nipple and begins nursing. As the sucking practice is repeated during the activity of feeding the infant forms a mental image accompanied by the soothing emotions — warm milk, full stomach and close sense of nurture with nursing mother's breast. The mental image is that of a good breast. When the infant is hungry, cold, or in discomfort, and experiences the distressing emotions that accompany this phenomenon, the lack of 'good breast' generates the mental image of a 'bad breast'. The infant creates two individual mental images of Objects, existing as unrelated individual entities.

The bad breast exists when the mother is unable to satisfy the infant's needs immediately, causing a desire to destroy this Object. The good breast exists when needs are fulfilled, causing feelings of love towards the Object. Repeated experience of 'lack of good breast' experienced as bad breast, gives rise to a dynamic in which all internal bad feelings, because they cannot be tolerated, are projected outwards. A paranoid fear arises, however, namely that the 'bad' projected out onto another

---

[9] Information on Klein in next paragraphs taken from: Learning Theories, 'Object Relations Theory (Melanie Klein)'.

will return to seek revenge. Klein calls this complex dynamic the paranoid-schizoid position.

In Klein's explanatory framework, after the six month mark the basis for an integrated ego begins to form as the infant starts to develop the capacity to view Objects as including both good and bad. That is, the mother who frustrated the infant by being absent when he or she needed her is the same mother who satisfied the infant by meeting his needs. 'The infant realizes, that the mother whom he phantasized of destroying, is the same mother he or she loves'. Klein calls this the depressive position. Feelings of anxiety which previously overwhelmed the infant in the paranoid-schizoid position are joined by the depressive position. The depressive position is characterized by feelings of guilt, and of mourning lost omnipotence. The fear of being destroyed is exchanged by the fear of destroying another. The infant thus engages in reparation to restore and fix Objects he previously phantasized destroying. The ability to view the self and Objects with complexity and engaging in appeasement efforts is crucial for the development of healthy relationships in adulthood.

In the light of research in neuroscience, one way to understand Klein's theory is to view her observation that there is a split between good and bad in the young child that has manifestations throughout the whole of life is basically correct. The account of its origin, however, is more akin to a story or myth that tells a truth, as opposed to an explanation. As previously noted, from the viewpoint of neuroscientific research the development of the unconscious occurs because bodily-based affects impact on the brain patterns of a person but are expressed at a pace well beyond the limited capacity of conscious awareness to process the data. Brain patterns formed outside the purview of conscious awareness lead to the formation of a fundamental split between conscious patterns and unconscious brain patterns.

The hypothalamus works to maintain the body's status quo by dividing positive and negative affects. Klein names this brain dynamic structure the paranoid-schizoid position. From the point of view of neuroscience, the integration of positive and negative affects can occur when the maturing child has developed a higher level of limbic structures and functions that involve the engagement of the prefrontal cortex.

Klein names this brain structure the depressive position. For Klein the paranoid-schizoid and depressive positions are not simply transitory or passing phases or stages, but they set up the basis of the psyche's enduring orientation throughout life. For the neuroscientist, the interaction between the limbic—that is fight, flight, freeze—mechanisms to keep ourselves safe and the cortical or executive parts of the brain occurs across a person's whole life.

Returning to Klein's framework, depending on the level of personal integration and the amount of subjective stress, elements of oscillation between the paranoid-schizoid position and the depressive position is a phenomenon that can be observed. The potential for oscillation is often actualized when a person is in a state of heightened anxiety and subjective stress. In such a state, primitive emotional experiences are activated. In terms of observable behaviour examples of splitting in adults include the emotional vacillation from love to hate and back to love that can be experienced from time to time in intimate relationships.

Klein observed this dynamic between individuals in the process of therapy and named it, projective identification. The dynamic of projective identification can be understood as when the Object of projection intro-jects, or takes in to him or herself the material projected on to him by the other and experiences this material as if it originated internally. In other words, the receiver of the projection feels what the person projecting feels, and over time, the receiver of the projective process has difficulty discriminating the origin of the feelings. In time the recipient of the projection begins to believe that the feelings that have been projected onto them by another originated within him or herself. The recipient of projections then begins to construct reasons to make sense of the experience searching for the origins of the feelings in his or her own psychic history. The dynamic of bullying leading to the one bullied self-harming is an example of this dynamic in action.

Splitting can also manifest in groups and organisation with factions developing where all that is viewed to be unacceptable in members of one faction is evacuated and projected onto the opposing faction with the dynamic also occurring in reverse. A significant development of Klein's psychoanalytic model was advanced by Wilfred Bion and is expressed in the concept of a 'relational unconscious', 'whereby one unconscious mind communicates with and interactively regulates another unconscious mind'.[10] Bion went on to developed Klein's notion of projective identification and applied it to the dynamics he observed in the groups and organisations.[11]

Various parts of the brain are richly connected and as such it is difficult to precisely identify specific parts that are responsible for specific functions. That said, broadly speaking, the right side of the cerebrum, that is the right side of the top two hemispheres of the brain that we are most aware of through popular representations, has been identified more strongly with the emotions. Reflecting on the dynamics of the therapeutic alliance that occurs in context of therapeutic encounters, Schore observes that 'rapid communications between the right-lateralized "emotional brain" of each member of the therapeutic alliance allow for moment-to-moment "self-state sharing", a co-created, organized, dynamically changing dialogue of mutual influence'.[12] Generalizing the insights gained from critical reflection on the therapeutic alliance and informed by research in neuroscience, the dynamic of projective identification or unconscious influencing of each other occurs rapidly and outside of conscious awareness, right brain to right brain. In the right brain to right brain 'relational matrix, both partners match the dynamic contours of different emotional-motivational self-states, and simultaneously adjust their social attention, stimulation, and accelerating/decelerating arousal in response to the partner's signals'.[13] In summary, Klein observed projective identification as operating between individuals. Bion observed that the dynamic of unconsciously impacting on each other's unconscious can occur in groups and organisations. Schore notes that unconscious influence occurs directly, that is outside of conscious awareness, right brain to right brain.

The explanatory framework of right brain to right brain confirms the basic tenets of Klein's notion of projective identification and Bion's insights in relation to the dynamics of groups and organisations. In terms of therapeutic and pastoral practice, there is evidence emerging

---

10 Schore, 'Foreword', xiii.
11 See Bion, *Experiences in Groups*.
12 Schore, 'Foreword', xx.
13 Schore, 'Foreword', xx.

with regard to the clinically observed dynamics of transmission of the family trauma in which the children of parents suffering from PTSD come to experience symptoms of PTSD including suicidal ideation.[14] The notion of intergenerational trauma, where the trauma experienced by parents is, in some measure, transmitted to their children,[15] may also benefit from such an explanatory framework.

This section has explored the main contours of relevant insights from neuroscience as related to the psychoanalytically informed Objects Relations theory. It provides an explanatory framework for theological reflection on original and personal sin as related to the notion of social sin. We now turn to the notion of social grace as the remedy for the accumulated effects of social sin.

Part 2: Social Grace as developed by Robert Doran.

According to Doran 'the universal gift of grace occurs in invisible missions of both the Word and the Holy Spirit'.[16] The invisible mission of the Word is independent from, and is historically prior to, the visible mission of the Son in Jesus of Nazareth. God as Trinity did not come into existence at the time of visible mission of the Son in Jesus of Nazareth. What changed following the visible mission of the Son in Jesus of Nazareth was our understanding of God as Trinity, not God as Trinity *per se*. Outside of time and space the Father eternally sends the Word invisibly. The invisible Word is received by human beings historically, 'through divinely originated insights and judgments of fact and value'.[17] The Hebrew Scriptures record the fruit of divinely originated insights and judgments of fact and value as an instance of a special manifestation or record of the invisible mission of the

---

14 See After the Call, *Mental Health Awareness for First Responders*.
15 See Ginot, *The Neuropsychology of the Unconscious*, 189–210.
16 Doran, 'Social Grace and the Mission of the Church', 171.
17 Doran, 'Social Grace and the Mission of the Church', 171.

Word.[18] The universal invisible mission of the Holy Spirit is the Father and the Son sending the Holy Spirit, in whom human beings participate through acts of charity.[19]

The Holy Spirit is the gift that the Father and the Son eternally give to each other as together they communicate the divine nature in the relation of love that unites them. The mission of the Holy Spirit which proceeds from the relationship of the Father and the Son historicizes and universalizes the eternal gift of the mutually uniting relationship of the Father and the Son.

The mission of the Holy Spirit is the divine eternal gift present in all human history.[20]

What marks Christianity as special within the universal invisible missions of the Word and Holy Spirit, is the recognition and affirmation of six movements of the Holy Spirit in the historical Christ event:

i) In the fullness of time the Father sends the Son in Jesus to be conceived by the Holy Spirit in the womb of the Virgin Mary. The work of God eternally performed in the invisible missions of the Son and the Spirit is made visible in the incarnate mission of the Son.[21]

ii) As the incarnate Son, Jesus of Nazareth was drawn by the Holy Spirit into the desert for forty days.

iii) In time and space, the Holy Spirit invited Jesus to return from the desert to preach the coming of God's reign.

iv) Prompted and strengthened by the Holy Spirit, Jesus, the incarnate Word, reveals the mysterious Law of the Cross, a Law embodied in the concrete instance of non-violent resistance and the return of good for the evil of the crucifixion.[22]

---

18 'From ancient times down to the present, there is found among various peoples a certain perception of that hidden power which hovers over the course of things and over the events of human history; at times some indeed have come to the recognition of a Supreme Being, or even of a Father. This perception and recognition penetrates their lives with a profound religious sense'. Vatican II, 'Declaration on the Relation of the Church to Non-Christian Religion'.
19 Doran, 'Social Grace and the Mission of the Church', 171.
20 Doran, 'Social Grace and the Mission of the Word'.
21 Doran, 'Social Grace and the Mission of the Church', 171.
22 Doran, 'Moving Vatican II Forward', 9.

v) In the power of the Holy Spirit, Jesus is raised to new life from a self-sacrificial death by the Father. In the resurrection of Jesus, the mysterious Law of the Cross, manifested as non-violent resistance and the return of good for evil, is confirmed as the divine solution to the problem of evil.

vi) In the Pentecost event the Father and the risen Jesus send the Spirit in a visible, palpable form to confirm, celebrate and continue the revelation of the mission of the incarnate Word.[23]

Pentecost marks the beginning of the ongoing act in the drama of the salvation wrought by Jesus. Pentecost begins an act that concludes with the realisation of the 'totality of the divine missions, visible and invisible, in the establishment of the reign of God'.[24] It is the Pentecost event that marks the beginning of the community that knows the divine missions of the Son and the Spirit in human history. It is this knowledge that distinguishes the church from all other communities. 'What was hidden is now revealed. What was conscious but not Objectified or what remained imperfectly articulated is now known and can be clearly spoken, proclaimed, announced'.[25] Pentecost marks the beginning of the church and its mission which is inseparable from its existence, the realisation of totality of the divine missions, visible and invisible in the establishment of the reign of God.

The ongoing Pentecost event in the drama of salvation includes us, here and now, as actors in history. In the drama of salvation the mutual interplay of divine and human freedom can now be carried out in explicit recognition of what, prior to the revelation that occurred in the mission of the incarnate Word, had been implicit, but not recognized, conscious but not known, or understood. Pentecost is a manifestation of the twofold mission of the Son and the Spirit. The universal invisible mission of the Holy Spirit becomes visible in the Pentecost event. This event confirms that the revelation which occurred in the visible mission of the Word in the incarnation, death and resurrection of Jesus, was indeed the revelation of the triune God in history.

---

23   Doran, 'Social Grace and the Mission of the Church', 171.
24   Doran, 'Social Grace and the Mission of the Church', 171.
25   Doran, 'Social Grace and the Mission of the Church', 174.

As already noted, the gift of the Holy Spirit is a universal offer. Reception of the gift may be implicit or explicit. Explicit reception actualizes and thus strengthens the effect of the gift. Implicit reception of the Word and Holy Spirit can be recognised in manifest goodness, made concrete in the actions of those beyond the Christian community.[26] The naming of 'unjust social structures' as social sin is now broadly accepted.[27] Social sin is the fruit of a collective coalescence of individual refusals or failures to do what is right or to reject what is wrong. When individuals coalesce to produce actions that gain collective attention because they are manifestly good, the observed actions are the social Objectification of grace, or in shorthand, social grace. In biblical terms, this is the in-breaking of the reign of God in human history.[28]

What then is the relationship between the fruit of sinful social structures, or social sin, and social grace? The fruit of individual sin works its way into personal subjective states, inter-personal relationships, society, culture and indeed history. The universal gift of the Holy Spirit is actualized in the reception by individuals and manifested as elevating and healing divine grace. This grace works its way into personal subjective states, inter-personal relationships, society, culture and history.

Doran defines social grace as 'our created relations with the three divine subjects (that) establish the state of grace as an interpersonal situation whose formal effects extend to the establishment of a genuine community of meaning and value among human beings'.[29] Unpacking the notion of social grace, Doran draws on a hierarchy or scale of values as the mechanism for understanding its operation. It was Bernard Lonergan who identified the scale of values.[30] For Lonergan, feelings are

---

26 An example of manifest good that has an ongoing legacy is the work of Australian ophthalmologist Fred Hollows who worked tirelessly to restore sight to many people suffering from the impact of curable blindness and the organisation that has succeeded him the Fred Hollow's Foundation.
27 In 1984 John Paul II wrote: 'One can speak of a communion of sin, whereby a soul that lowers itself through sin drags down with itself the church and, in some way, the whole world. In other words, there is no sin, not even the most intimate and secret one, the most strictly individual one, that exclusively concerns the person committing it. With greater or lesser violence, with greater or lesser harm, every sin has repercussions on the entire ecclesial body and the whole human family. According to this first meaning of the term, every sin can undoubtedly be considered as social sin'; John Paul II, 'Reconciliation and Penance'.
28 See Doran, 'Social Grace', 134.
29 Doran, 'Social Grace and the Mission of the Church', 173.
30 Lonergan, *Method*, 32.

intimately connected to values. Specifically, feelings respond to values in accord with a scale of preference, with vital, social, cultural, personal, and religious values operating in an ascending order.[31] Vital values refer to things such as health and strength, grace and vigour and in the context of social grace availability of the basic conditions for sustaining life; food, water, shelter and security. Vital values are normally 'preferred to avoiding the work, privations, pains involved in acquiring, maintaining, restoring them.'[32]

Social values create the environment in which the vital values of the whole community might be met and it is for this reason that social values are 'to be preferred to the vital values of individual members of the community.'[33] It is good for an individual to have breakfast this morning. This example is an instance of a vital value in operation. Creating a social system in which everyone in a community has access to sufficient food every day is an example of a social value in action.

Moving up the scale to cultural values, Lonergan asserts that 'over and above mere living and operating, men and women have to find a meaning and value in their living and operating.'[34] 'One does not live by bread alone' (Matt 4:4, NRSV). It is the function of culture to discover, express, validate, criticise, correct, develop and improve community meaning and values. As such cultural values rank higher than social values. The function of culture unfolds on two levels: infrastructure and superstructure. Infrastructure with respect to culture refers to the realm of common sense as society goes about the business of practical affairs concerned with everyday life in terms of existing economic, technological, and political structures.[35] The superstructure is constantly engaged in transforming the infrastructure, for better or for worse. The work of the superstructure involves critical reflection on theory. It is through deep reflection as promoted in institutions such as universities, theological facilities, and think-tanks that intelligent and thoughtful individuals work together to overcome the negative influence of the general bias

---

31 Lonergan, *Method*, 34.
32 Lonergan, *Method*, 31.
33 Lonergan, *Method*, 31.
34 Lonergan, *Method*, 32.
35 Doran, 'Social Grace and the Mission of the Church', 175.

of common sense which is often dismissive of theory, is only concerned with immediate issues, and is impatient with ultimate questions.[36] The infrastructure is constantly either aiding or interfering with the superstructure as it attempts to do its authentic work. The ideological system of economic rationalism is an example of superstructure impacting on the way a government attempts to shape a society or the actions and attitudes of citizens. The theoretical framework of economic rationalism has a concrete impact on infrastructure manifested in the level and type of economic support provided for citizens, viewed through the lens of economic rationalism, as seen to be unproductive. The use of the phrase 'lifters and leaners' by political leaders in relation to persons as economic units of production and consumption has concrete effects with regard to the formation of attitudes by fellow members of the shared society, towards those who, for a great variety of reasons, are not benefiting from the working through of an economic system grounded in what is sometimes referred to as market fundamentalism.

Personal value is manifested in the person as an originator of values in him or herself and in his or her milieu, as an inspiration and invitation to others to do likewise.[37] As originators of values, persons in their self-transcendence as loving and being loved 'can be principles of benevolence and beneficence, capable of genuine collaboration and of true love'.[38]

Perhaps a significant number of people have the capacity to be originator of values occasionally, by fits and starts. Rock or sports stars working together to raise funds for a worthy cause and then quickly returning to their primary purpose once the event is over, provide an example of originating value in fits and starts. To think and act as a virtuous person is far rarer. The virtuous person initiates genuine collaboration and true love, regularly, easily, and spontaneously in a manner that manifests benevolence and beneficence. The state of being a virtuous person is only achieved by those for whom such a manner of being in the world is the fruit of hard-won, long-term conscious and thoughtful

---

36 Doran, 'Social Grace and the Mission of the Church', 176.
37 Lonergan, *Method*, 32.
38 Lonergan, *Method*, 35.

practice.[39] 'It is only by reaching the sustained self-transcendence of the virtuous man or woman that one becomes a good judge, not on this or that human act, but on the whole range of human goodness.'[40]

According to Lonergan, to maintain self-transcendence the virtuous person needs to be sustained by religious values. These are the values that form the ground of the meaning and significance of a person's life and world. Such values also provide an orientation with regard to a person's ultimate horizon. It is for this reason that religious values rank highest in the ascending scale of values. Religious values help overcome bias and a tendency to moral impotence. The gift of God's love, that is, the gift of the Holy Spirit, manifests as religious values create the condition of the possibility of sustained personal integrity or personal value. Persons of integrity represent the condition of possibility of genuine meanings and values that in turn, inform ways of living, manifest as cultural values. The pursuit of superstructural cultural values is a constitutive dimension in the establishment of social structures and intersubjective habits or social values. These render more probable something approaching an equitable distribution of the necessities of life, or vital values, to the whole human community. Social values are informed and purified by authentic cultural values, which are nourished and sustained by religious and personal values. The consistent and persistent application of social values serves to gradually realise the reign of God in history.

This section has explored the notion of the scale of values as applied to politics as broadly understood. We now turn to a concise examination of the relationship between God and politics through a historical lens so as to provide background for Part 4 which examines the application of the scale of values in history.

Part 3: God and Politics

This part draws extensively on 'Globalization and the Mission of the Church' written by Ormerod and Clifton and published in 2011. After the conversion of the Roman emperor Constantine to Christianity,

---

39 Lonergan, *Method*, 35.
40 Lonergan, *Method*, 35.

the intertwining of church and state gradually produced Christendom. The intellectual foundations for Christendom were laid by Augustine of Hippo. 'The two categories which dominated Augustine's thought were grace, revealed in Jesus Christ and mediated by the church, and sin, manifest in human corruption and weakness and leading to damnation'. Augustine had an all or nothing approach, either grace or sin, either church or heresy. 'For Augustine, the State was an instrument of the church and enforced religious decrees. One was either in the City of God leading to salvation, or in the City of Man leading to hell'. Augustine's framework provided a simple and direct solution to the problem of the relationship between church and State.[41]

Following the philosophy of Aristotle, in the 13th Century Aquinas introduced a middle term, which he called 'nature'. 'For Aquinas, grace was gracious not simply in relation to sin, but also in relation to human nature. Human nature, for Aquinas, was "good" though not capable of achieving salvation by its own power. For Aquinas, goodness remains, if only in potential or orientation, in all human beings'[42]—pagans as well as Christians. 'The theoretical distinction between grace and nature allowed for the recognition of a realm or order of human activity in which the Church or faith had no direct say'.[43] In this understanding the competence of the Church in matters of faith 'did not necessarily extend to the organization of human affairs, of politics (e.g. forms of government) and the economy (e.g. on interest rates and usury), or of science and technology'.[44]

In the 16th Century, among the many things promoted by Luther was the notion of 'freedom of conscience' and a separation of Church and State. For Luther, the State had no right to violate the freedom of conscience of a religious believer. In another response, John Calvin established a virtual theocracy in Geneva.[45] One of the unintended fruits of the Protestant Reformation and the Catholic Revival was a splitting of the emerging nation states into Catholic and Protestant camps. The

---

41 Quotations from Ormerod & Clifton, *Globalization and the Mission of the Church*, 107.
42 Ormerod & Clifton, *Globalization and the Mission of the Church*, 107.
43 Ormerod & Clifton, *Globalization and the Mission of the Church*, 107.
44 Ormerod & Clifton, *Globalization and the Mission of the Church*, 108.
45 Trueman, 'John Calvin'.

structure of the new nation states meant that those who lived within the boundaries of the nation adopted the religious affiliation chosen by the prince or ruler of the nation. As the new states went to war with each other over territory, religion was used then, as it is sometimes used now, to mask political expediency.[46] The bitterness and interminable nature of these conflicts, however, contributed to a generalized disillusionment with religion. The experience of a widespread disappointment with the fruits of religion and the rise of new progress-orientated philosophical frameworks gradually led to 'our more modern position of a secular State, where religion is largely privatised and marginalised from the public realm'.[47] Leading up to the Enlightenment, religion in the form of Catholicism in conflict with various strands of Protestantism was viewed by some as a source and contributor to social conflict and upheaval. The response from many was the view that, 'the political order could survive quite well without Christianity. At the same time the State put aside attempts to regulate religion, except in the most minimal ways needed for good social order'.[48]

For the philosophers of the Enlightenment the church represented medieval tradition, superstition and ignorance. The modern state represented reason, intellect and social progress. According to Ormerod and Clifton, 'the Enlightenment marks the beginning of the systematic exclusion of religion from the public realm'.[49] Religion, church and faith were seen by the philosophers of the Enlightenment as part of an intellectual milieu that was dying. The Enlightenment project was marked by a desire to 'introduce scientific reason into human affairs, eliminate religious metaphysics and substitute them with a scientific account of human existence'.[50] Theology, previously viewed as the queen of the arts and sciences, lost its crown to sociology, political science, economics and other human sciences.

---

46 The imprisonment of Ahok; the popular Christian candidate for Mayor of Jakarta in Indonesia for blasphemy in 2017, I suggest, is a contemporary example of using religion for political expediency. See www.theguardian.com/world/2017/may/09/jakarta-governor-ahok-found-guilty-of-blasphemy-jailed-for-two-years
47 Ormerod & Clifton, *Globalization and the Mission of the Church*, 108.
48 Ormerod & Clifton, *Globalization and the Mission of the Church*, 108.
49 Ormerod & Clifton, *Globalization and the Mission of the Church*, 108.
50 Ormerod & Clifton, *Globalization and the Mission of the Church*, 108.

A recent illustration of a position on the relationship between church and State is contained in the second part of Pope Benedict XVI's encyclical, 'On Christian Love' which deals with the question of the relationship between church and State, in the context of the church's charitable works and agencies. The encyclical clearly rejects the Christendom model of Church-State relationship noting that: 'it is not the Church's responsibility to make [its] teaching prevail in political life … the Church cannot and must not replace the State'.[51] For Benedict, the Church's task is to 'inform consciences', 'stimulate greater insight into the authentic requirements of justice', and foster 'greater readiness to act accordingly'.[52] The Church's social teaching is based on 'reason and natural law', 'rational argument', so that a 'just society must be the achievement of politics, not the Church'. [53] Indeed 'the direct duty to work for a just ordering of society . . . is proper to the lay faithful . . . called to take part in public life as a personal capacity'.[54] It appears that with these statements Benedict was rejecting the idea of the Church as a separate perfect society, a safe haven, if you will, from the secular world. This is consistent with Doran's view that church is not a separate entity set apart from society but indeed part of society, a sector that is charged with a mission to influence the way the society operates in terms of culture, policy, and governance. The Pentecost mission given to the original community of disciples of Jesus Christ is to form and inform the lay faithful as it is their role to take part in public life in a personal capacity, that is, not as representatives of the church. One of the tasks of theology, as an academic discipline, is to work towards influencing culture. Theology is to engage with the cultural superstructure in order to influence policies and plans with regard to the manner in which a society may organize its infrastructure to ensure the just distribution of vital values. One of the tasks of ministry is the formation of the lay faithful in terms of personal and religious values so that they exercise their direct duty to work for a just ordering of society in the myriad of contexts in which they work and recreate. Having briefly outlined the broad sweep

---

51 Benedict XVI, *Encyclical Letter, Deus Caritas Est*, 28.
52 Benedict XVI, *Encyclical Letter, Deus Caritas Est*, 28.
53 Benedict XVI, *Encyclical Letter, Deus Caritas Est*, 28.
54 Benedict XVI, *Encyclical Letter, Deus Caritas Est*, 29.

of history in terms of God and Politics we now move to applying the insights gained from an examination of the scale of values as they have operated in history.

Part 4: Scale of Values in History

This part draws extensively on the work of Neil Ormerod, particularly his book 'Re-visioning the Church: An Experiment in Systematic-historical Ecclesiology'. The human spirit (nature) works creatively from below up. As noted in Part 2 of this article, the supply of vital values is a function of existing economic, technological, and political structures (infrastructure). Practical intelligence creates new situations, new technologies, new political and economic systems which change existing patterns of distribution of vital values, creating new opportunities for human living. New social values, however, must be sustained by developments in cultural values which help us 'make sense' of the new emerging social reality. New cultural values demand new levels of personal integrity if the social and cultural matrix is not to be subverted by old alliances and corruptions. Lonergan refers to this upwards movement as the creative vector in human history.[55]

There is also a movement from above to below.[56] Religious value or grace heals the distortions of consciousness which result from the breakdown in personal values. Remedying distortions in the cultural superstructure assists in the restoration of individual, moral, intellectual, and affective integrity. One appropriate response to such personal transformation is to seek to heal distortions in cultural values which have contributed to the process of personal decline of many members of a society. Healing the distortions of cultural values creates a superstructure which can also challenge and criticise the distortions in social values. The distortions in social values is expressed through biased common sense in our political, economic, and technological institutions. Healing of the distortions of cultural value can correct the short-term

---

55 See Lonergan, 'Healing and Creating in History', 100–109
56 Ormerod, *Re-Visioning the Church*, 78.

expediency of common sense and the power politics of group bias.[57] Healing of the social level of values can then lead to the just distribution of vital values to all groups within society. Lonergan refers to this movement as the healing vector in human history. Both healing and creative processes are needed in human history. Human creativity needs healing to liberate it to be itself, that is, freed from the blocks and biases which undermine its energy. The healing vector, though divine in its origin, has its own purpose within the domain of human history.[58]

Political engagement is the proximate outcome of a cultural transformation, and the more remote outcome of psychic, moral and religious conversions. It is only at the end of this multiple mediation through personal and cultural values that we can speak of a 'direct duty to work for a just ordering of society', a task 'proper to the lay faithful'.[59] The temptation, often enough succumbed to, is to move directly from the religious to the political, as if a political program can be read straight out of one's religious beliefs.[60] Examples of this dynamic include statements such as 'The Bible says' or 'Catholic Social Teaching says' with strident calls for society and culture to align itself with these revealed statements. Another approach is co-relating selected biblical or doctrinal statements with selected insights from the human sciences to create a vison for a new order. Such attempts at correlation presume that the scriptural or doctrinal texts were produced in contexts that were not limited by their own biases and distortions. Such attempts also fail to adequately acknowledge that the culture that is to be co-related with revealed insights has in at least some measure been shaped by the same religious tradition. In short, the method of theological correlation reflects the tendency to 'split' the secular and the sacred, as outlined in Part 1 of this article.[61]

It is at this point, Part 5, that we return to Object Relations theory noting an ever-present temptation for the church and religious people generally to tend towards the paranoid-schizoid position as proposed

---

57 Ormerod, *Re-Visioning the Church*, 79.
58 Ormerod, *Re-Visioning the Church*, 79.
59 Ormerod & Clifton, *Globalization and the Mission of the Church*.
60 Ormerod & Clifton, *Globalization and the Mission of the Church*.
61 See Ormerod, 'Quarrels with the Method of Correlation'.

by Klein. The basic split manifesting in perceived oppositions between the church and the world, between idealised past and demonized present, between Christianity and Islam, men and women, heterosexual and homosexual, clerical and lay states. As noted in the first part of this article, the observed phenomena named by Klein as the paranoid-schizoid and depressive positions have been largely affirmed by research in neuroscience. What has also been affirmed is that these 'positions' are not simply transitory or passing phases or stages, but they set up the basis of the psyche's enduring orientation throughout life. Further, it was noted that depending on the level of integration and the amount of subjective stress, elements of oscillation between the two positions is a phenomenon that can be observed. It was also noted that the potential for oscillation is often actualized when there is a state of heightened anxiety and stress. For the Church and religious people generally to be instruments of creative nature and conduits of healing grace to a splintered culture and social realm, there is a need for those who rhetorically proclaim peace and reconciliation in Christ, to mourn their own historic and current failures, lest they fall into the trap of cycles of collective unconscious projection of sin onto the 'other' and collectively, unconsciously, fear that the other will return to seek revenge.

Post the Royal Commission into Institutional Responses to Child Sexual Abuse, in Australia the churches and religious people generally have much to feel guilty about. Many ecclesial communities manifestly and tragically failed to live up to their own self-proclaimed ideals in terms of pastoral care of children. A result of the findings of the Royal Commission is that the churches have certainly lost their previous sense of omnipotence. One response to the finding of the Royal Commission has been the combination of an acknowledgement of guilt, seeking forgiveness, working at reparation, including just monetary compensation, the development of programs designed to ensure structural and cultural change and mourning the loss of an imaged image of the church as totally benign. Such a stance characterises Klein's depressive position. Another response to the Royal Commission and its report is to perceive the whole process as an attack and respond with some of the following strategies. Answering the changed relationship between the church and other elements of society some Catholics desire to 'return to a mythical' liturgical Latin past in terms of worship. Mythical in the sense that many of those working to restore a 'traditional Latin liturgy' have little or no understanding of the ecclesial situation prior to the liturgical reforms that were the fruit of the Second Vatican Council. The context of the pre-Vatican II Latin liturgy was an ecclesial culture permeated by individualism, fear, sectarianism, and distorted food laws closely tied to religious identity. Another response is that of radical orthodoxy which is characterized in terms of a call for clarity of doctrinal positions with certain derivative moral issues such as contraception and governance issues such as the call for women priests. In this response, these issues act as proxy indicators for dogmatic orthodoxy. Yet another response is Evangelical Catholicism, in which all Catholics are expected to be active evangelisers in their Church community. Such a view confuses discipleship with ministry and forgets that the appropriate role for most Catholic laypeople, indeed their direct duty, is to work for a just ordering of society consistent with the inbreaking of the reign of God in the many contexts in which they work and recreate. Another response to perceived persecution includes calls for 'home schooling' in the context of families and individuals living in monastically inspired, metaphorical 'arks' designed to ride out the floodwaters of postmodernity. Consistent with Augustine's all or nothing approach such responses illustrate a communal manifestation of the paranoid-schizoid position. Schizoid in the sense of a clear split between us and them, right and wrong. Paranoid in the sense of once the 'other' has been socially constructed, all the unacceptable elements of those in the groups and movements are unconsciously projected on to (into) the other and as such are to be feared. Such a dynamic is evident in both ecclesial and civil structures throughout the contemporary world. Perhaps its apotheosis in the political situation is in the USA under the presidency of Donald Trump and ecclesially, manifest in the factions for and against Pope Francis.

For the church to be effective in assisting in the task of healing political division and creating a new social order consistent with the reign of God, it needs the ability to view itself and other institutions as marked by present and historical complexity. Informed by the insights from Klein as confirmed by research in neuroscience on the dynamics of splitting, Christians who constitute the church need to catch themselves in the act of projecting what they find unacceptable in themselves onto the 'other' or others. As a complex, divinely inspired, human and sinful organization the church has the potential to operate as both a destructive force leading to division, or to be a healing and creative instrument of justice, peace and reconciliation to a culture and social order so much in need of such things. To act in this way however the church as a mature organization, needs to accept: a) That while it is founded by the Spirit to continue the mission of the incarnate Word, as an institution it no longer holds the omnipotent role it did in Christendom; b) As a divinely inspired institution constituted by individuals whose religious, moral, intellectual and psychic conversion is ever precarious, the church has the potential to be an instrument of both division and sin, and/or an instrument of grace and reconciliation to the world — a world, which, while damaged by the effects of sin, remains good, if only in potential, and which is being constantly offered participation in the invisible mission of the Holy Spirit.

The relationship between the church and the world of politics, culture, and society is extraordinarily complex and involves issues and sets of relationships that are influenced by both the historical effects of sin as well as the free gift of God's grace. As a discipline, Theology is one, among other, useful disciplines. Informed and inspired by the mysterious Law of the Cross, manifested as non-violent resistance and the return of good for evil, one of the tasks proper to Theology is to recognize complexity and cooperate with other disciplines in making sense of the impact of sin on the world. Another theological task is to work towards convincing those who hold positions of authority in churches and civil institutions to resist the ever-present tendency to split between good and bad under the influence of institutional stress and avoid the consequent result of proposing simple, common sense solutions to complex historically conditioned situations.

In terms of mission and ministry, in the absence of psychic, moral, and intellectual conversion, religious conversion can lead to magical thinking and a tendency to observe, or indeed create, a split between good-bad, church-world, saved-damned world-views. In the absence of moral conversion, religious conversion can lead to a privatised sense of personal salvation rather than a call to mission to work with the Holy Spirit to create a social order consistent with the in-breaking reign of God as proclaimed by the incarnate Word. In the absence of psychic conversion or psychic healing of the basic split in the psyche, religious conversion runs the risk of drawing on intellectual faculties to repeat and perhaps amplify psychic splits by simply changing the categories and labels for good and bad to heaven and hell and saved and damned, sacred and secular with little or no personal psychic healing or integration. Without intellectual conversion—in the sense of restricting one's judgement to that which, while mediated by meaning, can be affirmed as real—religious conversion runs the risk of tending towards the formation of a cult or sect, complete with sophisticated literature to justify beliefs, practices and patterns of worship. Passing live venomous snakes from one to another in the context of worship is perhaps not the only example of inauthentic Christian worship.

For those who live at this particular time in history as actors in the ongoing Pentecost event, the task is to promote and nurture integrative religious, psychic, moral, and intellectual conversion in those to whom we are called to minister or teach. The formation of authentic carriers of the meaning and message of Jesus Christ is foundational to the process of facilitating social grace in history. It is authentic carriers of the meaning and message of Jesus Christ who will influence, educate, and govern in a way that facilitates the action of the Holy Spirit through social grace, to co-create a world that aligns more closely to the vision of the reign of God as proclaimed by the Word made flesh, Jesus of Nazareth, during his historical mission on earth.

For those looking for a quick fix to complex problems such a proposition will appear to take too long and there will be calls for direct action echoing the cry of the two-year old 'I don't know what I want but I know I want it NOW!'

> When I was a child, I spoke like a child, I thought like a child, I reasoned like a child; when I became an adult, I put an end to childish ways. (I Cor 13:11 NRSV)

Given the multiple mediations involved and given the time and energy needed to shift cultures towards some normatively perceived political goal, church and religious people generally, often fall for the temptation of seeking quick and simple solutions to complex problems. The truth however is that the church and religious people in general, need to mourn their own current and historical failures before promoting solutions. The current call is for adult Christians to be members of an adult church. Adults are those who understand that it is only at the end of multiple mediation through personal and cultural values and through individual religious, psychic, moral, and intellectual conversion, that they can take up the task of co-creating with the Holy Spirit a society and culture that makes the basic necessities of life available to all. This task is, in fact, proper to the adult lay faithful. The task of clergy and hierarchy is to serve the lay faithful by constantly resourcing and inviting them into adult relationships with each other, with God, with the Church and the common humanity of which we are all members.

Bibliography

After the Call — *Mental Health Awareness for First Responders.* www.afterthecall.org/mental-health-awareness-booklet/mental-health-awareness-for-first-responders.

Benedict XVI. — *Encyclical Letter, Deus Caritas Est of the Supreme Pontiff Benedict Xvi : To the Bishops, Priests and Deacons, Men and Women Religious and All the Lay Faithful on Christian Love* (Strathfield, NSW: St Pauls Publications, 2006).

Bion, Wilfred R. — *Experiences in Groups, and Other Papers* (London: Tavistock/Routledge, 1989).

Bragdon, A., & D. Gamon — 'Your Brain and What It Does'. www.brainwaves.com.

Dahlitz, M. — 'The Limbic System'. NPT. Last modified 2016. Accessed 21/09/2018, 2018. www.neuropsychotherapist.com/the-limbic-system.

Doran, R. M. — 'Social Grace and the Mission of the Church', in C. Denny, P. Hayes, and N. Rademacher (eds.), *A Realist's Church: Essays in Honor of Joseph A. Komonchak* (Maryknoll: Orbis Books, 2015), 169–84.

Doran, R. M.	'Moving Vatican II Forward: The Multi-Religious Context', in F. Lawrence (ed.), *The Promise of Vatican II after Fifty Years* (Chestnut Hill: Boston College, 2014), 127–138.
Doran, R. M.	'Social Grace', *Method: Journal of Lonergan Studies* 2, no. 2 (2011), 131–42.
Doran, R. M.	'Social Grace and the Mission of the Word'. *lonerganresource.com* (2010). www.lonerganresource.com/pdf/contributors/Doran-Social_Grace_and_the_Mission_of_the_Word.pdf.
Ginot, Efrat	*The Neuropsychology of the Unconscious: Integrating Brain and Mind in Psychotherapy* (The Norton Series on Interpersonal Neurobiology; New York: W.W. Norton & Company, 2015).
Vatican II	'Declaration on the Relation of the Church to Non-Christian Religion', Documents of Vatican II. www.vatican.va/archive/hist_councils/ii_vatican_council/documents/vat-ii_decl_19651028_nostra-aetate_en.html.
John Paul II	'Reconciliation and Penance'. http://w2.vatican.va/content/john-paul-ii/en/apost_exhortations/documents/hf_jp-ii_exh_02121984_reconciliatio-et-paenitentia.html.
Kernberg, Otto F.	'Neurobiological Correlates of Object Relations Theory: The Relationship between Neurobiological and Psychodynamic Development'. *International Forum of Psychoanalysis* 24, no. 1 (2015): 38-46. http://dx.doi.org/10.1080/0803706X.2014.912352.
Lamb, Kate	'Jakarta governor Ahok sentenced to two years in prison for blasphemy', *The Guardian* 9/5/2017. www.theguardian.com/world/2017/may/09/jakarta-governor-ahok-found-guilty-of-blasphemy-jailed-for-two-years.
Learning Theories	'Object Relations Theory (Melanie Klein)'. Last modified 2017. Accessed 4 March 2017. www.learning-theories.com/Object-relations-theory-melanie-klein.html.
Lonergan, Bernard J.F	'Healing and Creating in History', in Fredrick E. Crowe (ed.), *A Third Collection* (Mahwah, NJ: Paulist Press, 1985), 100–109.

Lonergan, Bernard J.F.   *Method in Theology* (London: Dartman, Longman & Todd, 1972).

Ormerod, N.J.   *Re-Visioning the Church: An Experiment in Systematic-Historical Ecclesiology* (Minneapolis: Fortress Press, 2014).

Ormerod, N.J., & S. Clifton   *Globalization and the Mission of the Church* (London: Bloomsbury Publishing, 2011).

Ormerod, N.J.   'Quarrels with the Method of Correlation'. *Theological Studies* 57, no. 4 (D 1996), 707–19.

Schore, Allan N.   'Foreword', to Efrat Ginot, The *Neuropsychology of the Unconscious : Integrating Brain and Mind in Psychotherapy* (The Norton Series on Interpersonal Neurobiology; New York: W.W. Norton & Company, 2015).

Trueman, C. N   'John Calvin'. *History Learning Site* (2018). www.historylearningsite.co.uk/john-calvin.

CHAPTER 15

Reformation and Vatican II: Challenge of a Ministry-Centred Understanding of Jesus of Nazareth

Jacob Kavunkal SVD

Abstract

The close occurrence of the fiftieth anniversary of Vatican II and the five hundredth anniversary of the Martin Luther-inspired Reformation, the chapter argues, is a challenge for the Christian community and scripture scholars to retrieve the roots of Christian discipleship, the ministry of Jesus of Nazareth. After outlining the significance of ecumenism, the paper underlines two key emphases of Luther, the centrality of the Bible and the common priesthood of Christians, which had an impact on Vatican II as well. This, in turn, is a challenge to the Christian community to focus on the ministry of Jesus with its priority of wholeness of life for all, especially for those on the margins.

Introduction

The year 2017 is the five hundredth anniversary of the Reformation that Martin Luther gave rise to. It almost coincides with the fiftieth anniversary of the great Ecumenical Council Vatican II. Triggered by that confluence this chapter argues how the double celebration must help the church to retrieve the roots and fruits of Christian discipleship from the ministry of Jesus Christ.

The quincentennial commemoration of the reformation movement is an invitation to revisit some of the principles that Luther emphasised and which are also basic to Christian Faith. The course of events and developments that have transpired during the past five centuries, as well as the distance in time, enable one to review what Luther said with a certain equanimity but also with a view to enriching the church's life and mission today.

As Hans Kung has pointed out[1] the Reformation may be attributed to several persons and factors though basically it was Luther who initiated the event by his questioning of the church's granting indulgence, that is, remittance of punishment due to a dead person, in return for the money a living person gives to the church. The conflict concerning the indulgences developed into a question of spiritual authority which Luther understood in terms of the Scripture.[2]

The five hundred-year anniversary of the Reformation must prove to be an event strengthening ecumenism, eventually paving the way for the unity of the Church. 'Commitment to ecumenism responds to the prayer of the Lord Jesus that "they be one" (John 17:21)', wrote Pope Francis in his Apostolic Exhortation *Evangelii Gaudium* (The Joy of the Gospel) (no. 214). The Pope went on to say: 'The credibility of the Christian message would be much greater if Christians could overcome their divisions and the Church could realize the fullness of catholicity proper to her'.

Charting that path of ecumenism, this chapter will argue how the

---

1 Kung, *Christianity*, 525. The humanistic revival that began during the late middle ages, to a large extent, paved the way for the Reformation. People wanted to hear more enlightened sermons from the ministers. See Dillenberger, *Martin Luther, Selections from his Writings*, 166. Similarly, John Wycliffe (1320–1384), a century before Luther, had advocated the translation of the Bible into English and it influenced Jan Hus (1352–1445) who, though, was burned at the stake.
2 Luther, in his struggle, sought the help of the Nobility of Germany, as he felt powerless before the well-entrenched institutional power of the church of the time. Luther was convinced of the need for a General Council to discuss and usher in reform, especially with regard to the spiritual authority that the Church claimed to have, namely, to change divine will regarding a person who is in purgatory to be taken out by a substitutionary order of the Church in the form of a total indulgence which one could win for oneself or for one in purgatory, by paying money for the construction of the basilica of St. Peter.

Catholic Church can draw inspiration from Luther to make the Church ever more missionary, especially with regard to the role of the Laity as outlined by Vatican II. Together they invite all Christians to have a ministry-centred approach to the Lord as presented in the gospels.

Significance of Ecumenism

It is widely recognized how the world at large is changing in interactions and collaborations, tending to greater unity, despite the fissiparous tendencies fostered by narrow-minded vested interests. This has not left the Christian churches unaffected, as shown by the many joint study groups and inter-ecclesial commissions to usher in greater unity among Christians. The ecumenical ideal is upheld by all churches, more so by the Catholic Church, the World Council of Churches and the Orthodox Churches.[3]

Christian service has to take into account the socio-cultural context. A core element of many cultures is harmony and interdependence. This is further compounded by the plurality of religions in the midst of which Christians are called to render their service. The Lord of the Church reminds Christians how they are to be one so that the world may believe in them (John 17:21). The vexing problems that churches face with regard to ecumenism must be relativized in terms of the missionary priority. This missionary priority makes inter denominational confrontation obsolete and insignificant. The common Christian call to mission compels Christians to make use of ecumenical opportunities to be faithful to the Christian call to witness to the Gospel. While the past cannot be changed, what the churches remember and celebrate today can affect Christian mission vitally.

No wonder, on the occasion of the commemoration of the 500 years of the Reformation the Lutheran World Federation and the Catholic Church have taken further steps towards reconciliation and move forward in the field of joint service to express and strengthen their commitment to seek unity. This is amply expressed in their joint study

---

3   See the Declaration on Ecumenism (*Unitatis Redentigratio*) of Vatican II. *The Church: Towards a Common Vision* (Faith and Order Paper 214, WCC).

document, 'From Conflict to Communion'.[4] It advocates how Catholics and Lutherans should witness together to the mercy of God in proclamation and service to the world. No. 243 of the document reads: 'Ecumenical engagement for the unity of the Church, does not serve only the Church, but also the world, so that the world may believe.'

In the same spirit Pope Francis in his address to the Ecumenical event in Malmo Arena, Sweden on 31 October 2016, remembering the 500th anniversary of the Reformation, said: 'We remember this anniversary with a renewed spirit and in the recognition that Christian Unity is a priority, because we realize that much more unites us than separates us'.[5] In this the Pope was only following one of the leading guidelines of Vatican II saying that the Church of Christ has to be unique and one (UR 1).

As disciples of Jesus both the Catholics and the Lutherans have the irreplaceable duty to be best advocates of human lives, animated by the Christian faith, in a secularised world. Christians believe that the God who sent Jesus Christ is working through his Church, the community of his disciples, to confront evil and rebuild lives. The two churches are looking forward to working together in harmony and collaboration.

The commemoration is a fitting occasion to look back on the events that occurred 500 years back, putting the Gospel of Jesus Christ at the centre with the intent how this Gospel can be celebrated and communicated to the people of contemporary times, so that the world may believe how God gave God's self to humans and calls them into communion with God and with one another. In that spirit the present paper builds on Luther's contribution in order to make every Christian responsible in his/her vocation. This, in turn, can reinvent the ecumenical dialogue and the common journey.

The joint commission of Catholics and Lutherans pointed out in its statement in 1983, on the occasion of the 500th anniversary of Martin Luther's birth, that Christians, whether Protestants or Catholics, cannot

---

4 'From Conflict to Communion'. Lutheran–Catholic Common Commemoration of the Reformation in 2017. <www.bonifatius.de>.
5 <https://w2.vatican.va/content/francesco/en/speeches/2016/october/documents/papa-francesco_20161031_svezia–evento–ecumenico.html> (accessed on 20.01.2017).

disregard the person and message of this man.⁶ 'Luther's reforming agenda poses a spiritual and theological challenge for both contemporary Catholics and Lutherans'.⁷ They offer us both opportunities and obligations. This paper will emphasise the implications of Luther's teachings for the mission of the church especially with regard to the laity.

The 2017 quincentennial of the Reformation has added significance due to the fact that it was the first ecumenical celebration of the Reformation in which Catholics also participated. Equally, it offers Catholics the opportunity to interpret their theological tradition and mission adopting and accepting Luther's influence.

It is to be acknowledged that even if initially Catholics firewalled themselves against Luther's ideas, in the long run they had their impact on the Catholic Church as well. A major area of this impact was Scripture. With his encyclical *Divino Afflante Spiritu,* (Inspired by the Holy Spirit) (1943) Pope Pius XII opened the floodgates of the study of the Scripture in the Catholic Church.

The joint declaration, From Conflict to Communion, underlined that the Reformation should be freed from the notion of separation or division in the Church. What Luther intended was reform— not division, which was the result of various factors, including the institutional failure to read the signs of the times. Equally, it was due to the political climate of the Supreme authority of the Holy Roman Empire from which many wanted to free themselves. Nor was it a 'rediscovery of the gospel' as many of the followers of Luther traditionally claimed.⁸

Even if the present cannot cancel what has happened in history, the remembrance can enable Christians to recreate the past for the present. They can narrate that history in a fresh way. The many secular events like the Universal Declaration of Human Rights by the United Nations (1948), the growing phenomenon of secularization, the revival of world religions as well as the mutual influence of Catholics and Protestants, more so in recent times, all invite Christians to a new era of collaboration

---

6   'From Conflict to Communion', no. 2.
7   'From Conflict to Communion', no. 3.
8   As mentioned in footnote 1, persons like John Wycliffe and Jan Hus had already advocated the need for translating the Bible into the languages of the people and the place of the Bible in the lives of the faithful.

and unity. They impel Christians to search for what is common among them rather than what is dividing them and pursue ways of working towards overcoming the differences.

Centrality of Scripture

Until John Gutenberg's (1394–1468) discovery of the printing press, the Bible remained for ordinary Christians, by and large, a closed book, except for the occasional sermons and through art works. True, there were trail-blazing minds such as that of John Wycliffe and Jan Hus that attempted to popularize the Bible by translating it into local languages but were met with stiff opposition. However, it is Luther's merit that he made scripture the integral part of Christian life.

Luther along with colleagues from the University of Wittenberg translated the New Testament into German, and with the help of the newly introduced printing press, made it easily accessible to ordinary Christians. Luther was a biblical scholar and was convinced of the power of the Word of God in his own life.[9]

Luther recommended for the study of the scripture a process of three steps: prayer, meditation and affliction. One should read the Scripture in the presence of God, in prayer, and while meditating on the words of the Scripture one must be attentive to the situations in life that often seem to contradict what is found in the Scripture. Through this process the Scripture proves its authority by overcoming those afflictions. 'Note that the struggle of the Scripture is this, that it is not changed into the one who studies it, but that it transforms one who loves it into itself and its strength'.[10] A person not only interprets the Scripture but is also interpreted by it, which is the power and authority of the Scripture.

Luther's central teaching that the Bible is the core source of religion and authority opened a rising wave of interest and study of the Scripture and this has continued to the present.

---

9 Cf. Witterup, *Rediscovering Vatican II: Scripture*, 5.
10 Luther, 'Commentary on Psalms', in Herbert J. A. Bouman, *Luther's Writings*, WA 3, 397, 9–11, quoted in Conflict and Communion, no. 197.

The Common Priesthood

An associate idea of Luther, and flowing from the centrality of the Scripture, is the dignity and responsibility of every baptized person. In contrast to the prevailing medieval division of Christians into spiritual (hierarchy) and temporal (the laity), Luther insisted how all Christians are priests in the eyes of God and that they have direct access to God. In his letter to the German nobility he put forward the doctrine that all baptized Christians were priests and spiritual, dismissing the existence of two classes of believers, the spiritual and the secular.[11]

Luther understood the relationship of believers to Christ as a 'joyful exchange, in which the believer takes part in the properties of Christ, and thus also in his priesthood'.[12] Commenting on 1 Peter 2:9, 'You are a chosen race, a royal priesthood, a holy nation, God's own people,' Luther insisted, 'We are all consecrated priests through baptism'.[13] Similarly, in his writing, *On the Babylonian Captivity of the Church* (1520) he wrote: 'In this way we are all priests, as many of us are Christians. There are indeed priests whom we call ministers'.[14]

Luther held that all Christians are truly of the spiritual estate, and there are no differences among them, except that of office.[15] 'There is no true basic difference between layman and priests, princes and bishops, between religious and secular, except for the sake of office and work, but not for the sake of authority'.[16] Commenting on 1 Corinthians 12:12, 'For just as the body is one and has many members, and all the members of the body, though many, are one body, so it is with Christ', he explained, 'This applies to all of us because we have one baptism, one gospel, one faith, and are all equally Christians. For baptism, gospel and faith alone make men (sic) religious, and they create a Christian people'.[17]

However, Luther's teaching on the Common Priesthood of the

---

11 See 'An Appeal to the Ruling Class', in *Reformation Writings of Martin Luther,* Woolf, B.L. (ed.) (Library of Ecclesiastical History, 1952), 114.
12 See 'From Conflict to Communion', no. 162.
13 'Letter to the Christian Nobility', in *Weimar Ausgabe* 6, 407. See 'From Conflict to Communion', footnote no. 3.
14 I may add that this idea is foreshadowed already in the Old Testament when God reminds the people just before the making of the Covenant that they are to be a holy, priestly and kingly people at the service of God (Exod. 19:5–6).
15 See Lehmann, *Luther's Works,* 5.
16 Lehmann, *Luther's Works,* 14.
17 Woolf, 'An Appeal to the Ruling Class', 113.

baptized was not at the expense of the ministerial priesthood. Thus, in article 14 of his *Augsburg Confession*, he wrote: 'No one should publicly teach or administer sacraments in the church unless properly called'.[18] It may also be pointed out how all through his career at the University of Wittenberg there used to be ordinations for the ministerial priests.

Even if Luther made a distinction between priesthood and ministers who have an office in the Church as a preacher, the fact of sharing in Christ's priesthood is an invitation to share in Christ's ministry, to witness to the Gospel that Christ did all through his ministry. This is significant for the mission of the Church today which the paper will develop in the following pages.

Some Key Teachings of Vatican II

The Catholic-Lutheran joint document, From Conflict to Communion, points out how today Catholics and Lutherans are able to narrate the story of Luther and his reformation together, overcoming traditional mutual prejudices that, in the past, frequently afflicted the interpretation of each (no 35). In fact, some of the fresh teachings of the Second Vatican Council have their remote incubation beginning with Luther.

A major aspect of Luther's call for reform was his invoking the importance of the Bible and its role in Christian life. The Bible is so fundamental to Vatican II that most of its teachings are founded on the Bible, in contrast to the earlier Councils. Already in 1943 Pope Pius XII, through his encyclical *Divino Afflante Spiritu*, had liberated Catholic biblical research that had suffered a setback due to the fear of 'modernism', and encouraged Catholic Scholars to use critical methods in the study of Scripture and this in turn paved the way for one of the key texts of Vatican II, *Dei Verbum*, the Dogmatic Constitution on Divine Revelation.

The very opening sentence of *Dei Verbum* signals the biblical spirit that envelops the Council as well as this document specifically: 'Hearing the Word of God reverently and proclaiming it confidently...' (DV1). The Bible is the narrative of salvation history in terms of the words and deeds of God, intrinsically bound together (DV 2). *Dei Verbum* made the Word

---

18 Wengert, Priesthood, Pastors, Bishops, v.

of God central to the life and worship and spirituality of the Church and affirmed how the teaching authority of the Church is not above the Word of God but stands at its service (DV 10). 'The force and power in the Word of God is so great that it stands as the support and energy of the Church, the strength of faith for her sons, the food of the soul, the pure and everlasting source of spiritual life' (DV 21). Therefore, *Dei Verbum* admonishes the faithful to read Scripture through which God speaks to them (DV 25). It calls for a biblical revival in the formation of priests, in liturgy, in the Church's mission and in every aspect of the Church's life. In short, the document set in motion a biblical culture that underpinned the huge renewal program that the Council gave rise to.

Vatican II was a reforming Council and the greatest impact of this was felt in the very self-perception of the Church as 'a sacrament of God's reign in the world' (LG 8). Its identity is to serve as a sign to the world, its vocation is to actualize and to symbolize God's reign in its life and thus invite the world to be transformed to this divine reign, and this is done by the Church as a whole. In contrast to the previously held view of perceiving the hierarchy as the main part of the Church, Vatican II defined the Church as 'the people of God, (LG 10) with different ministries. This is an acknowledgement of the significance of every member of the Church. No wonder, in the decree on the Religious Life, the Council spoke of the 'Universal Call to Holiness,' in sharp contrast to different states of perfection!

The Church as a sign, with the same call to holiness of all members, reminds all Christians how they all share in the same mission of bringing the message of the good news of God's reign to the world. *Lumen Gentium,* the Dogmatic Constitution on the Church, rather than beginning with the Pope and the hierarchy and working downwards, in the first two chapters describes the Church as a mystery and as the people of God. The following chapters speak about the hierarchy, situating it as a service to the people of God. Further, *Lumen Gentium* (and later the Mission Decree *Ad Gentes* as well) showed how the Church, as the continuation of God's mission to the world through Jesus Christ and God's Spirit, is missionary by its very nature. To be involved in mission is the very purpose of its existence.

The Council, thus, was a liberating and, hence, an exuberant event in the life of the Church, of the Catholic Community. The new starting point is the fresh perspective on mission, as projecting the image of the Kingdom, always inviting the world to be conformed to the Kingdom. Equally significant is the description of the Church as a community, sharing in the priesthood of Christ, making every Christian responsible to witness to the Good News. The Council's teachings 'make a serious claim on the conscience of the Catholic Christian', wrote the German theologian and Cardinal Walter Kasper.[19]

Inasmuch as the Council found it appropriate to enact a decree on the laity, *Apostolicam Actuositatem*, (AA) and lay concerns were treated in many Conciliar discourses, one can qualify the Council as a 'Council of the laity'.[20] The laity came a long way from the status: 'pay, obey and pray' or better in the words of Pope Pius X, 'the one duty of the laity is to allow themselves to be led and, like a docile flock, to follow their pastors',[21] to that of being called to assume their responsibility to be actively involved in the church's mission (LG 30, 33).

As the internationally recognized Canadian Canonist Ladislas Orsy pointed out, already in 1938 Pope Pius XI said, while addressing a group of seminarians in Rome: 'The Church, the mystical body of Christ, has become a monstrosity. The head is very large but the body is shrunken. You the priests must rebuild that body of the Church and the only way in which you can rebuild it is to mobilize the lay people. You must call upon the lay people to become, along with you, the witnesses to Christ. You must call them, especially to bring Christ back to the workplace, the market place'.[22] The prophetic words of the Pope about rebuilding the Church got under way with Vatican II by rectifying the disproportionality of the various parts of the body of the Church. No doubt, the efforts of Catholic Religious Orders like the Dominicans, the Jesuits and others, as well as the writings of many theologians like Yves Congar, Joseph Cardign and others,[23] prepared the way for Vatican II in its retrieval of the role and dignity of the laity in the Church.

---

19 Kasper, *Theology and Church*, 9.
20 Lecky, *The Laity and Christian Education*, 1.
21 Lecky, *The Laity and Christian Education*, 1.
22 Orsy, *Receiving the Council*, 36, quoted by Ormerod, 'The Laity in the Australian Church', 62.
23 The late Cardinal Valerian Gracias of Bombay made a presentation at the World Congress for the Lay Apostolate in 1951 advocating a theology of the laity who shared responsibility for the Church's mission. Others like Cardinal Newman, Cardinal Suhard, G.K. Chesterton, Frank Sheed, Maisie Ward *et al.*, had their formative impact on the Council.

Dolores R. Lecky has shown, 'By the time the Second Vatican Council was convened in the fall of 1962, the movements and organizations that had been promoting increased responsibility for the laity within the Church and those that had been exploring the new frontiers of Christian education converged in significant ways'.[24] For the first time the Council was attended also by laymen and women, even if only as 'auditors'. Similarly, qualified lay persons like Patrick Keegan, President of the Catholic Workers' Movement, addressed the Council. No wonder the Decree on the Laity stated: 'Since in our time women are taking an increasingly active share in the whole life of the society, it is very important that their participation in the various sections of the church's apostolate should likewise develop' (AA no 9).

AA no 4, while situating family life within secular concerns and as a means of holiness in the life of the laity, makes use of the idea of vocation. The very use of the word 'vocation' is significant in so far as it was a word used almost exclusively to refer to the call of priests and religious. The laity are called by God to forward the reign of God in the world and in the church (AA no 4). The spirit of God is making the laity more conscious of their calling and their responsibility. The Council made it foundational that the laity share in the redemptive responsibility of the Church, participating in the priestly, prophetic and royal office of Jesus Christ confirmed by the sacraments of Baptism and Confirmation (AA no 2). There is a diversity of ministry in the Church to fulfil the one mission (AA no 2).

Laity and the Mission of the Church Today

Vatican II's affirmation of the vocation of the laity, anchored on Baptism and Confirmation, is very much scriptural. Already in the Old Testament, just before Israel is made as God's people through the covenant (Exod. 20–24), God informs the people of the very purpose of the whole process: 'That you may be holy and a priestly people, and a kingly nation...' (Exod. 19:5–6). Israel is constituted as God's people for the sake of a mission, that they may serve as light to the nations (Isa. 42:

---

24 Lecky, *The Laity and Christian Education*, 11.

6, 49:6). The role of a priest and a king is that of service to the people.

Exodus 19:5–6 is almost verbatim repeated by St. Peter in his first letter to the Christian community: 'You are a chosen race, a royal priesthood, a holy nation, God's own people that you may declare the wonderful deeds of him who call you out of darkness into his marvellous light' (1 Pet. 2:9). The purpose of the Christian community is precisely that it may declare the wonderful deeds of God.

The missionary vocation of the Christian community is reflected in every page of the New Testament. Evangelist Mark is very precise in his call narrative: 'He called unto him whom he was wanting to call and made them twelve—created a community—to be with him and to be sent out to proclaim and to cast out demons' (3:14–15).[25] Though there are individual differences among the evangelists the major elements are common to all: creation of a new community, presence of the community with the Lord and mission through word and deed. It is obvious from Acts 11:19ff that the Risen Lord's mandate to be witnesses to Him in Jerusalem and to the ends of the world (Acts 1:8) is discharged by the community as a whole. Interestingly, the very first Gentile community is the fruit, not of any of the Apostles' proclamation, but of the ordinary Christians (Acts 11:19–26).

However, the Post-Constantinian era witnessed a steady marginalization of the laity in the Church, especially with regard to their role in mission. This was aggravated also due to the changed understanding of mission. If mission in the Apostolic era was primarily a matter of sharing of an experience leading to transformation (see 1 John 1:1–4), gradually it becomes a question of conquest, displacement and expansion, especially, during the colonial days. It was executed by professional missionaries belonging to the Religious Orders, who were sent to the 'pagan lands' to save the souls of 'the natives'. That missionary era began to change with Vatican II.

Luther rightly insisted on the beauty and dignity of Christian baptism. However, due to his polemic against the Roman Curia, he did not devote equal space to the duties that baptism brings to every Christian, more so the missionary character of baptism. It is to the merit of Vatican

---

25 This is my translation of the original Greek text.

II that the Council spelt out the missionary nature of the whole Church, basing it solidly on God's love. The greatest insight of Vatican II, I would suggest, is its declaration that God is a 'fountain like love' (AG 2). The first five articles of the Mission Decree *Ad Gentes* spells this love further in terms of God's reaching out to the world through God's Word Incarnate, Jesus Christ, and through God's Spirit. As the nature of love is reaching out, the whole process of mission can be described as the divine dynamism of self-reaching out, beginning with creation. Thus, *Ad Gentes* goes beyond what some theologians name as *Missio Dei* (God's mission) and say how God, as self-diffusive love, **is Mission**. Church is missionary by nature because God in God's being is missionary!

True, *Ad Gentes* used the traditional concept of sending. In so far as sending is more congenial to a geographical sense of mission, not to mention of its colonial hangovers, and since the contemporary context of mission is much more complex than geography or culture, mission has to make use of the self-diffusive nature of love as reaching out. This would be more meaningful when we speak of the mission of the laity, in so far as they are not, normally, sent out as the professional missionaries.

In Jesus Christ God entered human history and Jesus told his listeners how in him God's reign has come (Mark 1:15, Matt. 4:17). Love and service are foundational to Divine reign. When a lawyer asked Jesus what was the basic norm of life, Jesus replied to him through the love command and outlined Christian life through the parable of the good Samaritan (Luke 10: 25–37). This is the good news of the Gospel. Vatican II's reform movement was precisely to take this good news to the heart of every human person, in his/her living context.[26] Every Christian is called to bring this good news to the neighbour through the practice of the Christian reaching out to the neighbour.

Christian living cannot be limited to certain devotional practices or the Sunday masses, but must include a genuine Christian outlook that does not shut out the neighbour. Mary's concern for the wedding host who ran out of wine must inspire any Christian. Reaching out to anyone who is in genuine need is the ultimate Christian value (Luke 10:37).

---

26 The Pastoral Constitution of the Church, *Gaudium et Spes,* which deals with this service to the world, begins with the words: 'The joys, the agonies and the aspirations of the world are our joys, our agonies and our aspirations' (GS 1).

The Christian preoccupation is not so much the salvation of one's soul as much as becoming a blessing to others even as Abraham is called to be a blessing to all the families of the world (Gen. 12:3). That is how, the common identity of the Church as the light to the world (Matt. 5:13–14), is concretized at the individual level. Only then can we appreciate the Lucan inaugural proclamation of the Lord (Luke 4:16–19).

The prophetic dimension of Christian baptism sharing in the mission of the prophet from Nazareth (Matt. 21:11) must be exercised by every Christian. In a world where there is so much self-seeking and lying, the very Christian life has to become an unsettling presence, powerful enough to effect a disturbance in the hearts and minds of the onlookers. Such a missionary perspective is present in most documents of Vatican II but more so in the Pastoral Constitution of the Church in the Modern World, *Gaudium et Spes*. Having said how the Church, 'coming forth from the eternal Father's love, founded in time by Christ the Redeemer and made one in the Holy Spirit', article 40 of *Gaudium et Spes* goes on to say: 'she serves as a leaven and a kind of soul for the human society[27] as it is to be renewed in Christ and transformed into God's family'.

All this spells out the baptismal foundation of mission rather than the priestly ordination or the religious vows, though the ordained ministers in their ministry can raise the awareness of the Christian community of its basic call to mission and to do everything possible that the community fulfils this vocation. Through their baptism Christians are 'reconfigured' (Gaillardetz) so as to have this constant habitual outlook of reaching out, even as the Good Samaritan did. The vocation of the laity for mission is not transitional or substitutional, i.e., temporary or filling a gap. It is the permanent call to make present God's other-centeredness experiential to people, and thus to become 'God with us, Emmanuel' (Matt 1:23).

This is a challenge that the Christian community refocuses its attention on the ministry of Jesus Christ rather than having an exaggerated concern for an other-worldly Saviour or similar theological preoccupations.

---

27 *Letter to Diognetus,* an early Church document, taught how Christians were to serve the world as soul did to the body (n. 6).

Retrieve the Ministry of Jesus

Dominic Crossan begins his magisterial volume, *The Historical Jesus: the Life of a Mediterranean Jewish Peasant*, with the assertion, 'In the beginning was the performance, not the word alone, not the deed alone, but both, each indelibly marked with the other forever'.[28] Similarly, Geza Vermes, an authority in Jewish studies, in the introduction to his book, *Jesus the Jew*, points out how the church in formulating its profession of faith has a 'passionate interest in Christ's eternal pre-existence and glorious after-life, but of his earthly career the faithful are told next to nothing, save that he was born and died'.[29] Granted that that situation is changing in the light of the scriptural research as well as the influence of liberation theology, there is still great need to return to the ministry of the Lord rather than focusing predominantly on the Paschal Mystery or similar doctrinal considerations. For, as Jose A. Pagola has spelt out, 'We begin to encounter Jesus when we begin to trust God as he did, when we believe in love as he did, when we come to suffering people as he did, when we defend life as he did, when we look at people as he did, when we confront life and death with hope as he did, when we pass on the contagion of the Good News as he did'.[30]

As a historical religion that bases its origin on the words and deeds of Jesus Christ, it is simply imperative that Christianity formulates its faith and mission in the light of the ministry of Jesus as the apostles did. Peter summarized the whole earthly life of Jesus in his very first address to a Gentile community by saying 'he went about doing good' (Acts 10:38). Similarly, he refers to Jesus in his Pentecost witness by stating how Jesus was 'a man attested to you by God with mighty works and wonders and signs which God did through him in your midst, as you yourselves know...' (Acts 2:22).

The Christian mission is nothing more and nothing less than what Jesus did, vs: manifest God his Father (John 1:18; 14:9) and usher in his Reign (Mark 1:14; Matt 4:17; Luke 4:18–19). The core message of Jesus was the in-breaking of the divine reign, that was available to all

---

28 Crossan, *The Historical Jesus*, XI.
29 Vermes, *Jesus the Jew*, 15.
30 Pagola, *Jesus*, 28.

those who cared to follow him.[31] John Shelby Spong has argued, what the gospels tell is 'the presence of God in a contemporary moment, they interpreted this moment by applying to it similar moments in their sacred story when they were convinced the presence of God had also been real to their forebears in faith'.[32] That was the only way they could understand and process the God presence they found in Jesus that was so powerful.[33] The gospels interpret the God-experience encountered in Jesus of Nazareth as the *good news* (Mark 1:1).

In the ministry of Jesus, we encounter 'the conduit through which the love of God was loosed into human history'.[34] In his ministry he became the expression of the very being of God. To have the courage to be himself, delivered from the need to please, to impress, to protect, to win, but to live authentically the self he was. The key question for Christians is not so much if Jesus was God, 'but whether they believe that God is Jesus-like', comments George Maloney.[35] In Jesus God becomes a 'God-toward-others by communicating Himself through His Word and His Spirit of love.'[36]

Jesus is the Kingdom of God, and the theme of the Kingdom of God, occurring over 50 times, is the most characteristic and the most distinctive 'feature of Jesus' preaching'.[37] James Dunn writes: 'More striking still, however, would have been Jesus' affirmation that the Kingdom had already come, or was already active in the present'.[38]

As scripture scholars like Tom Wright[39] have shown, at the time of Jesus one of the major challenges that Israel lived with was the Roman rule to which different groups responded differently. The Jewish leaders of the time, by and large, aligned with the Romans, while groups like the Essenes waited for God to act liberating them from the foreign rule, in contrast to the Zealots who had recourse to armed revolt. It is in

---

31 Chalke and Mann, *The Lost Message of Jesus*, 16.
32 Spong, *Liberating the Gospels*, 19.
33 Spong, *Liberating the Gospels*, 20.
34 Spong, *Liberating the Gospels*, 332.
35 Maloney, *Bright Darkness*, 6.
36 Maloney, *Bright Darkness*, 11.
37 Dunn, *Who Was Jesus?*, 16.
38 Dunn, *Who Was Jesus?*, 17.
39 Wright, *The Challenge of Jesus*.

this background that Jesus came with the message of the arrival of the divine reign (Mark 1:14–15). The good news that Jesus proclaimed was the arrival of the kingdom of God. 'This gospel,' writes Frank Matera, 'in which one must believe is God's good news (*euaggelion*) that the time is fulfilled and his kingdom has drawn near, or is at hand'.[40] In the Markan gospel the kingdom of God, though occurring only fourteen times, underlines everything that Jesus says and does and it serves as the leitmotif of his ministry.[41]

Jesus was not an abstract teacher of philosophical truths, but he acted as a prophet who explained the meaning of the kingdom that had been inaugurated in and through him. It was radically different from any of the prevailing notions and attitudes. Rather than finding refuge in isolation, he mingled with tax collectors and sinners. Instead of armed rebellion he took the path of peace, and forgiveness, turning the other cheek when struck (Matt.5:39), without abandoning justice (John 19:23).

Even as Jesus taught his disciples to pray for the arrival of the divine reign already now, his constant mission was the ringing in of this reign through his deeds of healing, feeding, casting out demons, forgiving, giving new lease of life as well as through his teaching. He made the kingdom visibly present through his all-inclusive table-fellowships, which we come across frequently in the gospels. 'Jesus', as Michael McCabe, writes, 'was not just pointing to the Kingdom of God, but was in his words, deeds and person actually embodying God's kingly rule'.[42] Jesus showed how he would win the messianic victory over evil and build the true temple through his ministry leading to the cross and resurrection. This prompted the Jewish scholar Ed Kessler to write: 'For Jews, the significance of Jesus must be in his life rather than his death; in his teaching rather than in doctrine; in the holiness of his life rather than in the sanctity of belief'.[43]

The Greco-Roman inculturation that began already with the Nicene Creed shifted the biblical realism on the understanding of Jesus as God's

---

40 Matera, *New Testament Ethics*, 14.
41 Matera, *New Testament Ethics*, 18.
42 McCabe, 'New Perspectives on the Historical Jesus and His Mission', 52.
43 Kessler, *Jesus*, 92.

presence ushering in the reign of God, to an abstract intellectualistic Christology. This reached its high-tides during the colonial period that went unchallenged due to the presumed cultural and social superiority of the Christian West. In the post-colonial period few are prepared to buy the claims of superiority or exclusivism. This, in turn, is an invitation to return to the Gospel realism that has its emphasis on the ministry of the Lord who went about doing good. Today, as Dominic Crossan has drawn our attention, a sapiential vision is needed 'for discerning how, here and now in this world, one can so live that God's power, rule, and dominion are evidently present to all observers'.[44]

The Kingdom that we encounter in the ministry of Jesus is not primarily an eschatological one to come about at the end of times, 'nor did it refer to a geographical area or a political entity but to a set of relationships that actually obtain or should obtain, between creator and creatures, between God and the world'.[45] The ministry of Jesus shows how the old age is crumbling and a new one is emerging right now. This is the meaning of the parables and the miracles of Jesus as narrated in the gospels. In contrast to the classical expositions of the doctrine of the person and expiatory work of Christ neglecting the earthly ministry of Jesus, we come across works like that of Leonhard Goppelt that portray the importance of Jesus' ministry for the church.[46]

Scripture scholar and theologian Sean Freyne underlines in his influential article, 'The Galilean Jesus and a Contemporary Christology', that only a historico-theological approach can 'illustrate the universal meaning that is disclosed in and through the particularity of Jesus' life. God did not become human as a universal, but in the particularity of the life and praxis of Jesus'.[47] Obviously, this particularity is revealed through his Incarnation and ministry.

The life of Jesus, with the emphasis on what he said and did, is the guiding principle for the church in so far as its basic vocation is to follow the Lord. Scripture scholars can shed ever new light on that life for each age to follow the Lord in his ministry so that the church becomes the

---

44 Crossan, *Jesus A Revolutionary Biography*, 56.
45 Funk, *Honest to Jesus*, 166.
46 Goppelt, *Theology of the New Testament*.
47 Freyne, 'The Galilean Jesus and a Contemporary Christology', 281.

light to the world (Mt 5:13–14). Though the church never advocated an exclusive Easter-Jesus, gnostic writings indeed caused to minimize the importance of the pre-Easter Jesus, with less reference to the historical Jesus. The evangelists, however, focus their readers' attention on the Jesus who began his ministry by announcing the arrival of the eschatological Kingly rule of God, with the 'fulfilment of time' (Mark 1.15).

A follower of Jesus cannot remain encased in his/her own world with little concern for the world outside, for discipleship is a call to be inserted into the very ministry of Jesus by following the same path (*halakah*) and thus to become a light to the world (Matt. 5:13–14). Referring to Jesus' practice of love, N.T. Wright comments: 'Jesus shares the pollution of sickness and death, by the power of his own love—and it is a love, above all, that shines through these stories—turns that pollution into wholeness and hope.'[48] Through his ministry Jesus becomes a divine manifestation, epiphany, and simultaneously, the manifestation of the humans, anthropophany. All this makes it imperative that the community of Jesus' disciples align itself with the point of view of God as manifested in Jesus' ministry, living under his kingship, and entering the kingdom of God that has made its appearance in Jesus' ministry.

Following the Lord can be only through following his ministry that brings one to the joy of the banqueting Lord (Mark 2:18–19), banqueting with the outcasts, compassionate association with the marginalized, and thus preaching the good news to the poor. Through that kind of mission Christians come face to face with Jesus, the epiphany of God.[49] Through such a practice Christians anticipate the end-times already now. To quote Tom Wright, 'Perhaps they are the sort of things that might just be characteristic of the *new creation,* of the fulfilled time, of what happens when heaven and earth come together'.[50]

By way of conclusion, the cleansing of the temple (Mark 11:15 ff., and Par) capsules what has been said: Jesus' ministry that led him to the cross and resurrection was a self-giving, out of 'zeal for God's house' (John 2: 17; Ps 69:1), God's reign, 'the divine house-hold'[51]. As Pope Benedict

---

48 Wright, *Luke for Everyone*, 105.
49 Borg, *Jesus*, 191.
50 Wright, *Simply Jesus*, 133.
51 Crossan, *The Greatest Prayer*, 3, 81.

XVI has shown evangelist Matthew concludes the account of the cleansing of the temple by observing: 'The blind and the lame came to him in the temple and he healed them' (21:14).[52] The purified temple, the community of his disciples, is to serve the cause of healing and wholeness of life, more so for those driven to the margins of life and society.

Bibliography

Benedict XVI — *Jesus of Nazareth* (San Francisco: Ignatius Press, 2011).

Borg, M. — *Jesus: A New Vision* (New York: HarperCollins, 1991).

Chalke, S., & Mann, A. — *The Lost Message of Jesus* (Grand Rapids, MI: Zondervan, 2003).

Crossan, J. D. — *The Greatest Prayer* (New York: HarperCollins, 2010).

Crossan, J. D. — *The Historical Jesus: The Life of a Mediterranean Jewish Peasant* (New York: HarperCollins, 1991).

Dillenberger, J. — *Martin Luther, Selections from his Writings* (Garden City, NY: Anchor Books, 1961).

Dunn, J. D. G. — *Who Was Jesus?* (London: SPCK, 2016).

Freyne, S. — 'The Galilean Jesus and a Contemporary Christology', *Theological Studies* 70.2 (2009), 281–97.

Funk, R. W. — *Honest to Jesus: Jesus for a New Millennium* (Rydalmere, NSW: Hodder & Stoughton Book, 1996).

Goppelt, L. — *Theology of the New Testament: The Ministry of Jesus in Its Theological Significance* (Grand Rapids, MI: Eerdmans Pub. Co., Vol 1, 1981 & Vol 2, 1982).

Kasper, W. — *Theology and Church* (London: SCM Press, 1989).

Kessler, E. — *Jesus* (Gloucestershire: The History Press, 2016).

Kung, H. — *Christianity: The Religious Situation of Our Time* (London: Collins, 1995).

Lecky, D. R. — *The Laity and Christian Education* (New York: Paulist Press, 2006).

Lehmann, H.T. (ed.) — *Luther's Works* (Philadelphia, PA: Fortress Press, 1970).

---

52 Benedict XVI, *Jesus of Nazareth*, 23.

Luther, Martin	'An Appeal to the Ruling Class', in B. L. Woolf, *Reformation Writings of Martin Luther* (Library of Ecclesiastical History London: Lutterworth Press, 1952).
Lutheran-Catholic Common Commemoration	'From Conflict to Communion'. *Lutheran-Catholic Common Commemoration of the Reformation in 2017.* <www.bonifatius.de>.
Maloney, G. A.	*Bright Darkness: Jesus the Lover of Mankind* (Denville, JJ: Dimension Books, 1977).
Matera, F. J.	*New Testament Ethics: The Legacies of Jesus and Paul* (Louisville, Kentucky: Westminster John Knox Press, 1996).
McCabe, M.	'New Perspectives on the Historical Jesus and His Mission', *Sedos Bulletin* 3/4 41 (2009), 51–53.
Ormerod, N.	'The Laity in the Australian Church', in N. Ormerod, et al. (ed.), *Vatican II: Reception and Implementation in the Australian Church* (Mulgrave, Vic: Garratt Pub., 2012), 62–75.
Orsy, L.	*Receiving the Council* (Collegeville: Liturgical Press, 2009).
Pagola, J. A.	*Jesus: An Historical Approximation* (Miami: Convivium Press, 2012).
Spong, J. S.	*Liberating the Gospels: Reading the Bible with Jewish Eyes* (New York: HarperCollins, 1996).
Vatican II	Declaration on Ecumenism (*Unitatis Redentigratio*) of Vatican II. *The Church: Towards a Common Vision* (Faith and Order Paper 214, WCC).
Vermes, G.	*Jesus the Jew* (New York: Macmillan, 1973).
Wengert, T.	*Priesthood, Pastors, Bishops: Public Ministry for the Reformation and Today* (Minneapolis: Fortress Press, 2008).
Witterup, R. D.	*Rediscovering Vatican II: Scripture* (New York: Paulist Press, 2006).
Wright, N. T.	*The Challenge of Jesus* (London: SPCK, 2000).
Wright, N.T.	*Luke for Everyone* (Louisville: John Knox Press, 2004).
Wright, N. T.	*Simply Jesus* (London: SPCK, 2011).

Websites

https://w2.vatican.va/content/francesco/en/speeches/2016/october/documents/papa-francesco_20161031_svezia-evento-ecumenico.html>